DATE DUE			

MODERN
LATIN AMERICA

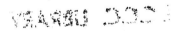

MODERN LATIN AMERICA

Thomas E. Skidmore
Peter H. Smith

New York   Oxford
OXFORD UNIVERSITY PRESS
1984

Copyright © 1984 by Oxford University Press, Inc.

Library of Congress Cataloging in Publication Data
Skidmore, Thomas E., 1932–
Modern Latin America.

Bibliography: p.
Includes index.
1. Latin America—History—1830– . I. Smith,
Peter H. II. Title.
F1413.S55 1984 980'.03 83-8007
ISBN 0-19-503366-3
ISBN 0-19-503367-1 (pbk.)

Printing (last digit): 9 8 7 6 5 4 3

Printed in the United States of America

For
David, James, Robert
And
Jonathan and Peter

ACKNOWLEDGMENTS

We have incurred countless intellectual debts in the writing of this book. We offer thanks to colleagues who gave us critical readings on various portions of the manuscript: Simon Collier, Florencia Mallon, Thomas McCormick, Lars Schoultz, Steve Stern, and Ralph Lee Woodward. For help in locating illustrations and obtaining permissions we are grateful to Michael Grow, Manuel Orús, Robert Potash, Adolfo Saracho, and Steve Stein.

Anita Genger provided valuable research assistance. The task of typing was shared by Maria Martínez, Genevieve Mittnacht, and Bonnie Walters. Ann Hartley helped with the index.

For her advice, encouragement, and tactful prodding, we owe special thanks to Nancy Lane of Oxford University Press.

We finished the writing in mid-1983. We alone are responsible for errors of fact or interpretation. We welcome comments and suggestions from readers.

Madison, Wisconsin   T.E.S.
Cambridge, Massachusetts   P.H.S.
August 1983

CONTENTS

Contents

Contents

MODERN
LATIN AMERICA

WHY LATIN AMERICA?

"The U.S. will do anything for Latin America, except read about it," according to James Reston, the dean of U.S. political commentators. Is there any reason why we should try to prove him wrong? There are several. First, our nation's economic interests are deeply involved in the region. Latin America is one of our major trading partners. It is the site of much U.S. investment and a source for oil and other critical raw materials. Rapid growth in key countries—such as Mexico and Brazil—may soon produce significant new powers on the world scene.

We also have political links. Revolutionary upheavals and repressive responses in Latin America directly challenge U.S. foreign policy. They raise difficult questions about how to protect and promote U.S. national interests (defined as not simply economic or strategic interests). President Reagan dramatized this fact shortly after his 1980 election by meeting with Mexican President José López Portillo on the U.S.-Mexican border, in what was the U.S. President's first such conference with any other head of state.

There is another important consideration closer to home. Large sections of our country have become Hispanized by the influence of migrants from Mexico, Puerto Rico, and the Caribbean. This is in addition to the Hispanic descendents of the original Spanish-speaking population of the formerly Mexican Southwest. Migration, both historical and recent, then brought peoples and customs from Latin America to the American Southwest (from Texas to California), Florida, and New York. Many major U.S. cities now have more children from Spanish-speaking families than from any other group. Bilingualism has become a political issue forcing us to rethink the meaning of Spanish-speaking America, both within our borders and beyond.

Most U.S. citizens (or "North Americans," as we are commonly known in Latin America) know little about our neighboring societies to the south. Many believe that the U.S. can impose its will on the region through "big-stick" diplomacy or military might. Others do not even care. Looking for an "easy" foreign language, high school or college students choose Spanish and then assume everything associated with speaking Spanish must be "easy." Such ignorance can be dangerous, and one purpose of this book is to help reduce misinformation. In fact, this lack of knowledge is felt just as keenly in West Europe. British journalists used to tell how some of their number once had a contest to think up the most boring newspaper headline imaginable and they came up with "Small Earthquake in Chile: No One Injured." Chile's tragic history over the last fifteen years puts that provincialism into painful relief.

By training and outlook, most North Americans and Europeans search for intellectual formulas that will yield clear-cut answers to our inquiries: the "Latin lover," the "Frito Bandito," the soulful Ché Guevara, the Brazilian mulatto carnival queens—these are the images that often first come to mind. But when we move beyond these caricatures

---

U.S. STEREOTYPES OF LATIN AMERICA

On December 10, 1940, the Office of Public Opinion Research conducted a nation-wide poll in which respondents were given a card with nineteen words on it and were asked to indicate those words that seemed to describe best the people of Central and South America. The results were as follows:

Dark-skinned	80%	Imaginative	23%
Quick-tempered	49%	Shrewd	16%
Emotional	47%	Intelligent	15%
Religious	45%	Honest	13%
Backward	44%	Brave	12%
Lazy	41%	Generous	12%
Ignorant	34%	Progressive	11%
Suspicious	32%	Efficient	5%
Friendly	30%	No answer	4%
Dirty	28%	No opinion	0%
Proud	26%		

Since respondents were asked to pick as many descriptive terms as they liked, percentages add to considerably more than 100.

Sources: John J. Johnson, *Latin America in Caricature,* (Austin: University of Texas Press, 1980), page 18; Hadley Cantril, ed., *Public Opinion, 1935–1946* (Princeton: Princeton University Press, 1951), p. 502.

(which have their own truth to tell), we find Latin America to be a complex region.

Latin America is not an easy place to understand, despite the fact that the same language, Spanish, is spoken everywhere except Brazil (Portuguese), the Andes (Quechua and other Indian languages), and the Caribbean (French, English, and Dutch). The term Latin America covers a vast variety of people and places. Geographically, Latin America includes the land mass extending from the Rio Grande border to Texas and Mexico to the southern tip of South America, plus some Caribbean islands: a total area two-and-one-half times the size of the United States. Brazil itself is larger than the continental U.S.

Physical features present sharp differences: from the Andean mountain range, stretching the full length of western South America, to the tropical forest of the Amazon basin; from the arid plains of northern Mexico to the fertile grasslands of the Argentine pampa. The people of Latin America contain elements and mixtures of three racial groups—native Indians, white Europeans, and black Africans. In 1980 the total population came to 364 million, compared with 222 million in the United States.

Latin American society displays startling contrasts—between rich and poor, between city and country, between learned and illiterate, between the powerful lord of the hacienda and the deferential peasant, between wealthy entrepreneurs and desperate street urchins. Politically, Latin America includes 25 nations, large and small, whose present-day experience ranges from military dictatorship to electoral democracy to Fidel Castro's socialist regime in Cuba (see Map 1). Economically, Latin America belongs to the "developing" world, beset by historical and contemporary obstacles to rapid economic growth, but here too there is diversity—from the one-crop dependency of tiny Honduras to the industrial promise of dynamic Brazil.

Throughout their modern history Latin Americans have sought, with greater or lesser zeal, to achieve political and economic independence from colonial, imperial, and neo-imperial powers. Thus it is bitter irony that the phrase "Latin America" was coined by mid-nineteenth century French, who thought that since their culture, like that of Spanish and Portuguese America, was "Latin" (i.e., Romance language-speaking), France was destined to assume leadership throughout the continent.

As these observations suggest, Latin America resists facile categorization. It is a region rich in paradox. This insight yields a number of instructive clues.

First, Latin America is both young and old. Beginning in 1492, its conquest by the Spanish and Portuguese created a totally new social order based on domination, hierarchy, and the intermingling of European, African, and indigenous elements. The European intrusion pro-

MAP 1 CONTEMPORARY LATIN AMERICA (pop. as of 1980, in millions)

foundly and ineradicably altered the Indian communities. Compared with the ancient civilizations of Africa and Asia, these Latin American societies are relatively young. On the other hand, most nations of Latin America obtained political independence—from Spain and Portugal— in the early nineteenth century, more than 100 years before successful anticolonial movements in other Third World countries. Thus by the standard of nationhood, Latin America is relatively old.

Second, Latin America has throughout its history been both tumultuous and stable. The Conquest began a tradition of political violence that has erupted in coups, assassinations, armed movements, military

6

interventions, and (more rarely) social revolutions. Ideological encounters between liberalism, positivism, corporatism, anarchism, socialism, communism, fascism, and religious teachings of every doctrinal hue have sharpened the intensity of struggle. Despite the differing forms of political conflict, old social and economic structures have persisted. Even where modern revolutions have struck, as in Mexico (1910) and Bolivia (1952), many aspects of traditional society survive. The Cuban Revolution (1959) seems at first an exception, yet even in Cuba the pull of history has continued strong, as we shall see.

Third, Latin America has been both independent and dependent, autonomous and subordinate. The achievement of nationhood by 1830 in all but parts of the Caribbean basin represented an assertion of sovereignty rooted in Enlightenment thought. Yet a new form of penetration by external powers—first Britain and France, then the United States—jeopardized this nationhood. Economic and political weakness vis-à-vis Europe and North America has frequently limited the choices available to Latin American policymakers. Within Latin America, power is ironically ambiguous: it is the supreme commodity, but it has only a painfully limited effect.

Fourth, Latin America is both prosperous and poor. Ever since the Conquest, the region has been described as a fabulous treasure house of natural resources. First came the European lust for silver and gold. Today the urge may be for petroleum, gas, copper, iron ore, coffee, sugar, or soybeans, but the image of endless wealth remains. In startling contrast, there is also the picture of poverty: peasants without tools, workers without jobs, children without food, mothers without hope. An aphorism oft repeated in Latin America summarizes this scene: "Latin America is a beggar atop a mountain of gold."

One can easily think of additional contrasts, but these should illustrate the difficulty—and fascination—in trying to come to grips with Latin America. To understand Latin American history and society requires a flexible, broad-gauge approach, and this is what we try to offer in this book. We draw on the work of many scholars, presenting our own interpretation, but also acquainting the reader with alternative views.

Interpretations of Latin America

Most historians of modern Latin America have stressed the area's political instability, marked frequently by dictatorship. North American and European observers have been especially fascinated with two questions: Why dictatorships? Why not democracy? This preoccupation is not recent. In 1930, for example, a U.S. economic geographer specializing on the region observed, "the years roll on and there arise the anxieties and disappointments of an ill-equipped people attempting to establish true republican forms of government." A year earlier an English scholar had noted that "the political history of the republics has been a record of alternating periods of liberty and despotism." Implicitly assuming or explicitly asserting that their style of democracy is superior to all other modes of political organization, North American and European writers frequently asked what was "wrong" with Latin America. Or with Latin Americans themselves.

What passed for answers was for many years a jumble of racist epithets, psychological simplifications, geographic platitudes, and cultural distortions. According to such views, Latin America could not achieve democracy either because dark-skinned peoples (Indians and blacks) were unsuited for it; or because passionate Latin tempers would not stand it, because tropical climates somehow prevented it, or because Roman Catholic doctrines inhibited it.

Each charge has its refutation: dictatorial rule has flourished in predominantly white countries, such as Argentina, as well as among mixed-blood societies, such as Mexico; it has appeared in temperate climes, such as Chile, not only in the tropics, such as Cuba; it has gained support from non-Catholics and nonpracticing Catholics, while many fervent worshippers have fought for liberty; and, as shown by authoritarian regimes outside Latin America, such as Hitler's Germany or Stalinist Russia, dictatorship is not restricted to any single temperament. Such explanations not only failed to explain; when carried to extremes they helped justify rapidly increasing U.S. and European penetration—financial, cultural, military—of the "backward" republics to the south.

The scholarly scene improved in the late 1950s and early 1960s, when North American social scientists formulated "modernization theory." As applied to Latin America, this theory held that economic growth would generate the social change that would in turn make possible more "developed" politics. The transition from a rural to an urban society would bring a change in values. People would begin to relate to and participate in the voluntary organizations that authentic democracy requires. Most important, a middle class would emerge—to play both a progressive and moderating role. Latin America and its citizenries were not so inherently "different" from Europe and North America. Instead they were simply "behind." Modernization adepts thought the historical record showed this process was well under way in Latin America.

Thus historians went to work describing Latin American history in the light of modernization theory. One optimistic and widely read U.S. scholar found in 1958 that the "middle sectors" had "become stabilizers and harmonizers and in the process have learned the dangers of dealing in absolute postulates." The author of a late 1970s textbook on

Latin American history saw "Latin American history since independence . . . as modernization growing slowly against the resistance of old institutions and attitudes."

Reality, however, proved harsher. Instead of spreading general prosperity, economic growth in the 1960s and 1970s (and it reached sustained high rates in Mexico and Brazil) generally made income distribution more unequal. The gap in living standards between city and countryside grew. Domestic capital's ability to compete with the huge transnational firms declined. Meanwhile, politics were hardly following the model predicted by many experts of modernization. The middle strata, relatively privileged, forged a sense of "class consciousness" which, in critical moments of decision, such as in Argentina in 1955 or 1976, Brazil in 1964, and Chile in 1973, led them to join the ruling classes in opposition to the popular masses. Politics took an authoritarian turn, producing military governments. And in stark contradiction of modernization theory, these patterns emerged in the most developed—and most rapidly developing—countries of the continent. What had gone wrong?

Two sets of answers came forth. One group of scholars focused on the cultural traditions of Latin America and their Spanish and Portuguese origins. These analysts argued, in effect, that anti-democratic politics was (and remains) a product of a Roman Catholic and Mediterranean world view that stressed the need for harmony, order, and the elimination of conflict. By failing to grasp these continuities in the Iberian experience, scholars had confused form with substance, rhetoric with reality. Latin America's constitutions were never as democratic as they appeared, party politics were not as representative as they might have looked. The North American and European academic community, afflicted by its own myopia and biases, had simply misread the social facts.

A second group of scholars accepted modernization theory's linking of socioeconomic causes with political outcomes but turned the answer upside down: Latin America's economic development was qualitatively different from that of North America and Western Europe, and therefore it produced different political results. Specifically, these scholars argued, Latin America's experience was determined by the pervasive fact of its economic dependence. "By dependency," as one scholar (Theotonio dos Santos) has explained,

> we mean a situation in which the economy of certain countries is conditioned by the development and expansion of another economy to which the former is subjected. The relation of interdependence between two or more economies, and between these and world trade, assumes the form of dependence when some countries (the dominant ones) can expand and be

self-sustaining, while other countries (the dependent ones) can do this only as a reflection of that expansion, which can have either a positive or a negative effect on their immediate development.

By its intrinsic character, "dependent development" generated inequities, allocating benefits to sectors participating in the world market and denying them to other groups. A typical case might involve a country whose economic growth relied on a single export crop, such as coffee or sugar. A national landowning elite, the planters, would collaborate with export-import merchants, often foreign, to sell the goods on an overseas market. Most profits would be restricted to those groups. The planters would use much of their money to import high-cost consumer goods from Europe or the U.S., and the merchants (if foreign) would remit profits to their home countries. The export earnings would therefore provide precious little capital for diversifying the local economy, thus creating a situation that some observers have labelled "growth without development." Because of a labor surplus, field workers would continue to receive low wages; groups outside the export sector would get little benefit. Consequently, regional imbalances would intensify and income distribution would become more unequal than before. What growth occurred, moreover, would be subject to substantial risk. If the overseas market for coffee or sugar contracted—for whatever reason, as it did in the 1930s—then the entire economy would suffer. It would in this sense be "dependent" for its continued growth on decisions taken elsewhere and it would be, as dos Santos says, "conditioned by the development and expansion of another economy."

The proponents of *"dependencia* theory," as it quickly came to be known, maintain that economic dependency led to political authoritarianism. According to this view, the "dependent" location of Latin America's economics placed inherent limitations on the region's capacity for growth, especially in industry. The surest sign of this economic trouble is a crisis in the foreign accounts—the country's ability to pay for needed imports, as occurred dramatically in Mexico, Argentina, Chile, and Brazil in late 1982 and early 1983. Exports lag behind imports, and the difference can only be made up by capital inflow. But the foreign creditors—firms, banks, international agencies such as the World Bank—deny the necessary extra financing because they believe the government cannot impose the necessary "sacrifices." Backed against the wall, the country must take immediate steps to keep imports flowing in. Political strategy falls hostage to the need to convince the foreign creditors.

The most frequent solution has been a military coup. The resulting authoritarian government can then take its "hard" decision, usually highly unpopular anti-inflation measures, such as increased public utility prices, cuts in real wages, and cuts in credit. Hardest hit are the lower classes. To carry out such policies therefore requires a heavy hand over the popular sectors. Thus, the coups and repressive authoritarian regimes that emerged in Brazil, Argentina, and Chile came about not in spite of Latin America's economic development, but because of it.

Analytical Themes in This Book

This book is a survey of modern Latin American history, not a formulation of social theory; but we cannot escape the need for concepts in approaching our material. From "modernization" theory we take the causal premise that economic transformations induce social changes which, in turn, have political consequences. From the dependency school we borrow the ideas that:

1. a country's place in the international division of labor defines the shape of available paths to economic growth;
2. functional location on the "periphery" of the world system, as distinct from the commercial-industrial "center," and development at a stage when the North Atlantic system was already far advanced, meant that economic transformations in Latin America would be different from patterns traversed earlier in Europe and North America;
3. these differences in economic processes would produce different forms of social change—with respect, for example, to the nature of the "middle classes," the urban and rural working classes, and the relationship among these classes;
4. this combination of social and economic forces would define the options available to political leaders and help explain the recurrence of authoritarian, nondemocratic regimes.

We believe that this approach can be applied not only to 1960s and 1970s, but also to the entire modern era. We shall be looking for these key features throughout the book.

But we see limits to the utility of this approach. The farther we go back in Latin American history, the harder it is to find the data on economic relations and social class behavior. We do not accept the all-embracing theoretical claims put forward by some dependency analysts, and we do not share the view of many that only socialist revolutions can break the cycles of dependency. Satellite nations on the periphery of the socialist system are highly dependent on central powers, in ways parallel to the dependency of Third World countries under capitalism (could there be a more dramatic example than the fate of Solidarity in Poland?), although the nature of the links may well differ. (East Europe's subordination to the Soviet Union derives not from Russian ownership of local property but from government-controlled commercial links and, most importantly, from political and military domination.) More fundamentally, we believe that historical transformations are complex processes and to understand them we need to adopt a multicausal approach. Cultural influences, for example, are not merely adornments or superstructures; they have important effects on the perceptions, attitudes, and actions of the people who make history. Anyone who has ever tried to compare the political traditions of Argentina and Brazil can vouch for this truth. Demographic factors, such as rapid population growth, also have far-ranging social and political effects. In our portrait of Latin American history, we hope to integrate a "modified dependency approach" with consideration of other, noneconomic forces.

Our narrative begins by describing first the Conquest and the colonial period, 1492–1825, when Latin America entered the periphery of the capitalist world-system through subordination to Spain and Portugal. We then describe how the disruption of this connection led to independence, followed by a phase of economic and political consolidation between 1830 and 1880.

In the late nineteenth century Latin America increased its links to the global system, this time providing raw materials (especially foodstuffs and minerals) to Great Britain, continental Europe, and the United States, and it is the formation of these export-oriented economies and their successors that occupies the major share of our attention. Why have we chosen this approach to modern Latin America? It is because by the best-known indicators—export growth, urbanization, life expectancy, literacy, political participation—Latin America around 1880 entered a period of more rapid change than anything it had experienced since the Iberian conquest in the sixteenth century.

Chapter Two is an overview of this process. It traces some common processes and patterns that accompanied the emphasis on exports and, later on, the drive toward "delayed" industrialization. We then turn to case studies: Argentina, with its traditional emphasis on beef and wheat, wracked by internal strife and military intervention (Chapter Three); Chile, a leading source of nitrates and copper and, eventually, the site of an abortive socialist experiment (Chapter Four); Brazil, so well-known for coffee and, more recently, its rapid industrial growth under a military-dominated regime (Chapter Five); Peru, with its strong Indian tradition and its uncertain lurch toward nationhood (Chapter Six); Mexico, with its proximity to the U.S., the scene of a popular upheaval in 1910 (Chapter Seven); Cuba, so dependent on sugar and so close to the U.S., the one Latin American society that has undergone a socialist revolution (Chapter Eight); Central America, a region of highly stratified societies long ignored until the political explosions of the late 1970s and early 1980s (Chapter Nine). We attempt to give full consideration to social and political themes in these country studies, and each chapter can be read independently. Taken together they represent 83 percent of Latin America's population and roughly the same fraction of its territory.

In Chapter Ten we summarize recent and current relationships between Latin America and the international community, particularly the United States, and in the Epilogue we speculate about likely developments in the next twenty years.

This book offers a picture of Latin American history, not a definitive catalog of facts. Our goal is to trace patterns and trends that help us to understand the complexities and variations in Latin America's paths to the present. We hope our presentation will stimulate discussion and debate, and we expect that students and colleagues will disagree with many of our interpretations. Above all, we want to introduce our readers to the excitement and fascination of the history of an area that is intriguing in its own right and has its own role to play on the world stage.

ONE

THE COLONIAL FOUNDATIONS, 1492–1880s

When Europeans reached present-day Latin America they found three important civilizations: Mayan, Aztec, and Incan. That we should still call the native peoples of this hemisphere "Indians" perpetuates the error of sixteenth-century Spaniards who wanted to believe they had reached the spice-rich Indies.

The Mayan people, who occupied the Yucatán peninsula, southern Mexico, and most of present-day Guatemala, began to build their civilization around 500 B.C. The most famous achievements of this group were cultural—not only the building of exquisite temples, but also pioneering accomplishments in architecture, sculpture, painting, hieroglyphic writing, mathematics, astronomy, and chronology (including the invention of calendars). Normally organized into a series of independent city-states, some with populations of 200,000 or more, the Mayans seldom fought among themselves. (This serenity, evident in the elegant harmony of their artwork, contrasts sharply with the bloodthirsty motifs in Aztec art.) For reasons unknown, classic Mayan society collapsed, falling victim to domination (972–1200) and then absorption (1200–1540) by Toltec invaders from the central Mexican highlands. Yet, the direct descendants of the Mayans have survived in southern Mexico and Guatemala down to our own day.

Mexico's spacious central valley later became the seat of the Aztec empire. One of the Chichimec tribes that came from the north to subdue the Toltecs in the twelfth and thirteenth centuries, the Aztecs engaged in constant war with their neighbors, finally constructing the city of Tenochtitlán around 1345 (on the site of contemporary Mexico City). After gaining control of the entire valley of Mexico, they created a major empire—one that was just reaching its peak as Columbus touched shore in the Caribbean.

Aztecs were noted for their military organization and prowess at ceremonial city-building. Their art, except for their haunting poetry, was inferior in subtlety and craftsmanship to many other ancient Mexican civilizations.

In its final form, Aztec society was rigidly stratified. At the bottom were slaves and at the top was a hereditary nobility. Education, marriage, and labor were meticulously programmed, and the economy was owned communally. Kings, such as Moctezuma II, exercised immense political power. Despite centralization of authority, however, conquered states in neighboring areas were not incorporated into the empire. They were treated as tribute-paying vassals, and some—such as nearby Tlaxcala—were allowed to maintain a perpetual state of war with Tenochtitlán. One reason for this warfare was that the Aztec religion required human sacrifice, and prisoners of war could be served up for the bloody rituals.

Incas adopted a very different pattern of organization. Their empire stretched for 3000 miles along the Andes, from northern Ecuador through Peru to southern Chile. After consolidating their hold in the Cuzco Valley in Peru, the Incas began expanding their empire in the early 1400s and continued until the Spanish Conquest in 1532. Once defeated, groups became integral parts of the empire. To obtain support for the emperor, or Inca, local nobles from conquered areas were brought to Cuzco and treated as royal guests, while resistant elements in recently conquered zones were transferred to areas controlled by loyal followers. Political power belonged to a tightly organized, highly disciplined bureaucracy, with teams of local officials on the bottom and a single supreme ruler at the top. Incas were thereby able to command effective authority over most of the Andes.

Incas were master engineers, building a vast road system (for human and animal transit, since they did not know the wheel), an intricate irrigation system, and impressive terraced agriculture on mountain sides. The Incas also excelled in textile design and in treating head injuries, the latter made possible by extraordinary skills at trepanning the human skull.

Aside from the Mayans, Aztecs, and Incas, there were many other Indian cultures. In the area of modern-day Mexico alone there were over two hundred different linguistic groups. Estimates of the size of Latin America's indigenous population have varied widely. One scholar has set the figure at 90 to 112 million, with 30 million each in central Mexico and Peru. Though this calculation may be too high, it is clear that by European standards of the late fifteenth century the Indian societies had grown very large. Then the Spanish arrived.

The European Context

Europe's "discovery" of America (the Indians presumably knew where they were) was part of the remarkable European expansion in the fifteenth century. Europe was coming to know the rest of the world, as its navigators and explorers pushed back the frontiers of then-current knowledge of the globe. By the early 1600s they had woven a network of communications all the way around the earth, and had established the economic dominance that would shape the modern world.

This burst of European expansion was made possible by a combination of factors. One was technical skill. Cartography and navigation were notable examples, as was the ability to adapt coastal ships to the challenges of the open ocean. And another example was weaponry, which was to fortify the Europeans against the occasionally well-armed native peoples, as in Mexico.

A second factor was the economic base. Technology alone was not enough. Vikings had shown the technical ability to reach America, but they lacked the resources to carry out settlement and colonization, which required men and capital. In short, the New World was not to be had by speculators of small resources or fragile nerves.

Third, there had to be a European power interested in more than technical expertise and profit. It had to be ready to pursue the unknown with an abnormal determination. Spain and Portugal fit this description. These Catholic monarchies, with their crusading ideal of converting heathen masses to the true religion, had a unique motivation. Spain in particular had come late to the consolidation of its territory against the infidel Muslim occupier. Portugal, although earlier rid of the Muslim intruder, was equally committed to the militant spread of the Christian faith. Their boldness set a precedent for European intruders into Latin America over the next four centuries. However much Latin America struggled, it was to remain an extension, at times a contradiction, of the Europe that had sailed west in the fifteenth century.

Spanish America: From Conquest to Colony, 1492–1600

It was no coincidence that Columbus reached America in the same year as the Spanish liquidated the last Moorish stronghold in Spain. The reconquest down the Iberian peninsula saw the warring Christian nobles acquiring land and the crown strengthening its political control. The result by 1492 was a nobility and would-be nobility anxious for more conquests, and a crown ready to direct these subjects overseas.

The Spanish therefore reached the New World in a conquest spirit already well-developed at home. Spain had presented moderate opportunity for upward social mobility, and there is considerable evidence to suggest that the New World conquerors—Hernán Cortés, Francisco Pizarro, and their followers—came to America in order to win social status as well as wealth. Spanish motivation was no doubt complex. Ferdinand and Isabella and successive monarchs thought the wealth of the New World could strengthen their hand in Europe. Many dedicated missionaries hoped to save the souls of heathen Indians. The conquerors had multiple purposes in mind: as one conquistador said, "We came here to serve God and the King, and also to get rich." But their central motive appears to have been the achievement of noble rank and wealth. (About one-third of the conquerors of Peru came from the lesser or "common" ability; two-thirds were of plebeian origin. These were people with status to gain.) Thus driven, they set out for they knew not what. In a few short years they had toppled the mighty empires of the Aztecs and the Incas.

How did they do it? How could a few hundred Spaniards overthrow empires with millions of Indians? When Cortés set out from Cuba toward Mexico in 1519, he had only 550 men and 16 horses. Within two and a half years he and his battered Spanish contingent (bolstered by several hundred reinforcements) had reduced to rubble the magnificent Aztec capital of Tenochtitlán and accepted the surrender of their disheartened and bewildered man-god, Cuauhtémoc. One explanation for their feat was the superiority of Spanish equipment and tactics—gunpowder (for muskets and cannons), horses, organization, and the confidence to stay constantly on the attack. Another factor was the propensity for the Aztecs to identify Cortés and his followers with the god Quetzalcoatl, whose return to the valley was predicted by myth. Important also was the role of non-Aztec peoples, such as the Tlaxcalans, who had grown restive under Aztec domination and who supplied the Spaniards with troops and advice on appropriate military tactics. Finally, and perhaps most important, an outbreak of smallpox, previously unknown in the Americas, ravaged an Indian population lacking natural immunity. By 1521, two years after the start of the Cortés campaign and less than 30 years after Columbus's first voyage, the Aztec empire had fallen under Spanish control. Cortés lost no time in asserting his authority. He extracted pledges of allegiance from neighboring chieftains and directed a vigorous reconstruction effort.

Some factors that favored the Spanish in Mexico operated also in Peru, but Pizarro's task was simplified by the civil war then wracking the Incan empire: the Inca Atahualpa, preoccupied by the local conflict, never took Pizarro as seriously as warranted. The small Spanish band had accomplished the takeover by 1533. They carted off as their booty a hoard of gold and silver large enough to fill a 12' × 17' room to the height of a man's arm. The dream of El Dorado had come true in the Andes.

The Spanish Conquest was centered in the Caribbean and the strongholds of the two great Indian empires—Aztec and Incan. The Spanish also launched explorations from the major population centers, but they lacked the men or resources to establish direct control in many such areas. Primary Spanish attention focused on their new realms in Mexico and Peru.

It did not take long for Spaniards to recreate many aspects of their own society in the Americas. They laid out typically Spanish designs for cities and created richly complex societies. Coopers, bakers, scribes—people from all walks of life in Spain—came, under tight immigration control, to make their way in the New World.

But there was a shortage of Spanish women. According to a recent study on Peru, for instance, white males outnumbered white females by least 7 to 1. This not only created intense competition for the hands of Spanish women, it also led Spaniards to take Indian women as their consorts. Their mixed-blood children, usually illegitimate, came to be known as *mestizos*. In time, the *mestizo* race would become the dominant ethnic component of much of Spanish America, including Mexico, Central America, and the Andean countries.

The Spanish crown soon realized it had a conflict of interest with the independent-minded conquerors and promptly created an elaborate bureaucracy, designed to keep the New World economy and society under firm control. In Spain the key institution for New World affairs was the Council of the Indies. Overseas the main unit of organization was the viceroyalty, headed by a viceroy ("vice-king") appointed by the king. The first viceroyalty was established in Mexico (then known as New Spain) in 1535, the second in Peru in 1544; two others were set up in the eighteenth century (see Map 2). The church had parallel structures, led by the archbishop and by the officials of the Inquisition.

In practice, this bureaucracy led to intense conflict over matters of jurisdiction, but the genius of the system was that stalemates, once they developed, could always be transmitted to a higher authority, such as the viceroy or the Council of the Indies. This meant that the various institutions would serve as watchdogs over each other (aside from periodic reviews and investigations of performance in office). Another feature of the system was, surprisingly, its flexibility. Virtually all groups had some measure of access to the bureaucracy. And though the crown retained ultimate authority, local officials possessed considerable autonomy, as shown by their occasional responses to royal decrees—*obedezco pero no cumplo* (roughly, "I accept your authority but will not execute this law"). Despite its seeming idiosyncrasies, the Spanish bureaucracy

MAP 2 COLONIAL LATIN AMERICA: POLITICAL ORGANIZATION

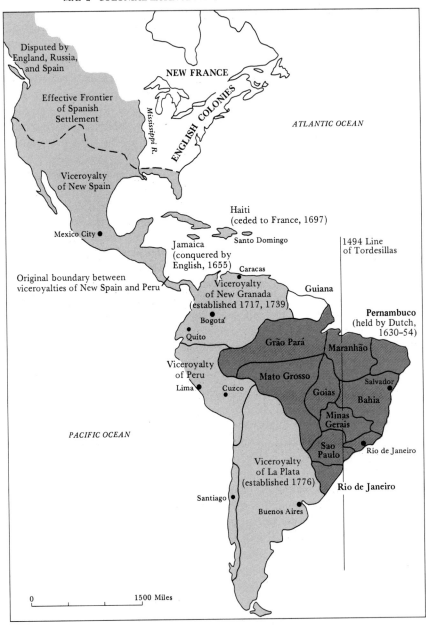

Disputed by England, Russia, and Spain

NEW FRANCE

Effective Frontier of Spanish Settlement

Mississippi R.

ENGLISH COLONIES

ATLANTIC OCEAN

Viceroyalty of New Spain

Mexico City ●

Haiti (ceded to France, 1697)

Santo Domingo

Jamaica (conquered by English, 1655)

1494 Line of Tordesillas

Caracas

Original boundary between viceroyalties of New Spain and Peru

Viceroyalty of New Granada (established 1717, 1739)

Guiana

Bogotá ●

Quito ●

Pernambuco (held by Dutch, 1630–54)

Grão Pará

Maranhão

Viceroyalty of Peru

Lima ●   Cuzco ●

Mato Grosso

Goias

Salvador

Bahia

Minas Gerais

Sao Paulo

Rio de Janeiro ●

PACIFIC OCEAN

Viceroyalty of La Plata (established 1776)

Rio de Janeiro

Santiago ●

Buenos Aires ●

0   1500 Miles

☐ Spanish America: Viceroyalties

◼ Portuguese America (Viceroyalty of Brazil): Captaincies-general ca. 1780

The viceroyalties of La Plata and New Granada originally belonged to the viceroyalty of Peru.

operated rather well in the New World, keeping the colonies under royal rule for nearly 300 years.

Underpinning this political structure was a set of values and assumptions that legitimized monarchical, elitist rule. They stemmed from the fundamental Roman Catholic premise, most clearly articulated by Thomas Aquinas, that there were three kinds of law: divine law, that is, God's own heavenly will; natural law, a perfect reflection or embodiment of divine law in the world of nature; and human law, man's thoroughly imperfect attempt to approximate God's will within society. Born in original sin, humanity was fallible by definition, and it was only by the grace of God that some people were less fallible than others. The goal of political organization, therefore, was to elevate the less fallible to power so they could interpret and execute God's will in a superior way. And the ruler, once in power, was responsible to his or her own conscience and to God—not to the will of the people.

This rationale provided convincing justification for the supremacy of the Spanish monarch. Its theological origin revealed and fortified close links between church and state. Resuscitated in the postcolonial era, as it has often been, the code also furnished, as we shall see, a devastating critique of democratic theory. In time, political rulers would thus legitimize their power on the basis of residual aspects of traditional Roman Catholic doctrine.

The empire's economic structure reflected the prevailing mercantilist theory that economic activity should enhance the power and prestige of the state, measured on the basis of gold or silver bullion. The good mercantilist was supposed to run a favorable balance of trade, thus acquiring species or bullion in payment. Following this logic, Spain attempted to monopolize the access to wealth discovered in the New World. The first target was mining, first of gold and then mainly of silver. Another goal was to maintain complete control over commerce. Agriculture, by contrast, received little initial attention from crown officials (unless it competed with Spain), and manufacturing, when later considered, was actively discouraged.

The central foundation for this economy was Indian labor, obtained from the natives by one form of coercion or another. They paid tribute to the crown and its appointed emissaries. Since cheap labor was so critical, the Spanish crown, colonists, and clerics fought bitterly for control of the Indians. In 1542, seeking to curtail the colonists, the king decreed the "New Laws," aimed at protecting the Indians by removing them from direct tutelage of the conquistadores and bringing them under the direct jurisdiction of the crown. By 1600 the crown had largely succeeded in this task, at least in legal terms. In reality, however, these changes altered only the legal form of oppression; the fact of oppression persisted.

For the Indians, the Conquest meant above all a drastic fall in population. Scholars have argued long and hard about the size of the indigenous population when the Spanish arrived. The most reliable studies of central Mexico place the preconquest populations, as of 1519, at around 25 million; for 1523 the figure is 16.8 million, for 1580 it is 1.9 million, and for 1605 it is 1 million—a total decline of 95 percent! Data on Peru are less complete, but they also show continuing decline, from 1.3 million in 1570 (40 years after the Conquest) to less than 600,000 in 1620, a drop of more than 50 percent. However uncertain the exact magnitudes, the Conquest clearly resulted in demographic calamity, largely attributable to diseases such as smallpox, measles, and influenza.

The Indian survivors saw their social order undermined and distorted. Forced to give their labor to the Spaniards, the Indians struggled to maintain their traditional social networks. The most fertile land was seized by the conquerors—who, in many cases, converted the land to raising livestock. Indians saw the symbols of their old religion destroyed and they clung to such syncretistic practices as they could devise. Diseases took a heavier toll of men than of women, and the resulting sex imblance further disrupted marriage patterns and family structure.

To offset the decline in Indian population, especially in tropical lowland regions, Spaniards began importing black slaves from Africa—a practice already familiar in Spain and Portugal and their Atlantic islands. Between 1518 and 1870, Spanish America imported more than 1.5 million slaves—over 16 percent of the entire Atlantic slave trade—mostly through Cuba and the northern tip of South America, destined for labor in the lowland coastal areas. Brazil, with its extensive sugar plantations, brought in about 3.7 million.

As we shall see later, Latin America produced largely multiracial societies, in contrast to the highly polarized biracial society that developed in North America.

The three ethnic components of colonial Spanish American population—Indians, Europeans, Africans—fit together in a social structure that divided itself along lines of race and function. The white sector, which included less than 2 percent of the sixteenth century population, was the most powerful and prestigious. In the same period the mixed bloods contained free blacks, *mestizos,* and mulattoes—all told, less than 3 percent of the total. The Indians, over 95 percent of the population, were placed in a unique position carefully limited and protected by a battery of royal laws.

There were additional important social relationships. One was the rivalry between whites born in Spain (*peninsulares*) and whites born in the New World (*criollos* or creoles). Another was the structure of occupations, such as the church, the army, merchants, and sheep farmers.

22

These overlapping social categories produced in colonial Spanish America a complex stratification system in which social status was the major prize. Conflict between the *peninsulares* and creoles would eventually shape the struggles that led to independence.

Interaction between the racial groupings was less tension-filled, but still tenuous. Though interracial concubinage was widespread, interracial marriage was probably rare, and even then it followed gradations—whites might marry *mestizos,* and *mestizos* might marry Indians, but whites seldom married Indians. As civil and religious consecration was extended to interracial liaisons, especially those involving whites, they tended to blur social boundaries, legitimize aspirations for mobility, and foment uncertainty about the system of stratification. Movement definitely existed, both socially and geographically, and individuals could experience considerable change during their lifetimes.

Marriage and family customs generally assumed male domination of females. The cult of masculine superiority (*machismo*) appeared early in Latin America, within a broad range of social and ethnic strata, and many women led restricted lives. But contrary to the stereotypical image, the standard family was not always headed by a male patriarch presiding over a large brood of children. More often than not families consisted of married couples reasonably close in age with two to four children.

But not all women married, and those who did, often did not remain married for life. Data on the sixteenth century are sparse, but by 1811, according to census results, only 44 percent of the adult females in Mexico City were married. Many women were widows, and approximately one-third of the households in Mexico City were headed by single women. This was due in part to the lower life expectancy for men. For whatever reason, many Mexican women spent much of their lives as single women.

Spanish America: The Transformation of Colonial Society, 1600–1750

Spanish American colonies underwent profound changes soon after 1600. The first impetus came from Europe, where Spain began to lose the power it once had in the late fifteenth and sixteenth centuries. After the defeat of the *armada* by the English in 1588, the royal treasury repeatedly went bankrupt, the nobles challenged the crown, Catalonia erupted in revolt, and in 1640 Portugal—since 1580 governed by the Spanish monarch—successfully reasserted its independence. At the same time, Spain and Portugal began losing their monopolies on the New World. The English, Dutch, and French established settlements in North America and also gained footholds in the Caribbean.

With Spain's decline, the rest of seventeenth century Europe sought to counterbalance France, now the leading power. The New World became a vital element in the European power equation. This became clear in the War of the Spanish Succession (1700–1713), which installed the Bourbons on the Spanish throne and gave the British the contract (*asiento*) for the slave trade to the Spanish colonies.

Far-reaching changes were also taking place within the colonies. The ethnic composition of society underwent profound transition. Continued immigration and natural increase turned the whites, mainly creoles, into a sizeable segment of the population, perhaps 20 percent by 1825. Much more dramatic was the relative growth of the *mestizo* and mixed-blood category, from less than 3 percent around 1570 to approximately 28 percent by 1825. The shift in the Indian population was even greater, although in a different direction—down from over 95 percent to barely 42 percent. By the same year (1825), blacks accounted for about 12 percent of the Spanish American population.

As time passed, the creoles began to assume active roles in key sectors of the economy, such as mining and commerce. Especially striking was their increasing ownership of land (something the early Spanish monarchs had discouraged) and, in some areas, the appearance of great landed estates, or haciendas. Typified by vast territorial holdings and debt peonage, the haciendas often became virtually autonomous rural communities governed by the owners or their foreman. Land titles were hereditary, and most were held by creoles. The hacienda in Spanish America brought a reversion to some of the values (although not the structure) of a classic feudal society. By the mid-eighteenth century, the crown was confronting a proud New World nobility.

The political role of the creoles was less obvious. In the late seventeenth and early eighteenth centuries they held many important political posts, mainly on the local level, such as in town councils or *audiencias*. Upper-level positions were still reserved for *peninsulares*. With the decline of Spain as an imperial power, however, political institutions ceased to function as before.

Portuguese America: A Different World?

The colonial history of Portuguese America contrasts with the story of colonial Spanish America. Under the royal House of Aviz, Portugal had established a far-flung empire with outposts in India, China, Africa, and some Atlantic islands. In fact, Portugal had become the European leader in exploration by shrewd use of its superior technical skills in cartography and navigation. In 1494 the Treaty of Tordesillas between Spain and Portugal granted Portugal the eastern half of South America (the dividing line could hardly be precise in the unknown territory), and in 1500 Pedro Alvares Cabral, the Portuguese sea captain

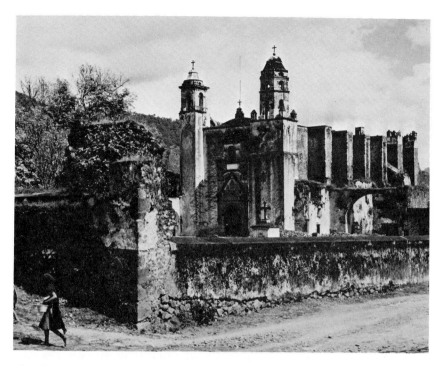

The fortress-like construction of this sixteenth century Dominican monastery in south-central Mexico aptly illustrates the alliance of church and crown in the conquest of New Spain. (Courtesy of the Library of Congress.)

credited with "discovering" Brazil, claimed that vast territory for his monarch. (See Map 2.)

This New World incursion differed from Spain's in two fundamental respects. First, there was no Indian civilization in Brazil comparable to the Aztecs or the Incas. The Tupí-Guaraní, the largest language group, lived along the coast from what is now Venezuela into southern Brazil and Paraguay, and Tapuias inhabited the interior. Some Indians were cannibalistic and most were semi-nomadic—which meant that Brazil would have to be settled gradually, rather than taken at a single blow. More important, it meant that the Portuguese, unlike the Spanish, did not face a highly organized, settled indigenous civilization. These Indians had built no imposing cities and they had no mythic explanations for this sudden alien intrusion.

Furthermore, there was no trace of silver or gold, and consequently no easy path to fabulous wealth. The first important economic activity was the export of brazilwood (hence the country's modern name), prized in Europe for its qualities as a source of dye. And in time, contrasting sharply with most of colonial Spanish America, agriculture, especially cane sugar cultivation, predominated in the Brazilian colonial economy.

The scarcity of human and mineral resources forced the Portuguese crown to resort to unusual means in trying to persuade or entice its subjects to occupy the New World holdings. In the 1530s the kings started making massive grants of effective power over (almost totally unexplored) land, usually to military men with prior experience in India or Africa or to hand-picked personal favorites, and in either instance to men "of gentle blood." The land donations were huge, averaging about 130 miles along the coastline and running all the way back (as much as 500 miles or more) to the imaginary Line of Demarcation that divided Portuguese from Spanish America.

Not until 1549 did the crown begin to establish an effective imperial bureaucracy—but the purpose was to protect the area from French and British intrusions and not, as in the case of Spanish America, to reconquer the possessions from the conquerors. On the contrary, it was the lack of a Portuguese presence that forced Lisbon to act.

Partly because in its first century Brazil received a lower priority than Portugal's other overseas dominions (which were more profitable), monarchical control started out much looser than in Spanish America. Even when the Portuguese crown tightened up after 1549, the royal institutions were largely limited to the Atlantic coast, where the taxes on exports could be easily collected. Power on the local level rested with the landowners and the town councils. Even the church was weak in sixteenth century Brazil, compared to Mexico and Peru.

During the late sixteenth and early seventeenth centuries, landowners developed a lucrative sugar industry in the Brazilian Northeast. Having earlier made technological breakthroughs in sugar processing in their Atlantic islands, such as the Madeiras, the Portuguese had come to rely on the Dutch to retail the product in Europe. To grow sugar in America, however, required abundant labor. The Portuguese landowners first turned to the Brazilian Indians. As in Mexico and Peru, however, the Indians soon fell victim to devastating European diseases. The survivors often fled into the interior. Although the Portuguese continued to exploit the Indians until well into the eighteenth century, they had to look elsewhere for a satisfactory labor supply.

The obvious source was Africa. By the early 1500s the Spanish and Portuguese already had a half-century of experience with African slave labor, both at home and in their Atlantic islands, such as the Canaries (Spanish) and the Madeiras (Portuguese). It was not until the 1580s that the Portuguese saw enough potential profit to warrant importing African slaves. By 1650, however, Northeastern Brazil had become the world's greatest source of cane sugar, produced predominantly with

African slave labor. Her sugar exports were estimated at £2.5 million a year, which made Brazil's coastal Northeast probably the richest single region in the entire Americas.

Other European powers wanted in on the sugar boom. The British and Dutch brought new technology, which eventually made the Caribbean into the world's preeminent sugar cane producer. The Dutch invaded Brazil itself in 1624 and controlled the sugar-rich Northeast until an alliance of Portuguese planters, merchants, and mixed-blood troops pushed them back into the ocean in 1654. Yet the Portuguese were never again to duplicate the near monopoly on New World sugar production they had enjoyed earlier in the century.

In the central and southern regions of Brazil the economy first centered on cattle-raising and, more importantly, on slave raids against the Indians (who were often shipped to the Northeast). As one Jesuit missionary lamented, "the true purpose" of these expeditions "was to capture Indians: to draw from their veins the red gold which has always been the mine of that province!" Carried out by the *bandeirantes,* whose legendary status in national history resembles a mixture of the California gold prospectors and the American cowboy, these forays extended Portuguese control over the Brazilian interior. Furthermore, they led to the discovery of mineral wealth, which had so long eluded the Portuguese. In the 1690s gold was found in Minas Gerais ("General Mines") and people flocked to the area. Diamonds were located in 1729. Mining reached its peak in 1750, with a yearly output of £3.6 million, although the low level of technological expertise contributed to a decline in mining near the late 1700s. The era also brought a brief export boom in cotton, but Brazil would have to await the nineteenth century coffee boom before regaining much prosperity.

Brazil's colonial economy had been created for export. It was "the King's plantation." The resulting social structure reflected the investment the Portuguese crown had made. The most important single human consequence was the pervasive presence of African slaves. Over 2.5 million Africans had been brought to Brazil by 1810, nearly one-third of the Atlantic slave trade in that era. Blacks were a major component of Portuguese American society, in contrast to most areas of Spanish America.

As shown in Table 1-1, blacks amounted to nearly one-half of Brazil's total population around 1825, compared with 12 percent in Spanish America, and the mixed-blood group, mainly mulattos, added another 18 percent. All in all, perhaps as much as two-thirds of the entire Brazilian population in the early nineteenth century were of partial or total black ancestry.

The multiracial colonial Brazilian society was highly stratified, according to the relatively little research done to date. Racial intermar-

TABLE 1-1   Racial Composition of Early Latin American Population

	Spanish America		*Portuguese America*	
	1570 (%)	*1825* (%)	*1570* (%)	*1825* (%)
Whites (legally defined or by social convention)	1.3	18.2	2.4	23.4
Mixed-bloods (*mestizo* or mulatto)	2.5	28.3	3.5	17.8
Blacks	(included with mixed-bloods)	11.9	(included with mixed-bloods)	49.8
Indians	96.3	41.7	94.1	9.1
Total	100.1	100.1	100.0	100.1

Note: Some details may not add up to 100 because of rounding.

Source: Adapted from Richard M. Morse, "The Heritage of Latin America," in Louis Hartz, ed., *The Founding of New Societies* (New York: Harcourt, Brace & World, 1964), p. 138.

riage was rare, accounting for no more than 10 percent of all mar-riages, and, as in Spanish America, it followed lines of gradation—whites might marry mulattoes, but they almost never married blacks. Concu-binage and common-law relationships were more frequent among blacks than whites. As in Mexico City, about one-third the family units in a sample of colonial Brazilian communities were headed by single women.

A second major facet of the social structure was internal division within the white ruling stratum, particularly between Brazilian-born landowners and Portuguese-born merchants. This difference resem-bled the creole-*peninsular* conflict in Spanish America, and it had the potential for leading to an independence movement. As it turned out, European politics cut the process short. In any case, the looser crown control of Brazil had generated less resentment among the colonists than in most of Spanish America.

Portuguese America's integration into the Western economy as a pe-ripheral area resembled that of Spanish America, but with notable dif-ferences: first, for two centuries Brazil lacked the gold and silver that obsessed the Spaniards in Mexico and Peru; second, Brazil's main con-tribution until the eighteenth century was agricultural, not mining; third, and perhaps most important, Portugal had developed a simpler system for ensuring revenues from its prize colony ("the milch cow," as Brazil was known in Lisbon). Unlike Spain, Portugal did not develop a vast bureaucratic network aimed at taxing and controlling the domestic market. Instead, it concentrated almost entirely on taxing Brazil's ex-ports. As a result, Brazil offered less potential than Spanish America for breeding a powerful alliance of colonial interests which might rebel against the political authority of the mother country.

The Roots of Independence

The independence movements that led to the creation of most of present-day Latin America's nation-states owed their origins to events in Europe. Most were not radical and none brought cataclysmic changes in the social order. Much of the impetus proved to be conservative, thereby shaping the direction of the young republics in the early nineteenth century. Our story begins back in Europe.

The Bourbon monarchs of Spain, whose family had succeeded to the crown in 1713, had sought to reverse Spain's decline, both in Europe and America. Hoping to shore up New World defenses against rival European powers while also increasing revenues for the crown, the Bourbon kings imposed far-reaching administrative and political reforms. One was to create new viceroyalties—one at New Granada (first in 1717, then again in 1739) and another at Buenos Aires (1776).

In addition, Charles III (1759–88) replaced the complex administrative arrangement of the Hapsburgs with the intendancy system. In effect, this led to the replacement of the hated *corrigedores* in Spanish America with "intendants"—local governors who directly responsible to the crown, not to the viceroy. Almost all of the intendants were Spanish-born *peninsulares,* rather than American creoles, presumably thereby assuring loyalty to the monarch. The intendants greatly strengthened crown control over government, but also collided with prosperous creoles, many of whom had taken advantage of relaxed administration.

This trend could be seen in the administration of local courts. Desperately needing funds, the late seventeenth century Hapsburg monarchs put court appointments up for sale, as had Philip II earlier in the century. It was creoles who bought, and by 1750, out of 93 judges 51 were American-born. The Bourbon monarchs reversed this trend, and by 1807 only 12 out of 99 judges were creoles. Ultimately, creoles would decide to look elsewhere for positions of authority and prestige.

One place they looked was to the town councils or *cabildos,* which were barely functioning by the early eighteenth century. *Cabildo* offices did not always find eager buyers. With the arrival of the intendants, however, more efficient taxation gave the *cabildos* increased revenues— and they reasserted their role as local councils. The *cabildos* thus became institutional bases of creole authority.

Charles III also sought to increase royal power by tightening crown control of the church. The most dramatic step was the expulsion of the Jesuit order from all of Spanish America in 1767. Charles saw the

Jesuits as a state within a state, a rival source of power and wealth. The best properties of the Jesuits were auctioned off and the proceeds, of course, went to the crown.

The military was another power source. To ward off outside threats and to crush any potential rebellion, the king decreed the establishment of colonial militias, an excellent source of prestige for status-hungry creoles. But it also altered the military balance. By 1800, for instance, there were only 6000 members of the regular Spanish army in the viceroyalty of New Spain—compared to 23,000 American-born members of the colonial militia. This was the foundation of the patriot army that would later fight for independence.

The Bourbons wanted especially to promote colonial economic development, in order to strengthen their hand in Europe. In 1778, Charles III promulgated a Decree of Free Trade, which meant that the 24 ports of Spanish America could now trade directly with any port in Spain or with each other (but *not* with any port outside the Spanish realm). Commerce would no longer be restricted to four colonial ports (Veracruz, Cartagena, Lima/Callao, and Panama) or tied to the Cadiz monopoly in Spain. Buenos Aires immediately began to profit from the measure. In fact, contraband trade had long flourished on these formerly forbidden routes. But the crown increased its customs receipts, since it could now get at the goods that were once smuggled.

Partly for this reason, the colonial economy flourished under the Bourbons. The port of Buenos Aires, a small and lackluster town in 1776, grew to a city of 50,000 by the year 1800. Mexico was minting three times as much silver and gold in the 1790s as it had been in the 1740s. Commerce was thriving by the turn of the century.

The Bourbon policies appeared to be a success. Administration became more efficient, defenses improved, commerce swelled, and governmental revenues increased. But creoles were upset by many of these changes, which threatened (and often managed) to reduce their status and influence. It was the challenge to creole status, more than the influence of Enlightenment thought or the example of British colonies in North America, that ultimately prompted the Spanish American dominions to opt for independence.

There had been colonial resistance, to be sure. In 1780, Tupac Amaru II, claiming to be a lineal descendant of the Incas, led an Indian revolt with an army of nearly 80,000 men. It took nearly two years of brutal fighting to stamp out the insurrections that swept over southern Peru and Bolivia. In 1781 the citizens of Socorro, in New Granada, violently protested against a tax increase and the disruption spread through much of the viceroyalty. Although patriotic Latin American historians have often described these events as "precursors" to the creole-led independence movements of the nineteenth century, this was not the case. As for Tupac Amaru II, some strands in that insurrection pointed toward independence, but on terms of Indian leadership that would never gain solid creole support. In the 1781 rebellion in New Granada, the protestors did not seek independence from the Spanish crown. They were protesting within the system, not against it.

Then how did independence come? Once again Latin America's fate was determined by dynastic politics in the Old World. After having tried and failed to help the French Bourbons save their crown, Spain allied with the revolutionary French regime in 1796, a pact that led directly to the annihilation of the Spanish navy at the Battle of Trafalgar (1805). Meanwhile, Napoleon Bonaparte, now France's dictator, in 1807 occupied Portugal, England's long-time ally. Napoleon reached the hills above the capital city of Lisbon just as the English royal navy was whisking the Portuguese royal house of Braganza and its court off to Brazil. Napoleon then turned to Spain. In 1808 he occupied Madrid, planting his brother, Joseph, on the Spanish throne. This was the act that prompted the colonies to revolt.

There was Spanish resistance to Joseph, as supporters of Ferdinand VII rallied to the cause. A junta was set up in Seville to rule in Ferdinand's name. In 1810 there followed a parliament, or *cortes,* dominated by Spanish liberals who had moved into the vacuum created by the monarch's absence. In 1812 it proclaimed a new constitution, which asserted the authority of parliament and restricted the role of the king.

The Colonial Response

When Napoleon put his brother on the Spanish throne the creoles rejected him as an imposter, just as the Spaniards had done. Since Spain no longer had a government, the colonists argued, sovereignty reverted to the people. Could this logic be extended to an argument for independence?

Yet there was nothing inevitable about the train of events that overtook Spanish America. Neither the European Enlightenment nor the example of the American Revolution alone would have fomented rebellions in Spanish America. Without Napoleon's intervention the Spanish American colonies might all have remained Spanish until well into the nineteenth century, as did Cuba.

One of the focal points of resistance to Napoleon was Buenos Aires, the seat of the newest viceroyalty, whose *cabildo* had already acquired remarkable authority. In 1806, an English squadron occupied the city of Buenos Aires, sending the viceroy fleeing to the interior city of Córdoba. A citizen's army drove the British out, and in 1807 it made short shrift of a second British attack. So it was the creoles, not the viceregal authorities, who successfully defended Buenos Aires from invasion. This demonstrated both the weakness of the crown and the capacity of the local citizenry.

Another lingering issue to the La Plata region was free trade. The proclamation of 1778 had partially opened up trade for Buenos Aires, which could now ship goods directly to Spain—rather than along the long tortuous route overland to Panama and finally across the Atlantic. But it was England, not Spain, that offered the most promising market for hides and salted beef. A contraband trade therefore flourished and Argentine desire for open commerce with other European countries intensified.

In 1809, after Napoleon had ousted Spanish King Ferdinand VII, a young lawyer named Mariano Moreno called for a two-year experiment with totally free trade. Moreno argued that such a step would strengthen loyalties to the Spanish crown and provide increased revenues—since duties could be charged on legal trade, but not on contraband traffic. Late in the year the viceroy granted Buenos Aires limited freedom of trade with nations allied to Spain or neutral in the Napoleonic wars. Once again, the elite of Buenos Aires tasted political success.

When Napoleon's forces seized the centers of Bourbon resistance in Spain in 1810, leading citizens met and decided to create a "provisional junta of the Provinces of the Río de la Plata, governing for Ferdinand VII." Although it was not until 1816 that a congress formally declared independence, the pattern had been set.

In 1810 a similar movement emerged in Caracas, where the municipal *cabildo* deposed the Spanish captain-general and organized a junta to govern in the name of Ferdinand VII. As in Buenos Aires, the insurgent group consisted mainly of wealthy creoles. Their leaders had more decisive views. The most famous, Simón Bolívar, from the beginning wanted independence for America.

Born into a wealthy creole family in Caracas in 1783, Bolívar was orphaned at the age of nine. He was then sent to Spain to complete his education, and after three years he returned to Caracas with a young Spanish bride, who within months died of yellow fever. Bolívar was devastated, and never remarried. (He did not deprive himself of female companionship, however.) A magnetic, charming, persuasive personality, he inspired loyalty and confidence among his followers. Familiar with the ideas of the Enlightenment, he vowed in 1805 to free his homeland from Spanish rule. In July 1811, the congress that convened to govern Venezuela responded to his vision by declaring independence.

But the pro-Ferdinand junta in Seville proved more resilient than had been expected, sending troops to crush this upstart rebellion. Together first with blacks, then with *llaneros* (cowboys) of the Venezuelan flood plains, Spanish forces defeated colonial troops under Francisco de Miranda. Bolívar himself managed to escape to New Granada. In 1813 he returned to Venezuela and won a series of startling military victories, triumphs that earned him the title of "the Liberator."

Events in Europe again intruded. In 1814 Ferdinand VII returned to the Spanish throne, annulled the liberal constitution of 1812 and restored himself in an absolute monarchy. Many creoles concluded that since the king was back there was no reason to continue their mobilization.

Bolívar now saw his men and munitions dwindle. After a series of defeats he was obliged in 1814 to flee again to New Granada and then to the English island of Jamaica. He hoped that Latin America might become a single nation, but knew the odds were low. Here he was much influenced by the recent failures to establish republican government in Venezuela. Republican democracy "is overperfect, and it demands political virtues and talents far superior to our own. For the same reason, I reject a monarchy that is part aristocracy and part democracy although with such a government England has achieved much fortune and splendor." So Bolívar concluded: "Do not adopt the best system of government, but the one which is most likely to succeed."

In New Spain events took a different course. In 1808 *peninsulares* (rather than creoles) ousted the viceroy José de Iturrigaray, and promptly recognized the junta in Seville. Mexico City was firmly in royalist hands until 1821.

The provinces of New Spain, particularly north of the capital, were another story. By 1810 a group of prominent creoles, including a priest named Miguel Hidalgo y Costilla, were planning to seize authority in Ferdinand's name. When the plot was discovered, Hidalgo decided to act. On September 16, 1810, in the little town of Dolores, he gave an impassioned call to arms. And, curiously, it was not the local notables who rallied, but rather the long-suffering mixed-bloods and Indians. They flocked to the banner of the Virgin of Guadalupe, whom they had long ago appropriated as their own. This "colored plebe" now formed a massive, angry, undisciplined army—"a horde," in the eyes of the startled creole elite.

Hidalgo's men stormed into the city of Guanajuato, where they massacred 500 Spanish soldiers in an all-out assault on the municipal granary. After looting freely, they headed toward Mexico City. Hidalgo struggled to maintain control.

By November 1810 Hidalgo was on the outskirts of Mexico City with about 50,000 men in arms. In a decision that has prompted debate and speculation ever since, he then pulled back from the city. Surely he could have taken the capital. Why did he withdraw? Was he afraid of his own following? Instead Hidalgo moved north. After a defeat near

Guadalajara in early 1811 he went on to Coahuila where he was captured and subsequently executed by a firing squad at Chihuahua.

Leadership now passed to José María Morelos, another priest. Like Hidalgo, Morelos supported the abolition of Indian tribute and slavery, and even wanted agrarian reform. The latter was an explosive issue among the colonial elite. He insisted, too, that citizens had the right to choose their own form of government. Ultimately, Morelos envisioned "a new government, by which all inhabitants, except *peninsulares,* would no longer be designated as Indians, mulattoes, or castas, but all would be known as Americans." Thus Morelos combined nationalism with a commitment to social and racial equality.

In 1813 the Congress of Chilpancingo declared Mexico's independence from Spain (although it is September 16, the anniversary of Hidalgo's speech, that is celebrated as the country's independence day). The congress also decreed that slavery should be abolished and that Roman Catholicism should be the state religion. The constitution, adopted the following year, affirmed the ideal of popular sovereignty, created a system of indirect elections, and designed a powerful legislature alongside a weak three-person executive.

Meanwhile the Spanish were winning military victories. One of the Spanish commanders was the young Agustín de Iturbide, later to play a central role in Mexican independence. In 1815 Morelos was captured, tried (by the Inquisition as well as by secular authorities), and executed. Others continued to fight for the cause, but the Spaniards now held the upper hand.

Thus ended the first phase of the Spanish American independence movements. New Spain's Morelos and Hidalgo were both dead. Bolívar languished in exile in Jamaica. The junta in the Río de la Plata struggled to maintain unity and had yet to call for independence. By 1815, with Ferdinand back on the throne, the Spanish crown appeared to have snuffed out its colonial rebellion.

Achieving Independence

The Spanish military advantage in South America did not last long. In 1816 Bolívar returned to Venezuela and began duplicating his earlier victories. But now he had allied with José Antonio Páez, the brilliant leader of the fearless *llaneros* who had earlier fought for the royalists. Now Páez was fighting for independence from Spain. Bolívar's cause was further bolstered by the arrival of reinforcements from England, which by 1819 numbered over 4000. Thus strengthened, Bolívar established firm control of Venezuela by early 1819.

After defeating Spanish forces in New Granada, Bolívar attempted in 1821 to create a new state of Gran Colombia, uniting Venezuela,

New Granada, and Ecuador. It gained little support, so Bolívar marched southward, hunting for more royalists and Spaniards to defeat.

Meanwhile, José de San Martín was conducting an extraordinary military compaign in the south. The son of a Spanish officer, born on the northern frontier of present-day Argentina, he began a military career at the age of eleven. In 1812 he offered his services to the junta in Buenos Aires, having decided in favor of independence for the colonies. A soldier by training and outlook, he did not have the political acumen of Bolívar or the social commitment of Morelos, but he was a skillful military strategist.

As commander of the rebel forces, San Martín was ready by early 1817 to attempt one of the most daring exploits of this era: leading an army of 5000 across the Andes for a surprise attack on royalist troops in Chile. He caught the Spaniards completely off guard, won a major victory in the battle of Chacabuco, and triumphantly entered the city of Santiago. San Martín now prepared for the next step in his campaign, the liberation of Peru.

By 1820 San Martín reached the Peruvian coast. Lima was even more monarchist than Mexico City. As the capital of a major viceroyalty, the city had received numerous favors and privileges from the crown. Although the elevation of Buenos Aires to a viceroyalty in the Bourbon era had hurt Lima economically, its monarchist sentiment was still strong. Creoles and *peninsulares* both tended to favor the continuation of Ferdinand VII's rule. San Martín withheld his attack, noting: "I do not seek military glory, nor am I ambitious for the title of conqueror of Peru: I only wish to free it from oppression. What good would Lima do me if its inhabitants were hostile politically?"

Here, too, radical change in Spain catalyzed events. When Ferdinand VII suddenly endorsed the liberal constitution of 1812, the turnabout stunned his Lima supporters. They were especially distressed over the abolition of the Inquisition and the challenge to the dignity of priests. Many could accept limitations on monarchical authority, but not on the role and power of the church.

This turn of events in Spain drastically altered the climate of opinion in Mexico City and Lima. Independence from Spain was no longer a radical or even a liberal cause. Now it was a *conservative* goal, a means of upholding traditional values and social codes. As if acknowledging this fact, the *cabildo* of Lima invited San Martín to enter the city in mid-1821. On July 28, he formally proclaimed the independence of Peru.

After further skirmishes with royalist troops San Martín went to Ecuador for a historic meeting with Simón Bolívar. Exactly what happened there has never been established. Bolívar may have set the tone when he offered a toast "to the two greatest men in America, General San Martín and myself." Apparently Bolívar rejected San Martín's proposal for a monarchy in Peru, insisted on the federation of Gran Colombia, and declined San Martín's offer to serve under his command. In any case, San Martín then resigned all his offices and soon went to Europe, where he died in 1850.

In late 1823 Bolívar moved to Peru, where the Spaniards still maintained an imposing force. In 1824 the royalists were decisively defeated by colonial troops in the battle of Ayacucho. In 1825 Bolívar entered Upper Peru (present-day Bolivia) in the hope that Peru and Upper Peru might form a single nation, but he was too late. The regional leaders of Upper Peru were set on creating their own republic. They promptly did so, naming it for Bolívar and making him president for life.

After returning to Lima, Bolívar went on to Gran Colombia, hoping to patch up the failing federation. By now he had grown bitter and vindictive, upset that his dreams had failed to materialize. In 1830 both Venezuela and Ecuador withdrew from Gran Colombia. Suffering from tuberculosis, Bolívar looked back in despair. "America," he said, "America is ungovernable. Those who have served the revolution have plowed the sea." On December 17, at the age of only 47, the Liberator died of tuberculosis.

In Mexico the defeat of Morelos in 1815 stalled the independence movement—until Ferdinand VII declared allegiance to the constitution of 1812, thus pushing prosperous and prominent creoles to the side of independence. The cause was led by the same Agustín de Iturbide who had led the royalists against Morelos.

The opportunistic Iturbide persuaded the viceroy to give him command of royalist forces in the south. He then marched against a rebel leader with whom he immediately struck an alliance—for the sake of independence. In 1821 he issued a call for three "guarantees": of religion (the Catholic faith to be the official creed), of independence (presumably a monarchy), and union (fair treatment for creoles and *peninsulares* alike). Iturbide took Mexico City and established an empire—with himself, of course, as emperor. It lasted only two years.

In Central America the landed creole class became as worried about liberal dominance in Spain as had been their counterparts in Mexico. In 1822 the Central American landowners decided to cast their lot with Iturbide's empire and announced their annexation to royalist Mexico. When Iturbide abdicated in 1923, the modern-day Central American states, from Guatemala to Costa Rica (excluding Panama) became the independent United Provinces of Central America.

The Brazilian Path to Independence

Independence came to Brazil in a manner very different from that of Spanish America. That was partly due to the fact that Brazil was by 1800 far more populous and prosperous than the tiny mother country. By contrast, no single Spanish colonial territory equalled metropolitan Spain in economic or political power. When the colonials proclaimed independence, Spain fought back doggedly and Spanish Americans grew to hate the crown. The Portuguese, on the other hand, did not even have the military power to stop the Brazilians' move toward political autonomy.

The context of Brazilian independence pointed up another important difference. When the Napoleonic army invaded Iberia in November 1807 the entire Portuguese court was able to flee to Brazil, thanks to the British royal navy.

Upon arriving in early 1808, the Portuguese court found a colony which had no printing presses, no academic faculties, and no commerce, save with the mother country. The newly arrived Prince Regent and later Dom João VI promptly decreed the end of Portugal's commercial monopoly by opening Brazil's ports. His logic was obvious. Since Napoleon now controlled Portugal, the exiled Portuguese monarch could only continue to benefit from Brazil's foreign trade if the formerly exclusive link with Lisbon was severed. The prime beneficiaries were the British, who had, after all, brought the Braganza family and its retinue to Brazil.

Britain gained privileged access to Brazil in 1810 by official, fifteen-year agreements which: (1) gave Britain the lowest tariff (even lower than Portugal!) on goods entering Brazil; (2) committed the Portuguese crown to the gradual abolition of the African slave trade; and (3) guaranteed British subjects in Brazil the right of trial by British-named judges. These treaties soon caused deep resentment among the Brazilian elite.

The exiled Portuguese monarch now set about creating new institutions, such as a national library, a national museum, and a botanical garden, all in Rio. A French artistic mission was requested to speed professionalization in architecture, painting, and sculpture.

The crown also sought to attract foreign immigrants to Brazil. It had very limited success, and large-scale European immigration was not to begin until the late 1880s. There was a push to promote textile manufacture, including repeal of the 1785 royal decree that banned all industry. But such measures could not get at the deeper causes of Brazil's economic backwardness: lack of capital, technology, skilled labor, and a significant domestic market.

In late 1808 French troops were driven from Portugal, and an assembly (*Cortes Gerais*) was called to write a new constitution. The newly victorious Portuguese liberals, interested in exploiting Brazil's wealth, pressed for the return of the royal court to Portugal. Dom João soon did return to Lisbon, leaving his son Dom Pedro behind in Brazil as the Prince Regent of the Combined Kingdoms.

Attention now focused on the *Cortes Gerais,* which approved measures that would have restored Lisbon's royal trade monopoly in Brazil by setting lower tariffs for imports arriving in Portuguese vessels and/or trans-shipped from Portugal. The *Cortes* also approved measures returning the individual Brazilian provinces to direct and separate rule from Lisbon, thereby undermining the central rule created in Rio do Janeiro after 1808. However "liberal" the Portuguese Liberals were in Portugal, they abhorred the move toward autonomy of their American "co-kingdom."

The landowners and urban professionals who constituted the Brazilian elite had been preparing to confront the Portuguese recolonizers. Their passionate rhetoric overflowed the fledgling Rio press. They wanted the Prince regent, Dom Pedro, to refuse to return to Lisbon. By June 1822 Dom Pedro had decided to convoke a Constituent Assembly in Brazil. The *Cortes* in Lisbon then demanded the Prince Regent's immediate return and took new steps to reverse Brazil's growing autonomy. The Brazilian plantation owners' pressure on Dom Pedro now paid off: On September 7, 1822, in São Paulo, he defied the summons of the *Cortes.* "I shall remain!" he cried, giving birth to the only durable independent monarchy in modern Latin American history.

To win their independence the Brazilians had to fight, but not on the scale of the Spanish Americans. The fiercest combat came in Bahia, on the northeastern coast, and Grão Pará, in the eastern Amazon valley. In Bahia a junta proclaimed loyalty to Portugal and fought off the local pro-independence rebels. In 1823 the rebels triumphed, aided by Admiral Cochrane, one of the English military officers hired to give the rebel governments experienced help in combat. Another mercenary, Admiral Grenfell, led the victory over a similar loyalist junta in Grão Pará. His forces then mopped up a local rebel wing that was demanding more radical social change. In Brazil, as in Mexico, the elite was alert to repress any fundamental challenge to the socioeconomic establishment.

Portugal's military weakness partly explains why Brazil's struggle for independence proved less bloody than Spanish America's. Equally important, the Brazilian rebels did not split over the issue of republicanism because, with a few exceptions, the elite preferred a monarchy to a republic. Thanks to the exile of the court, the Brazilians could opt for an independent monarchy. Brazil thus entered independence with a unique legacy. Not least important, Brazilians did not associate independence with military prowess: no Brazilian Simón Bolívar or San Martín arose to dominate the patriotic imagination.

The Aftermath of Independence, 1830–50

The new Spanish American republics faced formidable problems as they embarked on independence in the 1820s. The physical violence of the wars wrought economic disaster. The destruction probably reached its highest point in Venezuela, where *guerra a muerte* ("war to the death") took a heavy toll of human life and reduced the livestock population by more than one half between 1810 and 1830. The early phases of the Mexican wars, particularly during the campaigns of Hidalgo and Morelos, took a similar toll on people and property. Uruguay, where José Artigas led bands of gaucho rebels against well-entrenched Spanish troops, also suffered grave losses. During the second phase of the movement the theater of operations shifted to other areas, especially Peru, where the fighting appears to have been less intensive than before—but the burden of supporting large armies was nevertheless heavy. The civilian labor force was decimated and, throughout the continent, capital was scarce.

The economies of the new nations were overwhelmingly based on agriculture and mining. This was equally true of most of the world outside west Europe. Yet, Latin America differed from most of Africa, the Middle East, and Asia in that over the past two-and-a-half centuries it had been partially brought into the world trading economy dominated by Europe. It was the exportable surplus from Latin America's agricultural and mining production that linked it to the North Atlantic economy. With the creation of separate countries this basic economic structure remained intact almost everywhere, slowly to be modified in succeeding decades.

Trade had come to an almost complete standstill between 1810 and 1826. Commerce with Spain had stopped, and trade among the former colonies was also greatly reduced. Northwest Argentina, for instance, suffered from the loss of trade with Peru. Montevideo, still under Spanish control, could no longer function as a commercial entrepôt. Guerrilla warfare in New Spain and other areas made transport difficult and dangerous. Communications systems within and between the former colonies, never much favored by the Spaniards, fell into near-total disuse.

There was also the factor of postindependence regional conflict within major areas of Spanish and Portuguese America. Mexico was wracked by battles which kept that country divided and without effective national direction before 1850. Brazil, at the same time, collapsed into a series of regionalist revolts that left the monarchy effectively neutralized until the 1840s. And in the Río de la Plata region the fierce rivalry between the province of Buenos Aires and the rest of the country was resolved by the dictatorship of Juan Manuel de Rosas (1829–52). Everywhere the move was to assert economic autonomy by locality or region. That meant fragmentation. In Spanish America it meant that Bolívar's dream would be buried under the advance of nationalism. One after another of the new republics claimed economic independence. They would soon find the world market a sobering test.

In many parts of Spanish America the new governments had to deal with public debts, even before they could attempt to rebuild their economies. To sustain the fighting, to equip the armies, the insurgent regimes frequently had to obtain or borrow funds. Tax collection, to put it mildly, was difficult. As a result, the national treasuries were empty and government authorities had to turn elsewhere for funds. A prime source was Britain, where bankers supported the regimes with loans—particularly in Argentina, Chile, Peru, and Mexico. Thus the new governments immediately ran up debts to foreign lenders. Managing the foreign debt has remained, down to our own day, a major problem for Latin American governments.

Another area in which foreign capital invested was the African slave trade, which continued on a large scale to Brazil (until 1850) and Cuba (until 1865). Both had an export-oriented agriculture that made slave labor profitable when it was being abolished elsewhere in the western hemisphere.

The years between 1830 and 1850 saw Latin America's exports to the North Atlantic economy increase. Key primary products were wheat and nitrates from Chile, tobacco from Colombia, hides, salted beef, and wool from Argentina, guano from Peru, sugar from Cuba, coffee from Brazil, and cacao from Venezuela. These same countries were heavily importing textiles and consumer goods, thereby often throwing local artisan producers out of work. It was the industrial producers in West Europe (especially Britain) competing against the small-scale Latin American producers who had survived from the colonial era. The result was a foregone conclusion.

This was all part of free trade, the dogma that had arrived in Latin America with Enlightenment philosophy and the postindependence commitment to the principles of liberalism. Applying this dogma was the most significant economic policy decision in nineteenth century Latin America. Along with a rapid inflow of foreign (primarily European) imports came a small cadre of foreign merchants, expecially British. They become key figures throughout Latin America in the import of goods and services, the latter including shipping, insurance, and financing.

Should we be surprised that manufactured goods from Europe

steadily displaced domestic products? Wasn't it inevitable that Europe's greater technology and economies of scale would prevail? Transportation costs should have helped protect local producers, but the supposed (or genuine) superiority of foreign-made goods posed a serious dilemma soon after independence and has continued down to today. Latin American economies often failed to make their own industry truly competitive. Why? Lack of a sufficient market was certainly a factor. But equally important was the system of values and the social hierarchy which made it possible for the elite to perpetuate a society based on an agrarian-oriented economy.

The economic record of the 1830–50 period is therefore one of slow adaptation to the world economy. Latin America was on the fringes of the North Atlantic economy, which was to expand rapidly in the nineteenth century. Both research and data on the economic history of this era are distressingly scarce—but it appears, on the basis of evidence available, that Latin America's republic took a passive stance. The dynamism came from outside.

The creation and maintenance of large armies in most Latin American republics also crucially affected the social order, because they created a channel for careers based on talent. As the fighting intensified and the stakes increased, creole rebel leaders had to recruit soldiers and commanders on ability, rather than on skin color or social status. Thus José Antonio Páez, a rough-hewn *mestizo*, became a valued military leader in Venezuela. In Mexico José María Morelos was *mestizo*. Other examples abound. Military prowess became a means by which members of marginal groups could gain social recognition. None of the newly independent governments retained legal disabilities for *mestizos* or other mixed bloods, a fact which helped to blur once-rigid social lines.

But if the wars opened a social avenue for ambitious *mestizos* and others, it was limited. Economic resources, particularly land, remained in the hands of traditional creole families. Commerce was modest in the years right after the fighting, and many merchant families retained their control of trade. Industry barely existed. As a result, there was only one way for men of modest origin to get ahead: through the military, and from there into politics.

This social dynamic helps explain much of the political turbulence in Spanish America between the 1820s and 1850. The new republics finished the wars with large military establishments, often led by *mestizos* who had no alternative careers. To get ahead they had to stay in the army—or move into government. In the meantime, creole landowners, in many parts of the continent, did not complete for political power. They withdrew to their haciendas, which could function as self-sufficient units, and tried to increase their landholdings. In effect they left government to the soldiers and to the bosses known as *caudillos,* partly because political power did not seem worth the trouble. Later in the nineteenth century, when governmental authority became a valued commodity, *hacendados* and *estancieros* came off their lands and took over.

So governments were toppled and run by *caudillos,* often soldiers (or ex-soldiers) who took power by force. Once in the presidential office, they usually found that sparse treasuries offered little reward for their followers. Their bands then dispersed, and new *caudillos* would come forward with new bands of followers. The governments did not have strong finances and as a result were highly vulnerable to being overthrown. From the 1820s until mid-century, the state in Spanish America was notably weak.

During this era another current emerged, a move to consolidate and centralize power. It usually came out in attempted dictatorships, not popular consensus. The first two decades after independence thus saw the appearance of real or would-be "strong men," like Diego Portales in Chile and Juan Manuel de Rosas in Argentina, who sought to impose their will on their countries, thereby strengthening the role of the state. The struggle between locally based power and the centralizers— military or civilian—became a basic theme in the political life of the new nations.

If the Wars of Independence opened narrow channels for *mestizos* and middle-range groups in Spanish America, they did very little for the Indian masses. In general, Indians had been ambiguous about the struggle: though they sided with Hidalgo or stayed neutral in Mexico, they supported royalists in southern Chile, and in Peru and Colombia they fought on both sides. The leaders of the new republics therefore did not feel indebted to the Indians. More important, the Indians now lost the special protection of caste status they had enjoyed under Spanish colonial law. Whatever its drawbacks, that status had been an oft-used refuge for the Indians. They also lost their communal lands (which had been inalienable) and were theoretically forced into the competitive market so praised by nineteenth century liberals. In fact, they became even more isolated and poverty-stricken.

Independence left a somewhat different social legacy for Brazil. Instead of *displacing* a ruling elite, as happened in Spanish America, Brazil *acquired* a ruling elite: the Portuguese crown and its attendants. Brazil also acquired a monarchy that would last until 1889. But these political trends had little effect on the black slaves who labored on sugar plantations and elsewhere in the economy. In fact, the institution of slavery was not abolished at independence or by the 1850s, as in Spanish America (except for Cuba and Puerto Rico) and it would later become a central issue in Brazilian politics. In Brazil, as in other new nations, independence did not change life much for the poorest segments of the population.

The Pull of the International Economy, 1850–80s

After 1850 Latin America moved from the postindependence consolidation phase to begin laying the foundations for its greater integration into the world economy. In political terms this required governments ready to create the infrastructure needed to export key primary products, such as guano from Peru, coffee from Brazil, henequen from Mexico, and sugar from the Caribbean. As the era of the *caudillo* gave way to the era of the administrators, the prime task was national unification.

The independent republics moved to strengthen the use of two elements in their economies: land and labor. Most governments sought to put land into the hands of entrepreneurs who would invest and make it bear fruit. In Brazil and Mexico that meant government pressure to sell off government (previously crown) land. The losers in Mexico and the Andes were the Indians, but such action could also hit white or *mestizo* owners who had failed to develop their lands.

To provide labor, the Latin American elites in several countries hoped for immigration from Europe. These years saw repeated proposals to attract European immigrants, who would supposedly contribute to national development with little further investment. In fact, the elite—in countries like Argentina and Brazil—soon found that immigration was a sensitive issue, both at home and in the countries sending the migrants. Before 1880 immigration was nowhere a major factor in increasing the labor force. But the strong elite impulse to recruit migrants demonstrated their belief that their countries' economic and social salvation was to be found in Europe. As will become apparent, this reflected Latin American doubts about their countries' viability.

The mid-nineteenth century also saw an effort to improve Latin America's transportation network. What was needed were railroads, canals, docks, and roads. Since the sixteenth century, cargo (including people) had traveled by pack-mule or burro. In only a few areas did navigable rivers or lakes offer an alternative. By mid-century Latin America was the target for numerous proposals to build railroads. The impetus usually came from foreigners, especially British and North American. But few railways were actually built before the 1880s, so the transportation networks remained about as bad as they had been on the eve of independence.

The rhythm of economic activity quickened, nonetheless, throughout Latin America after 1850. The stimulus came primarily from the dynamic economies of North America and West Europe, led by Britain. As Europe plunged ever more deeply into industrialization, it needed increasing imports of food, such as sugar, beef, and grain, as well as primary commodities such as guano and nitrate fertilizers, wool, and industrial metals. These were the decades when economic ties—trade, investment, financing, technology transfer, migration—deepened between Europe and Mexico, Argentina, Peru, Chile, Brazil, and Cuba (even though still a Spanish colony). By 1880 the stage was set for even greater economic expansion.

The economic upturn after 1850 had several important limitations, however. First, it resulted in very little growth of domestic industry. The rising Latin American need for metal tools, small machines, instruments, construction equipment, weapons, and similar light industrialized goods, was primarily met from Europe, not from home-country shops or factories. The trend was hardly surprising. The British, French, or U.S. products were of better quality than anything produced at home, although that advantage could have been narrowed if the domestic producers had had enough time and a sufficient market to upgrade quality. But that would have required government protection either through high tariffs or outright import prohibitions. No Latin American government was prepared or able to take such a step in these decades.

The reasons were several. First, imported products were superior and were thus strongly preferred by local consumers; second, most governments lived off tariff revenues, which tough protectionism would have cut off; third, the economically powerful groups, such as the landowners and cattlemen, were strongly committed to free trade, which their European customers preached as the only true road to prosperity; finally, Latin American merchants, who were strategically located in the largest cities, had an obvious stake in fighting protection. That motive was even greater when the merchant was a foreigner (usually British or French), as happened frequently by mid-century. Not surprisingly, the Latin American advocates of protectionism or state-aided industry could make little headway.

A second limitation on economic expansion between 1850 and 1880 was its reinforcement of the highly stratified socioeconomic structure inherited from the independence era: a thin elite at the top, a slightly wider "middle" group, and the other 90 percent or so at the bottom. The continued focus on agro-ranching and mining meant that most laborers would continue under working conditions and rates of pay that could never move them toward becoming the consumers that a "developed" economy both produces and needs.

Latin America was being pulled farther into the international economy in a way that would sharply limit its economic development. The nature of that economic link has continued to trouble Latin Americans for the last century, and will be a recurrent theme in the rest of this book.

TWO

THE TRANSFORMATION OF MODERN LATIN AMERICA, 1880s–1980s

Latin America has undergone a series of far-reaching economic, social, and political changes since the late nineteenth century. National economies have become integrated into the global system centered in Europe and the United States, social groupings and relationships have changed, cities have burgeoned, politics have witnessed reform and upheaval and sometimes stagnation. Variations on these themes have led to great diversity in national experience, and following this chapter we present seven case studies: Argentina, Chile, Brazil, Peru, Mexico, Cuba, and Central America. As we shall see, these countries illustrate the complexity of Latin America's modern history.

Yet there have been important uniformities as well as differences, and the purpose of this chapter is to offer an outline of the patterns and processes of change. It does not depict the history of any single country; rather, it presents a composite portrait that can provide a basis for understanding the context in which individual countries developed. It will also enable us to compare countries and generalize about the historical forces at work throughout the continent.

If we are to understand modern Latin America it must be placed within the context of global economic expansion, beginning with the Conquest of the sixteenth century. Within this system, Latin America has occupied an essentially subordinate or "dependent" position, pursuing economic paths that have been largely shaped by the industrial powers of Europe and the United States. These economic developments have brought about transitions in the social order and class structure, and these changes in turn have crucially affected political change. We thus begin with a set of simplified causal relationships: economic changes produce social changes which furnish the context for political change.[1]

---

1. It is for this reason that each of the case studies in following chapters contains an overview section on "economic growth and social change"—with the exception of Mexico, where the Revolution of 1910 exerted such a strong political impact on that country's history and obliged us to use a different format.

Phase 1: Initiation of Export-Import Growth, 1880–1900

It was the Industrial Revolution in Europe that precipitated change in the economies of nineteenth century Latin America. As shown in Chapter One, Latin America had seen its links with the world economy reduced after achieving independence from Portugal and Spain. Latin America's native landowners converted their holdings into autonomous, self-sufficient entities, rather than producing goods for domestic or foreign markets. Mining had come to a standstill, partly as a result of the destruction of the Wars of Independence. Manufacturing was modest, mostly done by artisans in small establishments.

By the late nineteenth century, however, industrialization in Europe was producing a strong demand for foodstuffs and raw materials. English and European laborers, now living in cities and working in factories, needed to purchase food they could no longer raise. And captains of industry, eager to expand their output and operations, were seeking raw material, particularly minerals. Both incentives led governments and investors in Europe to begin looking abroad—to Africa, to Asia, and, of course, to Latin America.

As a result, the major Latin American countries underwent a startling transition in the late nineteenth century, especially after 1880. Argentina, with its vast and fertile pampas, became a major producer of agricultural and pastoral goods—particularly wool, wheat, and, most notably, beef. Chile resuscitated the production of copper, an industry that had fallen into decay after the independence years. Brazil became famous for the production of coffee. Cuba produced coffee as well as sugar and tobacco. Mexico came to export a variety of raw material goods, from henequen (a fiber used for making rope) to sugar to industrial minerals, particularly copper and zinc. Central America exported coffee and bananas, while from Peru it was sugar and silver.

The development of these exports was accompanied by the importation of manufactured goods, particularly from Europe. Latin Americans purchased textiles, machines, luxury items, and other finished products in relatively large quantity. There thus occurred an exchange, though the prices of Latin American exports were far more unstable than the prices of Europe's exports.

As development progressed, investment flowed into Latin America from the industrial nations, particularly England. Between 1870 and 1913 the value of Britain's investments in Latin America went from 85 million pounds sterling to 757 million pounds in 1913—an increase of almost ninefold in four decades. By 1913 British investors owned approximately two-thirds of the total foreign investment in Latin America. One of the most consistent British investments was in railroad construction—especially in Argentina, Mexico, Peru, and Brazil. British,

French, and North American investors also put capital into mining ventures, particularly in Mexico, Chile, and Peru. This meant that the Latins themselves would not have to invest there. It also meant that control of key sectors of the Latin economies were passing into foreign hands.

Thus was established, in the late nineteenth century, an "export-import" form of economic growth that stimulated development in the raw-material sectors of the Latin American economies. The impetus and capital came largely from abroad. With the adoption of this alternative, Latin America took a commercial road to "dependent" economic growth—dependent, that is, on decisions and prosperity in other parts of the world.

The rapid expansion of Latin America's export economies was accompanied, even preceded, by the victory of an intellectual rationale that justified Latin America's integration into the world economy. That rationale was liberalism, a faith in progress and a belief that it would come in economics only through the free play of market forces, and in politics only through a limited government that maximized individual liberty. Latin American liberalism, like most ideologies in Latin America, was an import. Its principal sources lay in France and England. Unlike those countries, however, Latin America had not undergone significant industrialization by the middle of the nineteenth century. Latin America therefore lacked the social structure that had nurtured liberalism in Europe, a fact that was bound to make Latin American liberalism different.

In the second half of the eighteenth century Spanish America and Brazil underwent an abortive experiment in state capitalism. The upheaval caused by the French revolutionary wars had disrupted Spain's mercantilist monopoly in America. Havana had been captured by the English and its ports thrown open. The astounding increase in trade impressed all observers. The logic was inescapable: since smuggling had grown into a huge percentage of total trade throughout Portuguese and Spanish America, why not legalize free trade and gain taxes from the increase in government-monitored commerce?

The apologists of economic liberalism in Latin America quoted freely from European theorists who justified free trade and the international division of labor as "natural" and, indeed, optimal. Any deviation from its dictates would be folly—reducing trade and thereby reducing income. It is important to see that the great majority of those critics who attacked *political* institutions of monarchical governments (which they considered "illiberal") did not disagree with the ideology of *economic* liberalism. In Brazil, for example, Tavares Bastos indicted the imperial government on the charge that it stifled local political life but extolled the virtues of free trade and faithfully repeated European doctrines of laissez-faire.

One can say that throughout the later nineteenth century economic liberalism remained unshaken in Latin America. Attempts at protective tariffs were beaten back by politicians who argued that Latin America was not well-suited, either by her resources or by her relative bargaining position, to violate the principles of free trade.

The key debates about economic policy were largely restricted to the elites, who are defined here as that very small (less than 5 percent of the population) stratum that had the power and wealth to control economic and political decisionmaking on the local, regional, and national levels.

The elites' commitment to liberalism was reinforced by their deep concerns about the supposed racial inferiority of their native populations. They implicitly acknowledged the correctness of racist theories by constantly urging heavy European immigration as the solution to their lack of skilled labor. They preferred immigrants from northern Europe (although the vast majority in fact came from Portugal, Spain, and Italy), hoping that habits of self-reliance and entrepreneurship— the hallmarks of the liberals' ideal—could be reinforced in Latin America.

Added to the racist doubts was a general sense of their own inferiority. Until the First World War, Latin American elites frequently described themselves as little more than the imitators of European culture. Many doubted that their countries could ever achieve a distinctive civilization. For the tropical countries, their worries over racial determinism were reinforced by doubts about their climate, which European theorists constantly told them could never support a high civilization. This environmental determinism thus reinforced racial determinism, and the combination appeared to disqualify tropical lands as a stage on which the liberal dream could be realized.

Within Latin America the rapid growth of the export economies led to subtle but important transformations in the societies. First in sequence and importance was the modernization of the upper-class elite. Given these new economic incentives, landowners and property owners were no longer content to run subsistence operations on their haciendas; instead, they sought opportunities and maximized profits. This led to an entrepreneurial spirit that marked a significant change in the outlook and behavior of the continent's elite groups. Cattle raisers in Argentina, coffee growers in Brazil, sugar barons in Cuba and Mexico—all were seeking efficiency and commercial success. They were no longer a relatively enclosed, semifeudal elite; they became aggressive entrepreneurs.

New professional or "service" groups emerged to play additional economic roles. Particularly important was growth and change in the commercial sector. Merchants played an essential part in this transformation, as in the colonial era, but now many were foreigners—and this time they were tying the Latin American economies to the markets overseas, particularly in Europe. Another development concerned professionals, lawyers, and others who represented both foreign and domestic groups in their commercial transactions. Lawyers had always been important, but during the export-import phase they assumed crucial new roles in helping determine the institutional framework for the new era.

These economic and social transitions also led to political change. With so much at stake, Latin American elites—particularly landowners—began to take a clear interest in national politics. No longer content to stay on their fief-like haciendas, they began to pursue political power. The era of the traditional *caudillo* was coming to an end.

This elite quest for political authority in late nineteenth century Latin America took two basic forms. In one version, landowners and other economic elites took direct control of the government—as in Argentina and Chile. They sought to build strong, exclusive regimes, usually with military support, often proclaiming legitimacy through adherence to constitutions strongly resembling United States and European models. In both Argentina and Chile there was mild competition between political parties that tended, at least in this early phase, to represent competing factions of the aristocracy. But there was more agreement than disagreement about basic policy issues, and little serious opposition to the wisdom of pursuing export-oriented economic growth. Competition was restricted, voting was often a sham, and public debate was generally mild and genteel. One might think of such regimes as expressions of "oligarchic democracy."

A second pattern involved the imposition of dictatorial strongmen, often military officers, to assert law and order—again, for the ultimate benefit of the landed elites. Porfirio Díaz of Mexico, who took power in 1876, is the most conspicuous example—but the pattern also appeared in Venezuela, Peru, and other countries. In contrast to oligarchic democracy, where elites exercise direct political power, here it was the indirect application of elite rule through dictators who often did not themselves come from the upper ranks of the society.

In either case, the emphasis was on stability and social control. Dissident groups were suppressed and the struggle for power was contained within restricted circles. Indeed, one of the basic goals of these regimes was to centralize power, if necessary stripping it from regional *caudillos,* and to create powerful and dominant nation-states. These goals were not easily achieved, given the residual fragmentation of society and the social structure, but progress was made in the larger countries. In Argentina, for example, centralism triumphed with the establishment of the city of Buenos Aires as a federal district in 1881 (much as Washington, D.C., is under the direct jurisdiction of the federal government in the U.S.). In Mexico, the effective and often ruthless policies of Porfirio Díaz led to enhanced national power at the expense of local strongholds. And in Brazil, the imperial government of Dom Pedro II made significant headway toward the establishment of an effective nation-state (thereby also provoking a regionalist backlash that contributed to the empire's overthrow in 1889).

One intent of these centralizers was to promote further economic development along the export-import lines of growth. Political stability was viewed as essential to attract foreign investment which, in turn, could stimulate economic growth. And when the investment came, it helped strengthen the forces of law and order. Railroads are an example: British investors would be reluctant to put funds into a country threatened by political disorder; but once the railroads were built, as in Mexico, they became important instruments in consolidating central rule, since they could be (and were) used to dispatch federal troops to put down uprisings in almost any part of the nation.

Phase 2: Expansion of Export-Import Growth, 1900–1930

The success of these policies became apparent in the late nineteenth and early twentieth century, when export-oriented Latin American economies embarked on eras of remarkable prosperity. Argentina became so wealthy from its beef-and-wheat economy that the figure of the Argentine playboy became a watchword in fashionable European society—a free-spending young Latin in high-spirited pursuit of elegance. Plantations appeared and expanded in Mexico, producing henequen in the Yucatán and sugar in the central zones, especially in areas south of Mexico City; mining was also profitable, and the nascent industry of oil production was beginning to grow into a significant activity. Copper exports continued to grow from Chile, which produced some fruits and wheat for international markets as well. Technological improvements led to increased production of sugar in the Caribbean, especially in Cuba, as U.S. owners stepped up their investing in modern sugar mills. Brazil lived off coffee and natural rubber exports. The United Fruit Company expanded its huge banana plantations in Central America. In all these countries the money economy had become more sensitive to trends in the internatiional economy, where exports earned the foreign exchange to buy badly needed imports. Any major shock to the world economy would be bound to produce rapid and dramatic effects in the commercialized sectors. Although industrialization had not gone far yet, factories existed in such sectors as textiles, leather goods, beverages, food processing, and construction materials. The most dynamic service sectors were transportation, government bureaucracy, commerce, and finance.

Consolidation of the export-import model of growth prompted two fundamental changes in the social structure. One was the appearance and growth of middle social strata. Occupationally, these consisted of professionals, merchants, shopkeepers, and small businessmen who profited from the export-import economy but who did not occupy upper-strata positions of ownership or leadership. Most often found in cities, middle-sector spokesmen were usually relatively well-educated and were seeking a clearly recognized place in their society.

The second major change concerned the working class. In order to sustain expansion of the export economies, elites tried to import labor from abroad (as the Argentine Juan Bautista Alberdi once put it, "to govern is to populate"). As a result, Argentina began, in the 1880s, an aggressive policy to encourage immigration from Europe: the tide of arrivals in Argentina over the next three decades was so great, even allowing for the returnees, that it has been called by one historian the country's "alluvial era." Brazil also recruited immigrants, primarily to work in the coffee fields of São Paulo. Peru and Chile received a number of immigrants, though far fewer in both relative and absolute terms than Argentina. Cuba remained a special case, since the importation of black slaves from Africa had long since determined the composition of the country's laboring class (this had also been true in parts of Brazil, particularly in the Northeast where sugar plantations thrived on slave labor). Mexico presents an interesting exception to this pattern. Alone among the major countries, Mexico never sought large-scale immigration from abroad. One reason is obvious: the country continued to have a large peasant Indian population, making it unnecessary to import new recruits for the labor force.

The appearance of incipient working classes led to new organizations with important implications for the future. Workers often established mutual aid societies and, in some countries, started labor unions. The nature of the Latin American economies set the context for worker activism. First, because exports were crucial, workers in the infrastructure that supported exports—especially railways and docks—held a vital position. Any work stoppage posed an immediate threat to the country's trade viability and therefore to its capacity to import. Second, the relatively primitive state of industrialization meant that most workers were employed in very small firms, usually with less than twenty-five employees. Only a few industries, such as textiles, fit the modern image of huge factories with mass production techniques. The unions in question were usually organized by craft, rather than by industry.

The exceptions were the rail workers, miners, and dockers who, not coincidentally, were among the more militant workers.

The years between 1914 and 1927 saw a surge of labor mobilization. It was the high point of the anarchist, anarcho-syndicalist, and syndicalist influence, when the capital cities of every major Latin American nation were rocked by general strikes. Latin America suddenly seemed to be joining in the class confrontations shaking Germany and Russia, as well as the U.S. and much of the rest of Europe. It is at these critical moments—mass protests, general strikes, intensified ties between the unionized and the nonunionized—that we can see clearly the nature of the working class, its organizations, and the manner in which the dominant elites chose to respond.

What we shall need to compare, as the country studies unfold, are the similarities and differences in the patterns of interaction among employers, workers, and politicians, along with landowners, professionals, and the military. If there are similarities in urban labor's mobilization during the decade after the great protests that began at the end of the First World War, there were striking differences in the elites' response. In particular, we shall find that the legal framework of labor relations received much more attention in Chile than in Argentina and Brazil.

Another major change during the 1900–1930 era was in the balance between rural and urban sectors of society. The importation of labor and migration from the countryside combined, in this era, to produce the growth of large-scale cities. By 1900 Buenos Aires had established itself as "the Paris of South America," a large and cosmopolitan city with about 750,000 inhabitants. All told, just about one quarter of the Argentine population lived in cities with 20,000 or more inhabitants at the turn of the century; the same held true for Cuba. About 20 percent of the Chilean population resided in similar settlements, while the corresponding figures for Brazil and Mexico (the latter with a substantial indigenous population) were just under 10 percent. For Central America the figures were also under 10 percent and in Peru only 6 percent. The general fact is that expansion of the export-import economies brought with it the urbanization of Latin American society.

Because of national or ethnic origin, however, laboring classes did not gain much of a foothold on political power in the early twentieth century. Immigrants in Argentina and Brazil were not entitled to vote unless they went through naturalization, so politicians could afford to ignore them. In Mexico, workers of peasant background had little chance of influencing the Díaz dictatorship. And in Cuba, of course, the history of slavery left its own painful legacy.

What this meant, at least in the short run, was that Latin American elites, while promoting the export-oriented expansion, could count on a responsive labor force without an effective threat of political participation by the working class (although strike actions had proved worrisome). From then until the 1920s or 30s it seemed, for many, like the best of both worlds.

And as a result, elites in several countries permitted enough political reform to allow effective pursuit of power by members and representatives of the middle sectors. The idea was to gain the allegiance of the middle sectors and therefore strengthen the structure of elite control and power. Accordingly, the early twentieth century was a period of political reform in some of the larger countries: a voting law in 1912 in Argentina opened suffrage to large sectors of the population and permitted a middle-class party, the so-called Radical Party, to win the presidency in 1916. Changes in Chile, actually beginning in the 1890s, saw the imposition of parliamentary rule on a previously presidentialist system. In Brazil, the overthrow of the monarchy in 1889 opened a period of limited electoral politics. Cuba, after gaining independence from Spain in 1898 (and, many would say, then ceding it to the United States), remains a special case. And even in Mexico, where a large-scale revolution broke out in 1910, the generalization holds: the original goal of the revolutionary movement was not to transform Mexican society but merely to gain access to the political system for excluded fragments of the country's middle class.

The reformist movements often produced a "co-optative democracy"—in which effective participation spread from the upper class to the middle class, to the continued exclusion of the lower class. Such transitions usually reflected the attempts of ruling socioeconomic elites to co-opt the middle sectors into supporting the system, though they sometimes had unforeseen and unintended consequences—as in the case of Mexico, where events transpired to create a full-blown revolution. For the most part the goals were limited.

One significant side-effect was the creation of a cadre, in various countries, of professional politicians. Party politics created careers for men (women did not even have the vote anywhere in Latin America before 1929) who could devote their entire adult lives to the pursuit of political power. As often as not they represented the interests of the reigning aristocracy, but they also formed an identifiably separate social group. As prominent actors in the civilian political scene, they would also become targets for the disdain and wrath of the military establishment.

For many countries of Latin America, or at least for the elites, the reformist formula worked fairly well. European demand for raw materials during and for several years after World War I led to continued and sustained prosperity. The export-import model of growth appeared to offer a functional and profitable means of integrating Latin America into the global system of capitalism. Political adaptations seemed to assure the long-run hegemony of national elites.

In fact, liberalism—both political and economic—was soon found wanting. Its failure illustrates the phenomenon so familiar throughout modern Latin America: unsuccessful cultural borrowing, or "alienation" as latter-day nationalists have described it. Copy as they would the legal institutions and philosophical phrases of classical liberalism, Latin Americans found their reality did not lend itself to the simple application of dogma. They failed to understand that originally European liberalism was the ideology of a rising social class whose growing economic power gave it the political leverage to put its ideology into practice.

Does this mean anything more than that Latin America lacked a large middle class? Only in part. More fundamentally, Latin America had remained an agrarian economy whose export sector was matched, in most countries, by a huge subsistence sector. Liberalism had a chance only because, after 1850, a small but growing sector of the society *thought* it saw its interests as different from those of the traditional sectors.

Specifically, the professionals—lawyers, doctors, military officers, civil servants and the merchants—all constituted an urban interest. They rapidly absorbed the European liberal ideas without gaining the relative economic power which their counterparts had gained in France and England. Thus, even if they had seen their economic interests as antagonistic to those of the traditional agrarian sector, they would have been in a weak position. But often they did not. Their livelihood was usually tied to the agrarian sector even though they lived in cities. Their clients, customers, and employers were men whose incomes depended largely upon commercial agriculture. And the prosperity of this agriculture, in turn, depended upon foreign trade.

At this point Latin American liberals were stymied by their economic liberalism. Believing its abstract principles and uncomfortably aware of their patent weakness vis-à-vis their principal creditors and trading partners—the United States and England—they could not think their way to "illiberal" economic solutions. Furthermore, the latter would have cost them *personally* in the short run. For example, protective tariffs for industry undoubtedly would have saddled urban consumers with higher-priced, lower-quality goods. Protection would also have imperiled the profits of the export-import merchants, who were a powerful pressure group. Liberals were therefore disinclined to advocate industrialization, which alone could have increased their number sufficiently to give them the political power that might have made possible the realization of liberal political ideals.

Economic and political liberalism cross-cut in yet another way. Nonliberal ideas in economics, such as protective tariffs and controls on foreign investments, were often associated in practice with antiliberal political ideas. Thus the connection was easily established: deviation from liberal principles in economics must mean authoritarian government, and it was therefore held in low regard.

A further argument used against advocates of economic unorthodoxy (i.e., nonliberal measures) was politically difficult to answer. Whenever proposals for government support of national industry were made, opponents charged, often to good effect, that a small group of selfish investors were seeking to profit at the expense of the public. In addition, local entrepreneurs were almost invariably underfinanced and inexperienced. Just as everywhere in the developing world, these businessmen faced formidable competition from goods imported from the industrialized economies. Without protection and subsidies they had little hope.

Latin American liberals were debilitated for yet another reason. It was their uncertainty about an underlying assumption of liberalism: faith in the rationality and enterprise of their individual countrymen. In Brazil, for example, politicians had spent years justifying slavery on the grounds that it was a necessary evil for Brazil's tropical, agrarian economy. Only enslaved Africans could do the work. Now the argument came back to haunt liberals. Slavery's legacy was a labor force that fell far short of the rational world envisaged by Bentham and Mill. The event that transformed this atmosphere was the spectacular collapse of the world capitalist economy in 1929–30.

Phase 3: Import-Substituting Industrialization, 1930–60s

The Great Depression had initially catastrophic effects on the economies of Latin America. The precipitous economic decline in Europe and the United States suddenly shrunk the market for Latin American exports. The international demand for coffee, sugar, metals, and meat underwent sharp reduction—and Latin American leaders could find no alternative outlets for their products. Both the unit price and the quantity of Latin American exports dropped, with the result that their total value for the years 1930–34 was 48 percent below what it had been for 1925–29. Once again, events at the industrialized center of the world-system had decisive (and limiting) effects on the peripheral economies of Latin America and other Third World societies.

The ensuing world depression put great pressure on the political systems of Latin American countries, many of which suffered military coups (or attempted coups). Within a year or so after the October 1929 stock market crash in New York, army officers had sought or taken power in Argentina, Brazil, Chile, Peru, Guatemala, El Salvador, and

An American cartoonist depicts the Latin American military as a continuing threat to democratic institutions. (Roy B. Justus, *Minneapolis Star,* 1963. Reprinted with permission of the Minneapolis Star and Tribune Company.)

Honduras. Mexico was enduring a special constitutional crisis of its own, and Cuba succumbed to a military takeover in 1933. It would be an exaggeration to say that the economic effects of the Depression alone caused these political outcomes; but they cast into doubt the viability of the export-import model of growth, helped discredit ruling political elites, and made the populace more prepared to accept military regimes. From the early 1930s onward, the military reasserted its traditional role as a principal force in Latin American politics.

Latin American rulers had two options in responding to the global economic crisis. One was to forge even closer commercial linkages to the industrialized nations in order to secure a steady share of the market, whatever its size and dislocations. Argentina took such an approach, for example, struggling to preserve its access to the British market for beef. In 1933 Argentina signed the Roca-Runciman Pact, through which it would retain acceptable quotas in the English market in exchange for Argentine guarantees to purchase British goods and to insure profits on British businesses in Argentina. In this way, some countries tried to maintain the workability of the export-model despite the reduced demand brought on by the Depression.

An alternative tack, not necessarily inconsistent with the first, was to embark on industrialization. One of the goals of this policy, often supported by the military, would be to achieve greater economic independence. The idea was that by building its own industry, Latin America would be less dependent on Europe and the United States for manufactured goods. For the military, this meant arms. By producing industrial as well as agricultural and mineral goods, the Latin American economies would become more integrated and more self-sufficient. And, as a result, they would be less vulnerable to the kinds of shocks brought on by the worldwide depression.

A second purpose was to create jobs for the working classes that had continued to grow in size and importance since the beginning of the twentieth century. Concentrated almost entirely in cities, the Latin American proletariat was still struggling to organize and sustain union movements. And in contrast to the previous generation, it was now trying to exert power as a social force. In some countries, such as Chile, union movements were relatively free of arbitrary government involvement. Elsewhere, as in Mexico and Brazil, politicians recognized labor as a potential political resource and took a direct hand in stimulating (and controlling) labor organizations. Whether perceived as ally or threat, the urban working class was seeking secure employment, and Latin American leaders saw industrialization as one way to respond.

But the most plausible *form* of industrial development was not simply to copy the paths traced by, for example, nineteenth century England. Instead, Latin America's economies started producing manufactured goods that they had formerly imported from Europe and the United States. Hence the name for this type of development, "import-substituting industrialization" (ISI).

From the late 1930s to the 1960s, at least in major countries, ISI policies met with relative success. Argentina, Brazil, and Mexico developed significant industrial plants that helped generate economic growth. There were limitations and drawbacks in this form of development (discussed below), but the immediate result was to generate momentum for the national economies.

The social consequences of industrialization were complex. One result, of course, was the formation of an entrepreneurial capitalist class or, in Marxist parlance, an industrial bourgeoisie. In Chile, members of this group came principally from the families of the landed elite. In Mexico and Argentina, they comprised different social types and therefore presented a potential challenge to the hegemony of traditional ruling elites. But the basic point remains: industrialization, even of the ISI type, created a new power group in Latin American society. Its role was to be much debated as the century continued.

Of particular importance here was the role of the state in stimulating ISI growth. In contrast to the largely laissez-faire policies of nineteenth century England and the United States, Latin American governments actively promoted industrial growth. They did so in various ways: erecting tariff barriers and raising the price of imported goods to the point where local industrial firms could successfully compete in the marketplace; creating demand by favoring local producers in government contracts (involving, for example, purchases for the military); and, most important, establishing government-run companies and investing directly in industrial firms. Through protection and participation, the state in Latin America furnished critical impetus for the region's industrial growth.

As industry progressed, the working classes also grew in strength and importance. Whether autonomous or state-directed, union movements increased rapidly and the support (or control) of labor became crucial for the continuation of industrial expansion. The workers were needed to provide the labor under conditions that would yield profits for their employers. Organized labor was emerging as a major actor on the Latin American scene.

The political expression of these socioeconomic changes took two forms. One was the continuation of co-optative democracy, through which industrialists and workers gained (usually limited) access to power through electoral or other competition. One example was Chile, where political parties were reorganized to represent the interests of new groups and strata in society. Prolabor and proindustrialist parties entered the Chilean electoral process, leading eventually to the tragic confrontation of the 1970s. Under this system, they were co-opted into the governing structure, and as long as this arrangement lasted their participation lent valuable support to the regime.

The more common response involved the creation of multi-class "populist" alliances. The emergence of an industrialist elite and the vitalization of the labor movement made possible a new, pro-industrial alliance merging the interests of entrepreneurs and workers—in some cases, directly challenging the longstanding predominance of agricultural and landed interests. Each of these alliances was created by a national leader who used the power of the state for his purpose. Thus, as we shall see later, Juan Perón built a multi-class, urban-based populist coalition in Argentina during the 1940s; in Brazil, Getúlio Vargas began to do so in the late 1930s; and, under somewhat more complicated circumstances, Lázaro Cárdenas turned to populist solutions for Mexico during this same period.

Most populist regimes had two key characteristics. For one thing, they were at least semi-authoritarian: they usually represented coalitions against some other set of interests (such as landed interests) that were by definition prevented from participation, and this involved some degree of both exclusion and repression. Second, as time would tell, they represented interests of classes—workers and industrialists—that were bound to conflict among themselves. The maintenance of such regimes therefore depended in large part on the personal power and charisma of individual leaders (such as Perón in Argentina and Vargas in Brazil). It also meant that, with or without magnetic leadership, they would be hard to sustain in times of economic adversity.

Phase 4: Stagnation in Import-Substituting Growth, 1960s to the Present

The 1960s brought in the current era in Latin America. The economic strategy which grew out of the post-1930 industrialization politicies had begun to run into serious troubles, both economic and political. On the economic front, the problems arose in part from the nature of ISI development itself.

First, industrialization through ISI was structurally incomplete. To produce manufactured goods, Latin American firms continually had to rely on imported capital goods (such as machine tools) from Europe, the United States, and now Japan. If such capital goods could not be imported, or were too expensive, local firms were placed in jeopardy. Latin Americans slowly realized that ISI growth did not end the dependency of Latin America on the industrialized nations. It merely altered the form of that dependency.

This inherent difficulty became acute because of the uneven terms of trade. Over time, the world market prices of Latin America's principal exports (coffee, wheat, copper) underwent a steady decline in purchasing power. That is, for the same quantity of exports, the Latin countries could purchase smaller and smaller quantities of capital goods. Industrial growth therefore faced a bottleneck. And the answer did not lie in increasing the quantity of their traditional exports, since that might simply depress the price.

Second, the national demand for manufactured products was inevitably limited. Industries ran up against a lack of buyers, at least at prevailing prices and credit terms. Brazilians could buy only so many refrigerators (especially in view of the highly unequal distribution of income, which kept the popular masses from even contemplating such purchases). This problem of limited markets might have been met through the formation of multinational or regional trade associations, or something like a Latin American common market; there were efforts in this direction, but they did not resolve the issue. The industries in the major Latin countries tended to be more competitive than complementary, and such rivalries posed serious political obstacles to the formation of such associations. As time went on, industrial firms in Latin America continued to face the problem of limited markets.

Third, and closely related, was the relatively high degree of technology involved in Latin American industry. This meant that it could create only a limited number of jobs for workers. In other words, Latin American industrial development in this era had picked up the capital-intensive technology typical of the advanced industrial economies: in comparison to nineteenth century models of growth, it entailed more investments in machines and fewer in manual labor. Individual firms saw this as necessary to survive against the economic competition. One of the unintentional results, however, was to place a ceiling on the size of the domestic market for consumer goods, since relatively few wage-earners could afford to purchase them. A second result was the failure to reverse the growing unemployment, which, by the 1960s, began to pose a serious threat to the prevailing social orders.

As pressure mounted, ruling elites in several countries imposed highly repressive regimes, often through military coups—as in Brazil (1964), Argentina (1966), and Chile (1973). By early 1983 all three countries were still ruled by the military, with the degree of civilian collaboration varying from Brazil, where it is greatest, to Chile, where it is least. In all cases the most important decisions are made (or are subject to veto) by the top ranks of military officers. In view of economic stagnation the military and elites believed they had to stimulate investment. And in order to accomplish this, they reasoned, they would have to dismantle, perhaps even crush, the collective power of the working class. The more organized the working class, the more difficult this task became.

Each of these military-dominated governments has assumed the power to control decisions concerning labor's most vital interests—wages, working conditions, fringe benefits, and the right to organize. Labor has had to reconcile itself to the measures approved by the military-dominated government bureaucracies that set labor policies. Outright strikes were virtually non-existent in Chile between 1973 and 1979 or in Brazil between 1968 and 1978. Moves to organize strikes in those countries in those years invited harsh repression, although some relaxation occurred in Brazil beginning in early 1978. Argentina's stronger tradition of union initiative has been harder to suppress, but labor leaders there have been forced to show great prudence also. All three military regimes have created a "command economy" when it comes to labor relations.

Why this heavy hand toward labor? Viewed from the short term, all three cases could be explained by the need to undertake unpopular anti-inflation policies. These regimes came to power when inflation and balance of payments deficits had made their economies dangerously vulnerable. In all three cases international credit, both public and private from the capitalist world, had been virtually closed off. All three were required to launch stabilization programs. Since no capitalist country in recent years has succeeded in carrying out economic stabilization without producing a drop in real wages (usually very large), and since Argentina, Brazil, and Chile have all had extensive experience with organized labor's resistance to stabilization programs, it was no surprise these military governments sought tough controls over labor.

All three cases of anti-labor polices, however, had more profound causes. These governments have proclaimed themselves to be "anti-political." All blame their countries' distress on the alleged incompetence, dishonesty, or treachery of politicians. These military groups have been most aggressive against the radically leftist politicians and labor leaders. Few channels of political opposition are left open. Just as Chile had once been the most democratic system, its military regime has been the most draconian, abolishing all political parties and burning the electoral rolls. The generals repudiated the open pluralistic political competition for which that country had been famous. Chile was to enter an era "free" of politics.

Argentina's military government took stern measures in 1976, although less sweeping than the Chilean military in 1973. It suspended Congress and all political parties, thereby signifying a hiatus in competitive politics, but no complete repudiation. Brazil's military guardians, having come to power in a less radicalized political atmosphere than their counterparts in Argentina and Chile, also found themselves in their second year (1965) pushed to abolish the old political parties (replaced by two government-sanctioned new ones). A more repressive phase (although with fewer deaths than in Argentina or Chile) after 1968 was followed by a gradual "opening" after 1978 as the military sought some new form of co-optative democracy.

Regimes pursuing this path have become known as "bureaucratic-authoritarian" states, and they have several characteristics. One is the granting of public office to people with highly bureaucratized careers—to members of the military, the civil service, or large corporations. Second is the political and economic exclusion of the working class and the control of the popular sector. Third is the reduction or near-elimination of political activity, especially in the early phases of the regime: problems are defined as technical, not political, and they are met with administrative solutions rather than negotiated political settlements.

Finally, bureaucratic-authoritarian governments have sought to revive economic growth by consolidating ties with international economic forces—revising, once again, the terms of dependency on the global world-system. Specifically, leaders of these regimes often forged alliances with multinational corporations (vast international companies such as IBM, Philips, Volkswagen). To establish credit and gain time, they also needed to come to terms with their creditors, such as U.S. and European banks and international lending agencies (such as the World Bank and the Inter-American Development Bank). Tasks of this kind have commonly been delegated to the most internationalized members of the original coalition, frequently young economists trained at United States institutions—often identified by derisive nicknames, such as the "Chicago boys" in Chile.

The exact fate of these experiments has been much disputed and remains in doubt, although the crippling world recession of 1981–83 and its attendant financial crisis has given dependency a grim new meaning. It is clear that the coalitions behind bureaucratic-authoritarian regimes are relatively fragile: local industrialists feel threatened by multinational corporations, and the military's instinct to annihilate any militant opposition has aroused opposition from middle-sector supporters. By the early 1980s, in fact, there were tentative signs of liberalization. The Peruvian military gave way to an elected government in 1980. The Brazilian regime oversaw a series of hotly contested elections in late 1982, even permitting opposition candidates to win key gubernatorial posts. And in Argentina, partly as a result of military humiliation in the South Atlantic (and partly because of economic problems), the regime was preparing to hold elections in late 1983.

It was difficult to interpret the meaning of these events. Optimists saw them as clear indications of the irrepressibility of democratic beliefs in the western hemisphere. More cautious observers pointed out that, particularly in Brazil, electoral contests might lead only to the consolidation of right-wing rule. Outright skeptics claimed that Argentina had proved itself to be virtually ungovernable, either by juntas or elected governments, and they noted that Chile was maintaining its monolithic, hard-line approach. So the question remained: Was Latin America undergoing a process of democratization, a return to liberal institutions? Or was this another phase in the evolution of authoritarian rule?

Mexico, as we shall see in Chapter Four, represents a different situation, since the state had acquired effective control over the popular sectors before the economic turndown of the 1960s, and the country was therefore able to make the transition from "populist" authoritarianism toward "bureaucratic" authoritarianism without a brutal military coup. Central America demonstrates the volatility of social conditions where economic development took place under traditional dictatorship, without giving rise to incremental reform. And Cuba, with its socialist revolution, offers still another pattern of transition and change.

TABLE 2-1   Patterns of Change in Latin America

	Economic Development	*Social Change*	*Typical Political Outcome*
Phase 1 (1880–1900)	Initiation of export-import growth	Modernization of elite, appearance of commercial sector and new professionals	Oligarchic democracy or integrating dictatorship
Phase 2 (1900–1930)	Export-import expansion	Appearance of middle strata, beginnings of proletariat	Co-optative democracy
Phase 3 (1930–1960s)	Import-substituting industrialization	Formation of entrepreneurial elite, strengthening of working class	Populism or co-optative democracy
Phase 4 (1960s to the Present)	Stagnation in import-substituting growth	Sharpening of conflict, often class conflict	Bureaucratic-authoritarian regime

In summary, the evolution of leading societies in Latin America has followed a pattern in which economic, social, and political developments are linked. Adherence to a general pattern has varied from country to country, but it is nonetheless possible to discern the outline of a common historical experience since the late nineteenth century. (Table 2-1 presents a simple summary.) This set of patterns, one should remember, derives from the history of the largest and most economically developed nations of Latin America. Some of the economically less developed areas, such as Central America or Paraguay, have undergone only some of these transitions—and their trajectory is seriously affected by the timing of their start. Just as global factors have conditioned the historical experience of the larger countries, so will global factors condition the future development of less advanced countries. There is no guarantee, in other words, that the history of Argentina and Brazil foreshadow the future of Honduras and Paraguay—any more than knowing the history of the nineteenth century United States enables us to predict the evolution of Chile or Mexico.

Women and Society

If we are to judge by the conventional accounts, women have played only minor roles in the economic and political transformation of Latin America. That is certainly true, if we look at the prominent public positions. Why should this have been so? To answer, we need first to look into Latin American culture. A central cultural norm has consisted of the notion of *machismo,* a celebration of the sexual and social expressions of masculine power and virility. For centuries this idea has provided both a prescription and a justification for varied forms of aggression and assertiveness which have been linked, in turn, to the protection of honor. *Machismo* appears to have its origins in medieval conceptions of knighthood, including chivalry and *caballerosidad,* and it has undergone steady adaptation in the face of social change. In any event, it still lives.

The other side of this male-oriented stereotype has been, for women, the cult of *marianismo.* Named after the Virgin Mary, this myth exalts the virtues associated with womanhood—semi-divinity, moral superiority, and spiritual strength. For it is women, according to the Latin American conception, who are the custodians of virtue and propriety. They are pictured as having infinite capacities for humility and sacrifice and, as mother figures, they demonstrate unfailing tolerance for the impulsive (often childlike) antics of the *macho* menfolk. The typical female image thus becomes one of saintliness and sadness, often identified with the rituals of mourning: a wistful figure, clad in black and draped with mantilla, kneeling before the altar and praying for the redemption of the sinful males within her sheltered world.

Reality, of course, has not always complied with the mythologies of *machismo* and *marianismo.* But both cults have been integral parts of Latin American society, and they have consistently been used and exploited by members of both sexes.

The social role of females has typically been confined to the private sphere, particularly the family, and here women have often reigned supreme. Among the lower classes especially, women have from the colonial times onward often been the heads of household—because husbands have either moved elsewhere or died. And among the upper-class elite, extended families have frequently been dominated by forceful matrons, grandmotherly figures who wield unchallenged authority over such family matters as marriage, place of residence, and inheritance.

Over time the boundaries of acceptable social behavior for women have broadened a great deal. In the nineteenth century women of culture often hosted literary discussions, or *tertulias,* where guests would engage in discourse about novels and *belles-lettres.* Some, like Clorinda Matto de Turner and Mercedes Cabello de Carbonero in Peru, became distinguished writers (a tradition first set by a seventeenth century Mexican nun, Sor Juana Inés de la Cruz). But restrictions still persisted. Mariquita Sánchez, hostess of a well-known salon in Buenos Aires, described the female plight in ironic verse:

The only things we understand
Are hearing a mass, reciting a prayer,
Arranging our clothes,
And patching and repair.

During the twentieth century the process accelerated. Within middle-class strata especially young women ceased to be chaperoned on social occasions (partly because the family had less at stake in the event of an inconvenient marriage). Women have entered the job market and made their mark as teachers, professors, dentists, doctors, even lawyers. In large metropolitan cities, their lifestyle is often barely distinguishable from that of women living in Paris or New York.

Nonetheless, Latin American women have been slow in entering (or have been prohibited from entering) the public arena. As Table 2-2 reveals, women obtained the right to vote rather late in many countries, mostly in the 1930s or 1940s (and as late as 1961 in Paraguay). Survey research indicates that many women interpret the franchise as a matter of civic duty, rather than partisan involvement. On many occasions, it appears, they have voted in deference to their husbands' preferences.

TABLE 2-2   Female Suffrage in the Americas

	Year in which National Woman Suffrage Was Recognized
United States	1920
Ecuador	1929
Brazil	1932
Uruguay	1932
Cuba	1934
El Salvador	1939
Dominican Republic	1942
Guatemala	1945
Panama	1945
Argentina	1947
Venezuela	1947
Chile	1949
Costa Rica	1949
Haiti	1950
Bolivia	1952
Mexico	1953
Honduras	1955
Nicaragua	1955
Peru	1955
Colombia	1957
Paraguay	1961

Source: Elsa M. Chaney, *Supermadre: Women in Politics in Latin America* (Austin: University of Texas Press, 1979), p. 169.

But not always. In 1958, for instance, women in Chile tipped the balance in favor of the conservative presidential candidate (men having given a plurality to the radical opponent). And in 1970 in the same country, lower-class women provided an important base of electoral support for the victorious left. More research on the subject is needed (it is easy in Chile, where by law women and men vote in separate booths), but there is every indication that increasingly women are asserting independent stands in key elections.

They have also shown their influence in other ways. In Argentina, women formed an impressive bloc in the Peronist movement of the 1940s and 50s. They are active in the rituals of Mexican politics. They have participated in key demonstrations: one was a pot-clanging protest against Salvador Allende's government in Chile; another, since the late 1970s, has been the weekly vigil of the "mothers of the Plaza de Mayo" seeking information on relatives and loved ones who have "disappeared" in Argentina. And women have taken part in revolutionary movements—in Mexico, Cuba, and Nicaragua.

Ill, gaunt, and nonetheless compelling, Eva Perón waves to the crowd during a motorcade for the inauguration of her husband into his second presidential term in June 1952; she died the following month. (United Press International.)

Nonetheless, women have held relatively few important political posts, only 2–3 percent even now. There has been one female president (Isabel Martínez de Perón, 1974–76), although that position was obtained through the death of her husband. And while in office, Latin American women have often projected a distinctly female approach to their jobs. Listen, for instance, to Evita Perón, perhaps the most powerful woman in the history of the western hemisphere:

> In this great house of the Motherland, I am just like any other woman in any other of the innumerable houses of my people. Just like all of them I rise early thinking about my husband and about my children. . . . It's that I so truly feel myself the mother of my people.

Thus did Evita, willful and politically ambitious, harken to the themes of *marianismo*.

In the context of the constraints (and advantages) afforded by their culture, Latin American women have not developed a major feminist movement, although Brazil has made a beginning. For the most part, women have operated within prevailing socioeconomic and political categories. As Elsa M. Chaney predicted in 1979: "Latin American women probably will not replicate United States or Western European patterns of women's liberation. They have their own reality. . . . Whatever they do, Latin American women themselves will decide their own course of action in the context of their own culture and aspirations."

A Framework for Comparison

One of the aims of this book is to furnish a basis for the comparative analysis of contemporary Latin America. This involves three steps: first, identifying the patterns and processes shared in common by Latin American societies; second, identifying the differences between their individual historical experiences; third, and most difficult, ascertaining the reasons for those differences.

Thus far we have presented a general scheme for depicting socioeconomic and political transition in Latin America. To comprehend the similarities and differences between various countries we need to ask a common set of fundamental questions. We have, accordingly, approached the case studies that follow with several inquiries in mind:

1. How has the class structure evolved? What are the most important social classes? Are any classes missing? In some instances economic changes have conspired to create some groupings and to prevent the formation of others. Not every Latin society has had a peasantry or an industrial elite, for example, and the absence of a social grouping can have as important an effect on the social order as can the presence of others.
2. Which social classes have the most power? Who controls the econ-

omy and who dominates the political scene? How much effective competition takes place between existing groups?

3. Which groupings form alliances? Are there any social coalitions? On the basis of what interests? Are industrial workers more likely to join an alliance with entrepreneurial leaders, for example, than with peasants who share their lower-class status?

4. How autonomous is the state? Does the government represent the interests of only one social class (or coalition), or does it stand apart from such allegiances? If it is run by the army, for example, do military leaders strive to remain above and beyond the conflicts of civil society?

International factors have played key roles in the shaping of Latin American history, particularly in view of the economic "dependency" that we heve sketched out so far. This dimension gives rise to additional questions:

5. At any given moment, what kind of economic activity is taking place at the center of the world-system? What is the shape and form of industrialization in Europe and the United States, and what kinds of limitations and incentives does that pose for the countries of Latin America?

6. How does the relationship between the economies at the center and the periphery of the system affect the composition and arrangement of social classes within Latin American societies? Would a country exporting beef (Argentina), for example, be likely to have a different class structure from a country exporting copper (Chile)? What implications might this have?

7. How have Latin American countries managed to take advantage of their place in the economic world-system? Recent experience has suggested that the possession of oil, for example, can provide such countries as Mexico, Venezuela, and even Ecuador with economic opportunity and international influence. Have there been similar cases in the past?

8. What are the predominant political factors in the international scene? The presence (or absence) of an East-West Cold War, to take one obvious example, could help determine the plausible range of choices available to Latin American policymakers. In specific moments, too, this concern can translate into another factor: geographical proximity to the United States. Because of presumed "national security" considerations of a geopolitical nature, the U.S. may well grant more leeway to a country like Argentina than, let us say, to nations in the Caribbean basin.

We will offer a comparative analysis of key countries in the Epilogue. Our immediate task is to turn to individual case studies.

THREE

ARGENTINA
From Prosperity to Deadlock

Present-day Argentina was originally a backwater in the Spanish American colonial empire. Unlike Mexico or Peru, the region of the Río de la Plata lacked precious metals (although "Argentina" means silver in Spanish). Nor did the region have a settled native population. The Indians were few in number and nomadic, so the Spaniards had no ready large-scale source of labor. The area's greatest resource was the fertile land—some of the richest in the world, with loam over a foot deep in places. A further asset was the location of Buenos Aires, which was situated to become a great port if sufficient dredging were done. Yet these conditions produced no dynamic economy in the colonial era. Neither the technology nor the market for exploiting the fertile pampas was at hand. The port served largely to channel profitable contraband trade into Spanish South America.

Although Argentina's colonial economy was modest, its geography is important for understanding the region's later development. The most prosperous center was in the northwest of what is now Argentina—an area tied to Peru. Until 1776 Argentina was included within the viceroyalty of Peru, and its economic development was closely linked to the northward shipment of cotton, rice, wheat, and leather goods. The coastal region around Buenos Aires was less active. Its greatest industry was smuggling, since Lima's high customs rates made it attractive to avoid the authorities by using the route via the Río de la Plata. Only in 1776 did Buenos Aires assume importance, when it was made the seat of a new viceroyalty. Power then began to shift from the northwest to the southern coast, as Buenos Aires became the entry port for European imports, some of which directly competed with production in the northwest.

The Wars of Independence shook the viceroyalty of La Plata, but did not leave the damage to property that hit Mexico (and Uruguay). The anti-Spanish sentiment in La Plata united the local elite and produced what became an enduring myth of military prowess, as General José de San Martín defeated the troops loyal to the Spanish crown. With independence achieved in the 1820s, the landowning aristocracy contemplated their realm with satisfaction. Small-scale industries and trading communities continued to exist in the central and northwestern interior. The coastal areas had no such artisan base, but the adjacent ranchers produced hides and salted meat for export, and the city of Buenos Aires was growing into an active seaside port. Most important, Buenos Aires and the interior to the north and west grew steadily farther apart.

The Struggle Over Nationhood

The decades after independence saw a battle among Argentines about the direction of their new country's economic development. The competing groups came from different regions. One faction was made up of the "unitarians," mainly from the province (and city) of Buenos Aires. They wanted to nationalize the port city of Buenos Aires: strip it of its autonomy, then make it into a base from which to reduce provincial barriers to trade and thereby open the entire country to international commerce.

The second group was the "federalists," who were from the interior. They agreed on the need to nationalize the city of Buenos Aires because they wanted the city's customs receipts distributed to all the provinces. At the same time, they wanted to maintain provincial autonomy, especially the ability to levy interprovincial tariffs and thus to protect local industries.

The third group was also called the "federalists," but they were of a very different kind: they were from the province of Buenos Aires and opposed nationalization of the port city of Buenos Aires, since that would mean loss of their province's existing monopoly over the city's customs revenues. They also wanted free trade. In effect, the third group was advocating the status quo.

The conflict among these three groups lasted through the 1830s and 1840s. In the end the issue was decided by one of Latin America's famous dictators: Juan Manuel de Rosas, a politically ambitious cattle rancher from the province of Buenos Aires. A physically imposing figure who could intimidate the tough gauchos, Rosas won the governorship of his province in 1829. His ambitions did not stop there. He wanted to rule all of Argentina, and pursued his goal with policies favoring the *estancieros* (ranch owners), thus furthering the consolidation of a landed aristocracy. Rosas was an ardent Buenos Aires federalist. More important, he had the military leadership and the following to achieve his goal of subduing rival *caudillos,* "so that not one of this race of monsters may remain among us," as he proclaimed. As he consolidated his personal authority, he extended the power of the province of Buenos Aires over the country, in effect building up a nation on the principle of federalism. At the same time, Rosas built a powerful government machine, complete with a kind of enforcement squad (*Mazorca*) that terrorized all who dared oppose the dictator, even if only because they failed to wear the official color of red.

Along with his military and political skills, Rosas was such an ardent nationalist that many foreigners saw him as a xenophobe. He sought to apply in his foreign policy the tactics that had worked so handsomely in domestic politics. "Nourished in the monopolistic maxims of Spanish colonial law," noted a visiting French diplomat in 1850, "he neither understands nor permits trade except when it is hemmed in by protective tariffs and rigorous regulations." Unfortunately for Rosas, he had succeeded in arousing a powerful opposition alliance that included Brazil and Uruguay, as well as General Justo José de Uriquiza, who commanded the force that defeated Rosas in 1852. The Argentine strongman then immediately left for exile in England. Despite his ignominious fall, Rosas had succeeded in creating a united Argentina out of the disparate provinces. From the moment of his defeat Rosas became a legendary figure. Argentine nationalists adopted him as a prototypical Argentine patriot, who pursued national development against the alien forces seeking to subvert Argentina's rise to full nationhood. Rosas resembles Chile's Diego Portales and Mexico's Agustín de Iturbide, who also became strong-arm autocratic rulers in the decade after independence. Rosas ruled far longer than the other two.

During the rule of Rosas many Argentine intellectuals, such as Domingo Sarmiento and Esteban Echeverría, fled the repressive rule. They detested the gaucho leader's heavy-handed political success. Sarmiento described Rosas as the man "who applied the knife of the gaucho to the culture of Buenos Aires and destroyed the work of centuries—of civilization, law and liberty." These intellectuals dreamed of the day when they might capture the control of Argentina and steer it onto the course of liberal representative government. With the fall of Rosas in 1852 they got their chance.

Power was taken by Justo José de Urquiza, a federalist from the interior. He began by calling a constitutional convention, which promulgated a constitution in 1853, closely following the U.S. example. It was to be a federal system, with the president chosen by an electoral college whose members would be elected by popular vote. The federal congress had two houses, with the Chamber of Deputies elected by direct vote and the Senate elected by provincial legislatures. The provinces were to retain all powers not specifically granted to the national government, although a loophole provision authorized the central government to intervene in the provinces whenever it was deemed necessary.

The controversy over the status of the city of Buenos Aires was far from settled, however. Protesting the nationalization of the city in the new constitution, the province of Buenos Aires refused to join the new confederation. Defeated in a brief civil war in 1859, the province was forced to capitulate. Only two years later the province rose in revolt, led by Bartolomé Mitre, and captured control of the confederation.

In 1862 Mitre was inaugurated as president and he launched a new drive to unify Argentina. For the next two decades the liberals continued in power. Mitre was followed in the presidency by Domingo Sarmiento, author of *Facundo* (1845), the most famous literary attack on the *caudillo*-style gauchos. His real-life target was Rosas, whose rule Sarmiento had spent exiled in Chile. Sarmiento believed ardently in North-American–style public education and urged Argentines to follow the U.S. model. A diversion on the way was the drawn-out Paraguayan War (1865–70), in which tiny Paraguay held off Argentina, Brazil, and Uruguay for five years. At issue was the ill-advised attempt by the Paraguayan dictator, Francisco Solano López, to exercise a monopoly of control over access to the all-important Paraná River basin.

The third liberal president was Nicolás Avellaneda. In his term (1874–80) Argentina undertook its last major territorial conquest—the "Indian wars." The provinces to the south and west of Buenos Aires had long been plauged by Indian raids. Now an army force under the command of General Julio Roca subdued or exterminated the Indian bands. The year 1880 also brought a solution to the long troublesome question of the status of the city of Buenos Aires. It was detached from the province, rather like the District of Columbia in the U.S., but its citizens were given full voting rights in national elections.

About 1880 Argentina entered a remarkable era of sustained economic growth. Since ousting Rosas, the liberals had enjoyed power long enough to lay the basis for their country's rapid integration into the world economy. Their leader now was General Roca, hero of the "Conquest of the Desert." The symbolism could hardly have been better: the Indian-fighter presiding over the Europeanization of a South American republic.

The political elite had few doubts about its mission. Like their counterparts in Brazil and Mexico, the Argentine politicians and intellectuals saw themselves as applying the true principles of European science and philosophy. They believed in both economic and political liberalism. They quoted the pseudoscience of Herbert Spencer, arguing that if an aristocracy ruled Argentina, it was the result of natural selection. With the Indian and the gaucho safely subdued, the elite confidently looked torward to enriching itself, and, by liberal logic, thereby enriching their country.

Overview: Economic Growth and Social Change

Argentina's economic success in the 1880–1914 era was based on its ability to supply agricultural goods needed by the North Atlantic industrial world. With the industrial revolution, West Europe, especially England, was becoming a net importer of foodstuffs. Argentina had a comparative advantage in producing two key goods: meat and grain. Important technological advances had made it practical to ship foodstuffs the many thousands of miles from Buenos Aires to London and Antwerp. One was the steam vessel, with its faster and far more certain pace than the sailing ship. Another was the process for chilling meat (the plants in Argentina were called *frigoríficos*), which made possible a tastier and more substantial product than meat preserved by drying (beef jerky).

Thanks to one natural resource Argentina was ideally suited to furnish the needed foodstuffs: its pampas were among the most fertile lands in the world. But it lacked two other essential factors, capital and labor. England, Argentina's principal customer, soon sent the capital. It came in the form of investment in the railroads, the docks, the packing houses, and the public utilities. It also came in the form of English firms to handle shipping, insurance, and banking. Virtually the entire infrastructure of the export sector was financed by the British. This inflow of capital was exactly what the Argentine political elite saw as essential for their country's development.

The other missing economic factor was labor. Here the solution also came from Europe, although not from Britain. The badly needed workers streamed into Argentina from southern Europe, especially Italy. Between 1857 and 1930 Argentina received a net immigration (immigrants minus emigrants) of 3.5 million. This meant that during that time about 60 percent of the total population increase could be attributed to immigration. Of these immigrants about 46 percent were Italian and 32 percent Spanish. The demographic effect of immigration on Argentina was greater than in any other major country of the Western Hemisphere. By 1914 approximately 30 percent of the population was foreign-born. (At the same time in the U.S., another haven for European emigrants, only about 13 percent of the population was foreign-born.) The result was to give Argentina a distinctly European quality, with a resulting tension among Argentines as to their real national identity.

This immigrant labor force was a textbook example of the mobility of labor. The workers were hired and fired on primarily economic grounds, with a remarkable movement of laborers back and forth between Italy and the Argentine pampas (earning them the nickname of *golondrinas* or "swallows"). There was a fluid movement between city and country within Argentina, too, with Buenos Aires always attracting a large share of the foreigners.

This era also saw a modest industrialization, which, however, posed no threat to the basically agro-export orientation of the economy. Much of the industry processed products from the countryside, such as wool and beef, thereby leading the processors to identify their interests with agriculture.

The rapid economic growth of the 1880–1914 era had profound social implications. At the outset there was a landed elite on top, gauchos and wage labor on the bottom. With the epic tide of immigration, the national population swelled from 1.7 million in 1869 to 7.9 million in 1914. As the economy boomed, new economic niches appeared. The immigrants came first to the farms, but then often moved to the cities. The Italians and Spaniards arrived to become colonists, tenant farmers, and rural laborers. Other jobs opened in the urban sector: in transport (especially the railroads), processing, and the service industries (banking, government). Exploitation of Argentina's agricultural wealth produced an intricate network of economic interests and contributed to the creation of a complex rural-urban economy.

Argentina's economy thus entered its "golden age," an era of increasing prosperity based on the exportation of meat and grain and on the importation of manufactured goods from abroad. From the 1860s to 1914 Argentina's GDP (Gross Domestic Product) grew at an annual average rate of at least 5 percent (exact data for pre-1900 are sketchy). This is one of the highest sustained growth rates ever recorded for any country. Trade grew steadily from 1880 onward, while statesmen optimistically propounded the virtues of progress and commercial growth. It seemed to many that Argentina, so blessed with natural resources, was on its way to unending expansion.

But the country paid a price for this success. Argentina's integration into the world economy meant that sharp fluctuations abroad would have severe repercussions at home. A decline in European demand for foodstuffs brought a decline in exports, which could provoke a downturn throughout the entire Argentine economy—a fate shared with Australia, another exporter of temperate agricultural products. And as shown in Figure 3-1, the peso value of Argentine exports varied considerably during the period from 1915 to 1939: up during World War I, down in the early 20s, then up and down and up and down again when the Great Depression struck in the 1930s. This is one way in which Argentina, like other exporting countries of Latin America, came to be economically dependent on the industrialized center of the world system. Through the reliance on trade, the condition of the economy was largely determined by trends and decisions outside of Argentina.

But the international market for meat and grain was relatively stable, at least in comparison to the demand for such goods as sugar and coffee (as we shall see below). The meat trade, in particular, held fairly firm throughout the 1930s. After recovering from drought and other setbacks, demand for wheat and other cereals also bounced back. So Argentina was hit hard by the Depression, but not as quickly—or as completely—as some other countries of Latin America.

Another form of economic dependency appeared in the financial realm, since the Argentine banking system was periodically tied to the gold standard. Short-term fluctuations in trade caused sharp changes in Argentina's gold reserves, thus contracting or expanding the domestic money supply and making Argentina's economy a hostage to international currency movements.

Still another link to the world economy posed further problems: the large role played by foreign capital and foreign businessmen. Argentina's booming economy, along with government guarantees, attracted capital from abroad. From 1900 to 1929, 35 percent of the country's total fixed investment came from foreigners. Britain was the prime investor, followed by France and Germany. This high degree of foreign economic involvement later became a prime target for the economic nationalists. Such dependence on foreign resources also contributed to on-going Argentine self-doubt: a recurrent unwillingness to believe that Argentines could ever hope to achieve a more self-sufficient economy, especially in industry.

Argentina's export-import growth also created inequities at home, especially among geographical regions. While prosperity blessed the pampas and Buenos Aires, parts of the interior stagnated. Central and northwestern provinces such as Jujuy, La Rioja, Santiago del Estero, and Salta suffered economic decline and social decay. Only Mendoza, Tucumán and Córdoba escaped this fate, thanks to their wine and sugar production. Throughout the nineteenth century the interior had fought to prevent its demise at the hands of Buenos Aires. It lost, and the price of its defeat was poverty.

Of course inequities also existed even within the prosperous regions. In the rural sector the wealthy *estancieros* built elegant chalets, while foreign-born tenant farmers and displaced native workers scratched out a meager existence. In the cities, especially Buenos Aires, elegantly attired aristocrats met at their European-style clubs while workers struggled to protect their families from the inflation that always seemed to outpace their wages. The Argentine boom, like so many others in capitalist countries at this time, did facilitate considerable upward mobility.

FIGURE 3-1 Argentine Exports, 1915–39 (in thousands of pesos)

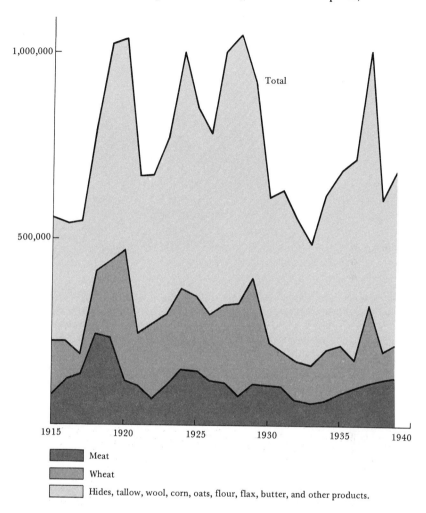

Source: Vicente Vázquez-Presedo, *Estadísticas históricas argentinas (comparadas)*, vol. II (Buenos Aires: Ediciones Macchi, 1976), 190–93.

But it also fostered huge income discrepancies, which were ultimately bound to create social and political tensions.

There were also tensions in the cultural realm. As Argentina experienced its impressive burst of economic growth, it became increasingly obvious that the Argentines did not yet have a clear-cut sense of nationality. Their nationhood was ill-defined because the flood of immigrants, mostly concentrated in Buenos Aires, had accentuated the long-

This difference in living conditions reflects the social inequality that accompanied Argentina's economic expansion after the 1880s. *Above,* luxurious residences of aristocratic families in Buenos Aires; *below,* temporary shacks for workers in the city's port area around 1910. (Courtesy of the Archivo General de la Nación, Buenos Aires.)

standing contrast between the densely settled, Europeanized, cosmopolitan capital city and the rough-hewn, cattle-oriented society of the vast and lightly populated interior. This contrast had been dramatized by the bitter battle between the liberals and Rosas, whom they saw as the incarnation of the primitive gaucho, who could never build, only destroy, a civilized nation.

In the early twentieth century this liberal dogma was challenged by a new generation of nationalist writers such as Ricardo Rojas, who sought, in his words, "to awaken Argentina out of its coma." Rojas pointed to the Indian and the soil as the true sources of Argentine nationality. He and other nationalists looked to *Martín Fierro,* the classic poem about the gaucho (first appearing in 1872), as a highly authentic document in the creation of a national consciousness.

One of the more famous works in the tradition of Rojas's nationalism was Ezequiel Martínez Estrada's *X-Ray of the Pampa* (1933), a lengthy indictment of the Argentine elite for having tried to cloak their country's reality in the trappings of European civilization. But Martínez Estrada added another dualism: "Race track and soccer field are two political parties: the former stands for adventure, instability, ambition, centralism, and monarchy; the latter represents work, passionate struggle, committee disputes, chaos, and democracy. The Jockey Club and the sports associations support opposing trends and recruit antagonistic forces."

Meanwhile the capital city was developing its own culture. The major foreign influence was Italian and in the dock area there emerged a unique dialect, *lunfardo,* a mixture of Spanish and Italian. It was a strictly working-class, as was also the tango, the famous sensuous dance and accompanying music, which originated in the suburbs (some said the brothels) and only became respectable in Argentina after it took Paris by storm on the eve of World War I. By the 1920s the tango had been adopted by the most fashionable Argentine circles and the music was brought to a high art form by Carlos Gardel, Argentina's immortal tango composer and singer. His death in an air accident in 1936 caused the greatest outpouring of grief Buenos Aires had ever seen. As the 1930s continued, North American popular culture penetrated urban Argentina at a quick pace, much to the fury of Argentine nationalist intellectuals.

One of the most crucial social effects of Argentina's expansion turned out to be a non-event: *the country never developed a peasantry,* at least not in the pastoral areas of the pampa and the crucial coastal provinces. The "Conquest of the Desert" in the 1870s virtually eliminated the Indian population, and the land was promptly distributed in large tracts appropriate for raising cattle and sowing grain. In contrast to the policy in the Great Plains of the United States, Argentina did not give its land to family farmers or individual homesteaders. Cattle ranching did not require a large-scale work force, since barbed wire was sufficient to contain the herds; and though wheat was often grown by foreign colonists who rented land, they did not constitute an influential social group. As a result, a classic peasantry—such as those of Mexico, Chile, or northeastern Brazil—did not exist in Argentina.

This fact would have far-reaching implications. It meant, for instance, that land reform would never become the vital and symbolic issue that it was in such countries as Mexico. It was not that land was so evenly distributed in Argentina; it was that there were no long-time rural dwellers to lay historic claim to the soil.

Further, the absence of a peasantry meant that there was no peasantry to form a power base and, perhaps even more crucial, there was no peasantry available for coalitions with other social groups. Landowners, when challenged, could not resort to the time-tested (if paradoxical) alliance with the peasantry that frequently occurred in other countries, and urban laborers could not enlist peasants in broad-based warfare between the "popular classes" and the social system at large.

In the big cities, however, wage laborers were numerous and prone to organization. According to one estimate, manual workers accounted for nearly 60 percent of the population in the city of Buenos Aires in the early twentieth century. And about three fifths of the working class, in turn, consisted of immigrants who retained citizenship in their home countries—mainly Italy and Spain.

The first efforts at organizing Argentine labor were influenced by European precedents. In the 1870s and 1880s European anarchist and socialist exiles began vigorous organizing, and in 1895 the Socialist Party was founded. The Socialists were molded on the European model: a parliamentary party, clearly committed to an electoral and evolutionary strategy. As of 1900 one might have expected the Socialist Party to become a major political voice for the Argentine working class. Yet it failed to attract the immigrant workers. Socialist pleas for reform through the political system fell on deaf ears.

The urban working class proved receptive to another message; it came from the anarchists. Their *Federación Obrera Regional Argentina* (FORA) caught the workers' imagination with its call for direct action. The FORA-sponsored local and general strikes were effective enough to worry the government, which assumed that any labor problems must be the work of foreign agitators. Congress therefore passed the *Ley de Residencia* ("Residence Law") in 1902, which empowered the government to deport all foreigners whose behavior "compromised national security or disturbed public order"—by participating in strikes, for example. It was an instinctive reaction of the lawmakers, who refused to believe that class conflict could arise among truly patriotic Argentines.

A few of the reigning politicians decided to try a different approach. In 1904 Joaquín V. Gonzalez proposed a general code for labor relations, which would have closely controlled labor action. Conservatives quickly attacked the bill because they opposed in principle labor's right to organize, while labor, led by the anarchists, opposed it because they feared that any government system would be manipulated against them. The combination killed the bill, thereby precluding the creation of any official labor relations system.

Political leaders continued their efforts to gain control of labor. In 1907 the Congress created a Department of Labor and invited the leading labor confederations, including the FORA, to participate in a tribunal created to adjudicate labor conflicts. But worker organizations refused to support the "corrupt bourgeois government" in this effort. Once again the Argentine labor movement escaped incorporation into a government-dominated system of labor relations.

Meanwhile the anarchists continued to organize. Their efforts reached a climax in 1910, the centennial of the declaration of Argentine independence, as a great public celebration was planned to glorify Argentina's progress. But the anarchist leaders had a different purpose in mind. As militant opponents of the liberal elite, they wanted to raise their protest against the farce of the European-oriented model of progress. The oligarchy and the middle class were indignant over the threatened disruption of a patriotic ritual. The protestors filled the streets and plazas, but were crushed and scattered by masses of police. The anarchist-led challenge was more than met. Government repression completely carried the day. The reaction against the protestors spilled over into the Congress, which approved a new law (*Ley de Defensa Social,* or "Social Defense Law"), making even easier the arrest and prosecution of labor organizers. A hunt began for urban protest leaders.

This was the death knell for Argentine anarchism, but not of urban protest. Strike activity in Buenos Aires reached another peak in 1918–19, and it would oscillate from time to time after that (see Figure 3-2). Even more significant is the persistence and continuity of worker agitation into and through the 1950s. Fairly early in this century, organized labor emerged as a key actor in Argentine society.

The Political System: Consensus and Reform

The liberal politicians later known as the "Generation of 1880" (so labelled for their emergence that year) drew their political power from several sources. First, they were themselves members of, or very close to, the landowning class that produced Argentina's riches. Second, they managed to monopolize the instruments of state power: they controlled

FIGURE 3-2   Strikes and Strikers in Buenos Aires, 1907–72

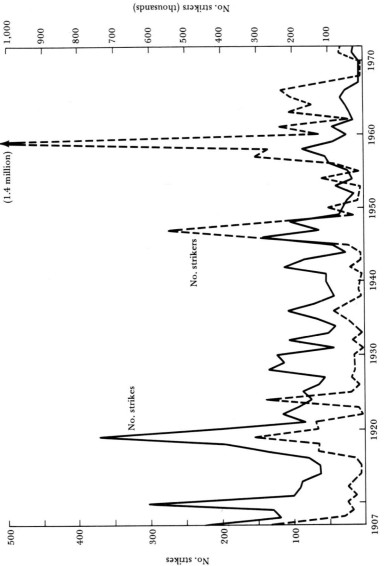

Sources: Departamento Nacional del Trabajo, *Estadística de las huelgas* (Buenos Aires, 1940), p. 20; Dirección Nacional de Inves-
tigaciones, Estadística y Censos, *Síntesis estadística mensual de la República Argentina*, 1, no. 1 (January 1947), 7; Vicente Vazquez-
Presedo, *Estadísticas históricas argentinas (comparadas)*, vol. II (Buenos Aires: Ediciones Macchi, 1976), 47; Guido di Tella and
Manuel Zymelman, *Las etapas del desarrollo económico argentino* (Buenos Aires: Paidós, 1967), pp. 537–38; International Labor
Office, *Year Book of Labour Statistics*, 11 (1949–40), 379; 16 (1956), 456; 25 (1965), 692; 33 (1973), 752.

the army and the elections, resorting to vote fraud when necessary. They also controlled the only authentic political party, the *Partido Autonomista Nacional* (PAN). The most important national decisions were made by *acuerdo,* or informal agreement among officials of the Executive. In this respect the Argentine liberals ignored one key aspect of the British/U.S. example—the central role of the legislature, which in Argentina had been rendered inconsequential in this period.

At first glance this political system seems to have admirably served the agro-export interests that profited from the post-1880 expansion. But the aristocrats in control did not go unchallenged. The spreading prosperity, which created new wealth holders in both country and city, helped feed political discontent among three groups: (1) newly prosperous landowners of the upper Littoral; (2) old aristocratic families, often from the far interior, who had failed to profit from the agro-export boom; and (3) members of the middle class doing well economically but excluded from political power.

These three groups joined forces to create the Radical Party, destined to play a major role in twentieth century politics. In 1890, just as the country entered a short but severe economic crisis, they attempted an armed revolt. An *acuerdo* ended the rebellion, but some intransigent leaders founded the Radical Civic Union (*Unión Cívica Radical,* or UCR) two years later. Able to make no electoral progress against the fraud routinely practiced by the ruling politicians, they resorted twice more to armed revolt. Both attempts failed. Nonetheless the Radicals, led first by Leandro Alem and then by Hipólito Yrigoyen, maintained their stubborn pursuit of political power. As for economic goals, they were by and large successful participants in the agro-export economy and were strongly committed to it. They simply wanted a share in the political direction of their society.

Not all the oligarchs endorsed the government position of freezing the Radicals out of power. A more enlightened wing won out in 1911 when President Roque Sáenz Peña proposed an electoral reform. Passed in 1912, the new law called for universal male suffrage, the secret ballot, and compulsory voting. This would significantly enlarge the electorate, especially in the cities. In effect, it was a shrewd attempt at co-optation by the oligarchy. Sáenz Peña and his colleagues saw labor organizers and the working class to be the real threat—not the middle classes, who would cooperate once incorporated within the system. The Argentine political bosses were acting here much like their British counterparts in the nineteenth century, who three times adopted electoral reform bills to widen the franchise and thereby incorporate new social sectors into the established political game.

The Sáenz Peña electoral reform thus extended the vote to the frustrated middle-sector citizens. The well organized Radicals immediately capitalized on the new rules and got their long-time leader, Hipólito Yrigoyen, elected president in 1916. Was this to be a new era?

An early test came in the government's behavior toward the workers. The Radicals began with an attitude different from that of their predecessors. They showed a genuine concern for the lot of the working class, partly because they hoped to win eventual votes in their struggle with the Conservatives. As labor-management conflicts arose, the Yrigoyen government followed an apparent pro-labor stance in its interventions. Labor organizers saw this as an improvement, but one that would depend on government action case-by-case.

The crisis came in 1918–19, when the entire western world was shaken by strike waves. The actions, which often included general strikes, were generally aimed at both the employers and the state. It was a confluence of specific grievances and generalized hostility. In Argentina, workers were aroused over the reduced buying power of their wages, caused by the inflation of World War I. Food prices rose sharply, stimulated by European demand, but wage increases lagged. The resulting squeeze hit Buenos Aires workers hard. Union leaders called a series of strikes in late 1918, and in early 1919 syndicalist organizers decided the time was ripe for a general strike—the syndicalist instrument for bringing down the bourgeois state.

Their idea had tragic consequences. The Yrigoyen government decided it had to act firmly, and the results were a rerun of 1910. Antilabor hysteria was promoted by a newly formed ultra-rightist civilian paramilitary movement, the Argentine Patriotic League (*Liga Patriótica Argentina*), which effectively exploited the middle- and upper-class fear of the popular challenge. League members took to the streets to attack workers; it was class warfare with a vengeance. Hundreds of demonstrators were shot. The labor leaders were again repressed, this time by the Radicals, with the heaviest blows falling on the syndicalists and the last remnants of the anarchist leadership.

Organized labor did not disappear. Although the anarchists were beaten and the syndicalists were weakened, two other ideological currents began to make headway among Argentine workers: socialism and communism. The former stressed political action, betting on the Socialist Party as the hope for change in Argentine capitalism. The Communists, on the other hand, placed emphasis upon the labor union movement instead of the ballot box, and they soon made modest progress in gaining key union positions.

The 1920s did not bring much success to labor organizers. Real wage rates increased steadily during the decade, but not because of union pressure. On the contrary, rising wages may have undermined unionization. The relative absence of conflict (seen in Figure 3-2) also meant that the government made no effort to create a new framework for

labor relations. By 1930 organized labor had become a relatively subdued actor on the Argentine stage.

At the other end of the political spectrum were the Conservatives.
They had hoped the Sáenz Peña electoral reform would make it possible to co-opt the Radicals. Their hopes were soon disappointed. Instead of sustaining the tradition of agreement by *acuerdo,* it led to basic
changes in the political system.

First, the electorate was steadily enlarged. All Argentine males over
eighteen years old now had the right to vote, and nearly 1 million people qualified in 1912. There continued to be a sharp increase in the
electorate, with the total reaching 3.4 million by 1946. Participation was
high, it being mandatory, and fraud was minimized. Between 70 and
80 percent of the eligible voters cast ballots in the presidential elections.
The elections were also highly competitive. Winners rarely emerged
with more than 60 percent of the vote. This relatively high percentage
of (male only) citizen participation distinguished Argentina from other
major Latin American countries such as Mexico or Brazil, whose far
more restricted electorates reflected lower literacy rates and more closed
political systems.

A further consequence of expanded voter participation was the increased importance of the political parties. Almost nonexistent under
the Generation of 1880, after 1912 the parties became primary vehicles
for the organized pursuit of power. The parties, in turn, spawned a
new kind of political elite: middle-class professionals who made careers
out of politics. Their favorite forum was the national Congress.

As innovative as the Sáenz Peña electoral reform was for its day in
Latin America, it left the political system still limited in basic ways. Restricting the franchise to male citizens not only excluded all women; it
also left out at least half of the adult males because so many were still
foreign citizens. Few immigrants underwent naturalization because most
never intended to settle permanently in Argentina and therefore did
not try. Those who did try were usually defeated by the labyrinthine
procedures and deliberately obstructionist tactics of Argentine officials.
Since the unnaturalized immigrants were more numerous among the
working class, the reform tended to help the middle class at the expense of the lower class.

The practical result of all these changes was to leave the Conservatives far from power. The Radicals, building upon their popular base
and employing machine tactics, displayed continuing electoral supremacy: Marcelo T. de Alvear became president in 1922, Yrigoyen was re-
elected in 1928, and the Radicals dominated both houses of Congress.
Intense partisan struggles replaced fluid party allegiances. The rise of
middle-class politicians threatened to end genteel, intra-class maneuvering. The political system came to represent an autonomous threat

to the socioeconomic system, even in the absence of major disagreements over policy, both through the hegemony of political professionals and through the accumulation of political power within an increasingly autonomous state. For Conservatives and their allies, Argentina's experiment in limited democracy was becoming distasteful and risky.

Tension in the political sphere was exacerbated by the world economic crash of 1929, though Argentina was not hit as soon or as hard as some other countries. The prices and values of beef exports held up until 1931. The wheat market was suffering badly, but mainly because of a drought; besides, farmers exerted scant political influence, partly because so many were unnaturalized immigrants (about 70 percent in 1914). In 1930 real wages underwent a brief decline and unemployment was starting to spread, but labor agitation was still at a moderate level (see Figure 3-2). The Depression no doubt exposed weaknesses within the political system, but it was not enough alone to have caused a coup.

The Military Turns Back the Clock

On September 6, 1930, a coalition of military officers and civilian aristocrats ousted President Yrigoyen on the grounds that his government was illegitimate. They then set up a provisional regime. Who were these soldiers? How had they come to intervene in what seemed to be a smoothly functioning constitutional order?

The answer is partly to be found in the history of the military's emergence. The liberals who came to power in 1852 believed that a professional army was indispensable for Argentina's development. They wanted a well trained military to crush provincial *caudillos* and to provide the order necessary for economic growth.

The professional training schools established were the *Colegio Militar* (1870) and the *Escuela Naval* (1872), which were to remain the basic training schools for Argentine officers. Like other Latin American military, the Argentines looked to Europe for their models. In 1899 General Roca and his colleagues negotiated the visit of a German mission to train staff officers in modern military technology. That collaboration with Germany was to last forty years.

The increased professionalization of the military led to a shift in the outlook of the Argentine officer corps. By 1910 there was a change in the criteria for promotion: now it became seniority and mastery of the new technology, rather than political favoritism. At the same time, there was a shift in control over promotions—from the presidency to an all-military committee made up of army division commanders and chaired by the highest-ranking general. The army was thus able to develop a new sense of its own efficiency, while acquiring a higher degree of institutional autonomy.

The increased emphasis on merit opened military careers to aspiring sons of the middle class. Not surprisingly, this soon included sons of immigrants, especially from Italy. The military offered an inviting avenue to upward social mobility. Successful recruits who made their way up the hierarchy forged a strong allegiance to the military as an institution—and a jealous regard for its independence, honor, and professional reputation. The reverse side of this loyalty was a deep suspicion of outsiders, especially politicians. Soldiers often regarded civilian officials with a mixture of scorn and apprehension. By 1930, officers concluded that the only way out of the political mess was to revise the rules of the political game.

Although agreed on that point, they were otherwise divided. One faction, led by General Agustín P. Justo, wanted to return to the oligarchical system of the pre–Sáenz Peña reform days. These officers thought it was merely Yrigoyen and the Radicals who had abused the electoral system. If they were removed from politics, then power would revert to the aristocrats and the specter of class struggle would disappear.

Another faction, led by General José F. Uriburu, suggested a more sweeping solution: the establishment of a semifascist corporate state. They saw the problem to be not Yrigoyen, or the Radicals, but the very attempt to try democracy in Argentina. Uriburu was reflecting the anti-democratic doctrines already rampant in Europe, especially in Italy, Spain, and Portugal. In essence, Uriburu and his sympathizers wanted a hierarchical order based on social function. Voting would be in the hands of the most cultivated members of society, and Congress would no longer be in the hands of the professional politicians—"agents of political committees," as he disdainfully described them. Uriburu envisioned a "functional democracy," where the elected legislators would represent functional (or "corporate") interests, such as ranchers, workers, merchants, and industrialists. This was the corporatist model in vogue in Mediterranean Europe. The theory was that a vertical structure would reintegrate the political system with the economic system, so that the political arena would once again reflect the distribution of power in the economic arena. It was also, quite obviously, a formula for stopping class-oriented politics. The corporatist answer to the ills of the congressional system was to radically redefine the bases of representation.

Although Uriburu directed the provisional government in 1930, the Justo group eventually won out. Elections took place but, as in the days before Sáenz Peña, fraud was freely practiced. After Justo became president in 1932 he created a pro-government coalition of parties called the *Concordancia,* and, in an effort to curry civilian support, he replaced a number of military men in sensitive posts with well-known politicians. Clearly, Justo was hoping to form a broad, national government that would give him the authority to respond to the socioeconomic effects of the world Depression.

This proved impossible. One reason for this failure was the expansion of an urban working class which, through strikes and other tactics, made repeated demands on the government. And on the elite level, political professionals—committed to partisan interests—refused to play by the old-fashioned rules. This became clear when Radical Party leader Roberto Ortiz, elected through *Concordancia* manipulation as Justo's successor in 1937, stopped electoral fraud and thereby allowed the Radicals to win control of Congress.

Ortiz' health forced him to leave office in 1940. His successor, Ramón Castillo, resorted to the technique of the embattled oligarchs when faced with elections: stuffing the ballot box. The cheating of course fooled no one. It only dramatized the illegitimacy of the incumbent civilian government.

Military officers watched the drama with increasing impatience. They saw how their counterparts in Germany and Italy had played key roles in displacing the wavering civilian governments. As the war spread in Europe in the early 1940s, and the Axis—which included Germany, Italy, and Japan after 1940—seemed to be carrying the day, the Argentine military chieftains saw the need for steady, sure leadership in their own land. The obstacle was the cabal of civilian politicians, whom the military had not sufficiently purged from power after 1930, and who had continued pursuing their petty interests and thereby rendering their country vulnerable.

Politics in Argentina was taking a path that did not appear in any other major Latin American country. The causes were several. There was first the strong Argentine antipathy to the Allies, especially the U.S. and Britain. In contrast to Brazil, whose government had, after a long flirtation with Nazi Germany, decided to cast its lot with the U.S. in 1942, Argentina wanted to preserve its "neutrality." In practice that meant it would continue to sell essential foodstuffs to besieged Britain while refusing to join the U.S.-led military effort. This reflected a strong sentiment among the Argentine elite, both civilian and military, that their country had most to gain by withholding its political and military allegiance in the world conflict.

Behind this rough consensus lay the continuing military impatience with the civilian politicians. Dissident officers mounted plots to seize power. The triumphant group was called the GOU (*Grupo Obra de Unificación* or *Grupo de Oficiales Unidos*) and justified its seizure of power as a response to popular demand: "We support our institutions and our laws, persuaded that it is not they but men [i.e., professional politicians] who have been delinquent in their application."

In fact, the ambitious officers wanted to revamp the entire political structure. They began, in 1943, by dissolving the Congress, that target of their oft-expressed scorn. The ascendant military, led by the first provisional president, General Arturo Rawson, grandly announced, "Now there are no political parties, but only Argentines." The military set themselves to rid Argentina of politics, as well as politicians. In 1944 they decreed the end of political parties, and they excluded from the cabinet all professional politicians, aside from a few "collaborationist" Radicals.

While the military were seizing control of the political system, class consciousness was growing among the workers. By the 1940s the urban working class, especially in Buenos Aires, had changed from the days of the Sáenz Peña electoral reform in 1912. It was now about 90 percent literate and it was mobile, with many of its members having recently arrived from the countryside. In contrast to the era of the great

Despite its historic importance, the military coup of 1930 was a relatively genteel affair—here a white flag of surrender flutters from the presidential palace (see arrow) as onlookers gather in the Plaza de Mayo. (Private collection.)

export boom (1880–1914), most urban workers were now native Argentines, not European immigrants. Buenos Aires hosted a proletariat not unlike those which had frightened the European bourgeoisie and military into turning to corporatist and fascist solutions. Indeed, political commentators in the U.S. and West Europe saw Argentina as an important test case in the ability of a New World republic to adjust to the social conflicts inherent in industrialization and development.

As the drama unfolded, the principal actors in Argentine politics turned out to be the military and labor. The military had its own institutional base, but the large and growing urban working class lacked effective political representation. Why? In part because of the electoral fraud. But more important was the way the existing party system worked. All the major parties, including the Radicals and the Socialists, were geared to the electoral system as modified by the Sáenz Peña law in 1912, when over half the adult male population remained excluded from the vote. So none of the major parties, with the partial exception of the Socialists, created an authentic working-class base. As a result, party politics offered no meaningful outlet for urban workers.

Enter Juan Perón. A man of middle-class origin, he had risen to the rank of colonel through a career in the Argentine army. Ambitious and outgoing, nearing 50, he had taken an active part in the GOU movement that ousted Ramón Castillo from the presidency in 1943. In recognition of his role he became secretary of labor, a fairly minor post, but one that he transformed into a bastion of strength. Using both carrots and sticks, Perón courted the support of industrial workers: old laboring groups as well as new, lifelong urban residents as well as recent migrants from the countryside. Thus he made the union movement a resource of his own, and partly because of this influence he later became minister of war and vice-president of the nation. A hero to the dispossessed, he won the presidential election of 1946 with a solid 54 percent majority—over the indiscreet resistance of the U.S. State Department, which denounced him for pro-fascist sympathies, and over the combined opposition of all the national political parties. The Argentine Communist Party was especially vehement in denouncing Perón as a fascist demagogue.

During this period Perón grew to rely on the political instincts of his mistress, later his wife, Eva Duarte. A former radio actress not long arrived from the interior, she was determined to make her mark in the world of Buenos Aires.

Peronism and Perón

Once installed as president, Perón proceeded to put into practice the corporatist principles the GOU officers had espoused. Argentina would now be organized according to functional groups: industrialists, farmers, workers. At the peak of this hierarchy would be the state. The government would act as the final arbiter in case of conflict among groups. The new government quickly issued a host of statutes regulating functional organizations, with Perón rapidly asserting an interventionist role for the state in the economy. A Five-Year Economic Plan was issued and a powerful new foreign trade institute (*Instituto Argentino de Promoción del Intercambio* or IAPI) was given a state monopoly over the export of key agricultural crops. Argentina was now positioned to undertake the most state-directed economic policy thus far seen in twentieth century Latin America.

Perón was carrying out the 1930s corporatist vision of General Uriburu, but with a vital difference: Perón made urban workers his most important political ally, flanked by industrialists and the armed forces. Uriburu would have reduced labor to a minor role. Perón created a political alliance completely unprecedented in Argentine history: a union of workers, managers, and the military.

Perón had campaigned for the presidency on a nationalist and populist note. "Argentina was a country of fat bulls and undernourished peons," as Perón later described Argentina in 1946. He promised to promote truly Argentine solutions while channeling to the workers the material and psychic rewards they had been unjustly denied. His government lost no time in rewarding the workers. Perón continued the tactics he had been perfecting since he took over the labor secretariat in 1943: the encouragement of strikes which the government then settled in favor of the workers. (Notice the upsurge in number of strikers in the late 1940s in Figure 3-2, though the number of strikes was not especially large: under Perón the average *size* of strikes went up as well.) Real hourly wage rates jumped 25 percent in 1947 and 24 percent in 1948. Labor's share of the national income increased by 25 percent between 1946 and 1950. Argentine urban workers received a sharp rise in their standard of living. The losers in this populist drama were the owners of capital, especially the landowners, since the government trade monopoly (IAPI) bought most of their products at low, fixed prices.

At first this bold strategy seemed to work well. The GDP grew by 8.6 percent in 1946 and at the startling rate of 12.6 percent in 1947. Even the lesser rate of 5.1 percent in 1948 was still very respectable by world standards. This growth was fueled in part by Argentina's booming exports, which produced healthy trade surpluses from 1946 through 1948.

Perón also made good on his promise to reduce foreign influence in the economy. In 1946 the central bank was reorganized so as to increase control over all foreign-owned monetary assets. In 1948 Argentina nationalized the British-owned railways, still the heart of the national transportation system. Also nationalized was the leading telephone company (from U.S.-controlled ITT) and the French-owned dock facilities. In every case the Argentines compensated the owners, at prices Argentine nationalists later claimed were too high. And in July 1947 Perón paid off Argentina's entire foreign debt, marking the occasion with a huge ceremony where he issued a "Declaration of Economic Independence."

Eva Perón also emerged as a political power in her own right. Snubbed by the society matrons (*señoras gordas*) who had always monopolized the political careers of past first ladies, "Evita" set up her own foundation in 1948. Dispensing cash and benefits personally from within her monumental marble building, Evita rapidly built up a fanatically loyal following. Her charisma complemented her husband's, and they together succeeded in building an imposing political machine. They presided over an elected government, but one that was steadily choking off any open political dissent.

By 1948 it seemed clear sailing for the Peronists. Social justice was rapidly being accomplished, and the regime would soon pronounce its "Justicialist" doctrine, the label used to describe the social welfare measures aimed at helping the urban working class. The economy continued to hum. The political opposition had been demoralized and humiliated. The streets were continuously full of the faithful. It was the realization of the "New Argentina" Perón had promised.

This success was soon clouded by economic problems. 1949 brought the first foreign trade deficit since the war, reducing foreign exchange reserves to a dangerously low level. Equally important was the sudden jump in inflation to 31 percent, double the previous year. A severe drought curtailed the production of exportable goods.

Perón ran into economic realities that had remained hidden during the first few postwar years. Profiting from the world economy seemed so simple in 1946, but now became problematic. World prices for Argentina's exports were dropping; prices for her imports, especially manufactured goods, were rising. Peronist policies also compounded the problem. IAPI, the government foreign trade institute, had set unrealistically low prices for agricultural goods. The objective was to keep down food prices in the cities, but the effect was also to discourage production, thus hurting exports.

Perón reacted to the economic crisis in 1949 by appointing a new finance minister who launched an orthodox stabilization program: tight credit, reduced government expenditure, and tough limits on wage and price increases. Perón was determined to get the economy under control and resume as soon as possible his ambitious social politics.

The onset of the economic crisis coincided with Perón's decision to strengthen his political grip. His first problem was the Argentine Constitution of 1853, which prohibited reelection of the President. Could there by any doubt that Perón wanted another six-year term? The Peronists had their way. The constitution was amended not only to allow reelection of the president, but also to reiterate a 1947 law which gave women the vote. In 1951 Perón was reelected with 67 percent of the 6.9 million votes cast, drawing especially heavily among women voters. A Peronist party was now founded, with a Tribunal of Party Discipline as one of its central organs. The government now reverted more frequently to authoritarian measures, such as the expropriation in 1951 of *La Prensa,* the leading opposition newspaper.

On one political front, however, Perón was defeated. In running for reelection in 1951 he wanted Evita to be his vice presidential candidate. Her political influence had grown enormously, as many workers had come to identify her as the heart of Peronism. She was brilliant at promoting this image, aided by huge (and largely unaccounted for) government funds. But the military put their foot down: they refused to accept the possibility that a woman might succeed to the presidency and therefore become their commander-in-chief. Evita was bitter about the decision, which suggested that there were limits to Peronist power.

The military veto of Evita's candidacy foreshadowed a far greater blow. Evita fell ill and eventually could not hide the fact that she was dying of cancer. She grew hauntingly thin, but fought the disease ferociously, and continued her exhausting vigil at the foundation, facing the endless lines of unfortunates begging for her help. In July 1952 she finally died, depriving Perón of a political partner who had become fully as important as he.

Evita now became larger in death than she had ever been in life. The government suspended all functions for two days and the labor union confederation, the CGT (*Confederación General del Trabajo*), ordered its members to observe a month's mourning. The outpouring of grief was astounding. Merely transferring her body from the presidential residence to the ministry of labor, where she was to lie in state, provoked such a crush of onlookers that eight people were killed. Over 2000 were treated for injuries in the following 24 hours. There were immediate plans to build a mausoleum 150 feet taller than the statue of liberty. Dead at the age of 33, Evita became a powerful myth binding together the Peronist faithful.

Meanwhile the tough austerity plan of Finance Minister Alfredo Gómez Morales was beginning to produce results by 1952. Perón and his advisers now opted for a second Five Year Plan, far less populist and nationalist than the policies of the late 1940s. There was a direct appeal for foreign capital, resulting in a contract with Standard Oil of California in 1954. There were new incentives to agriculture, previously a prime target for exploitation under the cheap-food strategy. Workers were asked to accept a two-year wage freeze, a sacrifice in the name of financing much-needed investment.

The political implications of this shift in economic strategy were obvious. In order to regain economic growth Perón believed he had to reverse, at least in part, some of his nationalist and redistributionist policies. As long as the economy was expanding it was easy to favor one social sector; with a stagnant economy, however, the workers could only gain at the direct expense of the middle or upper sectors. Class conflict threatened to tear apart Perón's carefully constructed populist coalition.

Perhaps for this reason, the Peronist political strategy seemed to become more radical. After 1949 the few aristocrats once found in the Peronist ranks disappeared. Perón moved to win control over the army by giving preferential promotion to political favorites. There was also a new program to indoctrinate cadets with Peronist teachings, and to dress up the lower ranks with flashy uniforms. Perón knew he had opponents within the army and in 1951 they attempted a coup against him. He easily suppressed them, but the germ of discontent remained alive.

After Evita's death in 1952 Perón shifted his attention from the army to the labor unions, led by loyalists. As the economic policy became more orthodox, Peronist rhetoric became more strident. A militantly "Justicialist" working-class tone became evident. In 1953 a Peronist street crowd pillaged the Jockey Club, the bastion of the Argentine aristocracy.

In 1954 the Peronist radicals took on another pillar of the traditional order: the church. Divorce was legalized and all parochial schools were placed under the control of the ministry of education. 1955 brought mass demonstrations against the church, orchestrated by the Peronists. Several famous cathedrals in Buenos Aires were burned by Peronist crowds. The Vatican retaliated by excommunicating the entire governmental cabinet, including Perón. The president vowed to mobilize his masses against the "conspirators" who menaced Argentine independence, threatening vengeance on five opponents for every Peronist who fell in political combat.

In fact, the Peronist government was out of control. The anti-clerical crusade could not possibly bear enough political fruit to justify its disruptive effect on the public, including some faithful Peronists. Most important, the ugly battle with the church had now given Perón's enemies within the military their chance. Many officers who had been disturbed by varying aspects of Peronism became convinced that he was bent on destroying the country. In September 1955 the military conspirators mobilized their forces and presented their former fellow officer with an ultimatum: resign or face civil war. Perón, so often given to extreme rhetoric, had no stomach for a bloodbath. Unlike Evita, he had never wanted to arm the workers. Now it was too late. He accepted the ultimatum and retreated to the refuge of a Paraguayan flying boat that took him across the Río de la Plata to Paraguay.

The Military Stewardship

As General Perón fled across the wide river, the mood changed in Argentina. Where were the workers, anxious to protect their leader? What had happened to the huge political machine? How could a relative handful of military officers so easily thwart the working class?

Perón had not really been defeated. He had left. He departed under duress, but he had made no effort to mobilize his followers against the men in uniform. The sudden vacuum created by his departure was indicative: neither Perón nor Peronism was finished.

The general who now became president was Eduardo Lonardi, a moderate who wanted to avoid a vindictive policy that would keep the Peronists united. But the hard-line military grew impatient with his conciliatory approach; they demanded tougher measures. In November these hardliners deposed Lonardi and installed General Pedro Aramburu as provisional president. The anti-Peronist zealots now got their chance to purge everything Peronist. The party was outlawed, Peronist functionaries were fired, and every scrap of Peronist propaganda became contraband.

The hardline military seemed to believe that Peronism could be eradicated in a relatively brief interval of military rule. Familiar pillars of pre-Peronist Argentina were quickly restored. The vehemently anti-Peronist *La Prensa* was returned to its owners, the Gainza Paz family. Former property owners hit by Peronist expropriations had their holdings restored. The Aramburu government pushed the crackdown on Peronist leaders, especially in the unions, on the assumption that repression could reverse their influence. In June 1956 the Peronists struck back. A revolt of pro-Peronist military took place in several provinces, and the government responded with force. In the follow-up some 40 leaders, including some military officers, were executed. Spilling of blood on this scale was ominous; however authoritarian Perón's government, it had never resorted to such a level of official killing.

The Aramburu political strategists believed that they could reshape the political system for a transition to a post-Peronist era. In October 1956 they created a "Board for the Defense of Democracy," which was to monitor all "nondemocratic" parties and movements. All parties were now required to commit themselves to democracy. Having to establish such a "requirement" was itself a dramatic proof of the fragility of Argentine democracy. Early 1957 saw a recrudescence of Peronist violence, met by government repression. Despite this conflict, the military still expected to transfer power to a civilian government capable of handling the Peronists.

On the economic front the military governments of 1955–58 found a sluggish economy which had fallen far short of its ability to extract gains from foreign trade. In fact, the economic policymakers summoned by the military took few bold steps. There was a devaluation, and the renegotiation of Argentina's many bilateral foreign debts. The years 1955–57 saw a healthy growth rate in the GDP, although agricultural output lagged. The military governments had not found a way to create convincing incentives for the landowners, still traumatized by the discriminatory Peronist policies. Notwithstanding their rhetoric, the military policymakers followed wage policies that resulted in virtually unchanged real hourly wage rates for 1955 and 1956 and in a 7.2 percent increase in 1957. Any attack on the major economic problems awaited a government with more legitimacy.

Unfortunately for Argentina, the anti-Peronist civilian politicians were deeply divided. The largest party was still the Radicals, the venerable party of Yrigoyen and his acolytes. At a party convention in 1956 the Radicals (UCR) split in two. One faction was the "Popular Radicals" (UCR del Pueblo—UCRP), led by Ricardo Balbín, the party's elder statesman who had run for president in 1951. The other was the "Intransigent Radicals" (UCRI), led by Arturo Frondizi, an economics professor. The Balbín faction was more fanatically anti-Perón, while the Frondizi faction advocated flexibility in dealing with the Peronists. This paralleled a similar split of opinion within the military.

In July 1957 Argentina held its first elections since Perón's overthrow. The two Radical factions won an almost equal number of seats in the constituent assembly, which promptly restored the Constitution of 1853. But the delegates wrangled and walked out so often that the assembly was finally disbanded.

The military were nonetheless determined to move to a civilian government. They held a presidential election in February 1958 and the victor was Frondizi, who had mounted an aggressively nationalist campaign. His wing of the Radicals, the UCRI, was still bitterly opposed by the Balbín wing (UCRP), so Frondizi had needed votes elsewhere. To get them he struck a deal with the Peronists, promising some Peronist-type policies and a willingness to work to restore their party to legality. Frondizi's wing won not only the presidency and the national Congress, but most provincial governments as well. It looked as if Argentina now had a strong centrist government that could take up the difficult tasks left by Perón and the inconclusive military government of 1955–58.

The major cloud hanging over Frondizi was the degree of his debt to the Peronists, and how he might have to repay them.

The Failure of Developmental Reformism

The Frondizi government (1958–62) was an all-important test of Argentina's ability to rejoin the ranks of elected civilian regimes. The new president seemed to be from the same mold as other democratic reformers then making their mark in Latin America, such as Eduardo Frei of Chile and Juscelino Kubitschek of Brazil. On both the economic and political fronts, Frondizi decided to take major gambles. The risks were great, but so were the potential rewards.

Frondizi had an ambitious economic program designed to accelerate industrialization while also stimulating agricultural production, thereby boosting export earnings. Much of the financing for new industry was to come from abroad, while at home the extensive state intervention in the economy was to be reduced, starting with the recognition of free collective bargaining in the labor sphere. There was one unfortunate catch to this plan: it could succeed only if there was a shift from consumption to investment. That meant that consumers, once so favored under Perón, must be prepared to make short-term sacrifices for the sake of long-term national development.

Frondizi disappointed the nationalists by one of his early investment decisions: to sign oil exploration and production contracts with foreign oil companies in an effort to correct Argentina's 50 percent dependence on imported oil. Argentina was potentially self-sufficient in petroleum and badly needed to save the foreign exchange spent on imported oil. Nonetheless the nationalists bitterly attacked Frondizi for his "sell-out" to the imperialists, especially since he had struck a dramatically nationalist note in his campaign.

The rest of the new president's economic plan soon came under a more ominous shadow. Only a few months into his presidency, Frondizi was faced with an acute balance of payments crisis. Since 1955 the military government had run consistent deficits on the commercial account, leaving the new civilian regime in 1958 with fewer foreign exchange reserves than any government since the war. Perón had faced a similar problem in 1949 and again in 1952 by undertaking a tough stabilization program without any commitments to foreign creditors. Most specifically, he had avoided the International Monetary Fund, which Peronist Argentina had chosen not to join. But Frondizi chose a different tack. He wanted to impress Argentina's foreign creditors, from whom he sought new investment. With Argentina now in the IMF (the military government had made a point of joining), Frondizi decided to accept the IMF's extreme medicine: a huge devaluation, stiff controls on credit, cuts in public spending, tough wage limits, elimination of subsidies on public services, and dismissal of redundant public employees.

Frondizi was now caught in a contradiction: he was trying to launch a major economic development program while at the same time cutting back in order to satisfy foreign creditors. His truncated presidency became a classic example of the political costs of economic stabilization.

The contradiction in Frondizi's economic policy was matched by a contradiction in his political strategy. He owed his election to Peronist support, and he was clearly hoping to coax Peronist voters over to his side. Yet the military, whose approval was essential for any government, was deeply suspicious of this conciliatory policy. Within a year Frondizi was forced by the military to fire his economic team and replace them with a dogmatic free-enterprise group headed by Alvaro Alsogaray, a rigid advocate of IMF-style monetarism.

Frondizi was now committed to carrying out the IMF-prescribed "shock treatment," beginning with a 200-percent devaluation and a sudden removal of price controls and subsidies. The objective was to jolt the economy into adjusting domestic prices to international prices. The shock-treatment advocates argued that this process would be painful in any case, so it should be done quickly. An important sectoral goal was to increase the real price of agricultural products, thereby presumably calling forth the increased production to satisfy both the external and the domestic market.

The inevitable effect of these policies was a sharp shift in income. The real income (or buying power) of industrial workers dropped by 25.8 percent in 1959, while the real income accruing to beef production rose 97 percent in the same year. Here was an exact reversal of Perón's *Justicialismo*. Even before their real wages had declined significantly, urban workers went into battle against the new government. There were general strikes in April, May, and September of 1959, and an extended railway strike in November. The latter was the most damaging, because the swollen employment rolls of the deficit-ridden nationalized railways were a prime target in the government's campaign to reduce the government deficit. Due to apparent public support for the strikers, Frondizi was forced to accept a compromise settlement in which labor was the effective victor.

The stabilization policy also came under attack from Argentine businessmen, especially those from smaller firms. They denounced the credit restrictions and the huge increase in import prices resulting from the massive devaluation. Businessmen from the larger firms, especially those linked to foreign capital, were happier, since government policy helped them. Farmers proved to be one of Frondizi's greatest disappointments. Having been guaranteed higher prices, they were expected to expand production, but they proved suspicious and refused to make the long-term commitment needed to boost output.

Despite the fierce public opposition, some of the Frondizi policies began to bear fruit. The stagnation of 1958–59 was followed by growth rates of 8 percent in 1960 and 7.1 percent in 1961. The rate of inflation, which rocketed up to 113.7 percent in 1959, declined to 27.3 percent in 1960 and only 13.5 percent in 1961. Industrial production was up sharply, and two key sectors showed success: the country's first integrated steel complex was finished in 1960 and domestic oil production was trebled, attaining virtual self-sufficiency.

Yet the fate of Frondizi's presidency would not depend on economic indicators. It rested on the strength of his political support. Here the odds were stacked against him. Labor and the nationalist left never forgave him for the orthodox stabilization policy, with its cut in real wages and its embrace of foreign capital. The congressional elections of March 1960 dramatized the problem. Frondizi's Radicals got fewer votes than the Balbín faction; Peronists cast blank ballots on instruction from their exiled leader. Frondizi was already losing his gamble that he could woo the Peronists to his side, and this increasingly obvious failure aroused the military.

The climax came in the congressional and local elections of March 1962. Now the Peronists were allowed to run candidates under their own banner (for the first time since 1955), as Frondizi fulfilled his commitment to restore the Peronist party to legality. The result was a disaster for the government. The Peronists led all parties in total votes, with 35 percent. They won a string of provincial governorships and a large bloc of congressional seats. The Frondizi Radicals got 28 percent and the Balbín Radicals 22 percent, the rest going to smaller parties.

The furious military quickly forced the president to annul the Peronist election victories in the provinces. The Frondizi Radicals then tried for a coalition with the Balbín faction, an obvious way out. Together, the Radicals represented half the electorate. But the Balbín followers rejected the Frondizi overtures, dismissing the gravely weakened president for his "anti-nationalist" economic policies. Once again the middle-class party, the Radicals, proved unequal to the task of governing Argentina, the most middle-class country in Latin America.

The military now saw Frondizi as discredited. He had gambled on converting the Peronists and lost; yet he stubbornly refused to resign. On March 29, 1962, the army tanks rolled onto the streets and removed Frondizi from the Casa Rosada. Into the presidency stepped the constitutional successor, Senate President José María Guido.

Guido served as acting president for a year and a half, but the real power was held by the military, still deeply divided on how to deal with the civilian politicians. These splits led to intra-military revolts and repeated small-scale bloodshed among the men in uniform. The fact was that the military were by no means united over the advisability or possibility of trying to "reintegrate" the Peronist masses into the political system. And complicating this was the exiled Perón himself, continuously sending instructions to his lieutenants in Argentina.

The military finally decided to annul entirely the election results of 1962, and to hold a new round of elections in July 1963. The voting followed a familiar pattern, although this time the Balbín Radicals won the largest total, with 27 percent of the ballots. The new president was Arturo Illia, a colorless provincial physician who was to lead the second Radical attempt at governing post-Peronist Argentina.

Illia's political style was decidedly low-key. This seemed suitable, since he had gained only slightly over a quarter of the popular vote, and would face a Congress in which the opposition held almost two-thirds of the seats. Unlike Frondizi, Illia had made no overtures to the Peronists. Nonetheless, the hardline military were ever vigilant to find any signs of softness toward Peronism or the left.

Illia was relatively fortunate in the economic situation he found. 1962 had seen a recession, but good agricultural harvests would soon improve the trade balance and increase foreign exchange reserves. The Illia government began very cautiously on the economy, announcing no overall program. It soon became evident, however, that the policymakers were set on expansion, granting generous wage increases and imposing price controls. These measures helped to swing Argentina into the "go" phase of the "stop and go" economic pattern (alternately stimulating and contracting the economy) it had exhibited since the war. The GNP showed small declines in 1962 and 1963, but spurted to gains of 10.4 percent in 1964 and 9.1 percent in 1965.

On the agricultural front the Illia government suffered through a downswing in the "beef cycle," when the depleted herds were withheld for breeding. The resulting shortage irritated urban consumers—always voracious beef eaters—and reduced the production available for export. Cattlemen were angry because the government did not let prices rise to the levels indicated by market demand. Illia, like virtually every other president since 1945, found the rural sector virtually impossible to harness for the national interest.

The Peronist unions were opposed to Illia from the moment he entered office, in part because the Peronists were barred from the 1963 elections. Despite Illia's initially large wage settlements, the Peronist-dominated CGT drew up a "battle plan" (*plan de lucha*), which included strikes and workplace occupations. Like Frondizi, Illia hoped his policies would attract some Peronist votes. That illusion was shattered in the congressional elections of March 1965, when the now legalized Peronist party won 30.3 percent of the vote, as against 28.9 percent for the Illia Radicals. As in 1962, the Peronists showed their ability to get out the vote in demonstration of loyalty to the movement.

Perón, in his Spanish exile, was encouraged by the vote and sent his third wife, Isabel, to Argentina to negotiate directly with the feuding Peronist groups. The hard-line military grew more worried over the apparent Peronist comeback. Illia had taken the same political gamble as Frondizi, with similar results. The economic scene had also taken a disquieting turn. Inflation had erupted anew, the government deficit was out of control, and investor confidence plummeted, with the Argentine stock exchange virtually closing down. In June 1966 the military intervened again. Illia was unceremoniously ejected from the Casa Rosada. Once again the officers had removed a Radical government unable either to court or to repress the Peronist masses.

The Bureaucratic-Authoritarian Solution

The military coup of 1966 appeared to mark a sharper break with the past than any coup since 1943. At a minimum, it was the most repressive, at least in the initial stages. Proclaiming the advent of "the Argentine Revolution," General Juan Carlos Onganía sought to implant a new kind of regime—a bureaucratic-authoritarian state. The goal was to attack the root causes of Argentina's problems, rather than deal with the symptoms: society must be transformed. The Onganía government shut down the recalcitrant Congress, ousted opponents from the universities, and set out to control (and purportedly "uplift") the tone of social life. Dismissing politicians from positions of authority, the military leaders forged alliances with technocrats and foreign investors, whose capital was sought as a means of spurring economic growth. A key part of the overall plan called for the suppression of the labor movement, since the increase in investment was to be provided in part by a decline in real wages.

The Onganía government attempted yet another economic stabilization program. Perón had been forced to adopt one in 1949 and again in 1952; he controlled inflation and improved the balance of payments, but the cost was economic stagnation. Frondizi tried in 1958, gaining limited success with inflation and the balance of payments, but only at the cost of stunting investment and sacrificing his longer-term developmentalist plan. Illia had simply ridden with the expansionary phase of the economic cycle, imposing quasi-Peronist wage and price policies. None of these governments had succeeded in getting at the root of Argentina's problem: the lack of sustained growth, based on a productive rural sector able to satisfy both export and domestic demand. Frondizi had put forward the most coherent vision, but it was immediately compromised by the need for painful short-term stabilization measures.

The Onganía government was determined to undertake a more profound economic program. After an initial pause the economics minister, Adalberto Krieger Vasena, announced a wide-ranging plan which one expert foreign analyst later called "the most balanced anti-inflationary program of the postwar era," one which "combined the expansion of production, price stability, and the improvement of the balance-of-payments objectives with an effort to increase the level of aggregate consumption, albeit very gradually." A key feature was a two-year wage freeze in 1967, which the government was able to enforce because of its authoritarian methods and its relative success in holding down price increases. (Note also the sharp reduction in strikes shown in Figure 3-2.)

The government had another factor working in its favor. A significant wing of organized labor, led by CGT executive Augusto Vandor, welcomed the coup against Illia and wanted to collaborate with the new military government. The Onganía-led officers in turn relished the prospect of dividing labor and thereby breaking the Peronist stranglehold. This tactic proved partially successful in 1967 and 1968. But in 1969 it was engulfed by explosive labor opposition.

In that year an opposition movement developed in the provincial city of Córdoba, the heart of the newly created Argentine automobile industry. There had been a series of anti-government protests and labor stoppages. The local army commander became nervous, his troops jumpy, and during a street protest the troops opened fire, killing some tens of protestors and bystanders. A howl of protest went up in the country, despite the authoritarian government's control of the media. The many enemies of the government's economic program, including some military who opposed the wage freeze, seized the occasion to lobby for Krieger Vasena's ouster. Onganía hesitated, the pressure grew, and Krieger Vasena was finally forced out in June 1969. The Onganía government lasted another year, but its credibility was shattered.

It was not only the labor opposition that doomed Onganía's regime. There was also a shocking rise in political violence, such as clandestine torture and execution by the military government and kidnapping and assassination by the revolutionary left. The Onganía coup began in violence and the victorious military immediately made clear that all normal legal guarantees were suspended. The labor policy, tinged with a conciliatory aspect at the outset, soon came to depend on coercion. This had happened before, as under Aramburu, and even under Illia, but now there was a difference. The left decided to reply with its own violence. Splinter revolutionary groups sprang up, kidnapping prominent businessmen and ransoming them for huge sums. Foreign multinational executives became targets. The firms countered by locating their people across the river in Montevideo, from where they would commute daily under armed guard. In 1970 leftist terrorists kidnapped ex-President Aramburu, who had ordered the execution of Peronist conspirators in 1956. Aramburu was later found murdered.

A deadly toxin had entered the Argentine body politic. There was now a revolutionary left, committed to traumatizing the nation by violence against those they identified as the oppressors: the military and the police, along with their collaborators, the well-tailored executives of the multinationals. And the government struck back with violence of its own. A civil war had broken out.

The Onganía government was by all standards a political failure. Although it brought off postwar Argentina's most successful economic stabilization program, it failed to meet a more difficult challenge: creating a broad-based political coalition which could give continuity to policy and make possible genuine planning for the future. The Onganía military regime could never have achieved such a coalition because it seized power against both the Radicals, chief voice of the middle class, and the Peronists, still the strongest voice of the working class. Unlike the Brazilian generals, whose apparent success the Argentines envied, the Onganía officers could not forge a military-civilian alliance capable of holding power long enough to carry out a policy that would bring sustained economic growth. No less important, the Argentine political scene had grown far more polarized than in Brazil. Onganía's failure left Argentina with few alternatives.

The new president was another general, Roberto Levingston, a little-known intelligence officer stationed in Washington, D.C., since 1968. Returning to Buenos Aires, Levingston faced a treacherous economic problem: inflation, which Krieger Vasena had gotten down to 7.6 percent in 1969, was on the rise, reaching 34.7 percent in 1971. Levingston pursued a moderately expansionary course, which was soon doomed by a downswing in the beef cycle that caused shortages and high prices. Never well endowed with military prestige, Levingston found himself isolated. Recurrent rioting in Córdoba in March 1971 sealed his doom. Yet another military coup removed Levingston, installing General Alejandro Lanusse, who had been the brains behind the ouster of Onganía eight months earlier.

Lanusse followed a moderate nationalist course in economic policy. Disinclined to take bold steps, he decided to ride along with rising budget deficits. Predictably, inflation increased, hitting 58.5 percent in 1972. The Lanusse government made no pretense at having an answer for the economy.

Lanusse's real ambition was to achieve a new political accord. He opted for a relegalization of the Peronists, along with a new electoral system which he hoped would favor pro-government parties. Lanusse took an even greater gamble: he decided to allow Perón to return. Elections were announced for March 1973. Perón briefly returned to Argentina in late 1972 and lobbied intensively for his stand-in, Dr. Héctor Cámpora, as his own presidential candidate. Meanwhile the violence continued, with business executives being kidnapped, ransomed, or murdered. The guerrillas became bolder and were directly striking at high-ranking military officers, as well as at prisons and barracks.

Cámpora received 49 percent of the popular vote, not an absolute majority, but far ahead of Balbín's 22 percent. The president and like-minded officers began to see Perón as the only hope against the left. They saw him as an essentially conservative figure, having nothing in common with the leftist guerrillas, some of whom claimed to fight in his name. When Héctor Cámpora was inaugurated in May 1973, more than a few officers felt that the first step toward a solution to the leftist threat might be at hand.

The Peronists Back in Power

Cámpora had left no doubt that he was only a stand-in until Perón could return and run in a new election. Notwithstanding Cámpora's thoroughly weak personality, his government launched a bold new economic policy. It had been largely drawn up by the CGE (*Confederación General Económica*), an Argentine businessmen's association; it was aimed at first stabilizing prices and then boosting workers' earnings back to the share of national income they had reached in the earlier Peronist era. It was to be done by (1) a one-time wage increase; (2) a price freeze agreed to by government, labor, and industry; (3) a two-year wage freeze; and then (4) a set of policies designed to improve the workers' real incomes. Obviously this would require extraordinary cooperation from all interest groups. The Cámpora government seemed to have negotiated agreement to that in their proposed "Social Contract" (*Pacto Social*), which was formally ratified by both the CGT and the CGE. They drafted a parallel compact with rural producers (except for the rabidly anti-Peronist cattle breeders) which promised price, tax, and credit incentives in return for a promise to double farm production by 1980. Surprisingly, the new Peronist regime had constructed a coalition that included almost every interest group in Argentine society. How was it possible? In part, because both exhaustion and realism had taken hold of Argentines. Indeed, more than a few long-time anti-Peronists looked to the new Perón government as perhaps their country's last chance to solve their problems by something short of naked force.

As every Argentine and foreign observer could see, the odds for success were not high. Political violence was rising steadily, as guerrilla forces scornfully rejected the new Peronist regime and tried through kidnappings and assassinations to destabilize the fragile political balance. A further liability was the age and health of the once charismatic figure around whom the new social consensus had to be built: Perón was now seventy-seven and in failing health.

New presidential elections were scheduled for September. Perón now succeeded in a political tactic which had failed in 1951: he got his wife, Isabel, nominated for the vice-presidency. They swept the election with 62 percent of the vote. Perón now began to turn on the revolutionary left, whom he had often encouraged in his comments from exile. The People's Revolutionary Army (ERP) was outlawed, in good part because of its repeated assassination of military officers. Perón gave his blessing to crackdowns on leftist rallies and publications. Lanusse's judgment seemed vindicated; Perón was proving the perfect sponsor to preside over a military and police counteroffensive against the revolutionary left.

On the economic front, the ingenious program launched by Cámpora seemed to be working. Early 1973 had seen an economic boom, fueled by high export earnings, as world meat prices rose and Argentina's grain production swelled. During 1973 inflation dropped dramatically and real wages rose 13.3 percent in the second half of the year. But 1974 brought trouble. The OPEC oil price increase hurt Argentina's balance of payments, although it was importing only 16 percent of its oil. Furthermore, some non-CGT unions won new wage agreements, in violation of the "social contract." Several CGT unions soon followed suit. Now under growing pressure from union leaders, Perón agreed to large year-end bonuses for all CGT unions, thereby undermining his own anti-inflation program.

Whether Perón could have yet worked his magic with the workers again was not to be known. In July 1974 he died; the president now was Isabel. Perón had met her when she was a nightclub dancer in Panama, during his leisurely journey after his 1955 overthrow. Isabel was no Evita, as her insecurity and indecision had already made clear. *La Presidente* assumed office as the Peronists were bitterly squabbling.[1] There was an immediate scramble to gain influence over the frightened woman who had succeeded to the presidential duties.

The advisor with greatest influence was Isabel's minister of social welfare, José López Rega, an ambitious and bizarre figure as well known for his fascination with astrology as for his militantly right-wing Peronist views. López Rega first helped convince Isabel to purge her cabinet

1. Isabel should normally have been referred to by the feminine form *la presidenta;* but the Argentine Constitution speaks only of *el presidente,* and her supporters did not dare take any chances. So legal nicety triumphed over grammatical logic, and she came to be known as *La Presidente.*

of the more moderate ministers in October 1974, then persuaded her to crack down on the left—including left-wing Peronists. This became the direction of policy in 1975, as unions began negotiating new contracts with 100 percent wage increases or more. Isabel mounted a counter-campaign, annulling the huge wage settlements and later, after a series of massive strikes, reinstating them. This dramatic reversal, on top of the increasingly bloody battle between leftist guerrillas and the military, led to López Rega's resignation. The president also lost her congressional majority as the Peronist delegation split apart.

The economy now careened out of control. Inflation rocketed to 335 percent in 1975, as the wage-price spiral picked up speed. 1975 also proved to be disastrous for exports, with a disappointing harvest compounded by a new European Common Market ban on imported beef. Foreign exchange reserves dropped by more than 50 percent. By early March 1976 Isabel's government was reduced to adopting a stringent stabilization plan in return for help from the IMF.

Deterioration of the economy was accompanied by increasing violence in politics. The guerrillas continued their deliberately provocative attacks on the police and military, bringing off some dramatic assassinations. The right answered through equally violent organizations such as the Argentine Anti-Communist Alliance. The "great accord," on which the new Peronist era was to have been based, now seemed a cruel hoax. The value of money shrank daily, almost hourly. Fear of terrorists, whether of the right or left, took hold of the populace, especially the urban middle class. The president was terrified, utterly unable to wield command, and increasingly bewildered. Only one question was in the air: when would the military remove her?

Isabel's term ran to 1977, and the military seemed determined to let her serve it out. If they seized power, then they would have formal responsibility for dealing with the economic mess. Better to leave her in office, especially since she was giving carte blanche to the security forces in their war on the guerrillas. By retaining her as president they had the semblance of civilian legitimacy. And there may have been another motivation at work. The military may have decided to let the national situation become so violent and the economy so chaotic that no one could doubt the need for the military to step in. If so, they had succeeded by March 1976. In Argentina's best predicted coup, the men in uniform placed *La Presidente* under house arrest (she would be investigated for corruption) and once again an elected government disappeared from the Casa Rosada.

The Military Returns

When the armed forces finally moved against Isabel, they were determined to impose a bureaucratic-authoritarian solution that would last. Under General Jorge Rafael Videla, the regime launched a vicious campaign, alternatively known as a "dirty war" or "holy war" against the opposition. The government began arresting "subversives" at will, at one point acknowledging that it held nearly 3500 prisoners. And then there were the *desaparecidos,* those who simply "disappeared," perhaps 15,000 or 20,000 in all. These people were abducted by heavily armed men who refused to identify themselves but who were undoubtedly "off-duty" security men or paramilitary operating with the military government's knowledge. Virtually none of the abducted were ever heard of again. The secrecy for this ghastly slaughter may have come from the Argentine military's study of how the Brazilian security forces in the early 1970s were highly criticized for mistreatment of political prisoners. The Brazilian mistake, according to the Argentines, was to place suspects under official arrest, thus leaving a legal trail.

We shall never know exactly how many of the "disappeared" were totally innocent and how many were involved in the guerrilla war against the government. At least 10,000 Argentines were actively involved on the guerrilla side, including couriers, gunmen, infiltrators, arms smugglers, and look-outs. From bank robberies and ransomings the guerrillas built a war chest of at least $150 million. The army and police faced a formidable challenge.

The guerrillas were so well organized and so adept at hitting the government (one bomb went off in an army mess, killing 15 and wounding many more) that the infuriated generals decided on an all-out offensive, without any legal restraints. The "disappeared" were victims in a tactic consciously designed to terrorize the country. Combat with the guerrillas was brutal, with even a conventional battle in the province of Tucumán. In the end the generals won, but at a terrible price. They thought they had had no choice, and savagely rejected criticism from every quarter. One of the most widely read exposés was by Jacobo Timmerman, a former Buenos Aires newspaper publisher, who described his torturers as abusively anti-Semitic and even pro-Nazi. Once proud Argentina became an international pariah along with Chile and South Africa, and its people, by habit articulate and argumentative, suffered the ignominy of silence and intimidation.

What had the guerrillas wanted? There were several groups, but all sought the violent overthrow of the government and the installation of a revolutionary socialist regime along Marxist-Leninist lines. They were predominantly middle-class and many were university students or recent graduates. Desperately idealistic and deeply alienated by the merry-go-round of Argentine politics, they were caught up in a passionate rebellion against a socioeconomic structure that was, ironically, one of the most "modern" in Latin America. Once locked in battle, there was no exit for the guerrillas. The military were so set on liquidating their tormenters that amnesty was never a remote possibility. It was a war to the death.

The war showed, as have others in Latin America, that a well-equipped and determined government can, barring any major split among the society's ruling elites, normally defeat a guerrilla movement. A key factor was the tacit (and often explicit) support of the middle class for the anti-guerrilla campaign. As a proportion of the society, the Argentine middle class was the largest in Latin America, and therefore a crucial actor in the political drama. It had watched with dismay the decay of order under Isabel from 1974 to 1976 and most of it supported the coup of 1976.

The March 1976 takeover was intended as a coup to end all coups. Videla and his colleagues proclaimed that their goal was not merely to terminate the chaos of the Peronist years, but also to restructure Argentine society. The junta promised to eradicate terrorism and thereby remove some potent actors from the political scene. They planned to revitalize the private sector, including foreign as well as domestic capital, to reduce the public sector, and consequently to rearrange relationships among business, labor, and the state. They affirmed Argentina's alignment with the "Western and Christian world" and, in keeping with these lofty principles, they promised to "reeducate" the populace by emphasizing values of "morality, uprightness, and efficiency." Thus the soldiers would lay the foundations for an eventual "democracy" that would be, in carefully chosen words, "suited to the reality and needs and progress of the Argentine people."

In pursuit of these ideas the military not only embarked on all-out war against the opposition. It also penetrated Argentine society more deeply than ever before: in addition to seizing command of major power centers, such as the national labor association, military officers also took over other institutions, such as sports and charitable organizations.

In 1978 the generals got a heaven-sent propaganda opportunity when Argentina hosted the world soccer cup matches. The quadrennial tournament has become the premier international sports event. The Argentine military invested $200 million in a new stadium and a face-lift for rundown Buenos Aires. Argentina won the cup, to the ecstatic cheers of the home crowd and the obvious pleasure of the heavy-handed generals. For a few weeks at least, ordinary Argentines could take pride in their country. But the euphoria was soon dissipated by the realities of Argentina's plight.

Among the gravest worries was the economy. The military junta led by Videla had started the economic policy on yet another of its dramatic swings. Economics Minister José Martínez de Hoz, an outspoken representative of the "neoliberal" view, immediately imposed a stabilization program designed to reduce inflation and win back the confidence of foreign creditors. Labor faced declining real wages, while businessmen found credit increasingly hard to obtain. The most favored sector were the banks and financial institutions, which earned huge profits because of record-high real interest rates (often 20–40 percent). Foreign capital inflow rose dramatically, but much of it was speculative. Martínez de Hoz also moved to denationalize a number of state enterprises, while slashing tariffs on almost all industrial goods.

These policies succeeded in bringing inflation down to 88 percent in 1980, and in achieving a surplus on the balance of payments for four successive years (1976–79). By 1981, however, the picture had darkened. A wave of bank failures provoked a huge outflow of funds. Inflation again exceeded 100 percent, and a recession set in. In 1981 industry operated at only half capacity and real income was less than it was in 1970.

Despite these economic troubles, the armed forces demonstrated an unprecedented degree of coherence and unity. This was an institutional regime, not a one-man show, and when Videla turned the presidency over to General Roberto Viola in March 1981 it was merely confirmation of the fact. Viola lacked the stamina needed in the pressured position, and passed the presidency in early 1982 to General Leopoldo Galtieri, the commander-in-chief of the army.

Galtieri soon proved more adventuresome than his predecessors. In March he chose to stake his government's fate on the Falkland Islands, controlled by the British but long claimed by the Argentines, who called them the Malvinas Islands. In the colonial era the French and English had both disputed claims to the islands by the Spanish crown. Once the wars of independence had passed, the British decisively occupied the islands in 1833, expelling some Argentine inhabitants. Britain subsequently argued that Argentina, by failing to exercise its claim, had forfeited any possible inheritance of the Spanish crown's sovereignty.

During his 1946–55 rule Perón reawakened Argentine passions over the islands, but Britain simply ignored him. In 1965 the United Nations invited Britain and Argentina to begin talks leading to a peaceful solution of the dispute. Progress was made on many practical matters, such as improved communications with the Argentine mainland. The sovereignty issue was not formally discussed until 1977, the same year in which British intelligence warned of an impending invasion. Britain sent a small war fleet, without publicity, and the threat faded.

In 1982 the Argentines thought the British had changed signals and would not bother to defend the desolate islands—8000 miles away from

Britain, populated by only 1800 British subjects and 600,000 sheep. On April 2 a large Argentine force invaded the islands and quickly overwhelmed the badly outgunned Royal Marine garrison.

British Conservative Prime Minister Margaret Thatcher, already following a hardline monetarist policy domestically, was not about to see Britain's sovereignty and subjects snatched away by a South American military dictatorship. The British denounced the invasion and mobilized a major naval task force. Britain justified her impending military intervention as needed to prevent the aggressor from usurping the islanders' right to self-determination.

Before the British task force reached the South Atlantic U.S. Secretary of State Alexander Haig feverishly shuttled between Buenos Aires and London, hoping to prevent the war. For the U.S. the war was a diplomatic disaster, since both protagonists were U.S. allies. Haig failed, as did the UN, and in late May the British task force landed thousands of troops onto Falklands/Malvinas beachheads. All but three other Latin American countries backed Argentina in an OAS vote condemning Britain as the aggressor.

Why had the Galtieri government decided to invade? Clearly the Argentine economy was on the rocks again, with inflation and her foreign debt rocketing upwards. Only days before the April 2 invasion there had been the largest anti-government demonstration since the military seized power in 1976. Galtieri, and the few fellow officers he consulted, undoubtedly saw the lure of a quick and certain military victory in the Falklands/Malvinas as a boost to the government's sagging popularity. Furthermore, Galtieri felt certain that he would have at least the tacit support of the Reagan administration, with which the Argentine generals had developed a warm relationship.

In the short run Galtieri was right about the Argentine reaction. The invasion brought an outpouring of patriotic sentiment in Argentina, even from bitter opponents of the military regime. The tonic seemed to be working. In part that was due to hyperbolic, government-controlled reporting that told of nothing but Argentine victories. Had long-fragmented Argentina finally found a way to come together?

The Argentine public soon suffered a rude return to reality. The better trained and more experienced British troops swept across East Falkland, encountering little resistance. They encircled and laid siege to the 7500 Argentine troops holed up in the capital, Port Stanley. After nervous consultation with Buenos Aires, the Argentine commander surrendered without a shot—the only sensible option given the poor morale, condition, and positioning of his troops. Yet the sudden surrender hit Buenos Aires hard. The government's propaganda now turned to ashes. Britain, supposedly enfeebled and unable to defend these distant islands, had decisively defeated numerically superior Ar-

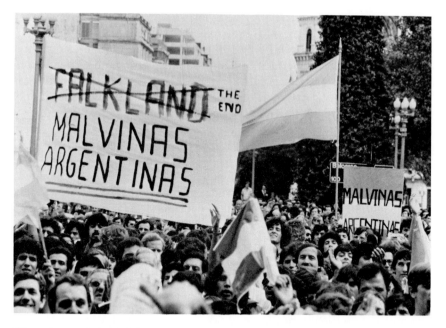

The seizure of the Falkland/Malvinas islands in 1982 led to a massive outpouring of national pride and defiance. (C. Carrión/SYGMA)

gentine forces. Only the Argentine Air Force emerged as having had both the skill and the courage to fight effectively.

The Galtieri-led junta had made a mortal error: as a military government it began a military adventure which it failed to win. The public reaction was inevitable: what good are generals if they can't even win a small war? Patriotic fervor turned into ugly demonstrations outside the Casa Rosada. Galtieri came under intense fire from his fellow officers. He resigned, as military unity began to unravel. The interim president was General Cristino Nicolaides, a tough-talking representative of the army's more authoritarian wing. The navy and air force withdrew from the junta, leaving the army holding power alone. General Nicolaides chose as the new president an obscure retired general, Reynaldo Bignone, an officer in the engineers corps. Upon assuming office in July 1982, Bignone bravely repeated Argentina's claim to the Falklands/Malvinas. He also promised elections in 1983 and a return to civilian government by 1984. It was as if the Argentine generals had by their incompetence restored legitimacy to the civilian politicians.

The Argentine economy went from bad to worse in 1982. Inflation shot up to 200 percent, workers lost about one quarter of their real income, and the country went into de facto default on its private foreign debt. By early 1983 the nominal take-home value of the minimum wage was one million pesos a week, worth only about $19. The Brazilians (their inflation rate was only 100 percent) thought it amusing when the Argentines printed their first one-million-peso note. The Argentines themselves grew frustrated. The 100-peso coin—worth far less than one U.S. cent—dropped out of circulation and proved useful only to irate soccer fans who threw them at referees, and to anti-government demonstrators who hurled them at police.

In order to obtain desperately needed external financing, the government agreed to an austerity plan outlined in collaboration with the IMF. But there was real doubt as to whether the military government could manage the transition to a civilian government. In December 1982 the opposition staged the largest anti-government protest in seven years of military rule.

Argentina was once more experiencing a pattern it had endured repeatedly since 1930: the military seizes power from civilians, rules for a while, fails to achieve legitimacy, then relinquishes its control. And as the Bignone regime was preparing its exit from office, there were fundamental questions about the rules of the forthcoming political game: precisely when the elections would take place and under what auspices; whether there would be an "official" candidate; whether the Peronists would be allowed to win; whether an elected government would be prohibited from investigating the repression of the mid-1970s; whether information on those who had "disappeared" (the *desaparecidos*) would ever be publicly released. It seemed unlikely that the military would give ground easily.

As the civilians prepared to come to power, they would unfortunately encounter all the familiar Argentine problems. In the economy it was high inflation, inadequate investment, and great difficulty in mobilizing support for any long-range economic program. No less important, the political parties remained anemic and ineffectual, hardly surprising in view of their suspension during the nine-year state of siege. It was still a face-off between the Radicals and the Peronists, just as it had been ever since the presidential election of 1946.

Most important, the debacle of military defeat in the South Atlantic gave another rude shock to Argentina's badly bruised sense of national identity. As one foreign journalist noted, "Like the dirty war, the repercussions of defeat will not fade quickly nor will rebuilding the nation be easy. Deep down, everyone knows that the Argentines must come to grips with who they are and what they want."

FOUR

CHILE
Democracy, Socialism, and Repression

The territory we now call Chile was one of the most distant realms of the Spanish empire in America. It evolved into a secondary center valued largely for its agricultural production. The Spanish found a native Indian population, but many perished under the onslaught of diseases brought by the Europeans. A relatively homogeneous population emerged from the colonial era, *mestizo,* although few of the "European" inhabitants wished to admit the extent to which their Spanish forebearers had mixed with the Indians.

When Napoleon invaded Spain, the colonists in Chile reacted much as their counterparts elsewhere, showing strong loyalty to the crown. They were indignant over Napoleon's cavalier treatment of Spain and her colonies: turning them over to his brother Joseph. As the French control of Spain dragged on after the conquest in 1808, the Chileans took matters into their own hands, holding a Congress in 1811. They seemed headed for independence, but the royalist forces regained the initiative and by the end of 1814 won control of Chile. It was against this royalist "reconquest" that Bernardo O'Higgins helped lead a revolutionary army from Mendoza. The rebels won Chilean independence from the Spanish and their royalist supporters in 1818 and their hero, O'Higgins, became the new republic's Supreme Director. He proved a decisive but autocratic leader. O'Higgins created a navy (to be one of Latin America's finest), promoted education, and won recognition of Chile's independence from the U.S., Brazil, and Mexico. The constitutional congress he had promised was rigged, however, and in 1823 the discontented Chilean aristocrats forced him to resign.

The following years saw political instability, as Liberals and Conservatives struggled for control. The latter won in 1830, beginning the three decades of the "Conservative Republic." The key figure was Diego Portales, who became the strong man of the regime, although never president in name. A Constituent Assembly was held in 1831, producing a constitution in 1833. It created a strong central government, with economic power in the hands of the landowners. Portales ruled unchallenged because the government controlled the electoral machinery and the landowners were happy to let Portales exercise power for their benefit.

Portales's undoing was a war with Peru (1836–39), which provoked a military rebellion at home and brought the dictator's assassination. Chile then went on to defeat the Peruvians. Chile's principal war hero was General Manuel Bulnes, who served as president for a decade after 1841, presiding over an era of ferment and creativity. Cultural life was enlivened by the presence of exiles from elsewhere in South America, especially Argentina, suffering under the dictator Rosas. In foreign policy, the Bulnes government took possession of the Straits of Magellan, initiating a territorial struggle with Argentina that has lasted ever since.

The 1850s brought another decade of fruitful consolidation for the new nation. The status of the church proved a key political question. Of all the legacies from the Spanish colonial era, none was to cause more controversy than this issue. One wing of the landowning elite wanted greater state control over the church, especially in education and finances. Their opponents defended all of the church's privileges. When the normally anti-clerical Liberal Party softened its stance in the late 1850s, dissident Liberals founded the Radical Party, an organization that would come to play an enduring role in the political life of the nation.

Overview: Economic Growth and Social Change

For Chile, as for many Latin American countries, the nineteenth century marked a period of far-reaching economic and social transformation. During the colonial era Chile played a relatively minor role in the Spanish American economy. Land in the fertile central valley was concentrated in the hands of a small number of powerful landlords. Their vast estates produced agricultural goods, especially fruit and grain, some bound for such cities as Santiago or Valparaíso but most destined for export to Lima and other urban markets in Peru. Maritime trade along the west coast of South America thus connected Chile to the centers of the Spanish empire.

The Wars for Independence interrupted this coastal trade, and Chilean agriculture promptly entered a period of relative stagnation. The situation was further affected by protectionist policies in Peru, which sought to encourage its own agrarian development by placing tight restrictions on imports from Chile. In the 1840s the California gold rush provided temporary stimulus for a boom in agricultural exports, which jumped from $6.1 million in 1844 to $12.4 million in 1850 and reached $25 million by 1860. But there they leveled off and then declined again. Completion of the U.S. transcontinental railroad helped to take away the California market, although export to England continued. With its advantageous location and fertile pampas, Argentina had better access to Europe. Agricultural production and commerce in Chile continued, of course, but they did not become the leading forces for economic growth.

Mining played that role. Between the mid-1840s and mid-1850s the production of silver grew by four or five times. Copper mining accelerated during this same period, and by 1870 Chile controlled about one-quarter of the world market for this product. Thereafter came a sharp decline. Chile would regain its preeminent position as a copper producer only after the turn of the century.

In the meantime it was nitrates, used for fertilizer and explosives, that became the country's leading export. This development was made possible by the acquisition of northern territory from Peru as a result of the War of the Pacific (1879–83). Foreign investors (especially British) quickly rushed in, and Europeans owned about two-thirds of the nitrate fields by 1884. But Chilean investors retained a hold in this area, reaping over half the total earnings by 1920. Eventually, however, the nitrate market declined. An increase in exports during World War I (for obvious reasons) was followed by a cutback in the early 1920s,

Though mining became the most dynamic sector of the Chilean economy, agriculture continued to play a significant role; here sacks of beans are loaded for export at the port of Valparaíso sometime after 1900. (Courtesy of the Library of Congress.)

then a brief recovery, then a steep and final reduction in the 1930s. Synthetic nitrates took over after that.

The nineteenth century growth of Chilean mining—in silver, copper, and nitrates—led to important changes in the country's social structure. One was the appearance of new elements within the elite, consisting of mine owners in the north and merchants from the growing towns and cities. Yet these elements did not truly rival the traditional landowners. For in Chile, more than in most Latin American countries, the landowning elite did not remain isolated and apart from the manufacturing and mining elites. There was, instead, a kind of merger, often achieved through family ties, so landowners frequently had relatives in upper levels of the other sectors if they did not take part themselves. Brothers, cousins, and brothers-in-law provided important links, and these connections tended to minimize conflict between the city and the countryside.

The growth of towns and cities led to a higher level of urbanization than in most of Latin America. In 1850 only 6 percent of the Chilean population was living in urban areas, but by 1900 the figure climbed to 20 percent. It would remain around this level, between 25 and 30 percent, until the 1930s. (By 1970 the proportion was over 60 percent, surpassed only by Argentina and possibly Uruguay.) Santiago retained its position as the nation's most important city, and bustling ports like Valparaíso became vital centers of commercial activity.

There also appeared a working class, first unionized in the nitrate fields of the north. Chile's economic development in the late nineteenth and early twentieth centuries did not require the massive importation of labor, however, and this fact points to a central feature of the country's working class: it was native-born. This stands in clear contrast to Argentina, where 25 percent of the population was foreign-born in 1895; for Chile this proportion was less than 3 percent. From the outset, Chilean workers had direct access to the political scene.

Copper production underwent a technological revolution just after 1900, due to the invention of a new smelting process, and this led to a major transformation in Chile. Investments required large amounts of capital, and these came from abroad. In 1904 the Braden Copper Company began exploiting the El Teniente mine near Santiago. British interests were soon taken over by the Guggenheims, and by 1920 the industry was dominated by only three companies, known from their initials as "the ABC": Andes Copper, Braden Copper, and the Chile Exploration Company–Chuquicamata. The first and third belonged to Anaconda, while Braden was a subsidiary of the Kennecott Corporation.

In less than 20 years the Chilean copper industry thus acquired characteristics that would affect the shape of national life for some time to come. It was concentrated in a few hands, and these hands were American. It came to constitute a foreign enclave, one that would provide relatively little stimulus throughout the rest of the economy. The heavy reliance on capital and technology meant modest levels of employment for Chilean workers. The importation of equipment and parts did not give much business to Chilean manufacturers. And most of the profits, often large, were returned to parent companies in the U.S. instead of being invested in Chile. It is little wonder that resentment grew.

An additional problem came from the great instability of copper prices on the world market. Indeed, copper prices could fluctuate as much as 500 or 1000 percent within a single year. This made it extremely difficult for Chile to anticipate the dollar amount of foreign exchange earnings, and this posed a serious problem for economic planning. Unpredictable gyrations in the world copper market could wreak havoc with the most carefully laid-out plans. As dependent on copper as it was, Chile could only accept the consequences.

And copper came to dominate the Chilean economy. By 1956 copper production accounted for half of all the country's exports, and taxes on the companies' profits yielded one-fifth of the government's entire revenue. As copper went, it was often said, so went Chile's economy.

In summary, these developments formed a complex social structure. The rural sector contained a traditional landowning elite, a peasantry tied by labor obligations to the estates where they lived, and a small but mobile work force that provided wage labor for the large commercial estates. There was a mining and industrial elite, many of whose members had kinship ties to the landed aristocracy. There were middle classes as well, and a growing, native-born, urban working class. Foreign investors were conspicuous from independence onward, but by the twentieth century their presence was epitomized by the preeminence of U.S. copper companies.

Tensions would appear between these various groups, but Chile has not had to face one problem that has beset so many other countries of Latin America: excessive population growth. Indeed, Chile has consistently had one of the lowest annual rates of population growth in the hemisphere: in 1900–10 it was just 1.2 percent, and in 1970–80 it was only 2.1 percent (compared to 2.8 percent for Latin America as a whole). Birth control and family planning have kept the country's population size within manageable limits, around 11.5 million by 1980, although there have never been enough jobs for even this limited population.

As cause or effect of this situation, women in Chile have enjoyed more opportunities than in many other countries. Females entered the work force with relative ease, and by 1970, for instance, nearly 16 percent of Chile's employed females held professional or technical jobs (higher than the U.S. rate of 14.7 percent). Social customs also re-

FIGURE 4-1   Chilean Copper: Production and Prices, 1912–1976
(Major Companies)

Sources: Markos Mamalakis and Clark W. Reynolds, *Essays on the Chilean Economy* (Homewood, Ill.: Richard D. Irwin, 1965), pp. 371–72; Ricardo Ffrench-Davis, "La importancia del cobre en la economía chilena," in Ffrench-Davis and Ernesto Tironi, eds., *El cobre en el desarrollo nacional* (Santiago: Universidad Católica de Chile, 1974), Cuadros 2, 7; Manual Lasaga, *The Copper Industry in the Chilean Economy: An Econometric Analysis* (Lexington, Mass.: D. C. Heath, 1981), p. 10.

flected fairly open and egalitarian standards in the relative treatment of the sexes.

Politics and Parliament

As nineteenth century Chile began to consolidate its place in the international economy, political crisis ensued. A civil war in 1859 had convinced the elite it was a time for quiet consolidation. They got it from José Joaquín Pérez, who began a ten-year presidential term.

The two most important political issues of this era were the structure of the constitution and the status of the church. On the first issue, the Liberals continued their campaign for equality of religion, while the Conservatives fought to protect the state-favored position of the Catholic Church. Slowly the Liberals won concessions, as non-Catholics received the right to have churches and religious schools. In effect, this was a modest opening of the elite, making it more pluralistic.

As for the constitution, the elite was struggling with the perennial problem of how to achieve effective government while avoiding despotism. In 1871 the constitution was amended to prohibit presidents from serving two consecutive terms. In 1874 further changes made government ministers more accountable to Congress, thereby strengthening the legislative powers. This dimunition of the power of the church and president led to labelling the years between 1861 and 1891 the "Liberal Republic."

The middle 1870s brought a severe economic depression, as mining output went into decline. They also brought Chile's most famous foreign conflict: the War of the Pacific (1879–83), when Chile fought both Peru and Bolivia. The ostensible issue was the treatment of Chilean investors in the desert territories governed by Peru. After extended fighting the Chileans won an overwhelming military triumph. As victors, the Chileans took control of the mineral-rich coastal strip that had belonged to Bolivia and Peru, justifying the war as the only honorable response to the ill-treatment of their countrymen by Peru and Bolivia. This conclusion had two important effects: to increase the self-confidence of the Chileans and to arouse deep resentment among the Peruvians and Bolivians. It also led to Chile's nitrate boom.

The 1880s saw much activity on the church-state issue. The liberal reformers made new gains. Civil registration of marriage, birth, and death was made compulsory, further eroding church control over daily life. In these same years the Congress extended the vote to all literate males over 25, eliminating the previous income test.

The second half of the 1880s brought the presidency of José Balmaceda (1886–91), the most controversial leader of late nineteenth century Chile. Although Balmaceda was a Liberal, the political lines fragmented so badly that disciplined political activity was endangered. The new president was soon engulfed in a bitter battle over food policy.

The issue arose when Chilean cattle raisers proposed a tariff on Argentine beef, which would have meant less meat and higher prices for Chileans. They were countered by the new middle-class led Democratic Party (founded 1887), which helped mobilize Santiago's artisans, small merchants, and skilled workers against the tariff. The opposition carried the day. Balmaceda convinced the bill's proponents to withdraw it.

This early triumph of the Democratic Party signalled the start of an important trend. It was a forerunner of populist politics, i.e., a direct appeal on economic grounds to the middle and lower sectors of the cities. Seeking a broad electorate, the Democrats argued for laws that would help workers while they also presented classic liberal demands for such items as compulsory free education and democratic procedures in electing governments. The party's articulation of mass demands showed how far Chile had already come on the road toward modern politics.

The fate of Balmaceda's presidency was sealed by the civil war of 1891. To this day Chileans argue passionately over the war, its causes, and its meaning. The origins lay in Balmaceda's efforts to push economic development faster than most of the oligarchy was ready to go. The president wanted to increase government intervention in the economy. In order to pay for the building of new railways, roads, and urban infrastructure (water and sanitation), Balmaceda needed growing tax revenues from the nitrate industry in the northern province of Tarapacá. The obstacle was the primarily foreign ownership, especially in the railways, where Balmaceda proposed to break a foreign monopoly.

His plans met with stiff opposition in the Congress. In fact, Balmaceda's boldness masked a deeper constitutional struggle, that of congressional versus presidential authority. Congress had been fighting to establish its supremacy in the constitutional structure. But Balmaceda was determined to impose his will. The result was extreme ministerial instability. Between 1886 and 1890 Balmaceda was saddled with thirteen different cabinets, and the battle between the two branches of government led to an impasse.

In 1890 the Congress failed to produce a budget, whereupon the president ruled that the previous year's appropriations would apply. Balmaceda had earlier ventured into an area which had always proved sensitive: the choice of a presidential successor, whom he tried to nominate himself. The Congress passed a law voiding any such nomination, which Balmaceda then refused to sign.

Congressional opposition was now ready to seek a remedy by force of arms. Its leaders sought out possible military conspirators but with no success. The emerging conflict had complex implications. First, Balmaceda had alarmed conservative Chilean interests by his economic plans. He wanted a national bank, an obvious threat to interests of the established oligarchy, which dominated the private banking system. Above all, Balmaceda was asserting the power of the presidency against a parliamentary system. Given his unorthodox economic ideas, this endangered the ruling landowner-merchant network.

The rebels against Balmaceda had the support of the navy, but not the army, which supported the beleaguered president. The mining region in the north proved a rebel stronghold, where the mine owners were happy to support a force that promised to depose the president who threatened to savage their economic interests. The owners also cut off export tax revenues which were vital to the Santiago government. A northern rebel army mobilized to sail south and depose the president.

The resulting combat at Con Con and la Placilla produced the bloodiest battles in Chilean history, with Balmaceda's forces going down in defeat. The President took refuge in the Argentine embassy, where he commited suicide one day after his presidential term ended.

In less than a month a new president was elected: Jorge Montt. But now the president's power was seriously circumscribed, as Chile now embraced the parliamentary system.

One of the key issues of the war—the status of foreign investors—had been settled. Nationalization was out, but the parliamentary victors continued pressure on the European investors. Nationalistic sentiment had penetrated all sectors of the Chilean elite.

The trauma of the 1891 civil war might at first seem a turning point in Chilean history. In fact, it only underlined the relative stability of the Chilean political system. The elite weathered the crisis of the Balmaceda challenge in a manner that promised stability at least equal to that in neighboring Argentina. Chile was poised to participate in the export boom that was carrying Latin America ever deeper into the North Atlantic economy.

Balmaceda's fall at the hands of the congressional rebels changed Chile's constitutional structure. The strong presidency gave way to a parliamentary system, but it proved impossible for any ministry to last long. Cabinets came and went at an average of four every year between 1895 and 1925. This instability was reinforced by the fragmentation of major parties, which proliferated to five by 1900.

Political control continued in the hands of an oligarchy representing primarily agricultural interests. It was dubbed *la fronda aristocrática* ("aristocratic front") in Alberto Edwards's classic book (1928) of that name. Occasionally they were challenged by urban interests, such as merchants. The workers, although not yet organized into political parties, were already beginning to make their weight felt. The issue that aroused them was rising prices. In 1905 workers staged a series of protests that led to direct confrontation with armed members of the oligarchy, and a miners' strike in 1907 in the northern city of Iquique similarly erupted into violence and bloodshed.

After 1910 workers became even more militant. The leading organizers were the anarcho-syndicalists, indefatiguable activists who excelled in organizing the many small firms. Although their long-term goal was the abolition of all government, they concentrated in the short run on winning immediate concessions for their followers. Centered in Santiago, the anarcho-syndicalist-led unions won significant improvements in wages and working conditions. But they were vulnerable to reprisals against their leaders, who were subject to firings or arrests or imprisonment.

These unions did not, however, represent a basic threat to the political system. In their wage demands, the workers sought to hold their own against inflation. As for working conditions and fringe benefits, the employers could undercut much of the militancy by granting social welfare benefits. The Congress did exactly this, legislating workmen's compensation in 1916, employer's liability in 1917, and a retirement system for railway workers in 1919.

After a slowdown in strike activity and a loss in bargaining power, organized labor began to revive in 1917. Economic recovery strengthened labor's hand, as World War I had greatly stimulated the demand for nitrates, a key ingredient in explosives. But inflation was again eating up wages, making workers receptive to the organizers' appeals. For the next three years unions grew steadily, despite the fact that Chilean law did not recognize labor unions.

This growth of labor strength worried the incumbent political oligarchy as well as the middle sectors. As in Argentina and Brazil, the elite presumed that discontent must be the work of foreign agitators. In 1918 the Congress passed a *ley de residencia,* much like the Argentine and Brazilian laws, designed to facilitate the deportation of aliens who were active labor organizers. But neither the politicians nor the elite had done their homework, because Chile had almost no such aliens! Since immigration from Europe had been minimal in Chile, the deportation strategy simply could not work.

The year 1919 marked the peak of labor mobilization. In January-February union leaders called huge rallies in Santiago to protest the high prices of wartime inflation. In August came another mammoth demonstration, with 100,000 participants marching past the presidential palace. The next month a general strike in Santiago failed, however, and worker morale was shaken. Thereafter the rate of strikes declined.

Surprisingly enough, the government response to strikers had been moderate since the labor upsurge began in 1917. In December an executive edict (the Yáñez decree) made the government a mediator in stalemated labor conflicts. Although rejected by anarchist and syndicalist leaders, it was heavily used, often for labor's benefit, in 1918 and 1919. That pattern continued into 1920, in part because the government was worried about the presidential elections scheduled for June.

Chile, like Argentina, had opened the door to middle-sector political participation, a process far less advanced in Brazil. The number of working-class voters, although still small, had begun to attract the attention of Chilean bourgeois politicians, especially in Santiago. Their support could be crucial, especially when the vote was divided among many parties, as in Chile. The political leader who saw this most clearly was Arturo Alessandri, who campaigned for the presidency by making a passionate appeal to urban voters, including workers. Alessandri represented an "enlightened" middle-sector view—accepting the inevitability of working-class participation, while also hoping to channel it into controllable lines of action. He proposed to legitimize unions, but also put them into an intricate legal framework determined by the government.

Alessandri won the election, if narrowly. With this democratic exercise past, the incumbent President Sanfuentes felt free in his few remaining days to answer the labor challenge. In July 1920 workers were harassed by the "Patriotic Leagues," paramilitary street activists recruited from right-wing middle- and upper-class families. Systematic government repression followed. Virtually all anarcho-syndicalist and other leaders who did not choose exile or go underground were arrested and imprisoned. The leaderless workers were further demoralized by a wave of lock-outs, as employers revoked many of the concessions made between 1917 and 1920.

There was hope that the anti-labor policy would change when Alessandri assumed office, and so it did. For the first half of 1921 the Alessandri government intervened (under authority of the Yáñez decree) in a number of strikes, favoring workers in their mediation. But conflict mounted and Alessandri drew attacks from all sides—from the right for being too soft on labor and from the left for winking at aggressive employer tactics. In July 1921 Alessandri finally opted for the employers. He intervened in a bitter tram strike in Santiago, helping the company to break the strike. A wave of successful lock-outs followed. By the end of 1921, the government had gone back to systematically repressing labor.

While organized labor was struggling against adverse economic and political conditions, President Alessandri pushed his proposals for a labor code and social welfare package, introduced in Congress in 1921. Conservatives balked at these ideas, since they preferred the status quo—

where unions had no legal status and therefore faced continuous assaults from both employers and government. Some Conservatives also feared that Liberals might pick up new voters among urban workers. The impasse between Liberal President and Conservative Congress continued until 1924. Then the military intervened.

From Instability to Popular Front

A military junta took partial control of the government in early September 1924, and three days later issued a manifesto listing legislative demands, with Congress dutifully approving every one. Included was a package of labor measures. Most important was an elaborate labor code that subjected unions to close government supervision.

Chile was following Bismarck's system of social welfare benefits created in the German Empire of the 1880s. As in the German case, this social advance was *not* the product of a political process where workers played a direct role. Rather, it was a preemptive move by the government, under military pressure, to head off further independent mobilization by workers' organizations. In Chile this apparently progressive step resulted from the pressure of a government cadre that had much to fear from worker mobilization—the military officer corps.

Alessandri, in the meantime, was losing ground in his struggle with the army and took a leave to Italy. He was recalled after a second military coup in January 1925. At this point, ironically, the officers now in control felt they needed both Alessandri and urban labor support to bolster their legitimacy. The new military government intervened frequently in strikes, usually on the side of the workers. It seemed that organized labor might be on the verge of gaining power; some even thought the revolution was at hand. Fear spread among the elite, which could see its power slipping away.

The revolution was not at hand. Alessandri returned from his leave in March 1925, and soon taught organized labor another lesson about its vulnerability. In a clash with nitrate workers in June 1925 the government cracked down. For the next two years labor battled not only government hostility, but also economic recession and unemployment. In January 1927 labor leadership ill-advisedly attempted a general strike. Its divisions became all too obvious and the strike failed.

Colonel Carlos Ibáñez emerged as the strongman from the political instability following Alessandri's resignation in 1925. In May 1927 he was formally elected president by the Congress, and he proceeded to consolidate a dictatorship that lasted to 1931. Chileans, having prided themselves on their relative democracy and free political competition, were shocked. The general-president jailed opponents, especially labor leaders, and suspended civil liberties.

Ibáñez had activist economic ideas to go with his authoritarian politics. The government now greatly enlarged its role in the economy. That meant speeding the construction of railways, roads, and power facilities. Not surprisingly, Ibáñez also stepped up spending for the military. Much of the financing came from abroad—loans and especially U.S. investment in mining. The world economic expansion of the 1920s made it all possible.

The Wall Street crash of 1929 abruptly ended that era, in Chile as elsewhere. Mineral exports fell disastrously and foreign financing dried up. Desperate attempts to create a national cartel for nitrate sales abroad failed. Protests against the government grew. An ever widening spectrum of the society, now including professional persons as well as workers, joined the attack on the dictator. Ibáñez finally gave in. In July 1931 he resigned, joining the ranks of the other South American heads of government who had the misfortune to be governing when the Depression hit.

For the next year Chile lacked a stable government. The interim regimes included a thirteen-day interlude of a "Socialist Republic" in which Colonel Marmaduke Grove became the best known figure. Although an ineffectual government, this regime dramatized the rise of a new institution, the Socialist Party, formally founded a year later. Another presidential election was finally held. The winner was a familiar face: Arturo Alessandri.

The once-fiery Alessandri was now more interested in order than change. His government cracked down on the opposition, especially the left. In 1936, when a wave of strikes broke out, Alessandri took tough measures. He proclaimed a state of siege, closed Congress, and sent labor leaders into exile. The army took over the railways, always a focus of labor conflict.

In economic policy the Alessandri presidency was quite successful. An ultra-orthodox finance minister, Gustavo Ross, drastically reduced public sector spending and dismantled some of the key government agencies that Ibáñez had created. Thanks to recovery of world demand for Chilean exports, especially minerals, the foreign trade balance improved dramatically. Unemployment, at 262,000 in 1932, dropped to less than 16,000 by 1937. Inflation remained a problem, however, as wage increases seldom kept pace with price increases.

Chile approached the presidential election of 1938 with apprehension. In 1935 the world communist movement, dominated by the Soviet-directed Comintern, had called for a coalition strategy in battling fascism, in effect encouraging communist parties to seek alliances with parties of the left and center (as quickly happened in Spain and France). In 1936 the idea bore fruit in Chile, as the Communists and Radicals joined forces in a "Popular Front," which by 1938 came to include a broad spectrum of parties: Radicals, Socialists, Communists, Democrats, plus a new Confederation of Chilean Workers. After the Socialist Marmaduke Grove withdrew his candidacy the nomination went to Pedro Aguirre Cerda, a wealthy Radical known for his reformist ideas on the agrarian question.

The incumbent political alliance nominated Alessandri's finance minister, Gustavo Ross. It was a choice bound to anger middle-class opinion. Ross presented an inflexible and backward-looking image, despite the relative prosperity brought by his policies. The campaign was bitterly fought, and Aguirre Cerda won by the narrowest of margins— a mere 4000 out of 241,000 votes cast.

Despite its narrowness, or perhaps because of it, this election set the political context for years to come. Centrist voters had tipped the balance by opting for the left. At the same time, however, they were voting for a reformist, so the outcome seemed ambiguous. What sort of a mandate would the resulting government have?

The Popular Front government soon suffered the strains inherent in such a heterogeneous coalition. The Radicals were the dominant element, and the least radical in ideology. They focused on economic development, not social welfare, and they were accused by some of exploiting power for the sake of old-style patronage.

The other elements in the Front were far from united themselves. The Communists and Socialists were natural antagonists, because many Socialists were ex-Communists who had refused to knuckle under to Party discipline. Both the Communists and Socialists tried to mobilize rural workers, thereby alarming the powerful landowners—and placing themselves in competition with each other.

The Congress was controlled by the right-wing opposition, but popular support for the left was on the rise. In the congressional elections of 1941 the Communists received 12 percent of the vote, up from only 4 percent in 1937. The Socialists (and kindred groups) got 20 percent. Although the rightist parties, when combined with the Radicals, won a majority, conservatives saw in the elections a growing threat from the left.

The policies of the Popular Front were anything but menacing. Economic policy concentrated on an expanded economic role for the national government. In 1939 a new state corporation was created: CORFO (*Corporación de Fomento*), which was to stimulate economic development by strategic investments in both the public and private sector.

The Popular Front lost even its titular leadership when poor health forced President Aguirre Cerda to resign in 1941. The following president was another Radical, Juan Antonio Ríos (1942–46), who had to face the uncertainties of wartime. Ríos struggled to keep Chile neutral in the spreading world conflict. Under U.S. pressure to join the Allies, he feared a reaction from the German colony in the south of Chile. In January 1943 Chile finally broke relations with the Axis. Chile had faced a dilemma much like that of Argentina, which delayed the break with Germany and Italy until early 1945.

The succeeding president, Gabriel González Videla (1946–52), was once again a Radical. He accepted Communist support in the campaign, and rewarded them with three seats in his cabinet. This modest throwback to the Popular Front did not last long. 1946 brought a series of violent strikes. Protest centered in the mining fields of the north, but soon spread throughout the country. A call for a general strike provoked strong police measures and riots ensued. A full-scale social conflict loomed. The government declared a state of siege and suspended civil liberties. Strikes continued into 1947.

González had by now purged the Communists from his cabinet. The strikes gave the right its chance to mount an offensive. The rightists had been alarmed by the steady rise in the Communist vote, which came to 18 percent in the municipal elections of 1947 (up from 12 percent in the congressional elections of 1941). The Chilean government now decided to move against the left, and in this it had plenty of support from abroad. The U.S. government was launching a major campaign in Latin America to isolate the left, especially the communist parties, and the U.S. embassy strongly encouraged the Chilean conservatives. The left fought back by attacking the González government and the U.S. The climax came in 1948: by an act of Congress, where the left was greatly outnumbered, the Communist Party was outlawed and its members banned from running for office or holding official posts. A witch hunt followed. The Radicals showed their true colors. Together with the rightists, the centrist Radicals had again shown how they were prepared to use "legal" means to eliminate their most dangerous adversaries from the political game. For the left, the Popular Front became an object lesson and they vented their anger on González Videla.

The Era of Party Politics

The final demise of the Popular Front ushered in a period of intense political competition based on party organizations. During this period the Chilean political system displayed several identifying characteristics.

First, elections were extremely competitive. There were many different parties, so it was rare for any one of them to receive more than one-quarter of the total vote. This fact accounted for a second feature: in search of governing majorities, the parties had to take part in coalitions. Alliances were fragile, however, and political leaders were constantly in quest of new arrangements and intent on mending fences. Underlying this was an increased tendency toward ideological polarization. In one opinion survey 31 percent of the Chilean population classified themselves as rightists, 25 percent described themselves as leftists, and the rest were centrists or undecided. Because of this fragmentation, the parties of the center could, through bargaining and skillful maneuver, have great leverage on coalition formation and electoral results.

Third, the system was highly democratic. In contrast to Argentina, where trade unions had uneasy relationships with political parties, the Chilean labor movement was closely identified with various parties, mainly on the left, so it did not form a separate power center. Measured as a percentage of registered voters, electoral participation was high (around 80 percent, compared to 50–60 percent in the U.S.), and registration grew rapidly in the early 1960s. And election results were accepted by almost all Chileans as binding.

The 1952 presidential election brought back another figure from the past: General Carlos Ibáñez. Now in his mid seventies, the former dictator proclaimed himself the only answer to Chile's many problems. This *caudillo* put himself forward as a true nationalist, but his appeal was really aimed at the right and center, who were once again worried about the left. Socialists and Communists formed another electoral alliance, although the latter were hobbled by their illegality. The election results were indicative of the path Chile was to follow for decades: a deeply divided vote with no candidate or party getting a clear majority. Ibáñez took office with a plurality of 47 percent.

Ibáñez had claimed to be the apolitical man able to solve all the political problems, but not surprisingly he failed to deliver on his promises. His prime economic problem was inflation, which had hit Chile earlier and harder than most of Latin America. Because he faced a major deficit in the balance of payments, Ibáñez had to look abroad for help. The logical source was the International Monetary Fund (IMF), created to help member countries with temporary balance of payments problems. Unfortunately for the Chileans, it was not simply a matter of arranging a foreign loan. The IMF was obligated by its charter to require evidence that any country getting help had a convincing plan for correcting the causes of the payments deficit. As applied in the mid-1950s, that policy meant the IMF must oversee the borrowing country's economic policies. As a result, the IMF came to be seen by most Chileans (and by most other Latin Americans) as an extension of U.S. economic and political power.

Ibáñez was thus caught in the typical policy dilemma produced by inflation. His government had to act because it was running out of foreign exchange and could not import much-needed goods from abroad.

Yet the sources of foreign financing offered their help only on the condition that they have a veto over basic policymaking. Financial-pressure was driving Chile to compromise her national autonomy. Ibáñez knew that the left would be in full cry against him if he acceded to the IMF terms. He decided to take the gamble.

His government soon paid the price. The initial measures were for austerity. An early target were the public utilities, which invariably charged very low rates in times of rapid inflation, since managers hesitated to pass rising costs on to customers and thus spark popular protests. An increase in bus fares, for instance, provoked a furious response. Riots began in Santiago and spread to other cities. Given the strength of labor and the leftist parties, Chile was a difficult place for anti-inflation policies. In the end Ibáñez was not able to live up to his grand claims. He had proved to be a tired old general who had little political base and even fewer political ideas.

The 1958 election produced a new president with a familiar family name: Alessandri. He was Jorge, the son of Arturo Alessandri. Jorge, although considering himself an independent, had run as the leader of the right, on a combined Conservative and Liberal ticket. His opponents were Salvador Allende, a medical doctor and long-time politician who represented the Socialist-Communist alliance (FRAP), and Eduardo Frei, an ambitious young idealist who headed the Christian Democrats (PDC), a relatively new party on the national scene. Alessandri won a plurality of the vote (31.6 percent), as against 28.9 percent for Allende and 20.7 percent for Frei, with the remaining 18.8 percent split between the Radical candidate and a maverick priest. The Congress readily confirmed Alessandri's election, as required by the constitution when no candidate won an absolute majority. The election had once again shown that the Chilean electorate to be deeply divided.

Alessandri was hardly the leader to bridge those divisions, even though he enjoyed personal popularity. An austere figure, he was the very opposite of the ebullient personality types who created the "populist" political style in Latin America.

The new president was an authentic representative of conservative political and economic thought in Chile. He strongly believed in free enterprise economics, including monetary orthodoxy and an open door to foreign investment. His government attacked the serious inflation with an orthodox IMF-style stabilization policy: budget cutting, devaluation (to a fixed exchange rate), and an appeal for new foreign investment.

Alessandri's stabilization efforts were undercut by a bitter battle over copper policies. The government tried to convince the U.S. copper companies to increase their investment. The idea was to get more of the processing of the copper to be done in Chile. This would increase the economic returns to Chile, as well as make Chile more self-sufficient in marketing the final product. But Chilean nationalists were incensed: they wanted to expropriate the companies, not just encourage their investment. Government policy carried the day, but copper company investments did not increase and Chile did no better at exploiting its only major asset in international trade.

Other orthodox economic policies showed some success in the short run. In 1957 and 1958 inflation had hovered between 25 and 30 percent. In 1959 it went up to 39 percent, but then came down to 12 percent in 1960 and only 8 percent in 1961. Export earnings failed to increase significantly, however, and a freeing of import controls led to huge trade deficits. A fixed exchange rate was supposed to restore confidence, but as the trade deficits mounted it only encouraged the speculators to abandon Chilean currency while there was still time.

Alessandri had also hoped his orthodox policies could make progress against the mounting social problems being created by Chile's slow and uneven economic growth. Large-scale public works projects were launched, financed mainly by foreign funds. A principal source was the U.S., where worry over the Cuban threat had led to hurried formulation of the Alliance for Progress. Alessandri even dared to tackle the agrarian question, long a forbidden subject in his political ranks. Although the law passed in 1962 was thought by all on the left to be ludicrously inadequate, in fact it did furnish the basis for an aggressive expropriation program.

Not surprisingly, none of the Alessandri policies did much toward solving the grave socioeconomic problems facing Chile. The steady exodus of the rural poor to the cities, especially Santiago, continued. There they were ill-housed, ill-fed, and ill-educated. Furthermore, there was little work. These "marginals" were the tragic underside of capitalist urbanization in a Third World country. By the 1960s about 60 percent of the Chilean population lived in urban areas.

Alessandri would have liked to govern a tranquil land. Events soon ruled out that dream. In the early 1960s the Chilean political scene began to change significantly. There was first the great growth of the electorate. Just over 500,000 in 1938, by 1963 it had reached 2,500,000—a fivefold expansion in twenty-five years. Second, a realignment of political forces had occurred. There were now four main groupings: (1) the right, including the Conservative and Liberal parties; (2) the centrist Radicals, long the masters of opportunism; (3) the Marxist left, comprised primarily of the Communists and Socialists; and (4) the Christian Democrats, located in the center, a reform-oriented party now building its electoral following. In the 1963 municipal elections each of these four won roughly equal percentages of the vote.

The biggest net gainers were the Christian Democrats, who were attracting votes from both left and right.

As the presidential election of 1964 neared, the polarization sharpened. A widely discussed indicator was a March 1964 special election to fill a congressional seat in the province of Curicó. Although previously a Conservative Party stronghold, its overwhelmingly rural voters gave the FRAP candidate 39 percent, while the center-right candidate got only 33 percent and the Christian Democrat drew 28 percent. Assuming these results were typical for the nation as a whole, Liberals and Conservatives quickly decided their only salvation lay in an alliance with the Christian Democrats. They dissolved their Democratic Front

FIGURE 4-2   A Genealogy of Major Political Parties in Chile

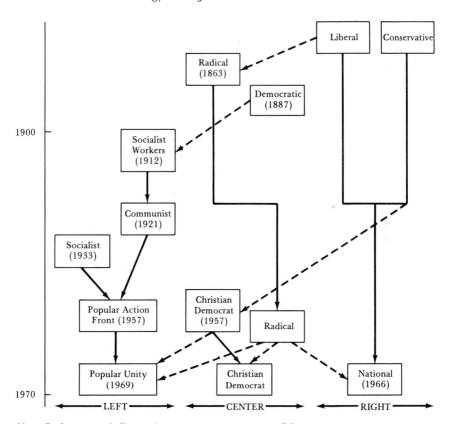

Note: Broken arrows indicate splinter groups or temporary coalitions.

and began courting the PDC. The political isolation of the Chilean countryside appeared to have ended. No longer could the landowners and their agents take the votes of the rural poor for granted.

The 1964 presidential election loomed as a crucial one for both Chile and Latin America. The left once again ran Salvador Allende. FRAP's strident criticisms of capitalism seemed all the more relevant, now that a classically conservative government had so recently failed.

The 1964 election was to be very different from 1958. A relatively new party, the Christian Democrats, had burst onto the scene. When the rightist parties decided to endorse the PDC candidate, Eduardo Frei, the Christian Democrats gained an enormous boost. It was a pragmatic decision, made out of the fear that the FRAP might win a plurality victory, as almost happened in 1958. The rightists decided this despite their misgivings about the PDC's reformist ideas, which many conservatives saw as dangerously close to the formulas of the left.

The campaign was hard-fought and aroused strong interest throughout the Americas. The FRAP called for a clear-cut repudiation of capitalism and imperialism. Chilean landlords and U.S. copper companies were depicted as the arch-villains. Allende called for nothing short of a sweeping transformation of Chilean society, in order to lead Chile to socialism.

The PDC campaign was a high-powered operation designed to convince the electorate that Frei could bring significant change without violating Chile's traditional freedoms. It was to be a "Revolution in Liberty." In fact, however, the Christian Democrats were promising reforms, not revolution. The reforms added up to a more efficient capitalist economy, to be achieved by limited government intervention to carry out such measures as agrarian reform (through the expropriation of underused land), increased public housing, and greater control over the U.S. copper companies (through Chilean purchase of part ownership).

Frei and the PDC wasted no time in branding FRAP as an extension of Moscow. Cleverly written campaign cartoons and radio jingles played on fears of "another Cuba" in Chile, fears known to be highly exploitable. The U.S. government, as well as West European Christian Democrats, also took a strong interest in this contest between reformism and Marxism. The Central Intelligence Agency would later admit to contributing more than 50 percent of Frei's campaign expenses. In this and other ways, probably including money and support from U.S. business firms, the Chilean voter felt the effects of strong North American interest.

It may have been a case of overkill. Frei won the election more handily than anyone had expected, with 56 percent of the vote. Allende got 39 percent, well over his share in 1958. The difference, of course, was that this time it was a two-way race. A third candidate, Julio Durán of the Radicals, was deserted by many from his own party and finished with only 5 percent. The triumph belonged to Frei, but the "Revolution in Liberty" owed its birth far more to the absence of a rightist candidate than to any sudden change of mind by Chilean voters.

Frei's government began with high expectations. The left had been decisively defeated. The voters had given a mandate for change. Now the Christian Democrats would have to move quickly and decisively.

Their plate was certainly full. First priority was given to economic policy. One of the hottest issues was copper: how to improve Chile's share in the exploitation of its most valuable export. Here, as elsewhere, the Frei strategists sought a middle way. Outright nationalization (with compensation) would be too expensive, they reasoned, since Chile would have to come up with enormous dollar payments. Simply encouraging the U.S. companies to increase their investment under the old terms was equally unacceptable, since it would be a backward step on the path toward greater national control. Their solution was centrist: the Chilean government would buy into part ownership of the companies, with the proceeds to be reinvested by the companies in expanded facilities, especially for processing. The goal was to double copper production by 1970. If successful, the plan would increase both national control and export earnings.

The proposal was savagely attacked by the left, which branded it a "sell-out." The Christian Democrats decided to make it a major issue in the congressional elections of March 1965, where they won an overwhelming victory. They promptly used their new congressmen to vote through the copper plan ("Chileanization") in November 1965. The opposition on the left and from many mine workers remained intransigent. Frei got his agreements with Anaconda (which became 25 percent government owned) and Kennecott (now 51 percent government owned), the two leading companies, but over the next five years copper production increased by only 10 percent. Export earnings doubled, but that was because of a rise in the world price of copper, not because of output. Furthermore, a big share of those higher earnings went to the companies, due to the terms of the new contracts. The company lawyers had thought ahead more skillfully than Frei's technocrats, a point made much of by the left.

The agrarian sector was another key policy area. Chile had long suffered under one of Latin America's most archaic rural structures, with the marginalized rural masses daily becoming more desperate. The Christian Democrats pushed through a land reform act in 1967 which was another compromise. Elaborate provisions were made for identifying land to be expropriated, compensation to be given, and land distributed to 100,000 peasants by 1970. Frei's planners hoped that cooperatives—always a mainstay in Christian Democratic thinking—could furnish the facilities necessary to get new farms running profitably. The program went more slowly than hoped, and by the end of Frei's term there were only 28,000 new farm ownerships, a number whose significance was obscured by the high expectations the Christian Democrats had aroused.

The U.S. continued to take a strong interest in the fortunes of the Frei government. It had all the marks of the kind of reformist regime that the Alliance for Progress was designed to support. The U.S., as well as the multilateral agencies such as the Inter-American Development Bank and the World Bank, gave Chile extensive financing. In the short run this helped Chile's annual balance of payments. In the long run it added to Chile's foreign debt.

In the political sphere the Christian Democrats attempted to deliver on their promise of a new kind of popular participation. Rejecting the massive state role that the solutions of the left would inevitably bring, they pushed for *promoción popular,* which was supposed to be a new kind of grass-roots political activity. In practice it meant a mixture of communitarianism, self-help, and cooperatives. Above all, it meant heading off the left, which had through its unions and party structures (both communist and socialist) gotten a head start in organizing at the mass level. The net effect was a dogfight to win elections throughout the society: in unions, student associations, cooperatives, bar associations, and every kind of professional group. Politics was penetrating more and more deeply into Chilean society.

The 1965 congressional election victory proved to be the high point of the Christian Democrats' political fortunes. In the 1967 and 1969 municipal elections they lost ground. In 1969 they lost their majority in the Chamber of Deputies. Efforts at reformist socioeconomic change proved difficult, and the odds on their Revolution in Liberty lengthened.

The left, so close to victory in the 1958 presidential election, was struggling to create another coalition for the 1970 campaign. The right, which had backed Frei out of sheer opportunism, now indulged its longstanding preferences. Conservative voices suggested that they could win with their own candidate, especially if he were the ever-popular Jorge Alessandri.

Time had run out on the Revolution in Liberty. The reformist gains had been substantial, if measured by past Chilean standards, but they were no longer enough. Because the constitution forbade consecutive reelection of the president, the Christian Democrats had to find a new candidate. Frei had been an overshadowing figure, but not without detractors within the party. In fact, the Christian Democratic left wing had veered sharply in the direction of radical change. As the presidential election of 1970 approached, it looked as if the electorate would return to the sharply fragmented voting pattern common before 1964.

The 1970 presidential election in some ways resembled 1964. But this time the right decided to run its own candidate, Jorge Alessandri, the magic name in twentieth century Chilean politics. The divided Christian Democrats nominated Radomiro Tomic, whose leftist stand precluded any possible electoral alliance with the right. The Communists and Socialists, now united under the rubric of *Unidad Popular* (UP or Popular Unity), once again chose Allende. The UP relentlessly attacked the Christian Democrats' record under Frei, charging a sellout to imperialism and domestic oligarchs. Alessandri offered an old-fashioned conservative recipe, almost oblivious to the bitter ideological controversy swirling about him. Tomic sounded remarkably like Allende. He favored radical change, including complete nationalization of the copper companies.

When the votes were counted, the tally looked a bit like 1958. Allende had won a plurality, but it was far from a decisive result. His vote total was 36.3 percent. Alessandri, whom the U.S. ambassador had confidently predicted would win, got 34.9 percent, and Tomic only 27.8 percent. The left was jubilant, but their more sober leaders were aware of the fragility of Allende's mandate.

Allende's first problem was the requisite confirmation from the Congress. The right saw Allende's impending presidency as a grave threat, and some militant members, especially within the army, began conspiring to block him. One military plot, initially supported by the U.S. government, aborted when General Schneider, the army commander-in-chief, was murdered in a bungled kidnap attempt. Allende was eventually confirmed by Congress three days later, and Chilean democracy seemed to have survived its first challenge after the election of a Marxist.

Socialism via Democracy?

Allende's three-year presidency was rich in significance, for both the history of Chile and that of Latin America, although the nature of that significance is still bitterly argued. The president and his advisers decided that despite the narrowness of their election victory they would seek radical change—but by legal means. Was such a course of action possible? How, asked the more radical UP militants, could socialism be introduced in a genteel fashion?

Allende's initial economic strategy was similar to that of Perón in 1946 and Castro in 1959: freeze prices and raise wages. The result was an immediate boom in consumer buying. This caused significant short-term redistribution of income. Merchants' inventories were quickly depleted, while producers put a hold on all production orders until they could see how long price controls would prevent them from recovering the inflationary costs they faced in producing new goods for the retail market. Here Allende had pursued an essentially populist strategy in order to expand his political support.

Allende's other economic policies flowed from campaign promises. Top priority went to the complete nationalization of the copper companies. Most significant, the congressional vote on this issue was unanimous. That spoke volumes about the growth of nationalist sentiment in Chile and the perceived failure of Frei's Chileanization policy. Later the Allende government argued that no compensation was due the companies because of what he charged were their previous illegally high profits. That aggressive stand provoked Christian Democratic opposition and furnished U.S. government hardliners with "proof" that Chile had declared war on private property in the hemisphere.

The UP government also extended state control into many other economic sectors. Coal and steel were nationalized, along with 60 percent of the private banks. As the "transition to socialism" continued, more and more firms and businesses were nationalized, with Allende's hand often forced by workers who occupied management offices and refused to leave until expropriation was announced. Foreign firms were a favorite target, with such well-known names as ITT and Ford falling victim.

This attack on foreign capital was bound to aggravate tensions with the U.S. The Chilean government could never hope to come up with the foreign exchange needed to compensate the owners. The refusal (and/or inability) to compensate gave the Nixon administration legal grounds to mount an "invisible blockade" against Chile in the international economy, although the U.S. took steps before the nationalization even began. This included a hold (with minor exceptions) on any loans from the World Bank or the Inter-American Development Bank, not to speak of the U.S. Export-Import Bank. Private foreign investment also came to a halt, so Allende faced a severe shortage of foreign financing. In his last year (1972–73) West European and socialist bloc countries began opening lines of credit to Chile, but their effect had yet to be felt.

In the rural sector the Allende government moved with speed. The expropriations came faster than the government's ability to ensure the services (credit, access to supplies, equipment) needed by the new small owners or by the state-controlled cooperatives. Furthermore, the government was increasingly outflanked by peasants, often organized by leftist radicals, who seized land on their own. By 1973 the Agrarian Reform Institute had lost control of the situation in many areas. Landowners hired armed guards, tried to fight back legally, or simply fled the country. The long-standing agrarian problem was being met by radical means, as the state rapidly displaced the *hacendados.*

In its overall management of the economy the Allende government took an early chance. Facing a majority opposition in the Congress, Allende's political strategists decided to go for a constitutional amendment that would create an assembly of the people in place of the Congress. The populist policies of 1970–71 (freezing prices, raising wages) were intended partly to build support for the amendment. It was a risk because the populist measures were bound to be inflationary. A great deal was riding on the gamble to win increased constitutional power, because the Congress could block so much of the program Allende sought to carry out.

Not surprisingly, the Congress rejected the amendment in 1972. At that point Allende and his advisers decided to pause in order to consolidate their political gains. They planned eventually to submit the amendment to a popular plebiscite—thereby bypassing the opposition-dominated Congress. The proper moment never came, however; at least they could never identify it. As 1972 continued, the government was preoccupied by the enormous dislocations hitting the economy. First, there were the distortions resulting from the attempt to enforce price controls. More and more products disappeared from the legal markets and made their way into black markets. Because it was a legal government in a system of limited constitutional powers, the Allende regime was ineffectual in combatting the burgeoning underground economy. Second, there was extensive sabotage or deliberate diversion by producers, landowners, and merchants who wanted either the UP experiment to fail or wanted to make quick profits, or both. Finally, there was the inefficiency of an inexperienced government trying to take over and run huge sectors of the economy. New and often untrained bureaucrats, frequently appointed for political rather than technical qualifications, could hardly master tasks that still bedevil their counterparts in tightly controlled socialist societies.

The result was that by early 1973 Chile was in the grip of runaway inflation. The annual rate was exceeding 150 percent (it would climb even higher than that) and the government looked helpless. Monetary authorities were simply pumping out money to cover huge budget deficits. An overvalued exchange rate was encouraging imports, while low world copper prices depressed export earnings. The balance-of-payments deficits in 1971 and 1972 could be covered out of the foreign exchange reserves left by the Frei government, but that recourse was gone by 1973. The new credits from the socialist bloc and West Europe were yet to materialize, so the foreign accounts had become a major economic worry.

The widespread nationalizations had demoralized the private sector,

137

while disorganization prevented rapid investment and expansion in the hugely augmented public sector. The economy was in a shambles.

But how could the transition to a socialist economy be smooth? In Cuba (see Chapter 8) there certainly was dislocation in the early years, and Chile faced much greater obstacles. Allende did not have the power Fidel enjoyed in Cuba. Chile was still a pluralist democracy. The opposition still controlled the Congress. The economy was still open to international blackmail.

Added to these inherent difficulties was the intransigence of the opposition. At no time, one should remember, did the Allende government get over half the vote. He became president in 1970 with a smaller percentage of the vote than he had received when losing in 1964 (36.3 percent compared to 38.9 percent). In the local elections of April 1971 the UP parties received 49.7 percent, their high point. Subsequent months saw furious battles in every political arena—elections in unions, students' groups, and professional associations.

The UP itself was weakened by splits within its own ranks. The far left, led by the MIR (the *Movimiento de la Izquierda Revolucionaria,* or Movement of the Revolutionary Left), pressed for more radical action. They wanted faster nationalizations, tough police action against the opposition, and rule by decree. The moderates within the UP, including the Communists, urged caution, arguing that precipitous action would play into the hands of the rightists who could manipulate the military and the middle class.

By mid-1972 the political climate had become superheated. Massive street mobilizations by both pro- and anti-Allende forces became routine. In August shopkeepers staged a one-day boycott to protest government economic policies. In October a series of protests began to sweep the country. They began with the truckowners' suspension of shipments. Small businessmen, private farmers, and pilots joined in strikes. Although often orchestrated by opposition politicians, these eruptions showed that widespread sectors of the Chilean public would confront the government in the streets. Virtually all of them stood to lose if a socialist society were achieved; they were determined not to go down without a fight.

The government had its own mass support. Especially in the major cities, UP could on command turn out several hundred thousand disciplined marchers. Their ranks included the many Chileans who had already begun to experience significant changes—higher real wages, subsidized fresh milk, a role in administering their community or workplace. They also responded to the new nationalism—the takeover of the copper companies, the tough line toward all foreign firms, the highly publicized welcome to Fidel Castro when he came to Chile in 1971.

March 1973 brought another political test. At stake was the composition of the Congress. It was a crucial moment, because the opposition hoped to gain a two-thirds majority and thereby be able to impeach Allende, or at least hold commanding legal leverage over him. The elections brought a huge turnout. When the votes were counted, the government had done better than even it had dared to predict: UP got 43 percent, reducing the opposition's majority from 32 to 30 (out of 50) in the Senate and from 93 to 87 (out of 150) in the lower house. UP leaders jubilantly pointed to the increase in the leftist vote over 1970, noting that no previous Chilean president had ever been able to increase his support in a mid-term congressional election. The opposition pointed to its 55.7 percent vote as equivalent to Frei's landslide victory in 1964; they also reminded UP that its 43 percent was down from the 49.7 percent it had won in the 1971 municipal elections.

The election returns could be used to buttress almost any political position. One thing was certain: the opposition had not gotten the big electoral boost it had sought. And since it lacked a two-thirds congressional majority, any attempt at impeachment was foreclosed. Allende may have lacked an absolute majority, but he had rock-hard support among the workers and an increasing number of rural laborers.

There had never been a shortage of plots to overthrow the elected Marxist government. The rightist *Patria y Libertad* (Fatherland and Liberty) had already been engaged in terrorist attacks against government officials and vital economic installations. By 1973, however, more and more of the middle class had come to think there was no democratic solution to the crisis. They saw Allende (or the more radical left, which he couldn't or wouldn't control) as threatening the very basis of private property in Chile.

In April a strike of copper workers began, giving the opposition ideal grounds to claim multi-class resistance to Allende. In July the truckowners struck again, triggering a wave of strikes by middle-class associations such as lawyers, physicians, and architects. The pro-Allende mass labor organizations staged huge counterprotests, with marches including hundreds of thousands. Chile was in the grip of a feverish political battle. Terrorist incidents became frequent. Few thought it could remain peaceful until 1976, when the next president would be elected.

Allende knew this. He had long since rejected his far left's advice to resort to extralegal means, and he knew the Christian Democrats were the only political force that was strong enough and possibly willing to reach an agreement to reduce levels of conflict and thereby keep the country's democratic system intact. Allende negotiated with Frei and his fellow leaders, but after extended deliberation they refused. They did not want to be drawn into joint responsibility for a collapsing government unless Allende promised them more than he was prepared to give; equally important, they suspected they had much to gain from further discrediting of UP. They may even have suspected that a military coup would restore them to power.

Allende then played his last and most dangerous card: increasing military participation in his government. Although it might give short-term stability, since the armed forces were obliged to carry out commands and maintain order, it might also open the way to military intrigue and to opposition charges of politicizing the armed forces. Allende sensed the danger and in August attempted to shuffle his army commanders. But it was too late.

By early September the military conspiracy to depose the UP government was in high gear. Santiago seethed with rumors about Brazilian money and "destabilization" experts pouring into Chile. Strikes and counter-demonstrations had further slowed an economy already hit by hyperinflation and capital flight. Allende now knew that the fate of Chile's socialist experiment was in the hands of the military. General Carlos Prats, army commander-in-chief and minister of defense, was a key figure. Unfortunately for Allende and the UP, Prats' military prestige was slipping badly. Late in August he was submitted to the indignity (from the military viewpoint) of a noisy demonstration in front of his residence by army officers' wives demanding he resign. Outvoted at a generals' council the next day, he resigned both his army and cabinet posts. His successor as army chief was General Augusto Pinochet, widely believed to be as constitutionalist as Prats.

The military now lost little time; on September 11 a well-coordinated coup began. Early that morning the Special Services *carabineros,* long thought to best embody Chile's tradition of nonpolitical police, were still guarding the presidential palace against possible attack. Ominously, they pulled out when informed that their commander had joined the unfolding coup. At 6 A.M. Allende was told that the navy had seized Valparaíso, and he decided to go immediately from his residence to La Moneda, the landmark presidential palace in the heart of Santiago.

The rest of the morning saw frenzied activity at the palace, as the defenses were prepared. Allende began receiving offers of safe exit to exile. To one air force general's offer, he reportedly replied, "Tell General von Schouwen that the president of Chile does not flee in a plane. As he knows how a soldier should act, I will know how to fulfill my duty as president of the Republic."

Allende had not lived the life of a revolutionary. He had spent three decades as a parliamentary politician, ceaselessly negotiating to create and maintain coalitions. Not a few cynics (on both left and right) had suggested he was too fond of the good life to make a revolutionary. But Allende now chose to stand and fight. Just before noon air force Hawker Hunters attacked the palace with rocket fire, spreading flames

The presidential palace in central Santiago burst into flames under rocket attacks by the Chilean armed forces during the coup of September 11, 1973. (United Press International.)

through the building that had seen so many peaceful transfers of power. Allende died inside, whether by suicide or by fire from the invading troops remains uncertain. In an early presidential speech Allende had noted "Our coat of arms says 'By reason or force,' but it puts reason first." That order was now reversed.

The military commanders expected resistance, especially from the industrial and workers' housing areas, but government supporters had few arms. Resistance was scattered but the repression was rapid and brutal. We shall never know how many died—probably between 5000 and 15,000. It was the most violent military coup in twentieth century South American history, and it had happened in a country that prided itself on its deeply grounded democratic traditions. The "transition to socialism" that so many on the left thought to be "irreversible" was about to be reversed.

In retrospect, it appears that Allende's downfall resulted largely from the interplay between social classes and political parties that characterized contemporary Chile. The left drew its support mainly from the urban working-class. It met opposition from a cohesive upper class whose agrarian and industrial components were united by family ties and objective interests, and this unified elite was able to gain the allegiance of middle-sector groups (and some traditional peasants) and, most important of all, militant lower-middle-class activists, such as storekeepers and truckers, in a common stand against a socialist order. Between 1970 and 1973 the worker-based Allende movement was unable to form an enduring coalition with other strata in Chilean society. That explains its inability to win a clear majority at the polls, and hence its ultimate vulnerability.

This is not to discount the effects of opposition from the U.S., which worked steadily at "destabilizing" (that is, overthrowing) the Allende regime by passing dollars (which were highly valuable on the black market) to conservative groups and subsidizing anti-Allende strikes. Whether this actually caused the government's downfall remains unclear, since the Allende administration had a mountain of troubles of its own. Nonetheless, the U.S. once again placed itself squarely on the side of counterrevolutionaries.

The Pinochet Regime

The new military government promptly set out to impose a bureaucratic-authoritarian regime on Chile. Proclaiming its goal as "national reconstruction," the junta set about to destroy—not merely reform—the country's political system. Congress was dissolved, the Constitution suspended, and parties declared illegal or placed "in recess": there was to be no more political bickering, no more *politiquería*. The junta further imposed a state of siege, called a 9 o'clock curfew, and set strict limits on the media. In October 1973, one month after the coup, the military took over the proud universities as well.

The armed forces thus sought to establish firm control of the country and, in so doing, to revamp longstanding relationships between state and society in modern Chile. One critical component of this plan was the unity of the military, led by army general Augusto Pinochet. Another was the disarray of civilian society, which made it possible for the regime to dismantle (or at least repress) such intermediate institutions as political parties and labor unions and to establish direct authority. Political activity in its traditional sense came to a halt. In January 1974 General Pinochet announced that the military would remain in power for no less than five years. It would turn out to be more than that.

As the generals consolidated their political power, a group of civilian technocrats introduced far-reaching changes in economic policy. Known as "the Chicago boys" because so many had been trained at the University of Chicago, these economists believed strongly in the efficiency and fairness of market competition. What had restricted Chile's growth, they reasoned, was government intervention in the economy—which reduced competition, artificially increased wages, and led to inflation. To put the laws of supply and demand back to work, they set out to reduce the role of the state and also to cut back inflation. The ultimate goal, Pinochet once said, was "not to make Chile a nation of proletarians, but a nation of entrepreneurs."

The regime's programs had a clear effect on inflation, which was running at an annual rate of around 500 percent at the time of the coup. By 1976 it was down to 180 percent, still an astronomic level; by 1978 it was around 30–35 percent, and by 1982 it was down to 10 percent. Chile enjoyed large foreign exchange reserves and in the late 1970s the growth rate was 6 to 7 percent. Here the junta could justifiably claim success.

Other policies did not work as well. In late 1973 the state owned nearly 500 firms. The junta returned about half to their original owners and opened bids for many of the rest. The absence of true competition meant that sale prices were low, and the chief beneficiaries were local businessmen and multinational corporations such as ITT.

Economic policymakers also reduced barriers to imports on the ground that quotas and tariffs protected inefficient industries and kept prices artificially high. The result was that many local firms lost out to multinational corporations. The Chilean business community, which strongly supported the coup in 1973, began to feel the pinch.

By far the hardest hit group was the working class, particularly the urban working class. Unemployment was rampant, close to 30 percent in Santiago and over 40 percent in the construction industry alone. By the late 1970s there were approximately 500,000 unemployed workers in a country of 11 million people. There were no strikes, but that was due to repression. There were hardly any wage increases either.

One consequence of this was a contraction of demand, since workers and their families could afford to purchase fewer goods. The reduction in the market further threatened the business community, which started producing more goods for export and less for local consumption. This posed yet another obstacle to economic growth and led to increased concentration of income and wealth in the hands of a small elite.

The price of this stagnation became apparent in the foreign debt, which by early 1983 was $17 billion, the highest per-capita level in the world. Though seeking private investment, the Pinochet regime had to rely on loans instead. Ironically, Chile was attempting to create a free-market economy with assistance largely drawn from international organizations and other governments, not private banks and companies. In 1981 the economy took a nosedive, however. A massive capital outflow shook the banking system, and growth was a negative 7 percent in 1982. Unemployment shot up and bankruptcies abounded. Contributing to the crisis was a sharp drop in the world price of copper, still Chile's principal export. (Note the production trend in Figure 4-1.)

The junta pressed on with its policies and continued its tight hold over the nation. Its brutal tactics earned widespread condemnation from the international community, as critics denounced repeated and persistent violations of human rights. In September 1976 the issue had erupted in Washington, D.C., with the murder (by car bomb) of Orlando Letelier, a respected diplomat who had served as Allende's ambassador to the U.S. The incident prompted an immediate outcry, and evidence plainly suggested that the Pinochet regime had sponsored the assassination. This put a strain on relations with the U.S., especially in view of President Carter's stress on human rights, and increased the international isolation of the Chilean government. But the election of Ronald Reagan came as a great relief to the Pinochet government, which soon found Washington seeking closer relations.

By 1983 the prospects for transition were unclear. Through clever political maneuvering Pinochet achieved supreme authority, and what had at first been a thoroughly institutionalized military regime became highly personalized—with Pinochet alone commanding power. A plebiscite in 1978 produced the widespread appearance of support for Pinochet's "defense of the dignity of Chile," and another plebiscite in 1980 approved a constitution that could leave Pinochet in office until 1989. The death in early 1982 of Eduardo Frei, leader of the Christian Democrats, removed one of the few remaining major opposition figures from the scene.

The economy continued its downward spiral in 1982, as production dropped 14 percent, and popular protests erupted in mid-1983. Pinochet responded with a mixture of mild concessions (ending book censorship, permitting exiles to return) and brute force (firing workers in government-owned copper companies, arresting opposition leaders—including Gabriel Valdés, the former foreign minister who succeeded Frei as head of the Christian Democrats). Pot-clanging citizens and student marchers clamored for a return to political democracy, but Pinochet dug in his heels. Said he of the demonstrations and their implication: "It's all over, *señores.*" It was becoming hard to envision perpetuation of a regime so contrary to a country's political traditions, but it was far from clear whether and how it might be displaced.

FIVE

BRAZIL
Development for Whom?

With an area of more than 3 million square miles, Brazil occupies nearly half of South America. The 3900-mile Amazon River reaches from the steamy jungles of the interior to the Atlantic coast. Land ranges from the semiarid northeast, plagued by recurrent droughts, to the rich forests and fertile plateaus of the center and the south. The country abounds in natural resources, including iron and other industrial minerals, and it has long been regarded as a potential world power—the "sleeping giant" of Latin America. Perhaps because of this anticipation, and perhaps for other reasons, Brazilians tend to have an optimistic, ebullient outlook on life. One saying sums it up: "God is a Brazilian."

Brazil's relatively nonviolent acquisition of independence from Portugal in 1822 left the country with an auspicious start. The lack of large-scale conflict meant that physical and economic destruction was minimal, especially in comparison to the devastation wrought in the Río de la Plata region, in Venezuela, and in central Mexico. Nor did Brazil have to cope with the problems of demobilizing a massive military apparatus in the postwar period. And most important, the transition of the Portuguese monarchy to Brazil provided a coherent political structure endowed with the authority of time-tested tradition. There were struggles, to be sure, and Brazil would meet a crisis of political legitimacy before the end of the century. But it did not face the same kind of instability that other Latin Americans faced at the outset of independence.

The economy was mainly agricultural, and sugar was by far the largest commercial crop. By 1822 the population included about 4 million inhabitants, roughly half of whom were slaves of African birth or descent. The social order consisted principally of two tiers, the landowning aristocrats and the labor-producing slaves, a dichotomy that would come to be aptly and sympathetically described by Gilberto Freyre in his classic book, *The Masters and the Slaves*. There were some merchants and lawyers and other professionals, mainly in the cities and especially in Rio de Janeiro, but society was dominated by the forces of the countryside.

Dom Pedro I (1822–31)

Too often we define historical eras by the rise and fall of heads of state or government. Yet at times it makes sense. Few would contest the label "Victorian" for the era of Queen Victoria's reign from 1837 to 1901. And in nineteenth century Brazil, many basic social issues were bound up with the fate of the crown. Most obvious was the consolidation of Brazil's independence. Related issues involved the centralization or decentralization of authority and executive versus legislature power. These questions had to be faced immediately after independence because both the elite and the emperor wanted to write a Brazilian constitution.

Dom Pedro I had become the first emperor of a newly independent Brazil in 1822, when the Brazilian aristocracy forced a break with Portugal. A year earlier Pedro's father, Dom João VI, had left Brazil to resume the throne in Portugal, but only after advising his son to remain in Brazil (to which the royal family had become very attached), even if it meant creating a separate monarchy. Dom Pedro I called for a Constituent Assembly and the resulting elections in 1823 revealed several political divisions. Most basic was the split between the Brazilian Party and the Portuguese Party, the latter consisting of those who had opposed Brazilian independence and wanted to resubordinate Rio de Janeiro to Lisbon. Its leaders were primarily Portuguese-born, mostly military officers, bureaucrats, and merchants. The Brazilian Party was led by José Bonifácio Andrada e Silva, a São Paulo landowner who was the leading spokesman for Brazilian liberalism and the leading minister of Dom Pedro's government.

Despite majority support in the Assembly, José Bonifácio's ministry had to resign after three months because the Emperor continually endorsed the Portuguese Party's protest over the government's anti-Portuguese measures. Heated polemics continued and street fights broke out, as an extremist faction of the Brazilian Party called for decentralized rule and piled abuse on the crown. Amid the furious debate the emperor simply dissolved the Assembly in November 1824. Shortly thereafter he unilaterally decreed a constitution for Brazil. It included many features from a draft prepared by Antonio Carlos Andrada e Silva, José Bonifácio's brother, but reserved greater powers for the *Poder Moderador* (the "Moderating Power"), which was to be the monarch himself. Most important was the power to dissolve the Chamber of Deputies and to appoint and dismiss ministers. Citizen voting was tied to a high minimum-property test, thereby severely limiting public participation in an imperial government that was to be highly centralized. Ironically, this unilaterally decreed constitution included passages from France's 1789 Declaration of Human Rights.

The story of this constitution demonstrated several things about the new nation of Brazil: (1) the monarch had seemingly preserved his absolutist initiative by dissolving the elected Assembly and imposing his own constitution; but (2) the constitution, while favoring the crown in the division of powers, was more liberal than absolutist, more akin to the contemporary English parliamentary system than to the French; (3) the commitment to human rights, however qualified by the real intentions of Dom Pedro and his loyalist advisers, thenceforth became a lodestar in Brazilian history, an ideal to which libertarians and reformers would continuously repair. The struggle over the new country's political structure had ended ambiguously: a liberal charter imposed by an emperor who was thereby establishing limits on all future governments.

The absolutist aspects of events in Rio stirred concern in the Northeast, the region that had proved most receptive to the liberal ideas of abolition, federalism, and republicanism. Back in 1817 republican conspirators in Pernambuco province had stubbornly resisted the discipline of Rio. Dom Pedro's imposition of the constitution in 1824 provoked a new rebellion, which dramatized the key issues at the heart of Brazilian politics for the rest of the Empire.

The Pernambucans declared their independence anew in a manifesto poetically proclaiming the "Confederation of the Equator." This climaxed a violent reaction to Rio's attempt to depose a locally popular junta and impose one less radical. After gaining the support of other Northeastern provinces, the rebels called for their own Constituent Assembly. The movement split apart on the slavery issue, however, as one leader shocked his colleagues by calling for an end to the slave trade through the Northeastern port of Recife. Most of the rebel organizers feared a mobilization of the lower orders, and not without reason. Discontent of marginal free persons, many of color, was threatening to turn the anti-Portuguese, anti-centralist agitation into a social revolution.

The rebels' internal divisions in Pernambuco came as the military pressure from outside was growing. The emperor had hired English and French ships and mercenaries, and they taught the insurgents a bloody political lesson. Most of the rebel leaders were executed. There were limits to the range of permissible social protest in Brazil.

Rio's domination came only with British help, and that aid had its price. Having secured a favored foothold in the Brazilian economy since 1810, Britain now found itself underwriting the transition to Brazilian independence.

Britain could help consolidate the newly independent Rio government by facilitating diplomatic recognition from the world's principal powers. That goal was achieved by a series of 1825 agreements Britain negotiated with Portugal and Brazil. They provided that the Portuguese king, now Dom João VI, was to recognize Brazil as a separate kingdom; that British exports to Brazil would continue to receive a preferential tariff rate; and, not least important, that Brazil would pay Portugal an indemnization of two million pounds sterling for damages suffered in the struggle for independence. (This was exactly the debt that Portugal owed to Britain; the negotiators kept this provision secret.)

The following year, 1826, Britain got from Brazil a treaty commitment to end the slave trade by 1830. The British wanted this commitment for several reasons. One, usually stressed by modern-day economic historians, is that Britain feared that slave-produced sugar from Brazil would prove cheaper in the world market than sugar from the British West Indies, where slavery had recently been abolished. Another reason, also important, was the pressure on the British government generated by British abolitionists. The new Brazilian government, with little enthusiasm and less genuine commitment, gave the British the clause they demanded. Further concessions to the British were made in an 1827 trade treaty which put Brazilian exports to England at a disadvantage with exports from British colonies. Much of the Brazilian elite saw the concessions as excessive and only explicable by Dom Pedro's apparent desire to retain British good will toward Portugal, which desperately needed continued British economic help. Criticism would have been even more strident if the two-million-pound payment had been made public.

In the end, Dom Pedro's loyalty to Portugal proved his undoing in Brazil. His imposition of the new constitution had by no means ended the struggle over the division of governmental powers. In 1826 the emperor became the target of a new wave of attacks, whose authors ranged from the "moderates" wanting more power for the legislature and revisions in the treaties with Britain, to the "extremists" demanding a decentralization of power and autonomy for the provinces. The emperor's critics dominated the expanding press with their drumfire of invective.

In this same period Dom Pedro suffered a serious reverse in foreign policy. What is modern-day Uruguay had been annexed to Portuguese America in 1821 as the "Cisplatine Province." But in 1825 local guerillas seized power and proclaimed union with the United Provinces of the Río de la Plata (present-day Argentina). The resulting war between Brazil and the United Provinces ended in 1828 with a treaty that created an independent state, Uruguay. The British, again intermediaries in arranging the treaty, hoped for a buffer state between Argentina and Brazil. This setback to Brazilian ambitions in the Río de la Plata basin was financially and politically expensive for the emperor. But it soon faded in significance when compared to the quagmire of the Portuguese royal succession into which Dom Pedro had been drawn since 1826.

When Dom João VI died in 1826, Dom Pedro, his legal successor, knew that the Brazilians would never agree to a reunion with Portugal. But the emperor had become increasingly absorbed in trying to protect his daughter's succession rights in Portugal. That drain of energy made him less able to deal with the aggressively anti-absolutist political forces in Brazil. He found his position increasingly untenable, as his opponents mobilized street crowds to protest his preference for an absolutist ministry. On April 7, 1831, Dom Pedro I abdicated, departing the land whose independence he had helped to secure less than a decade earlier.

Dom Pedro's abdication was a victory for the Brazilian Party and a defeat for the beleaguered absolutists. It also created a power vacuum, because the emperor's son, later to become Dom Pedro II, was only five years old. His father had deliberately left him behind in the care of other royal family members in order to maintain the Braganza family's claim to the Brazilian throne. Who would exercise power in his name? Would the huge and thinly settled lands of Portuguese America hold together? Or would it follow the example of Spanish America, which immediately fissured into the patchwork of nations we see today?

For nine years after Dom Pedro I's abdication, a regency, of varying structure and membership, exercised executive power. In 1834 the constitution was amended (by the "Additional Act") to give increased powers to the provinces, partly in response to separatist sentiments that were rocking key areas of the Empire. The most violent was in the province of Pará in the Amazon valley, although the most dangerous, because of its location in a province bordering Argentina, was the *Guerra dos Farrapos* in Rio Grande do Sul.

Dom Pedro II (1840–89)

Dom Pedro II's accession to the throne in 1840 unified the divided elite. Brazil had survived the separatist challenges and halted the drift toward social revolution. Decentralization was discarded as the emperor assumed the wide powers (the "Moderating Power") his father had spelled out in the 1824 constitution. The young emperor and the politicans now settled into an era of relatively harmonious parliamentary politics.

The two decades after mid-century were the golden years of the Empire. Executive power was exercised by the emperor and his ministry, the latter dependent upon retaining the confidence of the lower house. Yet the legislature's ultimate power was more apparent than real, because the emperor could dissolve the Chamber at will, thereby necessitating new elections. Until the late 1860s, however, Dom Pedro II exercised his power discreetly and the system seemed to function well.

By 1850 two distinctive political parties had emerged—both owing their origin to the Brazilian Party of the 1820s. The parties were Conservative and Liberal, although historians have long cautioned against taking these labels too seriously. In 1853 the two parties collaborated to form a "conciliation cabinet," which held power, except for the 1858–62 interval, until 1868.

The Empire's most important test in foreign policy came in the Río de la Plata basin, the site of a long-time rivalry among Paraguay, Uruguay, Argentina, and Brazil. The Brazilian government became alarmed over the strength and intentions of Juan Manuel de Rosas, the autocratic ruler of Argentina, who was claiming the right to control all traffic on the Río de la Plata. This was a grave threat to Brazil, since the economies of its southern provinces relied heavily on access to the Plata basin river system.

At the same time Brazil was being drawn into a dangerous political battle in Uruguay, where Brazilians had gained a financial and commercial foothold. Brazilian troops were sent into domestic Uruguayan battles on the side of the "Colorado" faction, which prevailed. The Brazilians then turned to face Rosas. They were encouraged by the French and British, who chafed over the tough terms Rosas had imposed for economic access to Argentina. The anti-Argentine coalition prevailed. Foreign troops, assisted by Argentine rebels (the latter representing the soon-to-be dominant liberals), defeated the Rosas forces in 1852, sending Rosas to a permanent exile in England.

But that did not bring all combat to an end. Even with Brazilian support, the Colorados lost control in Uruguay. Since the victorious Blancos could no longer look to Rosas for help, they turned to Francisco Solano López, the dictator of Paraguay. Argentina, now controlled by the liberals, joined Brazil in support of the Colorados in Uruguay. The deepening foreign involvement there soon led to direct military confrontation between the Brazilians and the Paraguayans. Solano López wanted to expand his rule by allying with the Uruguayan Blancos to conquer the Brazilian province of Rio Grande do Sul. He invaded both Argentina and Brazil in 1865, pushing them and the Colorado government of Uruguay into a military alliance.

The ensuing war lasted five years. The Paraguayan army proved to be well trained, superbly disciplined, and extraordinarily brave. The Brazilians bore the brunt of the fighting on the other side. At first they suffered humiliating reverses, but then triumphed after greatly expanding their army.

The war had several important consequences: (1) access to the Río de la Plata river network was guaranteed, thus pleasing European traders, Argentine liberals, and the Brazilian military; (2) the two major powers, Argentina and Brazil, cemented close relations; (3) Brazil consolidated her position—both political and financial—in Uruguay; and (4) Paraguay was left with half (it is thought) of its population dead and the country in ruins.

The war also had a profound effect on politics within Brazil. The long combat forced Brazil to enlarge her army, whose officers soon became important actors in Brazilian politics. It had also provoked the emperor into unprecedented steps in asserting his authority. Pedro II demanded Paraguay's unconditional surrender, while the Liberals, who held a majority in Chamber, wanted by 1868 to negotiate. He dismissed the Liberal cabinet, which had strong majority support in the Chamber, and called for new elections. Some radical Liberals reacted angrily by forming a splinter group that in 1870 became the Republican Party. And the war threw a new light on that most national of institutions, slavery. The slaves recruited for the Brazilian army performed well in battle and were given their freedom in compensation. Their combat effectiveness must have given pause to more than a few of the white officers who were later called on to hunt down fugitive Brazilian slaves.

The End of the Empire

The final two decades of the Empire were dominated by debate over the legitimacy of two institutions: slavery and the monarchy. Both came under scrutiny during the Paraguayan War.

Although the slave trade effectively ended in 1850, slavery was by no means dead twenty years later. The rapidly growing coffee plantations demanded labor, and the planters turned to an obvious source: slaves from the economically decadent Northeast. Slaveowners there became alarmed at this loss of "capital," and succeeded in getting provincial laws that forbade slave exports to other provinces. Such measures came late, however, and even if every slave in the Northeast had moved south they could not have furnished the labor needed in the coffee economy of the late 1880s.

The only solution, according to the coffee planters, was increased immigration. In 1886 the province of São Paulo launched a major effort to attract European immigrants to Brazil. But the *paulistas* found themselves unable to attract the amount of cheap labor they needed. Why? Partly because of the persistence of slavery. This conclusion led some of the elite to become pro-abolitionist on the pragmatic grounds that immigrants could never be recruited quickly enough unless Brazil's retrograde image in Europe was transformed. Abolition would be the most obvious step.

The manner in which Brazil carried out abolition was unique in the Americas. Brazilian slavery was a nationwide institution, thus preventing the kind of sectional conflict that occurred in the U.S. Furthermore, Brazilian slaves had worked in virtually every job category, including many "skilled" ones. No less important, a large number of free persons of color had already established themselves economically, providing examples to the newly freed. Brazil had also escaped the extreme racist view that dismissed all persons of color as irremediably inferior. The large mixed-blood population, a few of whom had reached prominent national positions by 1889 (such as the novelist Machado de Assis, and the engineer-abolitionist André Rebouças), showed that some mobility was possible.

Abolition in Brazil was a seventeen-year process marked by three laws. The first came in 1871, when the Congress passed the "law of the free womb," which provided freedom for all children thenceforth born of slave mothers. But the masters were given the option of retaining labor rights over these children until the age of twenty one.

It was not until the 1880s that the abolitionist movement was again able to force slavery to the center of the political arena. The abolitionists were led by urban professionals, especially lawyers. Prominent among them was Joaquim Nabuco, a Pernambucan deputy of impeccable social origins. Led by such orators as Nabuco, the abolitionists became the Empire's first nationwide political movement, organizing clubs, newspapers, and public rallies in the major cities. They raised significant sums to finance their propaganda and to buy the freedom of local slaves.

This mobilization had its impact on the Parliament, which in 1885 passed the second abolitionist law. This one granted freedom to all slaves sixty or older, without compensation to the masters. Cynics ridiculed the measure, pointing out that few slaves ever survived to such an age, and if they did their masters would be delighted to be freed from caring for them. The new law did little to defuse the agitation of the abolitionists, some of whom began inciting slaves to flee from or rebel against the masters. By 1887 slavery was visibly disintegrating. Soldiers in the army, charged with catching and returning fugitive slaves, found their job more and more repugnant. In 1887 army officers formally refused to carry out this mission any longer.

By 1888 slave owners had had ample time to prepare for the transition to free labor. The final step was the "golden law," passed in May of that year, which freed all remaining slaves without compensation. The law was approved by an overwhelming vote in both the Chamber of Deputies and the Senate. The political elite had managed to preserve a consensus while dealing with a volatile socioeconomic issue. This success at incremental reform helped to perpetuate the Brazilian elite's self-image as conciliatory. Remarkably enough, this image has come to be shared by many of the non-elites, showing how their modern-day rulers have manipulated Brazilians' understanding of their own past.

The other major drama of the late Empire was the rise of republicanism. It had erupted earlier in the century, usually linked to regional demands for autonomy. The Republican Party, founded in 1871, also had a strong regionalist cast, especially in São Paulo. The birth of this party could be traced to Liberal deputies' reaction to Dom Pedro II's imposing, in 1868, a Conservative ministry in the face of a Liberal majority in the Chamber. In 1870 a group of indignant ex-Liberals founded the Republican Party.

At first the Republicans appeared harmless. Up to 1889 they never controlled the Chamber of Deputies, and they had a very uneven following. It was strongest in São Paulo, Rio Grande do Sul, and Minas Gerais; weakest in the Northeast. The Republicans wanted to replace the Empire with a republic headed by a directly elected president, governed by a bicameral legislature (with direct elections for both) and organized on federalist principles. In effect the Republicans wanted to trade Brazil's English-style constitutional monarchy for a U.S.-style federal republic.

During the 1880s republicanism made great inroads among the younger generation—the university-educated sons of planters, merchants, and professional men. Often they combined republicanism with abolitionism. Both sentiments were reinforced by the teachings of the Brazilian Positivists, a dedicated group that had penetrated faculties of higher education, especially in military colleges. Thus the 1880s saw a convergence of intellectual and political movements that were simultaneously eroding support for the monarchy and for slavery.

However, it was not high-minded debate that sealed the Empire's fate. It was the discontent of an institution the emperor had too long neglected: the army. In the late 1880s recurring friction mounted between army officers and the civilian politicians—often over the officers' rights to express publicly their political views. Because of the Paraguayan War, Brazil had created a much larger military than wanted by the politicians or Dom Pedro II, who provided meager financing for modernization of the army. By the 1880s there was a disproportionately high ratio of officers to troops. That led to frustration over delayed promotions among junior and middle-level officers, who became especially receptive to the abolitionist and republican sentiments that were so influential among their civilian counterparts.

The final agony of the Empire came in 1889. The emperor had insisted on trying to rule with a Conservative ministry, despite its minority position in the Chamber. In June the emperor invited the Viscount of Ouro Preto to form a cabinet. He succeeded and formulated an ambitious reformist program including administrative decentralization. But it was too late. A military plot developed in November. Led by Marshal Deodoro da Fonseca, the conspirators demanded Ouro Preto's resignation. An ultimatum was given the emperor: the monarchy was finished and he must leave. Dom Pedro II and his family calmly left for exile in Portugal. The Republic was proclaimed the next day, November 16, 1889.

The Empire had fallen with little upheaval. Although the planters had long feared that abolition would doom agricultural exports, they soon came to their senses. They now realized they could preserve their economic (and therefore political) dominance in a world without monarchs or slaves. Neither the abolition of slavery nor the overthrow of the Empire in themselves brought fundamental change in Brazil.

Overview: Economic Growth and Social Change

In the mid-nineteenth century the Brazilian economy began a fundamental transition, not tied to any legal or constitutional changes, that has continued well into the twentieth century. It has also had a profound impact on Brazilian society and on relations between social classes.

Like most of Latin America, Brazil has exported a few primary products to the North Atlantic economies at the center of the world-system. But in contrast to many other countries of the continent, Brazil has passed through a chronological sequence of dependence on the exportation of different products at different points in time. The repeated pattern of boom-and-bust has made it difficult to achieve sustained growth. And since the various products have come from differing areas of the country, these cycles have created regional pockets of prosperity and decline.

After independence was achieved, sugar continued to be the most lucrative export, as it had been during the eighteenth century. Produced mainly on large plantations in the Northeast, where labor came from slaves, sugar accounted for 30 percent of Brazilian exports in 1821–30. It then began a long decline, as competition mounted in the Caribbean, and by 1900 it contributed only 5 percent of the overall export amount (though domestic consumption was and has remained substantial).

Rubber production started in the early nineteenth century, principally in the Amazon, and steadily increased. By 1853 the port of Belém was exporting more than 2500 tons of natural rubber. Demand in the industrial world grew enormously in the wake of Charles Goodyear's discovery of the vulcanization process—which prevented rubber from getting too sticky in hot weather and brittle in the cold. A spectacular boom arrived in 1900–13, when rubber amounted to about one-third of all the country's exports. Then the British capitalized on the more efficient rubber plantations they had developed in the East Indies, and the world price went into sharp decline. The Brazilians were unable to withstand the competition, and the rubber boom came to a sudden and permanent end.

It was coffee that provided the most durable stimulus to economic change in the postindependence era. Coffee production began to develop in the Caribbean in the early nineteenth century and then took hold in Brazil, where it enjoyed excellent natural conditions. The volume of Brazilian exports held fairly steady until the 1890s, then entered a period of spectacular growth. In 1901 Brazil exported nearly 15 million sacks of coffee (at 60 kilograms each) and produced nearly three-quarters of the total world supply. Early in the century coffee yielded about one-half of the country's foreign exchange.

Coffee thus became a central feature of Brazilian life. The state of the economy was directly related to the international market: when coffee prices were high, the prospects for Brazil were positive; if they were down, so was the national outlook. And the domestic consumption of coffee has long been an essential aspect of social life, as Brazilians conduct meetings and discussions over cup after cup of steaming coffee, usually taken with large quantities of sugar. A proverb gives the recipe

In the late nineteenth century sacks of coffee left São Paulo's plantations on mule trains and eventually reached overseas destinations. (Courtesy of the Library of Congress.)

for coffee: "As strong as the devil, as black as ink, as hot as hell, and as sweet as love."

Coffee production flourished in southern-central Brazil, particularly in the state of São Paulo. It requires ample land, a fair investment, and much labor. Coffee trees yield full production only after six years, and they need steady care. Berries need to be gathered, washed, and shelled. The beans inside the berries must be dried, sifted, sorted, sacked, and stored. This requires labor.

Like Argentina, Brazil turned its eyes to Europe. First the state of São Paulo and then the national government initiated programs that attracted millions of European immigrants, especially in the last quarter of the nineteenth century. The largest portion, perhaps a third of the total, came from Italy. But the relative size of the immigrant population never reached the same level as in Argentina. The peak for Brazil was 6.4 percent in 1900, and it declined after that.

In retrospect it is ironic to realize that this wave of European newcomers probably helped distort, at least regionally, Brazil's long-term economic development. Although ample labor was available in the Brazilian Center and Northeast, where the number of jobs had fallen disastrously behind the increase in workers, the prophets of immigration opted for Europeans, who would presumably be better workers and more reliable future citizens. So the Brazilian government paid the ocean passage of millions of Europeans, while millions of Brazilians in Minas Gerais, Rio de Janeiro, and the Northeast could not afford to move south. Great contributions were made by the transplanted Europeans and Japanese; but each of those jobs might have been held by a Brazilian who would have been rescued from the economically moribund regions.

Technology was harder to obtain. There was and is no quick substitute for technology—one of the most essential features of modern economies. In the capitalist world it has proved extremely difficult to buy technology by itself. The Brazilians, like other populations outside the dynamic North Atlantic industrial complex, found themselves having to accept direct investment by foreign firms in order to get technology. The telegraph system, for example, arrived with British and American firms, which installed and operated their own equipment. The same held true for railroads, electric utilities, and shipping—most of the infrastructure needed to sustain the growing agro-export economy. These were highly visible investments and later became convenient targets for nationalist attacks.

Capital was also sought abroad. Much came with the technology described above. It also came in the form of loans to Brazil on the state and national level. In 1907, for example, the states of São Paulo, Minas Gerais, and Rio de Janeiro signed a coffee marketing agreement to be financed by foreign creditors. The state governments planned to repay the loans with the receipts from export taxes on coffee. Such commitments obligated Brazil not only to repay loans, but also to finance the remission of profits (and eventually capital) on direct investments by foreigners. The crucial question was the *terms* on which all these transactions took place. Available data suggest that the profit rate on foreign-owned railways, to take an obvious example, did not exceed rates for comparable investments in Britain. But this question has yet to be systematically researched.

Throughout the years between 1889 and 1930 the center of the Brazil economy moved south and southwest. The primary push came from the "march" of coffee, as planters found it cheaper to break new ground than to recycle the plantation soils whose yields were dropping. The result was a path of abandoned plantations, stretching from Rio de Janeiro and Minas Gerais down into São Paulo and its vast interior.

The reliance on coffee entailed large-scale risks. One was overproduction. It was difficult to anticipate demand six years in advance, and therefore when trees should be planted. Furthermore, the yield would depend on weather and other unforeseeable factors. In 1906, for example, Brazil produced 20 million sacks of coffee for a world market that could absorb only 12 or 13 million. A political question promptly arose: What should be done with the surplus?

A related uncertainty came from the rise of foreign competition, especially in Africa and other parts of Latin America. Brazil's share of the world market declined from 75 percent in 1900 to 67 percent in 1930 to only 32 percent in 1970 and 18 percent in 1978. With time the country gradually lost its near-monopoly on supply.

A third source of vulnerability came from wide fluctuations in the world price. This reflected not only the effects of competition, but also changes in demand. Coffee is essentially a luxury, though habit-forming, and its consumption can be reduced in times of hardship. Between 1929 and 1931, after the Great Depression struck, the price of coffee plummeted from 22.5 cents a pound to merely 8 cents. Frequent oscillations led to wide variation in Brazil's foreign-exchange earnings from year to year—and in government revenues, which came primarily from export duties.

To illustrate both the growth and the uncertainty of the Brazilian coffee sector, Figure 5-1 displays the volume of the country's coffee exports during the period from 1860 to 1960. The rise in output and commerce is clearly visible. So are the fluctuations, which mainly reflect the instability of world demand.

A final hazard derived from the small number of purchasers. In the late nineteenth and early twentieth century Brazil sold between three-fifths and three-quarters of its exports to only three countries: the

FIGURE 5-1   Coffee Exports from Brazil, 1860–1960

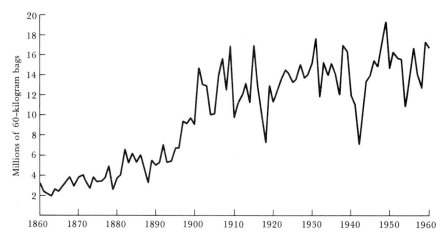

Source: Werner Baer, *Industrialization and Economic Development in Brazil* (Homewood, Ill.: Richard D. Irwin, 1965), pp. 266–267.

United States, Britain, and Germany. The U.S. was the largest single buyer and became as well the largest source of foreign investment (accounting for roughly half the total by 1960). The reliance on two or three customers created not only close but highly unpredictable ties to outside economies, as Brazil discovered after the crash of 1929. It could lead to political problems as well.

Prominent politicians and economists regarded this vulnerability as an inevitable result of Brazil's "agrarian vocation." Brazil, they argued, had no choice but to buy needed foreign finished goods with the funds earned by exports and augmented by direct foreign investments or loans. Any significant attempt to industrialize, they reasoned, would produce inferior goods and jeopardize relations with foreign buyers and creditors. Furthermore, Brazil could not hope to take the U.S. as a model for industrialization "because we don't have the superior aptitudes of their race," in the words of a Brazilian cabinet minister of the 1890s. Brazil must live, and would be forced to live, with what God gave it: a comparative advantage in a few agricultural exports.

Since the late Empire, however, a handful of intellectuals and men of business began disputing this logic. They argued that Brazil should stimulate home industry and monitor carefully economic ties with foreign countries, especially Britain and, later, the U.S. These critics had little influence on key policy areas such as tariffs or exchange rates. Yet they did succeed in creating a "nationalist" critique that was to prove important after 1930.

Official encouragement of industrialization came forth in 1890, when a tariff revision provided mild protection for local manufacturing from foreign competition (and also lowered the duties on capital goods required for production). Engineering schools sprouted in Recife, São Paulo, Pôrto Alegre, and Bahia. By 1907 the country had about 3000 industrial establishments, most of them small, textiles and foodstuffs being the principal products. By 1920 the number had grown to more than 13,000.

Brazil's industrial sector underwent large-scale expansion in the 1930s and 1940s, as the Great Depression and World War II both reduced the available supply of manufactured goods from abroad (as happened elsewhere in Latin America too). As with coffee, the center of industrial growth was in the state of São Paulo—where 15 percent of the nation's population was producing about 50 percent of the country's manufactured goods by 1940.

The upsurge continued thereafter, and Brazil moved into such heavy industries as steel and automobile production. Between 1947 and 1961 manufacturing output increased at an annual rate of 9.6 percent, compared to 4.6 percent for the agricultural sector. By 1960 industrial production amounted to more than 25 percent of the gross domestic product, and by 1975 it was up to nearly 30 percent. This diversification of the economy helped reduce Brazilian dependence on the outside world, and lent credibility to claims that the country would someday join the ranks of superpowers.

These economic transformations brought about far-reaching changes in the Brazilian social structure. One result was urbanization. In 1920 about 25 percent of the population lived in urban areas, and by 1980 about three-fifths lived in cities. But there are two unusual features in this trend. First, the tendency toward urbanization in Brazil has been *later* and *slower* than in many other Latin American countries. Second, Brazil does not have a single predominant city (like Buenos Aires or Montevideo, for instance). São Paulo and Rio de Janeiro have both become megalopises, with millions of inhabitants and the amenities and complications of urban life, but between them they contain only about 10 percent of the national population of 126 million. Urbanization has taken place in Brazil, but the cities coexist with a large and populous countryside.

Consequently Brazil has developed an intricate social structure. The upper-class elite includes landowners, frequently divided among themselves, as when *paulista* coffee planters rose up in the nineteenth century to challenge the sugar barons of the Northeast. In the course of the twentieth century there appeared as well an industrial elite, a new and vigorous group that would struggle for status and wealth, sometimes using the power of the state in pursuit of its means.

The popular masses were varied too. There has been, and remains, a large-scale peasantry, consisting of those who eke out meager livings from the soil. There is a rural proletariat, in the coffee fields and elsewhere, a stratum that performs wage labor in the countryside. And in the interior there are indigenous and other groups that have little contact with national society and who are for the most part marginal to it.

An organized working class of substantial size, perhaps 2 million by 1970 and certainly more by 1980, emerged within Brazilian cities. Its struggles with employers and its constant manipulation by the state provide one of the central themes in twentieth century Brazilian life. There is also a large stratum of chronically unemployed city dwellers, often migrants from the backlands who find shelter in the slums of Rio and São Paulo.

In between the upper and lower classes, middle sectors gradually appeared. Their size is difficult to estimate: they may now include as much as 30 percent of the people in some cities, though their share of the national population is less than that (perhaps 10 to 15 percent). They play important roles in commerce and the professions, and they have a particularly intimate relationship with one major institution: the military.

Social status in Brazil is not just a function of occupation or wealth. It is also a matter of race. The massive importation of slave labor from Africa brought an additional ethnic dimension into Brazilian society and this in turn has affected customs and attitudes.

There tends to be a strong correlation between race and social standing in Brazil: most on top are white, most blacks are on the bottom, and mixed-bloods are largely in between. Some institutions, such as naval officers and the diplomatic corps, long remained white. But in Brazil race is not defined purely on biological grounds. It is a social concept, open to interpretation. To be "black" one has to be totally black (in contrast to the U.S., where partly black in ethnic origin means black). Mulattos in Brazil have considerable opportunity for upward mobility, and for this reason miscegenation has been viewed by one scholar as a kind of social "escape hatch."

This is not to say that Brazil constitutes a racial paradise. Prejudice and bias have existed. For the last century most of the Brazilian elite has placed its faith in *branqueamento* ("bleaching"), with the unequivocally racist intention of purging Brazil of the presumably "negative" influence of black blood. The overall correlation between status and race continues to exist, despite the denial of well-to-do Brazilians. Several recent studies by a Brazilian demographer have shown significant differences in income by race (controlling for all other factors), based on official 1976 and 1980 data. The conclusion to be drawn is that race is a separate and significant variable in the Brazilian socioeconomic system. But mobility exists, marriage across color lines is common, and attitudes are more open than has been true in North American history.

Racial differentiation in Brazil has posed one obstacle, however modest, to the formation of durable coalitions between social strata and groups. Another obstacle is the sheer geographical size of Brazil. Distance (and poor communications) made it for a long time implausible to imagine a long-lasting alliance between urban workers of São Paulo, for example, and the landless peasants in the Northeast. Such natural divisions enabled Brazil to attempt political solutions that would have been immediately impossible in more densely populated and integrated countries such as Cuba.

The First Republic (1889–1930)

Although the military overthrew the Empire, civilian politicans shaped the new republic. A Constituent Assembly was elected and produced a new constitution in 1891. It was a virtual copy of the U.S. constitution, as its principal author, Bahian delegate Rui Barbosa, had intended. Brazil became a federation of twenty states and the Brazilian president was to be elected directly and empowered to intervene in the states in case of threatened separation, foreign invasion, or conflict with other states. Suffrage was restricted to literate adult male citizens. This resulted in fewer than 3.5 percent of the population voting in any presidential election before 1930, and only 5.7 percent in 1930.

After electing Deodoro da Fonseca president, and another Marshal, Floriano Peixoto, vice president, the Assembly rapidly collided with Deodoro over his financial policy and his interventions in the new state governments. In November 1891, plagued by ill health, Deodoro resigned, passing power to Floriano Peixoto, the so-called Iron Marshal. Floriano soon encountered a rash of revolts erupting over Brazil. In Rio Grande do Sul, revolt was part of the deadly conflict between local factions; in Rio de Janeiro, it was a naval revolt led by monarchist officers. Both rebellions were crushed, as the new republic used censorship, martial law, and executions. When Prudente de Morais of São Paulo was elected in 1894 as the first civilian president, the new regime had gained stability. But it came at the price of having to recognize the legitimacy of the entrenched oligarchical regime in each state.

Who were those oligarchs and how did they hold power? In every state a tightly organized political machine emerged, dedicated to monopolizing power. In states such as São Paulo and Minas Gerais, where the Republican Party had been strong before 1889, the "historic Republicans" controlled state government. In Bahia and the Northeast, which had few Republicans before 1889, power went to those politicans who most quickly established credentials as new-born Republicans. The resulting power structure was a "politics of the governors" at the national level, and "the rule of the colonels" (*coronelismo*) at the local level. The colonels were actually small-town and rural bosses who could produce bloc votes in any election. In return, they obtained control over state and national funds spent in their area of influence. At the state level the political leaders used their deals with the colonels to bargain on the national level with leaders from other states.

The chief prize in such bargaining was the presidency. As might be expected, the states enjoyed very unequal influence in this process. São Paulo and Minas Gerais were the most important, with Rio Grande do Sul able to tip the balance when the two larger states were at odds. Bahia, Rio de Janeiro, and Pernambuco were second-level states, often serving as power bases for dissident presidential nominees, although none was ever elected during the Old Republic (1889–1930).

The constitutional decentralization created by the republic allowed several states with dynamic economies, especially São Paulo, to gain virtual autonomy over their own development. Between 1890 and 1920 the state of São Paulo more than trebled its population. It had contracted a foreign debt larger than the national government and was accounting for 30 to 40 percent of Brazil's national output. Able to impose its own taxes on interstate commerce, it had, from the standpoint of the federal government, achieved a remarkable self-sufficiency. Only a loose federal structure could have allowed São Paulo's extraordinary burst of economic development ("the locomotive pulling the 20 empty boxcars," said *paulista* chauvinists), later to propel Brazil's rise to world prominence in the mid-twentieth century.

Brazil's relatively smooth-running political machine ran into trouble soon after the First World War. The political system created by the Republicans in the 1890s had not survived long in its original form. The first major crisis grew out of preparations for the 1910 elections. The "official" choice for president was Governor João Pinheiro of Minas Gerais, who died unexpectedly in 1908. The crisis deepened when the incumbent president, Affonso Pena, died in 1909, eighteen months before the end of his term. A bitter struggle ensued, with Marshal Hermes da Fonseca, son of the Republic's first chief executive, becoming the "official" candidate. He won, but for the first time there was a significant opposition movement. It supported Rui Barbosa, the liberal crusader from Bahia.

During Hermes da Fonseca's presidency (1911–15) many of the smaller states experienced bitter battles within the political elite—usually between the incumbent machine and dissenters. The lines of conflict often followed pre-republican patterns of family and class struggles. These battles made it impossible to return to the smoothly functioning "politics of the governors," not least of all because Presi-

FIGURE 5-2 *Café com Leite:* Brazilian Presidents by State, 1889–1930

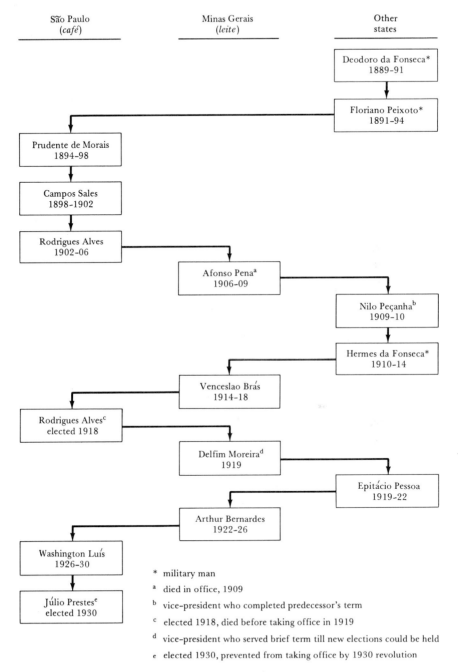

São Paulo
(*café*)

Minas Gerais
(*leite*)

Other
states

Deodoro da Fonseca*
1889–91

Floriano Peixoto*
1891–94

Prudente de Morais
1894–98

Campos Sales
1898–1902

Rodrigues Alves
1902–06

Afonso Pena[a]
1906–09

Nilo Peçanha[b]
1909–10

Hermes da Fonseca*
1910–14

Venceslao Brás
1914–18

Rodrigues Alves[c]
elected 1918

Delfim Moreira[d]
1919

Epitácio Pessoa
1919–22

Arthur Bernardes
1922–26

Washington Luís
1926–30

Júlio Prestes[e]
elected 1930

* military man

[a] died in office, 1909

[b] vice-president who completed predecessor's term

[c] elected 1918, died before taking office in 1919

[d] vice-president who served brief term till new elections could be held

[e] elected 1930, prevented from taking office by 1930 revolution

Explanation: The power of two preeminent states—São Paulo, a coffee-producing area, and Minas Gerais, a dairy state—led to a series of presidential bargains during the Old Republic (1889–1930) which Brazilians have nicknamed "the politics of coffee and milk" (*café com leite*). Rio Grande do Sul was another significant state, and the military played an important intermediary and supervisory role.

dent Hermes usually sent federal troops to the dissidents' aid. Formally, at least, the system continued functioning until October 1930. The "official" presidential nominees were invariably elected, and the federal Congress remained under the control of the state machines.

Yet the constitutional structure and political culture of the Old Republic had become targets for criticism and ridicule from every quarter. Prominent among the critics was a new generation of the elite, born with the Republic. Most were educated as lawyers. They denounced as corrupt the way the politicians were running the republic. Most traced this to the republic's founders, whom they accused of having imposed on Brazil a liberalism for which it was utterly unprepared. Necessary changes could be found only after a careful analysis of where Brazil stood—economically, socially, politically, and intellectually. In a word, Brazilian problems need Brazilian diagnoses and Brazilian solutions. They described themselves as "Brazilians who think like Brazilians: American, Latin and tropical." Leaders of this group included Oliveira Vianna, sociologist and lawyer; Alceu Amoroso Lima, literary critic and essayist; and Gilberto Amado, essayist and politician. Their mentor was Alberto Tôrres, a restless Republican of the older generation who had become disillusioned during his years as governor of the state of Rio de Janeiro and subsequently as a justice of the federal Supreme Court.

Criticism from intellectuals was paralleled by a mutinous mood among younger army officers. There was a series of barracks revolts in 1922 and 1924, led by lieutenants (*tenentes*). The 1924 revolts, which began in São Paulo and Porto Alegre, were the most serious. But the rebel officers fled and held out for two and a half years as guerrillas on a 25,000 kilometer march through the interior of Brazil. It was dubbed the "Prestes Column," after Luíz Carlos Prestes, a rebel lieutenant who was later to lead Brazil's Communist Party for more than thirty years.

The rebels' formal manifestos were vague, emphasizing the need for fair elections and honest government, along with attention to the nation's social needs. A more immediate complaint focused on professional concerns—anachronistic training, obsolete weapons, unresponsiveness from civilian governments, and poor prospects for promotion. This frustration was reminiscent of the late Empire, when army officers had both professional and intellectual reasons for supporting a coup against the crown.

Another powerful political current of the 1920s was the Democratic Party, founded in São Paulo in 1926. Its leaders, typified by coffee-baron Antonio Prado, agreed that the Old Republic was a fraud, not because of too much democratic liberalism, but because of too little. The party's support came from the urban professionals, disgusted at seeing their votes cancelled out by rural voters mobilized by the federal government's machine. They wanted what the European middle classes had won in the nineteenth century: political power through an electoral system that gave them a major role in government. It was no accident that this current of "liberal constitutionalism" made its strongest showing in São Paulo, the center of the fastest economic growth and urbanization. It was the voice of "modern" Brazil speaking out against the disproportionate influence of their country's "backward" regions.

Economic development in the late nineteenth century had created a working class in three or four major cities. Workers' first organization came in "mutual-aid societies," which did very little. They were superseded in the early 1900s by anarchist and anarcho-syndicalist organizers who were far more militant. In the decade after 1910, the anarchist and anarcho-syndicalist unions staged a variety of strikes, including several attempted general strikes. Sooner or later, they met heavy repression. The Spanish or Italian-born leaders were deported, while Brazilian leaders were jailed, beaten, and harassed. By 1921 the organized urban movement was a shambles.

In subsequent years social welfare laws were passed, as a tardy carrot to accompany the omnipresent stick. But Brazilian workers had many fewer organizing rights and welfare provisions than, for example, Chilean workers in the same era. One reason was the continuous labor surplus in Brazil, especially for unskilled or semi-skilled jobs. In the face of such numbers, Brazilian workers found it hard to organize themselves.

One result of the repression was the decline of anarchist and anarcho-syndicalist leadership and their replacement, in many cases, by communists, whose Brazilian party was founded in 1922. The communist presence furnished a new target for the authoritarians among civilians and military. By 1930 urban labor, although growing steadily in economic importance, was a political orphan. Meanwhile, employers saw no reason to change the autocratic manner in which they had long dealt with their workers.

Getúlio Vargas and the Estado Nôvo

The world economic crash of 1929 hit Brazil, like the rest of the Americas, very hard. As world trade contracted, the coffee exporters suffered a huge drop in foreign exchange earnings. Despite the crisis President Washington Luís clung to a hard-money policy. In effect that meant guaranteeing convertibility of the Brazilian currency (*mil reis*) into gold or British sterling. The Brazilian government should have frozen all transactions immediately. The gold and sterling reserves were quickly exhausted, forcing the government to suspend convertibility of the *mil reis*. The government was left in a deepening balance-of-payments crisis and the coffee growers were stuck with an unsellable harvest.

Given coffee's great importance to the Brazilian economy, one might have expected the government to rush in with help. But it did not. Instead, it tried to please foreign creditors by maintaining convertibility. Such were the money principles preached by the foreign bankers and economists who set the terms for Brazil's relations with the world economy. At a critical moment, the Brazilian government decided to stick with an economic policy which had no support from even one major sector in Brazilian society.

Not surprisingly, Washington Luís did not last out his term. As in 1889, it was the military that did the job. An opposition movement had coalesced around Getúlio Vargas, a Riograndense politician who had run for president earlier in 1930 and been defeated by Júlio Prestes, the "official" candidate who had been endorsed by Washington Luís. In this campaign Vargas had *not* challenged the political system. He ran strictly from within the elite. His supporters were dissenting factions in several states, outsiders anxious for their chance at power. It was only after the election, the loss of which Vargas had expected, that a successful conspiracy arose among the disgruntled politicians and officers.

The coup of October 1930 did not constitute a "revolution." The top military commanders deposed Washington and then passed power to Vargas as president of a provisional government. The cabinet invoked revolutionary power in order to take arbitrary and ad hoc steps they thought necessary. Yet 1930 is a watershed in modern Brazilian history, even if it was not comparable to the Mexican Revolution of 1910–20 or Cuba's transformation after 1959.

When Getúlio Vargas moved into the presidential palace in November 1930 few guessed how important a leader he would become. He was there only because a conflict within the national political elite was turning into armed warfare. It never reached a climax only because the military intervened. After the senior commanders had deposed Washington Luís, some officers wanted to retain power themselves, but the pressure whipped up by the Liberal Alliance's mobilization was too great: after only four days in power the three commanders transferred power to Vargas, who became provisional president. He held that post for four years. Since there was no legislature the president governed by decree. Meanwhile, important shifts were occurring among the nation's political forces.

First, Vargas moved swiftly to replace the governors in all the states except one, Minas Gerais. The replacements, or "interventors," reported directly to the president. This was a prelude to later battles over state autonomy, such as the president's drive to reduce the size of the state militia. Such activism from the central government often threw the state machines off balance and gave benefit to the dissenting factions, many of which had supported Vargas in the 1930 election. As in the Hermes da Fonseca presidency, political rivalries within states were being settled by decisions in Rio.

A second major development was a realignment of political forces in São Paulo. Vargas's interventor (João Alberto) had proved inept and tactless in handling the touchy *paulistas*. Their heightened sense of state loyalty and their fury at João Alberto united São Paulo against Vargas. Its leaders demanded that Vargas fulfill his promise to call a Constituent Assembly that would write a new constitution. In 1932 the *paulista* frustration finally erupted into an armed rebellion. The state militia, aided by enthusiastic volunteers, fought federal forces to a standstill for four months in the Constitutionalist Revolution. The rebels had to surrender because they were trapped by the federal forces' encirclement of São Paulo City. By their armed attempt at separatism, the *paulistas* further discredited the cause of decentralized government and strengthened the hand of the centralizers in Rio.

A third significant political development was the disintegration of the *tenente* movement. These young military officers had never achieved a cohesive organization. Some accompanied Vargas into power in 1930. Others founded the October 3rd Club to focus effort on achieving more radical social changes than those propounded in the 1920's, but their movement was isolated and vulnerable. Before long police raided the club premises and the group disintegrated.

Meanwhile, Vargas was strengthening his own network of political allies and collaborators. His success became obvious during the Constituent Assembly of 1933–34. The new constitution, the second for republican Brazil, was not startingly different from the first (1891). State autonomy was reduced: states could no longer tax goods shipped interstate. Yet it continued the bicameral legislature, which was to be directly elected, as was the president (except the first). Some nationalist measures appeared for the first time, placing restrictions on foreign ownership of land and on alien participation in professional occupations (such as law and medicine). The modest nature of these constitutional changes simply confirmed that the Revolution of 1930 had grown out of elite in-fighting and the continuous tension between centralization and state autonomy. The Constituent Assembly's most important act was to elect Vargas as the first president with a four-year term under the new constitution.

In 1934 Brazil entered one of the most agitated periods in its political history. Attention focused on two nationally based and highly ideological movements, both committed to mass mobilization. One was Integralism, a fast-growing rightist movement with affinities to European fascist parties. Founded in late 1932 and led by Plínio Salgado, an ambitious if minor literary figure, the Integralists claimed a rapidly growing membership throughout Brazil by 1935. Their dogma was Christian, nationalist, and traditionalist. Their style was paramilitary: uniformed ranks, highly disciplined street demonstrations, and aggressive rhetoric. They were essentially middle-class and drew support from military officers, especially in the navy. Unknown to the public, the Integralists' ambitious activities were financed in part by the Italian Embassy.

At the other end of the spectrum was a popular front movement, the National Liberation Alliance (*Aliança Libertadora Nacional,* or ALN), launched in 1935. Ostensibly a coalition of socialists, communists, and miscellaneous radicals, it was in fact run by the Brazilian Communist Party, which was carrying out a Latin American strategy formulated at the 1935 Comintern meeting in Moscow. The first stage of the strategy in Brazil would be an above-ground mobilization on conventional lines: rallies, local offices, and fund-raising efforts to forge a broad coalition on the left in opposition to the new Vargas government, the Integralists, and the Liberal Constitutionalists.

By mid-1935 Brazilian politics had reached a fevered pitch. The Integralists and the ANL were feeding off each other, as street brawls and terrorism increased. Brazil's major cities began to resemble the Nazi-Communist battles in Berlin of 1932–33. But the ANL was far more vulnerable than the Integralists. There could be little doubt where the government preference lay. In July 1935 the government moved against the ANL, with troops raiding offices, confiscating propaganda, seizing records, and jailing leaders.

The communists now moved to the second stage of their strategy: a revolutionary uprising. It was to be triggered by a barracks revolt, led by party members or sympathizers among officers in the army. The insurrection began in November 1935 in the Northeastern state capital of Natal, spreading within days to Recife and Rio. From the rebel standpoint, it was a disaster. Although the Natal rebels controlled the city for several days, their comrades in Recife and Rio, who lacked the advantage of surprise, were contained in their garrisons and quickly forced to surrender.

Vargas and the military now had a perfect opportunity to request a "state of siege," which would revoke normal constitutional guarantees. The Congress rapidly voted it. Vested with its new emergency powers, the federal government imposed a crackdown on the entire left—with arrests, torture, and summary trials. The Integralists were elated. With their chief rival eliminated, they began to smell power. What could be more logical than for Vargas to turn to the only cohesive nation-wide movement on the right?

It took two years for that illusion to be destroyed. Plínio Salgado and his collaborators were becoming more and more convinced that they would reach power by the 1938 presidential election, if not by other means. But Vargas had other ideas. On November 10, 1937, he took to the radio and read the text of yet another constitution to a nation that had just witnessed yet another military intervention. That morning the Congress had been dissolved, its premises occupied by soldiers. Brazil thus entered the *Estado Nôvo,* a legal hybrid combining elements of Salazar's Portugal and Mussolini's Italy. All the democratic hopes and promises that had grown since 1930 were gone. Brazil had succumbed to its own brand of authoritarianism.

Brazil's lurch into dictatorship in 1937 certainly fit the era. But was there more than a superficial similarity between Brazil's *Estado Nôvo* and European fascism? Where, for example, was the mass mobilization so typical of Hitler's Germany and Mussolini's Italy? Were the Integralists to play that role? Many—both inside and outside Integralist ranks—certainly thought so.

Like the Nazis in 1932, the Integralists in 1937 debated not *whether* they should enter government, but *on what terms.* Salgado, their leader, rejected Vargas's tentative offer of a cabinet post. Salgado thought he could hold out for more. In fact, Vargas and the military were playing their own game.

By early 1938 the greenshirts had become very frustrated. Soon after the coup the government had banned all paramilitary organizations. The obvious target was the Integralists, some of whom decided to take matters into their own hands. In February they organized an armed assault on the presidential residence. It was a *tour de force* of military incompetence, but the president's security forces seemed equally inept. There was a shoot-out and a stand-off during the early morning hours at the palace gates. The farce ended at dawn, when army units arrested the remaining Integralist besiegers. The government cracked down and the Integralist movement in effect disappeared, as Salgado fled into exile.

Vargas could now survey a political scene that no longer offered any organized opposition. In the coup Vargas had appointed himself to another presidential term, to last until the elections, scheduled for 1943. Few took that commitment seriously, given the ease with which Vargas had aborted the election that was to have been held in 1938. That skepticism was well founded. When 1943 arrived, Vargas announced that the wartime emergency precluded elections. He remained president until October 1945.

What was the significance of Vargas's authoritarian rule from 1937 to 1945? First, Vargas and his political and technocratic collaborators got a free hand in maneuvering to maximize Brazil's advantage in a capitalist world-system moving toward war. At stake were two central and related questions about Brazil's international role. Who could best help the Brazilians to modernize and equip their armed forces? And who could offer the most favorable conditions in foreign trade?

Before the coup of 1937 Nazi Germany had offered attractive terms in both areas. Brazilian generals, such as Pedro Góes Monteiro and Eurico Dutra, admired the German war machine and found the German arms-deal tempting. By the same token, Brazilian economic policymakers were intrigued by trade terms under the German "blocked" currency scheme, which was a form of barter. When Brazil sold to Germany it had to agree to accept only German goods in payment.

Strategy and ideology were also at stake in these negotiations. The pro-German faction within Brazil, strongest in the military, was countered by a pro-U.S. faction. The latter argued that Brazil had opted for the Allies in the First World War and had most to gain by sticking with the U.S. Many of the Brazilian elite therefore saw the flirtation with Nazi Germany as dangerous and short-sighted.

Meanwhile, the U.S. military and State Department were sparing no effort to pull Brazil back into the U.S.-dominated hemispheric orbit. They succeeded, but only after strenuous U.S. effort and German failure to offer the armaments Brazil wanted. From then onward Brazil became a vital cog in the Allied war machine, furnishing essential raw materials (like quartz and natural rubber) and air and naval bases that became critical in the "Battle of the Atlantic." Brazil even sent a combat division to Italy in 1944, where it fought alongside the U.S. Fifth Army.

Vargas had dealt shrewdly with the U.S. In return for its raw materials and bases, Brazil got the construction of a network of air and naval installations along the northern and northeastern Atlantic coast. The U.S. also promised to help finance construction of Brazil's first large-scale steel mill, at Volta Redonda. It was the first time an American government committed public funds to industrialization in the "developing world."

The *Estado Nôvo* furnished a centralized apparatus through which Vargas and his aides could pursue economic development and organizational change. The federal government assumed an aggressive role in the economy, organizing and strengthening marketing cartels (in cocoa, coffee, sugar, and tea), and creating new state enterprises, such as the National Motor Factory (to produce trucks and airplane engines). Vargas also overhauled the federal bureaucracy, creating a merit-oriented system to replace a patronage-ridden structure. Finally, one of the most important measures was a new labor code (1943), which spelled out rules of industrial relations that were to last until the 1980s. The law permitted unions to organize by plant and industry, although only on a local basis. Statewide and nationwide unions were forbidden. Only one union was permitted in each plant—under the scrutiny of the labor ministry, which controlled union finances and elections. Unions were in effect tied to the government, but the union leaders who "cooperated" could profit personally. This semi-corporatist labor union structure was paralleled by a semi-corporatist structure among the employers. These arrangements gave the federal executive a mechanism for controlling the economy. But Brazil of the early 1940s was *not* a modern, industrialized, urbanized society. Outside of a few key cities the corporatist structure left untouched most of the country, which was a vast, disconnected rural expanse.

The *Estado Nôvo* also had its darker side. The security forces had a virtual free hand. Torture was routine, against not only suspected "subversives" but also foreign agents (German businessmen were especially vulnerable). Censorship covered all the media, with a government news agency (*Departamento de Imprensa e Propaganda,* or DIP) furnishing the "official" version of the news. There were resemblances to Germany and Italy, but the Brazilians stopped well short of those extremes.

Brazil's economic history from 1930 to 1945 is not easy to capsulize. Coffee continued to be the primary foreign exchange earner, although helped during wartime by the boom in other raw materials shipped to the U.S. Industrial growth continued in São Paulo and, to a lesser extent, in Rio. The war cut off trade with Europe, with most shifting to the U.S. Brazil's wartime alliance with the U.S. also resulted in a U.S. technical mission to Brazil, which recommended programs for the country's economic development. Here again the U.S. government endorsed basic development in Brazil as the payment for the Vargas government's wartime cooperation.

Vargas had promised elections in 1943, for which he would be ineligible. As the war continued, Vargas knew that a wave of democratic opinion was building and he anticipated events by adopting a new, populist stance after 1943. The urban working class was now the object of government attention through such media as the nightly nationalist radio broadcast ("The Hour of Brazil"), and moves were made toward creating a Labor Party. Vargas was trying to create a new electoral image—something he had been able to neglect earlier in the *Estado Nôvo.*

Events moved rapidly in 1945. Vargas hoped to play down the contrast between the defeat of fascism in Europe and continued authoritarianism at home. He quickly demobilized the returning Brazilian Expeditionary Force, fresh from its sobering encounter with the Wehrmacht in Italy. In May 1945, with victory over the Axis a foregone conclusion, Vargas's government issued a tough anti-monopoly decree aimed at restricting the role of foreign firms in the Brazilian economy. It was part of the turn toward populism begun in 1943. The U.S. government was disturbed and put Vargas, and later Juan Perón in Argentina, on its list of Latin American presidents that had to go. There were plenty of Brazilians who shared the U.S. view. The liberal constitutionalists believed that foreign capital should be welcomed into Brazil. And they saw this issue as one that might help them gain the power they thought had been within their grasp in 1937.

There were other signs of Vargas's shift to the left. In early 1945 he decided to release leftist political prisoners. Most prominent was Luís Carlos Prestes, the leader of the Brazilian Communist Party who had been jailed since 1938. The relaxation of police control greatly helped the Communist Party, the best organized force on the left.

The polarization accelerated as the year went on. The anti-Vargas forces included the liberal constitutionalists, many military officers, and most state political bosses. On the other side were assorted populists, some labor union leaders, and the ideological left which included Socialists and Trotskyites, although the Communists were strongest. The confrontation climaxed in October 1945, when the army gave Vargas an ultimatum: resign or be deposed. He refused to step down, so the military declared him deposed. Vargas then acceded and flew off to a self-imposed exile on his ranch in Rio Grande do Sul.

The Second Republic (1946–64)

Three principal political parties emerged in 1945: the UDN (*União Democrática Nacional*), the PSD (*Partido Social Democrático*), and the PTB (*Partido Trabalhista Brasileiro*). The UDN was a coalition of anti-Vargas forces dominated by the liberal constitutionalists. The PSD was more heterogeneous; it included many political bosses and bureaucrats and some prominent industrialists. The PTB, smallest of the three, was created by Vargas in 1945, when he was still trying to shape the upcoming elections. The PTB was aimed at urban labor with a political approach supposedly modeled on the British Labor Party. These three remained Brazil's principal parties until 1965. They were often described as non-ideological, personalistic, and opportunistic—in short, not to be regarded as modern political parties. As we know from U.S. history, however, parties need not be ideologically precise to have sought and gained office according to consistent patterns.

Elections for a Constituent Assembly had been called before Vargas's fall, and when held in December 1945 proved to be among the freest in Brazil's history. The newly elected president, with 55 percent of the vote, was General Eurico Dutra, a close Vargas collaborator in the *Estado Nôvo*. The chief opposition candidate was Air Force Brigadier Eduardo Gomes, a throwback to liberal constitutionalism. He won 35 percent of the vote. The Communist candidate received 10 percent of the vote, which greatly encouraged the left. President Dutra and his advisers began watching closely the growth of the left and its links to urban labor.

In 1946 the Constituent Assembly produced another constitution, one that resembled the constitution of 1934. There was decentralization and a return to the classic guarantees of individual liberty. The elections that produced the Constituent Assembly had highlighted some other trends. They showed that the traditional political machines could still predominate in a national vote. That was hardly surprising, since Brazil was still a mainly rural society, and electoral manipulation was easiest in the countryside. Nonetheless, the extensive Communist vote showed that new forces were at work on the urban scene.

Soon after the war Brazil began struggling with the issue of how to finance its economic development. Total reliance on domestic capital was never seriously considered by Brazilian decision makers. One result of Brazil's involvement in the war had been to push the government toward economic planning. In wartime the objective was to maximize mobilization, but the same approach could be applied to peacetime economic development. Instead, the Dutra government (1946–51) avoided planning and returned to reliance on coffee exports, dropping most of the measures taken by Vargas to stimulate industrialization. This policy made Brazil once again highly vulnerable to changes in the world demand for coffee.

On the political front, the Dutra regime soon decided to repress the left. The Communist Party, legalized in 1946, had shown surprising strength in São Paulo and Rio. Labor unions, despite the corporatist legal structure, were gaining de facto autonomy, to the worry of employers and conservative politicians. Washington was closely monitoring these events, which had parallels elsewhere in Latin America. As would happen one year later in Chile, the Brazilian Congress in early 1947 voted to revoke the Communist Party's legality. Police raided its offices and seized its publications. The ministry of labor intervened in hundreds of labor unions and arrested or dismissed their officers, appointing government stooges in their place. The years 1945–47 had proven to be a rerun of 1930–35: a political opening, then a burst of activism on the left, climaxed by government repression. Henceforth the left was outlawed, and Communist Party candidates had to resort to electoral guises.

Vargas had not accepted his exit in October 1945 as the end of his career. Only two months later he was elected senator from two states, and chose to represent Rio Grande do Sul. During the Dutra presidency, Vargas worked steadily to retain national visibility and maintain his political contacts. Soon his friends and allies were urging him to run for president. He did not need much convincing.

In the presidential campaign of 1950 Vargas was supported by most of the PSD and PTB. His principal opponent was former *tenente* Juarez Távora, running under the UDN banner. There was also a splinter PSD candidate. Vargas conducted a shrewd campaign, attacking the Dutra regime for neglecting economic growth and for favoring the rich. Yet his position was moderate enough to appeal to the landowners who controlled votes in states such as Minas Gerais. Vargas won by a plurality (48.7 percent) and began his third presidency—the only one he gained by popular election.

In returning to power by popular vote, Vargas reversed the victory the anti-Getulistas, especially the liberal constitutionalists, had won in 1945. He had beaten them at the game they thought was theirs. They exploded, some even calling for the army to block the return of the ex-dictator. But it was to no avail.

Vargas made economic policy his top priority and he promptly assembled a team of young technocrats—engineers, economists, and planners. They formulated an eclectic strategy designed to maximize the inflow of capital and technology from both public and private sources abroad. The prospects looked favorable. In 1949 the U.S. and Brazilian governments had launched a joint study of the Brazilian economy. The commission's report in 1953 spotlighted inadequate energy and poor transportation as the prime obstacles to rapid economic development. The U.S. government indicated interest in channeling public funds for investment in these areas, and the Brazilian government created new federal agencies to handle the investment projects now in prospect.

Vargas's economic strategy also had its nationalist side. Profit remissions by foreign-owned firms were a frequent target for nationalist attack. By 1951 the remissions were high, encouraged by the growing overvaluation of the Brazilian currency (which progressively increased the value of the companies' earnings in U.S. dollars). In 1952 Vargas denounced the foreign firms and threatened new controls. The outflow slowed, however, and he held back from attempting to impose comprehensive controls.

Another target for the nationalists was oil. Since the late 1930s Brazil had been working on a national oil policy. Argentina and Mexico had already opted for state monopolies. In both cases, nationalist sentiment was a strong political force. Throughout Latin America international oil companies were regarded with strong suspicion. Brazil was no different. In 1951 Vargas proposed a mixed public-private corporation (to be called PETROBRAS) that would monopolize the exploration and production of oil.

The proposal touched off the most heated political debate since 1945. Nationalism proved very strong, especially among army officers. Bitter controversies arose, with state monopoly advocates questioning the patriotism of free enterprise defendants, and vice versa. In 1953 the Congress created an even stronger monopoly than proposed by Vargas. The debate had sharply polarized opinion, reducing the room for political maneuver.

Vargas had been elected in 1950 on a moderate platform and the party line-up in Congress required him to maintain that course. But economic pressures were forcing hard choices on the government. First, Brazil's rate of inflation turned up from 11 percent in 1951 to 20 percent in 1952. Second, her foreign trade balance went into the red. Third, the U.S. president elected in 1952, Dwight Eisenhower, threw into doubt the loan commitments the Brazilians thought the U.S. had made for the Joint Commission–endorsed infrastructural investments.

These reverses gave ammunition to Vargas's enemies on both the left and right. The left charged Vargas with selling out to the imperialists, who wanted to keep Brazil in the role of a primary-product exporter. The right, on the other hand, charged that Vargas was alienating the trading partners and foreign creditors on whom Brazil had to depend. Most politically conscious Brazilians fell between these extremes. Yet economic and political pressures were making moderation more difficult, spelling danger for Vargas and his government.

In 1953 Vargas reorganized his cabinet to face the economic crisis. Inflation and the balance-of-payments deficit were related problems because Brazil had clung to an overvalued exchange rate which, combined with Brazilian inflation, had made imports cheaper and exports more expensive. An economic stabilization program was urgently needed. In the short run that would mean falling real wages and strict controls on business credit and government spending. Such a policy was bound to be unpopular.

To lead the effort Vargas recruited Oswaldo de Aranha, his longtime political lieutenant, as minister of finance. Aranha pursued classic stabilization measures with apparent success in 1953. As 1954 approached, however, a bitter fight loomed over wage policy. Under the *Estado Nôvo* the ministry of labor fixed the minimum wage. It had not been increased for many years, despite the accelerating inflation. Aranha's objective was to prevent an increase so large as to wreck the anti-inflation program. For this Aranha would have to deal with the minister of labor: João Goulart, a young PTB politician and Vargas protégé from Rio Grande do Sul. Goulart was closely identified with the PTB left and the militant labor leadership.

By 1954 Aranha and Goulart were pulling in opposite directions: Aranha toward austerity and Goulart toward a populist, redistributionist path. Vargas had to decide the issue. In February, apparently opting for Aranha's austerity, he dismissed Goulart. The left, strengthened by its success in the fight over oil policy, now attacked Vargas for pandering to the imperialists with his stabilization program. Vargas cleared the air on May 1, 1954, when he announced a 100 percent increase in the minimum wage—higher even than Goulart had recommended.

This battle now merged into a wider political crisis. Vargas's bitterest enemies had found an issue on which they thought they could beat him: corruption. Evidence of financial scandals began to surface. The anti-Getulista propagandists closed in on the weary president. Unbeknownst to Vargas, his palace security chief had arranged an assassination attempt on Carlos Lacerda, a sensationalizing journalist who was leading the attack on Vargas. The bullet meant for Lacerda killed an air force officer who was a volunteer bodyguard for Lacerda, who suffered only a minor wound. The officer's death brought the military into the crisis. When their investigation pointed to the presidential palace, the senior officers demanded Vargas's resignation. Realizing he was trapped and isolated, Vargas put a bullet through his heart on August 24. He left behind an inflammatory suicide letter, blaming his demise on sinister forces, domestic and foreign, and proclaiming a highly nationalist position. By his sensational exit, Vargas exacted revenge on his tormentors. Lacerda had to flee Brazil and the anti-Getulistas, especially among the UDN and the military, found themselves on the defensive.

Caretaker regimes governed Brazil until the 1956 inauguration of Juscelino Kubitschek, elected to a full presidential term in 1955. Much to the surprise of both supporters and opponents, Kubitschek served out his full term. He was an ebullient PSD politician and former governor of Minas Gerais with a reputation as a skillful campaigner. Although he won the presidency with only 36 percent of the vote, he quickly moved to gain broader support.

Mindful of how often the military had intervened in politics, Kubitschek mollified them with large weapons purchases. He was also fortunate to have a war minister, General Henrique Teixeira Lott, who enjoyed great prestige among the officers and who proved staunchly loyal to the president. Kubitschek also had an effective PSD-PTB coalition in the Congress. Finally, the "Target Program" of economic development, plus the audacious idea of building a new capital, Brasília, in the interior, combined to generate enthusiasm which muffled the bitter political conflicts from the mid-1950s.

(The futuristic city of Brasília, built from scratch in four years on a completely undeveloped plateau site 600 miles from the old capital of Rio de Janeiro, also captured the imagination of the outside world. André Malraux called it "the capital of hope." President Eisenhower was one of many heads of state to attend its inauguration in 1960. Brazil was now on the world map for the daring, if controversial, urban planning and architecture developed in Brasília.)

The glittering capital of Brasilia boasts extraordinary modernistic architecture. *Above*, the headquarters of the foreign ministry; *below*, the legislative palace, whose twin towers and buildings contain the separate houses of the national congress. (Courtesy of the Consulate General of Brazil, New York.)

No small part of Kubitschek's political success was due to his own talents. It took great political skill to orchestrate the coalition that sustained his policies. Kubitschek's motto had been "fifty years of progress in five," and the economic leap forward was impressive.

Yet it would have been too much to expect Kubitschek's political strategy to endure forever. The PSD-PTB alliance in Congress was coming apart, growing discord among military officers precluded any repeat of General Lott's role, and the economy had once again run into inflation and balance-of-payments deficits. Kubitschek briefly tried economic stabilization in 1958–59, but scuttled it when the IMF demanded austerity measures that would have prevented Brazil from reaching the president's economic "targets." Kubitschek pressed on with his economic program and that created mammoth problems for his successor. When he left office in January 1961 no one doubted that a reckoning with foreign creditors was at hand.

The president who inherited this challenge was Jânio Quadros, one of Brazil's most talented and most flawed politicians. A whirlwind success as governor of São Paulo, Quadros won big in the 1960 presidential election, running with UDN endorsement. His campaign featured a broom as the symbol of his fight against corruption. That talk buoyed the liberal constitutionalists, who believed that at last power was near.

Quadros began by embracing a tough stabilization program, while at the same time launching an "independent foreign policy" especially aimed at new overtures toward the socialist camp. After seven months of idiosyncratic rule, however, Quadros suddenly resigned in August 1961. His reasons have never been entirely explained—apparently he expected the Congress to reject his resignation and offer him increased powers. He was wrong; the Congress promptly accepted his resignation. Quadros, the most charismatic populist politician of modern Brazil, faded into a retirement punctuated by occasional oracular pronouncements.

Quadros's self-engineered demise was demoralizing for the anti-Getulistas and other Brazilians who believed that his moralistic promises and his administrative success in São Paulo boded well for the new federal government. Worst of all from the UDN viewpoint, Quadros's departure meant power would now pass to the elected vice president—Vargas's former labor minister, João Goulart, the epitome of populism and anathema to the conservative military.

The military was in no mood to agree to Goulart's succession to the presidency. But the "legalists" among the officers argued in favor of observing the constitution. A compromise was reached. The Congress created a parliamentary system in which Goulart was president but was obliged to govern through a cabinet accountable to the Congress. It was an unworkable hybrid, designed solely to reduce Goulart's power.

The new president assumed his diminished powers in September 1961 and promptly started a campaign to get the parliamentary innovation repealed. January 1963 brought success when a plebiscite restored the full presidential system. By then Goulart had precious little time left from the 1961–66 presidential term.

Goulart's presidency proved ill-starred from the beginning. The odds were against him on almost every count, but he made them worse with his inexperience, weakness, and indecision. By 1963 inflation and the balance-of-payments deficit had grown even more difficult to deal with. Goulart chose his own stabilization team, headed by the brilliant intellectual-politician Santiago Dantas and the noted economist Celso Furtado. Dantas worked out a detailed plan, duly negotiated with the U.S. government and the International Monetary Fund. It called for the usual: reduction of government deficit, tough controls on wages, and painful reductions in credit. It was the same medicine that had been served up in the stabilization efforts of 1953–54, 1955–56, 1958–59, and 1961.

For Goulart, stabilization presented special problems. A tough wage policy, which always meant falling real wages, would strike at the social group to which Goulart was most committed. Furthermore, meeting the harsh terms of foreign lenders would invite attack from the nationalists, another area of his prime support. To what end should Goulart sacrifice his slender political capital? Even if he could bring off stabilization, his term would probably end before Brazil could resume rapid growth.

Notwithstanding the gloomy prospects, Goulart endorsed the Dantas-Furtado plan. But he did not stay with it for long. In a few months the political costs had become all too evident. Dantas quietly resigned, Furtado had already left Brasília, and any further serious stabilization effort was thereafter out of the question.

Stabilization was not Goulart's only worry. Since 1961 the Brazilian political scene had been heating up, stoked by passionate opinion on both left and right. The military, as always, was a key factor. Some of the officers who had fought Goulart's accession to power in 1961 were still fighting. They had begun an ongoing conspiracy to overthrow Goulart. Many of the ideas and personnel of the conspiracy could be traced to the 1954 military cabal against Vargas. What steadily increased the strength of the conspirators was the increasingly radical tone of the political combatants.

The left of the political spectrum had become very crowded. A rising sense of confidence had gripped the radical nationalists, who included Catholic literacy teachers, labor union militants, Trotskyist student organizers, and artistic idealists, all spreading a revolutionary message through popular culture as well as "high" art forms. By early 1964 the radical left had gained government blessing, sometimes even government financing and logistical support.

Conservatives were incensed over nationalist inroads among two groups. One was the military. Brazilian enlisted men had traditionally enjoyed only restricted political rights. Voting was not among them. The radicals began to organize among these "neglected" ranks to the point of advocating unionization of enlisted men. This scandalized the officers, who were hardly about to learn collective bargaining. Even politically centrist officers could understand that threat.

The other new area of mobilization was the countryside. In 1963 rural unionization was legalized and competing groups, including several on the left, vied to win sponsorship of local syndicates. Yet the rural sector was an unpromising arena for the Brazilian left to test its power. There was always excess labor, and landowners traditionally ruled with an iron hand. This rural unionization campaign, combined with a few land invasions, provoked landowners to take decisive action. They pressured the pro-landowner politicians, who were numerous in a federal Congress which overrepresented rural districts.

Although Goulart's opponents had made an impact in the Congress by early 1964, they did not have the votes to impeach him. The old PSD-PTB alliance still operated. It might not back a stabilization program, but it was also not ready to serve the anti-Goulart conspirators. The plotters saw only one way out: a military coup.

The president's military advisers had warned him about the conspiracy, but they assured him that only a minority of officers were involved. That may have been true but it was rapidly changing. Now even centrist officers were leaning toward a coup. The principal factor pushing them was the radical move to the left already under way, either by the president or by those who controlled him.

The U.S. government was taking a strong interest in Brazil's emerging political confrontation. Both the U.S. ambassador, Lincoln Gordon, and the U.S. military attaché, General Vernon Walters, were in close touch with the conspirators, both military and civilian. The U.S. had a contingency plan to support the anti-Goulart rebels with fuel and weapons, if needed. As it happened, they were not. On March 31 speculation ended as a military revolt, surfacing first in Minas Gerais, spread across the country. Within twenty-four hours João Goulart had fled into exile in Uruguay.

On April 1 the leader of the Congress, in Goulart's absence, declared the presidency vacant. Although his action lacked any legal foundation, the Congress acceded. Into the power vacuum moved the military conspirators and their civilian allies. Brazil once again opted for the authoritarian path to development.

In retrospect, the breakdown of Brazilian democracy (such as it was) bore a close connection to the interplay of social-class relations. The populist policies of Getúlio Vargas constructed a hierarchical order through which the state created and controlled institutions for organizing urban workers. This posed a significant but ultimately acceptable challenge to the upper and middle classes, the latter represented largely by the military. But in 1964 Goulart presented, or appeared to present, a much more fundamental threat. By mobilizing peasants as well as workers, and by using radical rhetoric, he seemed to be creating the conditions for a *class-wide* worker-peasant alliance against the socioeconomic establishment. Both the suddenness and the simultaneity of these movements startled and alarmed elites and onlookers, who recoiled at the prospect of such far-reaching and communistic alterations in the country's political structure. A class-wide coalition was simply not acceptable. The military exercised its long-standing veto power and went on to create a bureaucratic-authoritarian regime.

Military Rule

The conspirators of 1964 were surprised at the speed with which the Goulart government collapsed. The radical nationalists, so confident of their mobilization, found themselves without followers. The justice minister called for a general strike on April 1, but the response was minimal. Goulart's zig-zagging and the divisiveness within the left had undercut any effective mass support. The rebels encountered little or no resistance as their troops seized command of government.

Since 1964 Brazil has been governed by a succession of authoritarian regimes, each headed by a four-star general. Despite variations in structure and personnel, all were coalitions of military officers, technocratic administrators, and old-line politicians. In order to understand the record of their years we must look carefully at the key actors and forces.

The most important group has been the military. Army officers had a long history of intervention in politics since the Empire was brought down. There was the military regime of Floriano Peixoto (1891–94), and later the military interventions in state politics in 1910–14, followed by the revolts of junior officers in 1922 and 1924. In 1930 the military ended the Old Republic by delivering power to Vargas, whom they kept in power by the coup of 1937, only to depose him in 1945. It was a military manifesto that led to Vargas's suicide in 1954 and it was a "preventive" coup in 1955 that ensured Kubitschek's succession to the presidency. Finally, the military led the fight against Goulart's succession to the presidency in 1961 and then conspired to bring him down in 1964. Army officers were seen by all to be vital actors in Brazilian politics.

In the years after 1945 the army officer corps has been buffeted by conflicting political currents. The 1950s brought a polarization between nationalist and anti-communist positions. The former favored statist solutions in key economic sectors (such as oil) and a relative independence in foreign policy (strongly against, for example, sending troops to fight in Korea alongside the U.S.). As their label would indicate, the anti-communists identified with the U.S. in the deepening Cold War and saw the nationalist left as a stalking-horse for pro-Castroites or communists.

Officer opinion turned decisively against the populists, of whom Goulart was a principal example. The Goulart government's inability to get control of the economy (Brazil was near default to foreign creditors in March 1964); the mobilization of the lower sectors; and the direct threat to military hierarchy all pushed centrist military officers toward supporting a coup. By early 1964 the conspiracy was headed by General Humberto Castello Branco, the staunchly legalist army chief of staff who had supported Goulart's succession to the presidency in 1961.

Once the military had deposed Goulart, a new question faced the conspirators: the form and direction of the new government. The hard-liners' economic views were less easy to discern. They obviously self-seeking and subversive politicians. The country needed a long recuperation, which would necessarily require such measures as purging legislators, suppressing direct elections, and firing civil servants. The hard-liners' economic views were less easy to discern. They obviously detested the radical nationalists and the populists.

The moderate military composed another group. They believed a relatively brief interval of administrative and economic reorganization could return Brazil to the electoral democracy recently endangered by irresponsible politicians. The violation of democratic and constitutional principles bothered the moderates, who hoped for a rapid return to legal normalcy.

General Castello Branco was quickly chosen by the (purged) Congress as the new president and served until 1967. He considered economic stabilization to be his government's top priority. The immediate need was to bring inflation under control and to improve the balance of payments. Roberto Campos, a well-known economist-diplomat, was made planning minister and became the dominant figure in economic policy making. Inflation was reduced, but by much less than had been hoped, and a surplus was achieved in the foreign accounts, mainly because a government-induced recession greatly reduced demand for imports. Campos's team also attempted to reorganize and update Brazil's principal economic institutions. The banking system was overhauled (a proper central bank was finally created), a stock market and a government securities market were institutionalized for the first time, labor regulations were revised to make easier the discharge of employees, and export regulations were simplified. Campos had long argued that capitalism had not failed in Brazil because it hadn't yet been tried. This was his chance. The short-term results were disappointing, but Castello Branco and Campos did not despair; they saw their efforts as unpopular in the short run, but indispensable for sound growth in the future.

The hoped-for economic upturn did not occur in 1965–66 and Castello Branco was persuaded to extend his presidential term a year in the hope that the economy would improve. In fact, the country's economic problems could not be resolved even in his two-and-a-half years.

The second military government, that of President Artur Costa e Silva (1967–69), brought an ugly turn in politics. The president had hoped to preside over a liberalization, but events proved otherwise. Until 1967 the authoritarian government had shown considerable tolerance for the opposition, at least in comparison to Spanish American military governments of the 1960s and 1970s. But tolerance invited mobilization. In 1967 and 1968 the opposition mounted a series of protests, climaxing in mass demonstrations in Rio.

The hardline military, now opposing any compromise between democracy and a "tough" government, argued for a crackdown. In November 1968 a series of industrial strikes spread from Minas Gerais into the industrial heartland of São Paulo. The Costa e Silva government hesitated, then reacted by strongly repressing the strikers. A pattern was set: an authoritarian government resorting to dictatorial measures to carry out its version of rapid economic development. It was a growth strategy based on repression of labor unions, avid recruiting of foreign investment, and high rewards for economic managers.

In 1969 Brazil was hit with new levels of political violence. The militant opposition had produced a guerrilla network, mainly in the cities. In September 1969 President Costa e Silva suffered a debilitating stroke and the guerrillas made it the occasion to kidnap the U.S. ambassador, whom they subsequently released, in return for the government's releasing from prison fifteen political prisoners and the publishing of a revolutionary manifesto in all the media. For the next four years Brazil was wracked by guerrilla warfare. A small cadre of revolutionary activists kidnapped foreign diplomats, holding them hostage to ransom other revolutionaries in prison. The guerrillas also wanted to draw the government into a more systematically repressive role, thereby hoping that more of the populace would be alienated.

By 1973 the guerrilla movement was vanquished. They had exhausted their human resources to achieve meager results. They rescued a number of their revolutionary comrades from prison and torture, but in so doing they reinforced the repressive apparatus and made credible the hardliners' argument that any political opening meant civil war.

When General Ernesto Geisel assumed the presidency in 1974 he repeated the earlier moderates' hopes of a return to democracy and the rule of law. A major obstacle was the security apparatus, including both army and civilian units, which had gained great influence within the government. Their unsavory methods, including torture, had facilitated the liquidation of the revolutionary opposition, but had given them a powerful veto over liberalization.

President Geisel's commitment to redemocratization came from his close personal link to the legalist tradition of Castello Branco. Geisel saw this process not as a response to pressure, but as the working out of a democratic commitment inherent in the military intervention in 1964.

The fundamental problem for Geisel, as for all the preceding military governments, was the inability to win a free popular election. This would not have mattered if the military had not taken the democratic rules so seriously. But they did, and the result was an endless series of improvisations to make the voting results fit their preferences. The depth of the problem was shown in October 1974 when the new government, in contrast to its predecessor, allowed relatively free congressional elections. The result was a landslide for the opposition party. The lesson was clear: if given a choice, the public, especially in the urban industrialized centers, would vote against the government.

After 1967 the Brazilian economy returned to a growth path, duplicating the record of the 1950s. From 1968 to 1974 the growth rate averaged 10 percent, and exports more than quadrupled. As though to mark the end of an era, manufactured goods replaced coffee as the country's leading export product. Outside observers soon talked of the "Brazilian miracle." It was achieved by low wages and easy credit to purchasers of consumer durable goods.

But the "miracle" began to fade by the end of the decade. In 1980 inflation was more than 100 percent, and Brazil faced a serious and growing deficit in its international balance of payments. The foreign debt mounted and industrial production sagged. Furthermore, industrial labor had bestirred itself in São Paulo, staging a series of strikes in 1978, 1979, and 1980. The church, in the person of Cardinal Arns, supported the strikers and helped dramatize the disproportionate share of the sacrifice they had borne during the "miracle." To deal with the balance of payments crisis the government was forced to run a recession in 1981. Naturally this was unpopular, as unemployment spread in the industrial heartland of São Paulo. In 1982 Planning Minister

Delfim Neto and his fellow policymakers hoped to engineer an economic recovery, all the more since it was to be an election year.

These hopes were soon dashed by the world recession, which depressed the value of Brazilian exports, while high interest rates kept the cost of servicing the foreign debt at a crippling level. By the end of 1982 Brazil gained the dubious honor of having the largest foreign debt in the world ($87 billion—although many observers thought its short-term obligations ran the total up to $100 billion), and, like Argentina and Mexico, had to suspend payments on principal. To get the essential "bridging loans" to meet immediate obligations, Brazil agreed to an IMF-architected economic plan that involved a brutal reduction of imports in order to earn a trade surplus. The prospect by early 1983 was for the deepest domestic recession Brazil had experienced since the 1930s.

These bleak economic prospects spelled trouble for the "redemocratization" process begun during the years (1974–79) of President Geisel. After several false starts, President João Figueiredo (1979–85) worked hard to deliver on the promise of direct elections in 1982. For the first time since 1965, Brazil directly elected all its state governors in November 1982. Also elected were all the federal deputies, a third of the federal senators, and virtually all the mayors, state representatives, and local council members. The opposition won a smashing victory in the most developed states, winning the governorships of São Paulo, Rio de Janeiro, and Minas Gerais. The government party, the PSD, lost control of the Chamber of Deputies, but retained control of the electoral college, which will elect the new president in 1985. In effect it was a victory both for the opposition, which made huge strides despite persistent government attempts to stack the rules in favor of the government party, and for the government, which still held the trump cards in executing economic policy. Yet the government's margin had grown thin, and the opening up of politics—far more than in Chile or Argentina—had introduced uncertainty. By early 1983 Brazil presented an anomaly: an authoritarian regime in search of a new legitimacy that could only be created by a pluralism likely to undermine the foundation of authoritarianism.

Crucial to the political debates in Brazil have been controversies over the social consequences of the country's phenomenal economic growth. One of the hottest issues was income distribution. The 1980 census furnished the opposition with new evidence for its claim that inequality was the inevitable product of the official economic strategy. The percentage of the national income going to the top ten percent of the population had gone from 39.6 percent in 1960 to 46.7 percent in 1970 to 50.9 percent in 1980. Meanwhile, the poorest 50 percent of the population received 17.4 percent in 1960. which declined to 14.9 percent in 1970, and then only 12.6 percent in 1980. The message was unmistakeable: Brazilian capitalism, however dynamic, was exacerbating the economic inequalities in Brazilian society. This issue was at the heart of the debate as Brazilians battled over the shape of the society that might emerge in a more democratic era.

SIX

PERU
Soldiers, Oligarchs, and Indians

Any understanding of modern Peru must begin with a look at its geography. Located on the Pacific coast of South America, and approximately twice the size of Texas, the country has three geographical regions: coast, sierra, and *montaña*. The coastal area, arid and dry, has for centuries been dominated by the city of Lima, whose population in 1980 came to about 3.5 million (one fifth the national total of 17.7 million). The sierra is the Andean mountain range, a world of snow-capped peaks and chilly valleys that contain such ancient provincial cities as Cuzco and Ayacucho. And the *montaña,* on the eastern slope of the Andes, is a jungle region whose tropical forests extend to the upper reaches of the Amazon River, where the town of Iquitos is the major headwater port. Because of its inaccessibility the *montaña* has until recently seen little settlement, although today colonization has made it a dynamic and growing region.

These geographical features have helped to create disparate regional economies. The coast has given rise to commercial agriculture and fishing industries. The sierra has been an area for mining, livestock, and subsistence agriculture. Notwithstanding its natural resources the *montaña* has not enjoyed sustained growth; there has been a rubber boom and, in recent years, cultivation of coca leaves (for the international narcotics trade), but no sustained prosperity. More recently, however, the successful cultivation of coffee, sugar, and fruit (for the Lima market) has energized the regional economy.

Ethnic variations compound these differences. Once the center of the Inca empire, Peru continues to have a large Indian population. The 1940 census, the last to use racial categories, classified 46 percent of the population as Indian. This was probably an undercount in ethnic terms, since the definition of "Indian" depended more on physical appearance than ethnic heritage. The current figure is in all likelihood about 35 percent. It has been estimated that there are now about 3 million speakers of Quechua in Peru, and a sizable number of Aymara as well. Indians live (and have lived) mainly in the sierra, often in tightly-knit traditional communities, perpetuating folkways that go back to Inca days.

Peru has a relatively small layer of whites, a stratum that originated with the Spanish conquerors and now makes up about one-tenth the national population. Aside from blacks and Asians, most of the rest consists of *mestizos*—perhaps one-third or more of the total. As in other Latin American countries, the *mestizos* occupy an ambiguous position in Peruvian society, representing both the burdens of an oppressive past and, occasionally, the prospects for a radically different future. *Mestizos* are often known in Peru as *cholos,* a term sometimes used as a pejorative for Indians trying to pass as mixed-bloods.

Not surprisingly, this mixed ethnic background has led to widely divergent interpretations of Peruvian history and society. Some writers have violently denounced the country's Spanish legacy. Alberto Hidalgo, for instance, proclaimed in the early twentieth century: "I hate Spain because it has never done anything worthwhile for humanity. Nothing, absolutely nothing. . . . Spaniards are brutes by nature." But Spain has also had its apologists. Bartolomé Herrera, a nineteenth century priest, had only praise.

> The work which the Spaniards accomplished . . . was the greatest work which the Almighty has accomplished through the hands of man. To conquer nature, to master inward fears, to dominate far-off places through the formidable power of the intrepid heart, to accomplish all this and to take as the trophy of victory a new section of the world with an immense population which for thousands of years had been lost to civilization, and then to infuse this world with Christianity, to introduce the fire of life into millions of moribund souls, to broaden by millions of leagues the sphere of human intelligence, was an accomplishment of unparalleled splendor.

The implication was clear. Peru should place its power, and its hopes, in its citizens of European descent.

Such commentators also usually denounced the Indians. They were depicted as lazy, shiftless, hopelessly addicted to the chewing of coca leaves. The Indians stood beyond redemption; they posed an unyielding obstacle to national progress. If Peru had problems, they could be traced to the stubborn survival of the heirs of the Incas.

The *mestizo* has also come in for criticism. Just as José Vasconcelos was propounding his pro-*mestizo* ideas about "the cosmic race" in Mexico, Alejandro O. Deústua offered in 1931 a biting critique of Peru. "Among us," he said,

> the problem of the *mestizo* is much more grave than in other countries. The product of the Indian in his period of moral dissolution and the

Spaniard in his era of decadence, the *mestizo* has inherited all the defects of each without being able to conserve the remains of the gentlemanly life of the conqueror. . . . The mixture has been disastrous for the national culture.

Miscegenation was for Deústua not a sign of social progress but a symptom of backwardness. Peru was condemned by the racial composition it had inherited.

During the twentieth century, Peruvian thinkers have sought to resolve the haunting problem of national identity. Some have found inspiration in the country's Indian heritage. A notable case was José María Arguedas, the only novelist able to penetrate both the indigenous and creole worlds of Peru. He was a *mestizo* who had lived in Indian communities as a child and was fully bilingual in Spanish and Quechua. In *Canto Kechwa* (1938), he argued that

The indigenous is not inferior. And the day on which the people of the highlands who still feel ashamed of the Indian discover of their own accord the great creative possibilities of their Indian spirit, on that day, confident of their own values, the *mestizo* and Indian peoples will definitely prove the equality of their own creative ability with that of the European art which now displaces and puts it to shame.

Arguedas found the burden of his own ethnic heritage too much to bear and committed suicide in great despair.

Others have searched for a fusion of Spanish and Indian components, as did Víctor Andrés Belaunde in a book entitled *Peruanidad* (1957). Yet the basic question persists: Can Peru become a unified nation?

The Independence Period

During the colonial era Peru was a major source of income for Spain. The silver mines of Potosí in upper Peru (now Bolivia) produced vast amounts of wealth, particularly in the sixteenth and seventeenth centuries, and rich veins were subsequently found in the Peruvian sierra. The trappings of Spanish civilization soon appeared. The University of San Marcos was founded in 1551. The inquisition set up court in 1569, as the church became a powerful institution. Lima, an impressive metropolis for its place and time, was worthy of its name: the City of Kings.

Peru suffered a prolonged economic crisis during the late eighteenth century. Silver production slumped, although there was a short-lived boom in the 1790s. The Bourbon free-trade policies reduced Peru's share of trade with Upper Peru and Chile, as goods now came in overland from Buenos Aires. The creation of a viceroyalty in the La Plata region curtailed the activity and prominence of Lima's royal bureau-cracy. Tupac Amaru II (the *mestizo* José Gabriel Condorcanqui) led an unsuccessful, bloody Indian revolt in 1780–81. Although unrelated to the Spanish crown's administrative changes, many of the elite thought the revolt's message was clear: Peru was in decline.

Paradoxically, the economic trend did not produce a widespread in-dependence movement. Lima's intellectuals learned of the Enlighten-ment and launched a liberal journal, the *Mercurio Peruano,* in 1791. But they did not clamor for independence from Spain. Rather, they argued for concessions within the colonial framework, for policies that would bring back the privileges and prosperity of the pre-Bourbon era. There was a brief separatist movement—in the sierra, under a *mestizo* (socially known as an Indian) named Mateo García Pumacahua—but it was quickly snuffed out. While the cause of independence was sweeping through the rest of Spanish America, Peru remained a loyalist strong-hold of the crown.

When liberation came, it was from outside. Late in 1820, having led his troops over the Andes from Argentina to Chile, José de San Martín reached the southern coast of Peru. Several months later the Spaniards evacuated Lima and on July 28, 1821, San Martín proclaimed the in-dependence of Peru. Recognized as the "protector" by the local popu-lace, he began making plans to establish a monarchy—and commis-sioned an agent to search for a suitable European prince. This brought opposition from liberals, who wanted a republican form of govern-ment, and the project disappeared after San Martín's fateful meeting with Bolívar in late 1822 and subsequent withdrawal from the scene.

A special assembly passed a constitution in 1823 and José de la Riva Agüero became the country's chief executive, but independence still had to be won. The following year Bolívar resoundingly defeated the Spaniards at the battle of Junín, and Andrés Santa Cruz delivered the coup de grâce at Ayacucho. For all practical purposes Peru thus be-came free, though Spain refused to recognize the independence of her colony.

Bolívar then proposed a confederation of Peru with Upper Peru and Gran Colombia (Ecuador, Colombia, and Venezuela)—under his lead-ership, of course—and secured acceptance from a timid Lima assembly in 1826. Opposition mounted and Bolívar went northward to quell the criticism, having reluctantly approved a plan for a separate Bolivia.

Caudillismo and geopolitics took hold in Peru. A series of military chieftains battled for the presidency, with coups and counter-coups the order of the day between 1828 and the early 1840s. General Agustín Gamarra, having captured the presidency in 1839, attempted to sub-due and annex Bolivia, but met his death on a battlefield in 1841.

Peruvian politics in the postindependence era presented a paradoxical scene. Having defeated Spain through the help of outsiders, Peru found it difficult to assert autonomy from neighboring states. Having refrained from open conflict until the 1820s, Peru fell under the sway of military dictators. And having cast off the burdens of colonial rule, Peru found many saying its own society was in steady decline.

The economy was exceedingly weak. Fighting in the early 1820s had left Callao, the principal port (near Lima), in a state of ruins. Landed estates along the coast and in the sierra had been ravaged. Commerce remained in depression. The mines were in disrepair. The national treasury was nearly empty, and from the 1820s onward the government began to accumulate a series of foreign debts (mainly to British lenders) that would later prove to be nearly ruinous.

Nor had conditions improved for the Indians, who at this time composed about 70 percent of the total population (between 1 and 1.5 million). The traditional tribute, formally abolished with the expulsion of Spain, was replaced by a head tax, the so-called *contribución de indígenas*. And under the "liberal" doctrines of the era Indians were seen as individuals, not communities, so they no longer enjoyed their previous special protection. Some sought refuge as peons on estates or as workers in mines. Others tried to pass as *mestizos* and find employment in the cities and towns.

The Guano Age

Nature came to Peru's rescue. For centuries the coldness of the country's offshore waters, due to the Humboldt current, had attracted large numbers of fish. The fish in turn attracted birds, who left their droppings on islands near the coast. Atmospheric dryness aided the preservation and calcination of these deposits, known as guano, which had a high concentration of nitrogen. Guano, as the Incas had known, was a first-class fertilizer.

In 1841 the first shipment of Peruvian guano reached the port of Liverpool. Thus began a half-century of export-led growth in Peru, and a period of apparent prosperity.

It was a special bonanza for the hard-pressed government. The islands with the guano deposits were on public property, not private land. This posed both a practical and a theoretical question for liberal policymakers: How should a government committed to laissez-faire principles take advantage of this virtual monopoly?

The answer was found in the "consignment" system, through which the government would lease out (usually exclusive) exploitation rights to a merchant house or partnership. Under such contracts the government would obtain a fixed share of the total value of sales, perhaps two-thirds or so, rather than a tax on profits. The merchant, usually a foreigner, would receive reimbursement for costs plus a percentage of the sale. The strategy seemed sensible enough, since it involved the liberal state in a partnership with private enterprise to the advantage of both.

But the consignment system had some important ramifications. One was to place the state in constant conflict with the merchant houses. With complete control of supply, the government wanted to sell the guano for as high a price as possible. This could mean holding back on shipments in order to keep prices up. Because of the commission arrangement, however, the merchant was more interested in the total *volume* of sales than in the *price* of any individual shipment. After all, the merchant had the contract for a specified period of time—during which the point was to sell as much guano as possible. High prices would help, of course, but it would be more profitable from the merchants' viewpoint to sell large amounts of guano at moderate prices than to sell very small amounts at high prices. As a result, the Peruvian government and its consignees constantly bickered throughout the guano age.

A second factor derived from the size of required investment. Though the guano itself was readily accessible, piled in open-air mounds, its exploitation required large-scale capital investment: in ships, warehouses, transportation, lodging, and wages. Moreover the government continually demanded cash advances from its leaseholders. This restricted the pool of possible consignees to merchants with strong capital reserves, and given the plight of the local economy, few Peruvians could take advantage of the opportunity.

A third factor, related to the second, derived from the foreign debt. As early as 1822 the Peruvian government negotiated a loan of 1.8 million pounds sterling from a British banking house. Subsequent loans and accumulated interest led to a massive debt, and Peru fell behind on its payments. British bondholders became impatient, and quickly saw the guano bonanza as their salvation.

They were right. The guano trade eventually passed largely into British hands. In 1849, just as the Peruvian legislature was approving a resolution granting Peruvian nationals preference in the consignments, the government negotiated a contract with the London firm of Anthony Gibbs. The agreement authorized Gibbs to buy up debt securities from British bondholders at the going market price (about 40 percent less than face value) and then allowed Gibbs to use these bonds at face value to pay for guano shipments. The government thus took a sizable loss, while Gibbs could expect to make a handsome profit on sales of guano in the European market.

Peru became highly dependent on guano, thereby creating a single-product export economy. By the early 1860s the government was earning about 80 percent of its revenues from guano: this testifies to both the state's reliance on its consignments and the relative paucity of other exports. At the same time, about *half* the government's receipts on guano were destined for English bondholders. The guano boom therefore provided little stimulus for long-run economic growth: as Fredrick Pike has observed, "the greater the windfall gains became, the less self-sustaining the economy grew."

In 1845, as the guano trade was expanding, Peru came under the rule of its strongest nineteenth century leader: Ramón Castilla, 46 years old, the intelligent, dark-eyed son of a part-Indian mother and a Spanish-Italian father. A military officer who had distinguished himself at Junín and Ayacucho, Castilla sought to modernize the Peruvian armed services. Upon reaching office he submitted to congress a national budget, the first in the nation's history. He promoted public works, including the construction of Latin America's first railroad (extending from Lima to Callao). In foreign affairs he revived Bolívar's dream of Spanish American unity, partly because he feared the southward drive of the United States—which was bringing Mexico to its knees in 1846–48.

Castilla was succeeded in 1851 by José Rufino Echenique, whose main contribution involved consolidation of the domestic national debt. Under this policy the Echenique government recognized as valid all manner of claims from citizens, usually his upper-class cronies, who testified to losses sustained during the wars of independence and subsequent conflicts. The Echenique administration paid out about 19 million pesos in this fashion, and according to one estimate at least 12 million pesos went for unfounded claims. The source of the payments needed no explanation: the governmental share of guano sales. Notwithstanding the corruption, the financial reorganization led to some important internal capital accumulation.

In 1854 a disgusted Castilla ousted Echenique and resumed control. Castilla promptly issued two far-reaching decrees: one abolishing the *contribución de indígenas,* the other emancipating black slaves. Social legislation, too, was facilitated by the guano trade, since the government could now afford to forego the head tax on Indians and to indemnify plantation owners for their slaves. Peru promptly began to tap another source of labor—Chinese coolies, about 100,000 of whom came as indentured workers from the mid-1850s to the mid-1870s and worked primarily in the coastal economy (guano, sugar, cotton).

During this second term, which lasted to 1862, Castilla continued to support military professionalization and public education. He presided over assemblies that produced two constitutions, a federalist document in 1856 and a centralized charter in 1860. And he continued to press for continental unity. As Castilla explained his rationale: "The relative weakness of the South American republics, divided and isolated among themselves, is in the judgment of this government the deplorable cause of the fact that on many occasions we have been treated with grave lack of respect, as if for the great international potentates there did not exist a common law of nations."

After Castilla's exit, troubles developed with Spain, which had never officially recognized Peruvian independence. Spain protested the alleged mistreatment of Spanish immigrants in Peru and in retaliation seized some guano-rich islands about 100 miles south of Callao. A provisional settlement sparked protests and a revolt; Mariano Ignacio Prado came to power, and in 1866 he declared war on Spain. The conflict dragged on for several years and ended in 1869, when Spain at last extended official recognition of Peru's independence.

Governments continued to face a spiraling debt. President José Balta (1868–72) turned the problem over to Nicolás de Piérola, a 30-year-old *wunderkind* and something of a dandy, and Piérola negotiated an agreement with the Parisian firm of Adolph Dreyfus. Under the plan Dreyfus assumed complete responsibility for the government's foreign debt and forwarded additional loans—in exchange for a monopoly over the purchase and sale of guano. In time the agreement unravelled, after Dreyfus put his own shares on the open market, but in the short run it provided some stability to an ever-changing and chaotic situation. Piérola also made arrangements for Henry Meiggs, the adventurous and unscrupulous North American entrepreneur, to expand railroads throughout the country. The Dreyfus and Meiggs contracts were immediately attacked by nationalist critics as sell-outs, but they were approved anyway.

The foreign debt continued to grow. Manuel Pardo, candidate of the country's first political party, the *Civilistas,* held office from 1872 to 1876. Thoughtful and statesmanlike, a born aristocrat and self-made millionaire, he wrestled with the debt, promoted public education, and nationalized the nitrate fields. Clearly he was one of the most realistic and effective leaders of his era. Near the end of his term he supported an army general for the presidency, hoping such a president would be able to deal with the continuing insurrections. In 1878, at the age of 44, Pardo was killed by an assailant. Peru lost one of its finest leaders.

As it was, things became worse. The focus of the export economy shifted south. Nitrates began to yield profits in what is now southern Peru and northern Chile, then part of Bolivia, and Chilean investors refused to pay new taxes on nitrates claimed by Bolivian president Hilarión Daza. So Daza ordered the seizure of a Chilean-owned nitrate operation in Antafogasta. Chile sent in troops to occupy the region. After some hesitation, the Peruvian government of Mariano Ignacio Prado decided to honor an 1873 alliance with Bolivia.

Thus began the War of the Pacific (1879–83), pitting Peru and Bolivia against Chile. It was a total disaster for Peru. Chile won a stunning military victory and occupied Lima. In the ensuing peace treaty in 1883, Chile gained outright control of the nitrate-rich province of Tarapacá, including the city of Iquique; and it was to keep control of Tacna and Arica for 10 years, their subsequent fate to be decided by a plebiscite.

The War of the Pacific had far-reaching effects on all three countries. For Chile it ushered in a nitrate boom and boosted national confidence. For Bolivia it denied access to the sea. For Peru it was a humiliating defeat, which further discredited the politicians. Furthermore it increased the debt and disrupted commerce. It was a failure in every conceivable way.

In the wake of defeat came General Andrés Cáceres, who engineered a coup in late 1885 and governed from 1886 to 1890. Attempting to pick up the pieces at home and to placate angry bondholders abroad, the new president, like so many before him, looked beyond Peru for help. Cáceres began discussions with the London bondholders. Under their plan, named for Michael Grace, the British negotiator, Peru would satisfy its creditors by ceding control of its railroads for 66 years, turning over all guano not needed for domestic use, and making 33 annual payments of 8000 pounds sterling. The bondholders, for their part, advanced a new loan for 6 million pounds and promised to invest a fair share of earnings in the railroads. Amid disagreement and controversy, the Grace Contract was finally approved in 1889. Like the Dreyfus consignment, it has for nationalists remained a symbol of their government's excessive zeal to please foreign investors.

The Grace Contract marked the end of Peru's guano age. Deposits were nearing exhaustion in the early 1880s and after 1889 Peru had relatively little surplus available for export. The cycle came to a close.

The guano boom left a deep impression on Peruvian history. It provided a lure for foreign investors; it led to extravagance and corruption within the Peruvian government; and it altered social outlooks within the elite, particularly among coastal landowners. "Popular imagination endowed fantastic proportions to the improvisation of fortunes," one writer recalled. "It was the first time that the old forms of social life, more or less static even during political upheaval, suffered a severe shake-up. For the first time money emerged as the exclusive social value." Tempted by the prospects, landowners tried to emulate merchants, traders, and financiers. But this did not mean the creation of an independent middle class or entrepreneurial middle stratum. It meant, instead, the adoption of some entrepreneurial qualities by Peru's coastal aristocracy.

Overview: Economic Growth and Social Change

Since the early nineteenth century the Peruvian economy has undergone three long cycles of export-led growth. Figure 6-1, showing the volume and value of exports, illustrates the general pattern. The first phase, corresponding to the guano age, stretched from the 1830s to the late 1870s. After a period of oscillation the economy recovered in the 1890s and began a phase of expansion that lasted to the Depression of the 1930s. The conclusion of World War II re-opened international markets and precipitated another cycle of growth that continued to the mid-1970s, when world prices for agricultural and other commodities went into decline.

The pattern of these trends helps us to understand several key features of Peru's economic development. First, the country has remained highly dependent on exports as a stimulus to growth. Policymakers have almost always focused on the international market, not domestic demand. Second, Peru has therefore remained extremely vulnerable to price swings in the international market and thus to forces beyond its control. Third, as we shall see, each of the three cycles has reflected the rise (and fall) of one or more products, a fact which had led to boom-bust cycles for different regions of the country. Fourth, twentieth century Peru has created an economy in which links between the capital-intensive "modern" sector—dominating the export-import process and mainly on the coast—and the labor-intensive "traditional" sector—mainly low-income and in the highlands—do not lead to a systematic increase in the latter sector's income. And fifth, partly as a result of the domestic impact of this export-oriented economy, Peru had by 1972 a notably unequal pattern of income distribution. The top 10 percent of the population received 43 percent of the income, while the lowest 40 percent got only 7 percent of the income.

After the guano decline it was mining, along with sugar and cotton, two agricultural commodities both grown on the coast, that fed the 1890–1930 expansion. As in Cuba and elsewhere, sugar was by this time a capital-intensive operation. Machinery for the modern mills was expensive, and it took large amounts of land to feed sufficient cane to the mills. Along Peru's north coast, where most of the production centered, it was also a year-round activity (in contrast to most other areas, such as Cuba, where the rhythm of work is seasonal). As a result plantation owners, mostly Peruvian, developed a stationary labor force approaching 30,000 workers by the late 1920s. Some were descendants of African slaves; some were Chinese; others were Indians from the sierra who came under coercive conditions as *enganchados* (literally, "hooked ones"—indebted by cash advances).

Sugar production and exports grew especially rapidly in the mid-

FIGURE 6-1 Exports from Peru, 1830–1975: Indices of Volume and Dollar Value (1900=100)

Volume

Dollar earnings

Exports (logarithmic scale)

10,000
6000
4000
2000
1000
600
400
200
100
60
40
20
10

1830 1840 1850 1860 1870 1880 1890 1900 1910 1920 1930 1940 1950 1960 1970

Source: **Rosemary Thorp and Geoffrey Bertram,** *Peru 1890–1977: Growth and Policy in an Open Economy* (New York: Columbia University Press, 1978), p. 5.

1890s and again in World War I. By the 1920s productive capacity reached 320,000 tons, nearly double the pre-war level. Though the market collapsed by the end of the decade, most planters were able to survive. Their largest export market was the United States, however, where protectionism hurt imports, so Peru's sugar sector fell stagnant during the 1930s.

The other major source of growth was cotton, which could be grown all along the coast. Up to the late nineteenth century, Peruvian long-staple cotton could not compete with the short-staple North American variety, but technical innovations in the 1880s permitted blending of the Peruvian product with wool. World demand increased and land-owners responded. Production leapt from around 400 metric tons in 1890 to more than 2000 metric tons in 1910 to around 6000 metric tons in 1930, by which time cotton was accounting for 18 percent of Peruvian exports.

Cotton cultivation in Peru is a seasonal enterprise, in contrast to sugar, and this created two kinds of labor: sharecropping (*yanaconaje*), by far the most important mode; and independent production by small-scale peasants. Partly for this reason ownership remained Peruvian, since foreign investors were reluctant to get involved in neo-feudal, i.e., non-market, relations of production. By the 1920s the labor force in cotton included more than 40,000 people.

Foreign entrepreneurs made their mark not as landowners but as merchants, as they occupied crucial positions in the ginning, financing, and marketing of cotton. Up to the 1920s they also held a virtual monopoly on credit, and planters usually needed short-term loans from season to season. But most of the benefits went to Peruvian producers. In addition cotton cultivation provided stimulus for domestic investment in textiles and byproducts (such as soap, candles, and cottonseed oil), but it did not lead to a wide range of investments outside the cotton sector.

The sierra also played a part in agriculture. From the grazing lands of the Andes came wool accounting for more than 10 percent of exports in the 1890s, in 1903, and in 1918–20. The highest grade variety, from the alpaca, was produced mainly by traditional peasants. Sheep wool came from the large-scale haciendas, and conflicts over land led to a wave of peasant revolts early in the century. The collapse of the market in the 1920s brought on a recession, especially for sheep growers, but the coast-oriented central government did not offer any relief.

The Peruvian *montaña*, like the Brazilian Amazon, went through a short-lived rubber boom. Hard-driving domestic entrepreneurs such as Julio C. Arana amassed huge fortunes, and by the turn of the century the city of Iquitos, the key market town of the Peruvian Amazon, had grown to about 20,000 inhabitants. The boom was short-lived. Soon

Peru, like Brazil, was pushed out of the market by the more efficiently grown plantation rubber from the Far East.

From the 1890s onward the once-dominant sector of the Peruvian economy, mining, underwent major change. In the late nineteenth century small-scale operators concentrated on precious metals, first silver and then gold. But Peruvian ores, located throughout the sierra, are unusually complex, there often being more than one metal in a single mine. Industrial development in the United States created demand for nonprecious metals like lead, zinc, iron, and copper.

Copper became the most important mineral product up to 1930. Technological advances and railway extensions made it feasible to tap the Peruvian veins. Large-scale U.S. investment arrived in 1901, with the purchase of the complex at Cerro de Pasco, and production quickly accelerated. By 1930 nearly half the value of all metal production came from copper, with silver and gold now mined as a byproduct of copper. Migrant *serranos* provided the labor force, and ownership fell almost completely under the control of foreigners, especially the Cerro de Pasco Copper Corporation and Northern Peru Mining, a subsidiary of the American Smelting and Refining Company.

The search for, and exploitation of, petroleum also expanded in these years, especially during World War I. Coastal fields contained notably high-grade deposits, much sought after in the international market, and U.S. capitalists became active in the early stages. In 1913 the International Petroleum Company, IPC (a Canadian-registered subsidiary of Standard Oil), gained access to major fields at Negritos and La Brea-

Silver refining at Cerro de Pasco in the early 1900s featured large-scale technology. (Courtesy of the Library of Congress.)

Pariñas under terms later to become a source of continuing controversy. About 10 percent of output went for domestic sales (since Peru did not have any coal); the rest was for the export market, where it brought handsome profits to the owners. By 1930 oil made up 30 percent of total Peruvian exports. That same year an informed observer guessed that 50 percent of the wholesale price abroad was clear profit for the companies.

In comparison to these export products—sugar, cotton, wool, rubber, copper, oil—domestic activity had a minor role in the 1890–1930 cycle of growth. Textile production expanded early in the century and then levelled off. Some agricultural goods were grown for domestic consumption—meat, potatoes, sweet potatoes, maize—but a fair amount of production and exchange took place within subsistence economies and not in the money economy.

The Depression and World War II then altered the international picture and prompted a modest reorientation of the Peruvian economy, but—in contrast to their counterparts in Argentina, Mexico, and Brazil—national policymakers did not even try to embark on a sustained program of import-substitution industrialization. When opportunity beckoned in the late 1940s they turned instead to a tried-and-true strategy: export-led growth with ample room for foreign investment and integration of Peru's economy with the international economy, above all the U.S. economy.

Most economic sectors joined in the postwar cycle, albeit with some important changes. Sugar production expanded to the 1960s, when it received a boost from Peru's share of the U.S. market quota taken away from Cuba, and Peruvian sugar workers began to organize a militant union movement. Cotton output went up from 182,000 tons per year in 1945–49 to 381,000 tons in 1960–64 and then declined, partly because of oversupply in the world market and partly because of competition from synthetic textiles. *Yanaconaje* was joined by paid labor and cash rentals in the production process, and sharecroppers managed to enhance their bargaining position. Sheep wool virtually disappeared from the export list, though the high-grade alpaca trade continued on a modest scale.

Mining underwent its own diversification. Copper retained its preeminence. Iron ore received attention, and was developed by the Marcona Mining Company, a conglomerate whose major participant was the Utah Construction Company. Even as mining moved into other metals, U.S. investment remained predominant. The same was true for petroleum, though its relative weight among exports declined throughout the 1960s.

One new commodity contributed importantly to the overseas balance of trade: fishmeal, which came to be widely used in the U.S. animal-feed industry (especially for poultry and pigs). From a standing start in the 1950s Peru leapt ahead to become the world's leading fishing country by volume in 1964, with 18 percent of the total world catch, and it was producing about 40 percent of the world's fishmeal supply. The leading entrepreneurs were neither foreign nor elite: like Luis Banchero Rossi, the legendary anchovy tycoon, they were from the local middle class. Nature then played a cruel trick. Changes in the offshore ocean currents, first in 1965 and again in 1972, along with overfishing, led to the disappearance of the fishing grounds. Just as quickly as Peru had found a new source of wealth, it vanished.

Manufacturing added another dimension to the country's economic picture. Some industrial growth occurred in the 1950s but it tended to be export-supporting rather than import-substituting: it focused on by-products of export goods, often for the overseas market, rather than on the replacement of imported goods for the Peruvian market. This pattern started shifting around 1960, as industrial output began to include such items as cement, chemicals, and consumer durables. Because of liberal legal provisions it was the foreign sector, not local investors, that took advantage of this opportunity. During the 1960s at least 164 major foreign corporations, many of them multinational, came into Peru. By 1968 manufacturing accounted for 20 percent of the gross national product (compared to 15 percent for agriculture, 14 percent

TABLE 6-1   Composition of Peruvian Exports, 1890–1976

Products	*Percentage Share of Exports, by Value*		
	1890	*1930*	*1976*
Sugar	28	11	7
Cotton	9	18	6
Coffee	——	0.3	9
Fishmeal	——	——	13
Silver	33	4	11
Copper	1	10	17
Lead	——	7	4
Zinc	——		11
Rubber	13	——	——
Oil	——	30	——

*Columns do not add up to 100 because of exclusion of some export items.

Sources: Rosemary Thorp and Geoffrey Bertram, *Peru 1890–1977: Growth and Policy in an Open Economy* (New York: Columbia University Press, 1978), pp. 40, 153; James W. Wilkie and Peter Reich, eds., *Statistical Abstract of Latin America*, 19 (Los Angeles: UCLA Latin American Center, 1978), Table 2732.

for commerce, 6 percent for mining), and in 1970 the industrial sector included 14.5 percent of the labor force.

Exports nonetheless continued to be paramount and, as shown in Table 6-1, copper was the country's leading export by the mid-1970s. Metals made up 44 percent of the total. Fishmeal, having recovered somewhat from the setback of the early 70s, earned 13 percent. Sugar and cotton together came to 13 percent, and coffee came on the list with 9 percent.

Indeed, the table demonstrates that Peru has had a diversity of export products since the 1890s. The relative importance of products has changed—sometimes dramatically, as in the cases of rubber and oil— but Peru has not relied on a one-product export economy since the guano age. To this extent the country has been fortunate.

By the mid-1960s processes of economic change had led to fundamental changes in the country's social structure. At the top was the traditional elite, the so-called "44 families," but it was by no means monolithic. The coastal segment of the aristocracy had since the 1890s become involved in commercial agriculture and in export-import transactions. It was a cosmopolitan group, shrewd and well-educated, with its center of action in the capital city of Lima. It took a flexible, pragmatic approach to matters at hand, often collaborating with foreign investors and frequently permitting upwardly mobile newly rich and military officers to join its social circles.

The *serrano* elite was in general more traditional, both in its attitudes and in its insularity. The provincial *patrón* was bound to the land and maintained an intimate (though hierarchical) relationship with the working *peón*. At the same time, many of these landowners had carried out major innovations in agriculture, including dairy farming in the north and livestock raising in the center and south. This gave the sierra a new economic impulse.

In terms of political power, the *serrano* elite had since the 1890s relied on the support of the coast to shore up its position and help put down rebellions. By the 1960s the *serrano* oligarchy found its local authority eroding badly. For one thing, many peons had left the haciendas, looking for jobs either in the sugar or cotton plantations on the coast or in the mining camps of the mountains. Secondly, the rural gendarmerie was replaced by the national *Guardia Civil*. And in addition, Indians and Indian communities acquired increasing legal protection during the twentieth century. By the 1960s, as if in admission of defeat, frustrated landlords gave up dealing with recalcitrant peons and simply turned their haciendas over to pasture.

The lower class—probably 80 percent of the population, if not more— was heterogeneous. It included the rural proletariat on the sugar plantations, tenant farmers and hired hands in the cotton fields, and peasants and subsistence farmers in the sierra. It included wage-earners on fishing boats, miners in the mountains, and organized workers in the cities. It included domestic servants in Lima, peons in the countryside, and residents of suburban squatter settlements. It included speakers of Aymara and Quechua, on the fringes of national society, as well as workers taking part in downtown strikes. It was a large-scale stratum, divided along three dimensions: between workers and peasants, between coast and sierra, between non-Indian and Indian. Yet in practice, network and family lines often bridged these divisions, and migration helped to reduce once-major geographical gaps.

And there were, of course, people in between, middle sectors if not yet a middle class (in the sense of a cohesive, self-aware social class that emerged in nineteenth century West Europe), mostly living in urban areas. Significantly, according to one estimate for the 1960s, nearly one-half the income-earners in the middle sectors had positions in government—including the military. Bureaucracy, it seems, as well as commerce, had turned into the ultimate middle-sector occupation.

Through these transformations Peruvian society became more urban. The national population grew from 3 million in 1900 to 17.7 million in 1980, and the urban proportion increased in that same period from 6 percent to 45 percent (as of 1975). Lima maintained its preeminent position, with 4.5 million inhabitants in the metropolitan area, but other cities grew as well. Although not as urbanized as Argentina or Chile, Peru was on a level equal to Brazil. It was a complex and changing society, one that clearly held the potential for political conflict. Let us now turn back to Peruvian political history, to see how that conflict emerged.

Oligarchic Rule

The military continued to dominate Peruvian politics in the early 1890s. General Andrés Cáceres and Colonel Remigio Morales Bermúdez exchanged power between 1885 and 1895, as the Grace Contract received approval from the Congress, but then politics changed under the influence of new ideas. Just as Argentina gave birth to its "Generation of 1880" and Mexico was fostering its *científicos*, Peru produced a similar class of civilian leaders. Highly educated, neopositivistic by training and liberal by outlook, they comprised a curious breed: for lack of a better phrase, they might be classified as aristocratic technocrats.

Their initial spokesman was Nicolás de Piérola, who, as José Balta's brash young treasury minister, had negotiated the questionable Dreyfus contract of 1869. Now more experienced, and as both a mystical Catholic and a scientific revolutionist, he sought to reconcile idealism and materialism. To advance his position and gain supporters he created the Democratic Party—the country's second political party, the first being the *Civilistas*—and in 1895 he became president.

Eager to promote the export-led expansion starting in the 1890s, Piérola moved to strengthen Peru's credit rating. He tightened tax legislation, and increased duties on commerce led to a doubling of government income during his four-year term. The resumption of payments on the foreign debt restored the country's standing with merchants and creditors abroad. Piérola also established a ministry of development (*ministerio de fomento*) to assist local entrepreneurs and to establish a means for governmental participation in economic growth.

In politics Piérola put through a direct suffrage law and strengthened municipal governments. Perhaps hoping to diminish the prospect of military intervention, he undertook to professionalize the armed forces and in 1898, just as Chile and Argentina were bringing in German missions, he invited a French military advisory team to help modernize the Peruvian forces. A clever politician, intent on civilian rule and quick to seize advantages, Piérola earned an appropriately ambiguous sobriquet: "the democratic *caudillo*."

After Piérola stepped down Peruvian politics entered an era of "bossism" known as *gamonalismo*. Effective competition for power was restricted to the upper-class elite. Elections took place but ballots were not secret, so landowners could herd their workers and peons to the polls and be sure they voted correctly. *Hacendados* from the sierra had themselves elected to the national congress, where they customarily supported the president—in exchange for unchecked powers in their own local arenas. And the coastal elite, consolidating its control of economic policy, pursued the path of export-led growth. The careful alliances Piérola had formed with landowners were functioning well.

The untimely death of president Manuel Candamo in 1904 precipitated a brief succession crisis that was resolved by the election of José Pardo. An activist, Pardo supported education, increasing its share of government expenditure in his presidency from 9.6 percent to 17.2 percent, and he put forward proposals for social and labor legislation (which Congress greeted with skepticism). Through his able treasury minister, Augusto B. Leguía, he set up a series of public agencies to define and strengthen the state's role in the promotion of economic development. The most prominent of these was the Peruvian Steamship Company (*Compañía Peruana de Vapores*).

As though to ratify this economic policy, Leguía assumed the presidency after uncontested elections in 1908. He himself had been a highly successful businessman, with interests in insurance and exports, and he had served as president of the National Bank of Peru. Once in office he established a state-run agency for guano, now channeled entirely to domestic consumption. Confronted by a haphazard revolt in 1909, he jailed his opponents. Throughout his career, in fact, Leguía showed much more concern with the substance of policies than with the procedures of consultation. Disdaining politics, absorbed in administration, Leguía staked his claim for law and order.

Ironically enough, Leguía was succeeded by an erratic populist, Guillermo Billinghurst, who won the 1912 elections. Organized labor had made a timorous appearance in Peru in 1904, with strikes in textile mills and other factories, and 1911 witnessed some serious protests against inflation. A prosperous businessman and journalist, the grandson of a British naval officer, Billinghurst had been a popular mayor of Lima. Gaining the support of the masses—and of a segment of the ruling elite—Billinghurst campaigned on a platform that included the promise for a bigger loaf of bread for five cents. Hence his nickname, "Big Bread" Billinghurst.

Billinghurst's hope was to reconcile the interests of workers and owners under the mantle of enlightened capitalism. Having a touch of the demagogue, he was comparable in ways to Argentina's Hipólito Yrigoyen. He proposed public housing and proclaimed support for an 8-hour day, and in 1913 he secured congressional approval for labor legislation that guaranteed collective bargaining. He studied the condition of the peasants but, sensing his limits, took no action there. Billinghurst's following was in the cities, not the countryside, and he began to encourage street demonstrations in support of his policies. Aghast at such events, the elite closed ranks against the president. In 1914 Billinghurst fell victim to a military coup.

The next year power reverted to civilian technocrats and José Pardo, president in 1904–8, began another four-year term. Despite his own status as a practicing Catholic, he oversaw the promulgation of a law establishing religious toleration. As World War I continued he finally severed relations with Germany, partly in hopes of gaining U.S. support against technically neutral but pro-German Chile. Pardo put through some labor legislation, including regulations for women and children. Billinghurst was right to worry about this sector, as it was here that Pardo faced the greatest challenge. In January 1919, as labor protest erupted in Buenos Aires and Santiago and São Paulo, workers in Lima-Callao proclaimed a three-day general strike. Supported by students mobilized from the University of San Marcos, they demanded lower food prices, an 8-hour day, and enactment of other legislation. Pardo had to call out the army to disperse the workers, and in the wake of the violence he acceded in part to their demands.

The clashes of 1919 also led to the formation of Peru's most important labor organization, the Regional Peruvian Labor Federation (*Federación Obrera Regional Peruana,* or FORP). Its leadership was moderate and sought, unsuccessfully as it turned out, industry-wide and nationwide collective bargaining. By mid-1919 a Socialist Party and a Workers' Party had also appeared, more Marxist in approach, but labor organization and activism were still in early stages.

Leguía: The Oncenio

In the midst of this confusion, former president Augusto B. Leguía returned from abroad, gathered widespread support, and won the 1919 election. Then he executed a masterful plan. Claiming that Pardo and the congress were plotting to annul his victory, Leguía got military backing for a coup. On July 4 he and his comrades seized the national palace, sent Pardo off to exile, dissolved the legislature, and ensconced themselves in power. Thus began Leguía's dictatorship, a watershed remembered throughout Peru as the *oncenio,* or eleven-year rule.

After a hastily arranged inauguration Leguía defined the goals for his regime. "I have come not only to liquidate the old state of affairs," he is reported to have said, "but also to detain the advance of communism which, because it is premature among us, would produce dreadful consequences." Reacting to the red scare of 1919, Leguía proposed to siphon off working-class discontent by building a coalition between capital and labor, an alliance that would herald the foundation of a *nueva patria* (new fatherland) for Peru. Ironically Leguía was seeking to complete the task undertaken by Billinghurst, the chief executive who had himself sent Leguía off to exile some time before.

The first step was to tighten the grip on political power. In 1920 a pliant assembly devised a new constitution, a document that legitimized Leguía's rule and charted a course for the state's role in the economy. The government was given explicit powers to set prices, impose taxes, and monitor labor-management relations. It was to assume responsibility for the education and assimilation of the Indians. And it was to frame its policies without the tangled executive-congressional relations that had bedevilled previous administrations: every five years there were to be simultaneous elections of the president and both legislative houses, thus virtually assuring working majorities for the chief executive.

Leguía was able to consolidate such power in part because of the fragility and decline of the old-line political parties—*Civilista,* Democratic, Liberal, and Constitutionalist. In fact, they were never strong institutions. They had been personal vehicles, creations of individual *caudillos,* not stable and self-perpetuating organizations. By 1920 they were unable to meet current challenges, either from the masses or Leguía, and they quietly withered away. Indeed with one exception, described below, Peruvian politics has seen a relative absence of strong and durable parties.

Leguía aggressively silenced his critics. The minister of the interior,

Germán Leguía y Martínez, a cousin of his known as "The Tiger," had a free hand in forcing opponents out of the country. Leguía exiled Antonio Miró Quesada, the publisher of *El Comercio,* and he later seized *La Prensa* and turned it into a pro-government newspaper. He dismissed dissident professors from university chairs, and he turned as well against students who had once hailed him as their "mentor." In 1924 Leguía even appropriated religion to his side, when he dedicated the republic of Peru to the Sacred Heart of Jesus. The opposition demonstrators were easily repressed. He used the occasion to arrest and deport at least 30 university students, among them a rising young leader by the name of Víctor Raúl Haya de la Torre.

Other forms of discontent were dispatched with equal efficiency. In fulfillment of the 1920 constitution Leguía created an office of Indian affairs under the activist direction of Hildebrando Castro Pozo. As the bureau began investigating land titles and other ticklish matters, however, the *gamonales* reacted and Leguía took action. In 1923 he sent the army to crush an Indian uprising in the sierra. Despite public rhetoric, peasants and Indians had no genuine place in the Leguía coalition.

To construct the "new fatherland" Leguía undertook a vigorous program of public works. With earnings from the export trade he invested in transportation and infrastructure, improving roads and bridges and building 600 new miles of railroad. Some of the work force came from the infamous *conscripción vial* (highway conscription), which forced poor rural males into unpaid construction work. And he encouraged foreign investment. By 1925 the Cerro de Pasco holdings came to about 50 million dollars, and IPC was preparing to exploit the La Brea–Pariñas oil fields.

The cornerstone of Leguía's economic policy was, of course, promotion of the export-import model of growth. A post–World War I slump in foreign-exchange receipts put pressure on the system, but it did not lead to support for industrial development. Even before World War I Peru had begun to buy most of its imports from the United States rather than Europe, so the wartime cut-off in supply was not as severe as for some other Latin American countries. The postwar slowdown in trade reduced the amount of capital available for investment, of course, and entrepreneurs put what they had into relatively safe ventures—including areas favored by Leguía's public-works program, such as construction or real estate. Consequently all major partners in Peru's capitalist elite—merchants, bankers and importers—expressed alarm when the terms of trade began leading to the depreciation of the nation's currency. (Even though devaluation boosts exports and is often favored by commodity producers, the Peruvian elite on this occasion was more interested in retaining its capacity to import goods from abroad, or to invest in the international market.) The Leguía administration listened.

In 1922 the central bank sold off a large share of gold and foreign reserves, and in the mid-1920s a large-scale loan was raised for the express purpose of maintaining a high exchange rate for the Peruvian *sol.*

Leguía pursued an active foreign policy with bordering states. In 1927 his government settled a longstanding boundary dispute with Colombia. Two years later, in 1929, he reached an agreement with Chile: the northern province of Tacna would go to Peru, and Arica would remain under Chile. The War of the Pacific, so ignominious for Peru, finally came to an end.

Within this carefully constructed political environment Leguía had no trouble getting re-elected in 1924 and 1929. He seemed invincible. His supporters controlled the congress, while his opponents were in exile or jail. Throughout the 1920s he functioned as the quintessential aristocratic technocrat: Like the *científicos* of prerevolutionary Mexico, Leguía and his followers made economic policy to fit the prescription of export-oriented capitalist expansion. But, as in the case of Mexico, it could not last forever.

The Reformist Critique

Peru's checkered history since independence inspired various types of internal criticism. Some critics blamed the Indians, some denounced the Spaniards. Some sought to uplift the country with new ideals, or new embodiments of spiritual traditions, while others focused on the material base of national progress. Among these intellectuals three deserve special attention: Manual González Prada, José Carlos Mariátegui, and Víctor Raúl Haya de la Torre.

González Prada, born in 1848 of aristocratic Spanish parentage, hoped to rekindle patriotic spirits after the War of the Pacific. Peru had lost its moral bearing, he thought, and the false prosperity of the guano age had led to degeneration. "Riches served as an element of corruption," according to González Prada, "not of material progress. . . . No means of acquisition seemed illicit. The people would have thrown themselves into a sewer if at the bottom they had glimpsed a golden *sol.* Husbands sold their wives, fathers their daughters, mothers their sisters. . . ." Influenced by European socialism in the 1890s, González Prada excoriated both capitalism and Catholicism. Peru should seek renewal by joining forces with its Indians to topple, by violence if necessary, the prevailing system. The time to act was now. "Old people to the grave," he declared in a famous rallying cry, "the youth to work."

One of Leguía's sharpest critics was José Carlos Mariátegui, a writer and journalist of humble origin. At heart a socialist, he became a spokesman for pro-Indian *indigenismo.* "Socialism preaches solidarity with and the redemption of the working classes," he characteristically reasoned. "Four fifths of Peru's working classes consist of Andean Indians. Therefore, socialism means the redemption of these Indians." How? Land was the answer. "The Indian question derives from our economy. It has its roots in the system of land tenure. Every effort to solve it with administrative or protective measures, with educational methods or road-building projects, represents a superficial labor as long as the feudalism of the great landowners exists." As for those who agonized over Peru's supposed racial decadence, Mariátegui had a tart response: "The degeneracy of the Peruvian Indian is a cheap invention of legal lickspittles at the feudal table." In sum, he wanted to create a utopian society by drawing on and adapting the collectivism of the Incan empire, especially the communal *ayllu* form of organization.

In 1926 Mariátegegui launched an influential journal, *Amauta,* a wide-ranging review of art and politics. His most famous collection of writings appeared in book form as *Seven Interpretive Essays on Peruvian Reality.* In 1929 he helped found a Socialist Party which soon became an affiliate of the Communist International. In 1930, at the age of 35, he died of a chronic illness. Peru, and Latin America as a whole, lost one of its most creative political thinkers.

A colleague and rival of his was Víctor Raúl Haya de la Torre, who as a student had been exiled by Leguía in 1924. That same year, in Mexico City, Haya de la Torre founded what he called the American Revolutionary Popular Alliance (*Alianza Popular Revolucionaria Americana,* or APRA). Sharing some of Mariátegui's insights, Haya intended to create a practical instrument for action. A rather grandiose scheme, APRA proclaimed a five-point program for the redemption of "Indo-America": resistance to Yankee imperialism, political unity of Latin America (Indo-America), nationalization of land and industry, internationalization of the Panama Canal and, most generally, solidarity with the oppressed around the world. For Peru, he eventually declared a more specific program: state control of the economy, long-run nationalization of key sectors, and the protection of political freedoms and human rights.

A brilliant organizer and electrifying speaker, Haya de la Torre later founded the *Aprista* (APRA) party in Peru. Underneath its populist rhetoric lay a concern for the welfare of the middle sectors in society. As Haya once put it: "It is this middle group that is being pushed to ruination by the process of imperialism. . . . The great foreign firms extract our wealth and then sell it outside our country. Consequently, there is no opportunity for our middle class. This, then, is the abused class that will lead the revolution."

Revolution or not, because or in spite of its middle-sector base, APRA was to become the most enduring political party in the history of Peru. It was to have a lasting impact on the course of national politics.

Flirting with Alternatives

The Depression took an immediate toll on the Peruvian economy. Export earnings plummeted (as shown in Figure 6-1). Profits shrank and discontent grew. In the face of crisis, the helplessness and decadence of the Leguía government prompted anger and contempt. In August 1930 a young military officer, Luis M. Sánchez Cerro, led an uprising in Arequipa that ended by ousting Leguía (who later died in prison).

Sánchez Cerro became the presiding officer of a military junta, and Peru embarked on a new political era. Of modest background, unmistakably *cholo,* Sánchez Cerro brought a distinct touch to the executive office. As he campaigned throughout the country, both to gain legitimacy for the junta and to advance his personal ambitions, he built a strong popular following. He did not offer a coherent ideology, but he was clearly attempting to forge a populist coalition between selected aristocratic elements and the working masses. In March 1931, in a fit of frustration, he resigned his post and sailed off to Europe. A few months later he returned, this time as the presidential candidate of the Revolutionary Union. His main opponent was Haya de la Torre and the *Aprista* party.

The 1931 campaign proved to be one of the most fateful and controversial events in Peruvian history. Sánchez Cerro called for agrarian reform, rural extension programs, and assimilation of the Indians: "So long as we do not consider all of our people, Indian and non-Indian, to be Peruvians, with the same rights and duties, there will never emerge the unity which is the indispensable element of the nation." Haya de la Torre countered by stressing the evils of imperialism as well as the existence of social inequities. It was an intense campaign, marked by violence and mutual accusations. *Aprismo* (as the APRA movement was known) revealed an electoral stronghold in the northern coast, particularly in the sugar-growing areas around Trujillo, where economic modernization had led to social dislocation and popular frustration over the destruction of the traditional society; the party received ample support in Lima and elsewhere as well. But in the end it was Sánchez Cerro who won with an official tally of 152,062 votes to 106,007 for Haya de la Torre.

Polarization ensued. The *Aprista* movement, with its Marxist premises, offered a left-wing critique of Peruvian society. There was also a formidable movement on the right. As in Argentina, some conservatives openly sympathized with fascism. José de la Riva Agüero was elo-

An *Aprista* election poster expresses both the party's outlook and the intensity of the 1931 campaign; the slogans say "Only *Aprismo* will save Peru . . . vote for Haya de la Torre." (Private collection.)

quent on the subject. "Up with Catholicism," he declared, "up with the corporate state and fascism, with order, hierarchy, and authoritarianism." It was time, he said, for decisive action:

> There can be no middle ground. Either to the right or to the left. Democracy, capitalism, the liberal tradition, all represent a middle ground which is really disguised communism or else the certain road to it. . . . The only solution is to return to the medieval, Catholic, Hispanic tradition as now embodied in fascism.

Not surprisingly, Francisco Franco's right-wing movement in Spain had numerous adherents in Peru during the Spanish Civil War.

Tension continued to mount. In early 1932 a young *Aprista* tried to

211

assassinate Sánchez Cerro. The president was now determined to crack down on the *Apristas*. But they had their own plan—for an insurrection in the provincial city of Trujillo. The rebels succeeded in taking the entire city, including the army garrison. A powerful military column soon surrounded the *Apristas,* who decided to flee. In the ensuing panic, and perhaps even by top *Aprista* orders, the insurgents executed some ten military officers, fifteen policemen, and twenty-five civilians, all hostages. When the invading government troops discovered this atrocity, they summarily executed at least a thousand (the estimates ran as high as 6000) of the local residents suspected of giving armed support to the *Apristas.* This ugly exchange of murders set the tone for APRA-army relations thereafter. For the army it took on the character of a blood feud, and convinced many officers that they must never let APRA come to power.

Meanwhile, Sánchez Cerro was attempting to consolidate his power and pushed through a new constitution. In April 1933 another *Aprista* gunman succeeded in assassinating the president. Beset by yet another crisis, congress elected General Oscar R. Benavides to serve out the remainder of the presidential term.

As Benavides took office Peru entered a phase of economic transition, a period that held out the possibility of reducing the country's dependence on international markets and investments. Led by cotton, exports began to recover after 1933. But because of the Depression, and later on World War II, foreign capital beat a steady retreat: the proportion of exports produced by foreign-owned firms fell from around 60 percent at the end of the 1920s to 30 percent of less in the late 1940s. (By 1967 it would climb up to 50 percent.) Local entrepreneuers, sometimes with government help, gained increasing control of lead and zinc, and of some gold and silver as well. Petroleum output went up throughout the 1930s. Industrial capacity was modest but it nonetheless appeared that Peru was becoming able to redirect its economy if it so chose.

Benavides showed some desire to seize the chance. In 1934 his government began the state-directed development of petroleum. Trade doubled from 1933 to 1936, and the *sol* remained stable against the dollar. He used a fair share of governmental receipts for public works and social projects, including road construction, working-class housing, and a compulsory social-security system. He supported an agricultural bank founded in 1931 to give credit to cotton planters and other landowners, thus reducing the role of foreign merchant houses.

In the political arena Benavides tried to reduce polarization and to achieve a national consensus. Settlement of a border dispute with Colombia earned him both applause and time, but the going proved to be rough. At first he offered amnesty to imprisoned *Apristas* but then, as conflict intensified, he appointed the pro-fascist Riva Agüero as his prime minister. Crackdowns followed. In 1936 Benavides annulled elections won by an *Aprista*-backed candidate, and he held on to power for three more years.

In 1939 the presidency passed to Manuel Prado, a moderate civilian who adopted a conciliatory posture toward the *Apristas*. All major parties expressed support for Prado's pro-Allied stance in World War II. Peru also won a brief military clash and diplomatic triumph in a boundary conflict with Ecuador. Foreign affairs seemed to be having a healing effect.

Electoral triumph in 1945 went to José Luis Bustamante y Rivero, who ran as the candidate of the National Democratic Front—with APRA's support. He soon faced a series of political struggles, as *Aprista* delegates to congress sought to curtail executive authority. Inflation and food shortages prevented serious socioeconomic challenges. And amidst public controversy, Bustamante approved a contract giving IPC permission to search for oil in the Sechura desert.

Together, Prado and Bustamante furthered the modest reorientation of the Peruvian economy. They vastly increased government spending (which Benavides had tried to keep in check). They introduced a fixed exchange-rate system and they established import controls along with the rationing of foreign exchange. And they launched a scheme for a state-controlled iron and steel plant. In short, they modified the path of Peru's economic development in at least two crucial respects: they strengthened the role of the state, and they reduced the reliance on exports and imports.

All of which prompted the wrath of export producers, particularly the sugar planters. A central thrust of the Prado-Bustamante policy was the diversification of agriculture, and this entailed a series of measures which the sugar barons correctly saw as threatening: increased export taxes, rationing of guano, pressure to cultivate food crops, and, in 1941, an insistence that sugar producers satisfy domestic-market quotas before exporting to overseas markets. Taking advantage of the hullabaloo over the Sechura contract, which aroused strong nationalist sentiment, the coastal elite supported a military move against the Bustamante government. In 1948 General Manuel A. Odría seized power.

Economic Liberalism and Political Vacillation

The Odría coup of 1948 constitutes another watershed in contemporary Peru. In economics, it led to restoration of the open, export-led model of growth. In politics it ushered in an era of uncertainty, of dictatorial rule and electoral confusion. The contradictions in this system would eventually come forth with startling clarity.

Under the watchful eye of the elite, the Odría regime adopted pro-planter measures. The exchange-rate was freed, import restrictions were lifted, foreign investment was encouraged in mining and oil, advice was sought from U.S. experts on currency stabilization. All in all, as Rosemary Thorp and Geoffrey Bertram observe, the Odría government undertook to implement "that dream of orthodox development economists," a vision that would be pursued till 1968: "an export-led system in which cyclical balance-of-payments difficulties were handled by domestic demand restraint and exchange devaluation, in which the entry of foreign capital and the repatriation of profits were virtually unrestricted and in which government intervention and participation were kept to a minimum." Particularly in this last respect, Peru seemed out of step with the rest of Latin America. Notes another economist, Shane Hunt: "In a continent that was witnessing ever-increasing state intervention in economic life in country after country, Peru . . . turned around to begin a march in the other direction. . . ."

To tighten his hold on authority Odría immediately took after his opponents, particulary *Apristas*. Haya de la Torre managed to escape imprisonment by seeking refuge in the Colombian embassy where he remained for more than five years, awaiting safe conduct from the military. Dissent was stifled and civil liberties became precarious.

Odría consolidated his position by winning the 1950 elections—there was no opposition—and proceeded to impose his regime. Rather consciously, he began to emulate the style and manner of Argentina's Juan Perón. He courted working-class masses, more so in the coastal cities than in the rural sierra. He lavished funds on ostentatious public works, most notably in Lima. He developed a personalistic following. And with the aid of his wife, María Delgado de Odría, he sought to mobilize women in support of the regime, extending suffrage to females in 1955.

A decline in export earnings after the end of the Korean War in 1953 brought Odría's heyday to a close. Unemployment mounted, inflation increased, and workers went out on strike. Civilian oligarchs expressed apprehension over Odría's capricious form of rule. Under pressure, Odría finally consented to allow free elections in 1956.

The leading contenders that year were former president Manuel Prado, supported by the *Apristas,* and a political newcomer named Fernando Belaúnde Terry, candidate of the National Front of Democratic Youth. Belaúnde, a University of Texas–trained architect from a prominent family, began to articulate the hopes and frustrations of the country's educated middle sectors. But his time had not yet arrived. The winner was Prado, with 568,000 votes; Belaúnde, with 458,000, came in a respectable second.

Prado brought in a period of political liberalization, permitting trade-union organization and allowing Communists as well as *Apristas* to operate freely. By the end of his term organized labor could claim about 330,000 members. Through his economics minister, the aristocratic Pedro Beltrán, he continued Odría's policies, emphasizing exports and foreign enterprise. A program for "shelter and land" (*techo y tierra*) was proclaimed in the name of the peasants, but little was done about it.

The next presidential election, in 1962, offered a clear picture of political forces in Peru. Presidential candidates were Haya de la Torre, at last able to run on the *Aprista* platform; Belaúnde, who had created a new organization called Popular Action; and the always hopeful Odría, at the head of the *Union Nacional Odriísta*. The only genuinely institutional party was APRA; the others were personal vehicles for their respective leaders. Partly for this reason Haya won the largest number of votes (557,000), but his scant plurality of 33 percent meant the outcome would have to be decided by Congress. Ever the opportunist, Haya proceeded to reach an accord with Odría. The armed forces, who had never forgotten or forgiven the *Aprista*-inspired murder of their colleagues at Trujillo in 1932, refused to accept the prospect of an *Aprista* president, however, and the military suspended Congress and announced that new elections would be held.

The new elections came in 1963. Having obtained the support of Christian Democrats, Belaúnde emerged on top with 39 percent. APRA was next with 34 percent and the *Odriístas* garnered 26 percent. With the *Apristas* safely defeated, the military accepted the results and let Belaúnde enter the presidency.

Belaúnde revealed himself to be an appealing, sometimes even charismatic politician. Relishing the role of the visionary, he proposed building a trans-Amazon highway that would open up the lush Peruvian *montaña* region to development. He called on the memories of the Incas and urged his countrymen to aspire to greatness again. He traveled throughout the country, talking to peasants and workers as well as to planters and managers, tirelessly seeking to generate a national consensus.

On a more practical level Belaúnde recognized the need for adjustments in the Peruvian economic model. In particular, he began to increase the role of the state and to expand social services. He started to provide incentives for manufacturing. And he urged the need for agrarian reform.

Yet his efforts foundered. By the time his bill for land reform got through Congress it had been virtually emasculated. It emphasized technical improvement rather than land distribution, apparently in hopes that *hacendados* would increase production. And because of objections from *Apristas* and *Odriístas,* it exempted sugar estates on the coast—where the *Apristas* had built up solid unions, and where *Odriístas* had their right-wing support.

215

So land reform was more promise than performance, and peasants in the sierra finally reacted angrily. They started to invade the haciendas, seizing cultivated lands as well as fallow fields, and conflict raged throughout the Andes. Coinciding with the peasant protest was a Cuban-style guerrilla movement bent on establishing a rural *foco,* or nucleus. Ché Guevara and the young French intellectual Régis Debray had argued that a successful *foco* could be the spark to set off a country-wide revolution.

Within a year or so Belaúnde decided he had to suppress the peasant guerrillas. He sent the regular army on this mission, and by 1966 the movement was crushed. According to one account the repression left 8000 peasants dead, 19,000 homeless, 3500 in jail, and 14,000 hectares of land destroyed by fire and napalm. It was a traumatic experience— for both the 300,000 peasants who had risen up and for the soldiers who had put them down.

One of Belaúnde's other promises was to resolve the longlasting dispute with IPC, and here, too, he faced a no-win situation. After five years of protracted negotiations, during which the U.S. revealed continuing hostility to Peru's nationalistic inclinations, the Belaúnde government gave in. IPC surrendered its claim to the La Brea–Pariñas oil fields, by now exhausted anyway, while Peru gave up its claims to back taxes; IPC gained access to new fields in the Amazon; and the government agreed to sell crude oil to IPC at a fixed price for refining at the company's Talara complex. Amid a chorus of denunciation the Belaúnde administration published the agreement, all but the page containing the price for state-produced crude. The scandal created an uproar, as opponents accused the government of selling crude oil too cheaply to the foreign firm.

The economy was grinding to a halt. In August 1967 the government devalued the *sol* by 47 percent. Import controls and export taxes improved the balance of payments. As inflation declined so did growth. Belaúnde's optimistic vision, the dream of a united and prosperous Peru, was proving an illusory dream. In October 1968 the military once again decided to send their tanks to the presidential palace. This time, however, it would be no caretaker government they installed.

The Military Revolution

The military *golpe,* or coup, paved the way for one of Latin America's most ambitious military governments. Led by General Juan Velasco Alvarado, the junta immediately declared its intention to bring far-reaching changes in the structure of Peruvian society. A manifesto, issued the day of the coup, indicted the "unjust social and economic order which places the usufruct of the national wealth solely within the reach of the privileged, while the majority suffer the consequences of a marginalization injurious to human dignity." What Peru needed, the officers proclaimed, was a new economic order, "neither capitalist nor communist," a system that would abolish prevailing inequities and create the material foundations for harmony, justice, and dignity.

A combination of three qualities set this regime apart from earlier military governments in Peru—and, for that matter, in the rest of Latin America. One was its social and political autonomy. This time the Peruvian armed forces acted alone, rather than in collusion with civilian power groups; the middle-class military was beholden to no one but itself, and it consequently had an exceptionally free hand. Second, the leaders of the regime implicitly adopted the outlook and premises of the "dependency" school of analysis. One of their principal purposes, therefore, was to end what they called "the subordination of the Peruvian economy to foreign centers of decision, where actions originate which fundamentally affect the economic life of the nation and prevent an autonomous development process geared to the achievement of national objectives." And third, largely as a result of its anti-guerrilla campaign in the sierra, the Peruvian military had genuine sympathy with the plight of the long-oppressed peasantry.

The result was a revolutionary military regime. The prospect seemed startling, if not contradictory—in Fidel Castro's phrase, "as if a fire had started in the firehouse."

A key to the military government's program was agrarian reform. In mid-1969 the Velasco government announced the enactment of the most sweeping land reform program in Latin America since the Cuban Revolution. "Peasants," declared General Velasco, "the landlords will no longer eat from your poverty." All large estates, regardless of productivity, were subject to expropriation. The ax fell first on the highly mechanized sugar plantations of the coast, which were placed under the administration of worker-run cooperatives, called CAPS (Agricultural Production Cooperatives). For the sierra the idea was to create small or medium sized farms, but before long the government gave in to peasant demands for cooperative forms of organization. The principal form was the SAIS (Agricultural Society for Social Interest), the government-recognized unit that could combine former hacienda peons and villagers from surrounding communities. By the mid-1970s it was estimated that three-quarters of the country's productive land was under cooperative management of one sort or another. Reported one observer in 1974: "Practically speaking, the agrarian elite has disappeared as a power group." By 1979 half the 21 million hectares of agro-grazing land on the coast and in the highlands had been expropriated from the *hacendados* and delivered to the peasants. No land remained in the huge estates that had dominated the Peruvian agrarian sector.

The Velasco regime took firm steps to institutionalize these fundamental changes. The traditional association of the planter elite, the National Agrarian Society, was abolished by decree in 1972. In its stead appeared the National Agrarian Confederation (CNA), a peak organization for regional collectives.

In 1971 the Velasco regime created one of its most characteristic institutions, the National System for Support of Social Mobilization (*Sistema Nacional en Apoyo de la Mobilización Social,* or SINAMOS). Sometimes written as two words—*sin amos,* "without masters"—it was to serve as the integrating institution for peasant and working-class groups. It would thus link the regime with the masses, identifying the government with its constituent groups and promoting a harmonious set of leader-follower relationships.

This desire to organize and mobilize the peasantry became one of the hallmarks of the new military government. It reflected the extent to which Peru's new rulers intended to restructure the distribution of power—not only at the upper reaches of authority, but also at the bases of society.

A second area that captured Velasco's attention was the squatter shanty towns, the sprawling *barriadas* around Lima and other cities. By the late 1960s, it was estimated that about 750,000 recently arrived migrants lived in the environs of Lima alone. Peru's military officers concluded that this was an explosive situation. So they set about organizing the settlements, now renamed "young towns" (*pueblos jóvenes*), and enlisted the aid of the church in their efforts. Part of the solution was simple enough: the granting of property titles to the migrant occupants.

The other tactic was to bring the *pueblos jóvenes* under the umbrella structure of SINAMOS. The purpose was to create conditions for stability. As one official put it: "We want participation but it should be organized participation. We want to make as many people as possible homeowners, then they will act responsibly towards their community and have a stake in it." By 1974 the majority of urban squatters had been reorganized from above into state-chartered *pueblos jóvenes.*

This top-down pattern of organization and mobilization illustrates a crucial feature of the Velasco regime. It was not attempting to construct a socialist society, as did Allende in Chile or Castro in Cuba. Nor was it seeking to exclude and repress already organized working-class movements, as did military governments in Chile, Brazil, and Argentina. Instead, the Peruvian regime was intent on integrating marginal urban and rural masses into the national society in order to lay the groundwork for industrialization and autonomous development. The chief strategy toward this end was to incorporate such groups under the guidance and tutelage of the state, which would in turn regulate civil disputes. This would permit achievement of a major goal, one that has frequently appeared in Latin American settings: the reduction of class conflict.

In its stress on eliminating class struggle and establishing social harmony, the Peruvian regime emerged as a typical corporate state. In its emphasis on organizing and integrating lower-class groups, it was reminiscent of the Cárdenas government in Mexico (1934–40) and the early part of the first Perón rule in Argentina (1946–50).

The same basic principle applied to the manufacturing sector, for which the government promulgated an "industrial community" law. According to this scheme employees in every firm with six or more workers—members of the "industrial community"—were gradually to acquire 50 percent of the stock in each company, and to gain representation on the board of directors. Workers would become co-owners with management and, in principle at least, class conflict would disappear. Employers found various ways to get around this legislation, but by late 1974 there were approximately 3500 industrial communities with 200,000 members in control of 13 percent of all the shares in their firms.

To accelerate this process the government created the "social property" sector, through which firms would be controlled and managed exclusively by workers—with proceeds to go to the sector as a whole. Part of the income went to wages and housing and services, and part was reserved for reinvestment in other social-property industries.

While granting workers participation in the Peruvian industrialization, the military regime embarked on a series of measures to reduce the role of foreign capital. At the time of the 1968 takeover 242 firms with significant foreign investment were responsible for 44 percent of the country's industrial production. This was unacceptable to the government. Declared Velasco in 1970: "The moment has now passed when we judged the process of industrialization in the abstract as a panacea for all our problems. Now it is imperative to determine the type of industrialization. . . ." To curtail the role of foreign capital the government began to require approval of new investment by a regulation board, to prohibit the purchase of viable, locally owned firms, and to exclude foreign participation from sensitive areas. Peru also assumed a conspicuous role in the promotion of regional economic cooperation through the Andean Pact.

But the most decisive steps involved expropriation. Soon after the coup the regime announced the nationalization of IPC, to the delirious approval of the public, and the establishment of the state-supported *Petroperú*. In time the government took over other prominent foreign-owned firms: ITT (1969), Chase Manhattan Bank (1970), Cerro de Pasco (1974), and Marcona Mining (1975)—the latter two replaced by *Minoperú*. These actions met with hostility from the United States, but in February 1974 the two governments reached an accord through which Peru would pay $150 million as full settlement of all outstanding claims by North American business (including IPC) and the U.S. would withdraw its opposition to international loans for Peru.

Despite its populist stance the Velasco government met with considerable resistance at home. Pre-existing labor unions, such as the *Aprista*-dominated organizations among sugar workers, resented the inroads of their terrain. Peasants often found the top-down institutions unresponsive to their demands and began to stage protests in SINAMOS offices. The traditional elite expressed nothing but horror at the policies of the regime, of course; in response the generals seized control of the media. Four newspapers were taken over in 1970, TV and radio followed the next year, and six other Lima dailies were put under pro-government management in 1974. This only compounded the government's problem, as journalists and middle-sector spokesmen denounced these restrictions on dissent.

Obviously the military government was an authoritarian regime. Opponents were harassed, intimidated, exiled, and jailed. It was furthermore staffed by a cadre of technocrats intent on achieving economic growth and development. So it was a "bureaucratic authoritarian" regime to this extent, but it differed from the prototypical forms in Argentina and Brazil in at least three respects: first, it began as an extremely autonomous military government that did not involve a coalition with foreign investors and domestic capitalists; second, it was attempting to build support through the inclusion of lower-class groups; third, it did not engage in the campaigns of systematic terror that were occurring in the southern cone.

Economic conditions added to Velasco's woes. Export earnings declined, as shown in Figure 6-1. The fishmeal industry disappeared, petroleum explorations yielded no new oil deposits, world prices for sugar and copper dropped. The balance of payments deteriorated, the foreign debt swelled, and inflation struck. Workers began to demonstrate their discontent. In 1975 there were 779 strikes, compared to 414 in 1967.

As these problems first loomed on the horizon, Velasco himself succumbed to ill health in 1972: the diagnosis was serious circulatory problems. His grasp on power weakened, if slowly, and his colleagues eventually concluded that he had to go. In August 1975 Peru's joint chiefs replaced him with General Francisco Morales Bermúdez (who happened to be the descendant of a former president). An era thus came to an end.

In effect, Morales Bermúdez presided over the modification—if not the dismantling—of the 1968–75 experiment. SINAMOS was permitted to wither away. Under pressure from the IMF, the government imposed an economic austerity program that reduced the proportion of adults with adequate employment to 42 percent. The real income of the urban working-class declined by 40 percent between 1973 and 1978. In February 1977 Morales Bermúdez unveiled Plan Tupac Amarú, a program rhetorically committed to "fully participatory social democracy" but actually designed to undo much of the Velasco scheme. It called for, among other things, economic decentralization and austerity, the encouragement of foreign investment, and transfer of the state-controlled press to private hands. And it sounded the death knell of the regime. There were to be a constituent assembly in 1978 and general elections in 1980. The officers were getting out.

What this revealed, in retrospect, was the regime's inability to gain solid support from any social class or grouping and thereby establish institutional foundations for its authority. By reaching into so many areas of Peruvian society the military government succeeded in alienating almost everyone: No group felt safe from intervention or control, no stratum offered its unconditional adherence. Ironically, the feature which had given Peru's revolutionary military government so much freedom of action—its autonomy—also led to its eventual demise.

Back to Normal?

The 1978 elections for the constituent assembly produced several surprises. Not surprising was APRA's 35 percent of the vote, evidence of the party's continuing appeal. But no one had expected the five main parties on the left to win 33 percent. The left was apparently benefitting from the wave of popular mobilization in 1976–78. There was also a new party on the right, the Popular Christians (PPC), which won 24 percent. Would the left and right be able to hold to these gains in the 1980 presidential elections?

The top two parties were APRA, whose ticket was now led by Armando Villanueva (Haya de la Torre having died), and Popular Action, still under Fernando Belaúnde Terry, which had boycotted the 1978 elections. After an arduous and open campaign the 68-year-old Belaúnde captured a commanding plurality with 42 percent of the vote, partly because of his reassuringly statesmanlike image. APRA took only 28 percent, a substantial setback; the right, represented by the Popular Christian Party (PPC), received 11 percent; an assortment of left-wing parties amassed about 16 percent. Thus the left and the right each dropped to less than half their percentage of two years earlier. Belaúnde had clearly picked up votes from both. Villanueva declined Belaúnde's offer to take part in a coalition government, preferring to maintain APRA's time-honored role in the congressional opposition.

So Belaúnde became president again. The scene had a familiar touch, but there were some novel features too. In contrast to 1963–68, Belaúnde had virtual control of the legislature, with a clear majority for Popular Action in the Chamber of Deputies (95 seats out of 180) and room for maneuver in the Senate (26 of 60 seats). APRA began to fall apart and no longer resorted to purely obstructionist tactics. The right was relatively isolated. And the parliamentary left, though growing in strength, was divided into multiple factions. Belaúnde could claim a mandate almost by default.

One set of challenges came from the economy. Peru had a number of serious economic problems: inflation, unemployment, and a mounting foreign debt. Agricultural production was down, partly because of the recent reforms but more often because of decapitalization carried out by landowners in anticipation of expropriation. The massive state sector required close administrative scrutiny. To cope with such matters Belaúnde appointed as prime minister (and finance minister) Manuel Ulloa, a well-known financier with Wall Street experience. Other key members of the economic team were Pedro Pablo Kuczynski, minister of energy and mines, and Richard Webb, director of the central bank, both prominent economists. Most of the other cabinet portfolios went to political hacks and hangers-on.

Soon after the inauguration Ulloa announced a four-point plan for economic recovery:

1. reduction of the government's role in the economy—some state firms, including *Petroperú,* were to become limited liability companies;
2. strengthening of the private sector, which would receive a 48 percent increase in credit in 1981;
3. a scaling down of taxes; and
4. encouragement of foreign investment.

Ulloa's approach received support from APRA as well as the right-wing PPC. Only the left voiced apprehension about its effect on workers and peasants.

The economic team did its best to implement the program. A December 1980 law offered tax credits for reinvestment to foreign-owned oil companies, and the strategy seemed to pay off: An agreement soon followed with the Superior Oil Company of Houston for exploration and development of petroleum fields in the *montaña* region. Industrialists claimed to be threatened by overseas competition (particularly textiles from South Korea and Taiwan), but the government in effect sustained protection by devaluing the *sol* (thereby making imports more expensive). Webb and Ulloa collaborated smoothly with the IMF in re-negotiating the external debt. Price controls were lifted on most basic goods, including oil and electricity, and wages were held in check. In these and other ways Peru re-opened its economy to the forces of the national and international market.

In mid-1982, starting his third year in office, Belaúnde could point with pride to some achievements. The Gross Domestic Product had increased by 3.9 percent in 1981, compared to 2.7 percent for population growth. The foreign debt was down from nearly half the size of the gross domestic product in 1978 to 31 percent in 1981—still an excessive burden in Belaúnde's view, but the situation appeared to be under control.

Not quite. For the austerity measures of the Ulloa group brought special hardship to the working class, which reacted strongly. At one point in July 1980, the month of Belaúnde's inauguration, as many as 100,000 workers were out on strike. Labor leaders called general strikes in January 1981, in September 1981, and again in November 1982. The middle class was also hard-hit by the government's anti-inflation policy. White-collar workers, including doctors, jointed in protest with petroleum workers and agricultural laborers. The reason was simple enough. Inflation continued at a rate of 70 percent for 1982, while wages and salaries fell behind.

The criticism took its toll. In December 1982 Ulloa resigned from the cabinet—partly because of widespread opposition to his policies and partly, some thought, to prepare his own candidacy for the 1985 presidential election. (Kuczynski, too, had left office earlier in the year for personal reasons.) Ulloa was replaced as finance minister by Carlos Rodríguez Pastor, a long-time associate of Belaúnde. The moves did not appear to herald any major shift in policy, but they underscored the extent of social discord over economic issues.

Violence mounted too. In 1981 Belaúnde sponsored a draconian anti-terrorist law that called for 10 to 20 years in jail for convicted terrorists *and* their supporters or defenders. Later in the year he approved a police crackdown in Ayacucho and, to emphasize the point, put a retired air force general in charge of the Ministry of Interior. Nonetheless anti-government activities continued to increase, in both the countryside and in the urban centers. Guerrillas were especially active around Ayacucho, and their attacks provoked ferocious repression of the peasants by the police and army. Between January and late August 1982 there were reported to have been 263 terrorist incidents in the city of Lima, which was then struck by an electricity blackout and a bombing spree. Most of the raids were attributed to a movement called *Sendero*

Luminoso ("Shining Path"), a Maoist group intent on bringing the social system to its knees.

Consolations for the government were few and far between. The election of a Peruvian, Javier Pérez de Cuéllar, as secretary-general of the United Nations, brought well-deserved recognition to the country's diplomatic corps, and Cuéllar's level-headed (though unsuccessful) efforts to head off the Falklands/Malvinas War between Argentina and Britain in mid-1982 won further admiration. And on the domestic front, Belaúnde had won one major triumph: He was still in office.

By early 1983 Peru was in a delicate position. The centrist government was receiving sharp criticism from both right and left. Continued assaults by *Sendero Luminoso* prompted rumors of a military coup—this time, observers predicted, of a thoroughgoing right-wing variety. The society was polarized and the political system was feeling the strain. Indeed, the legacy of the 1968–80 experiment had yet to be assessed. Said one experienced observer: "The chances for violent swings to the left or the right are much greater than they were [in 1968]. Peru's generals and colonels may not have achieved a successful revolution, but it may yet turn out that they made one possible."

SEVEN

MEXICO
The Taming of a Revolution

The history of Mexico offers a study in contrast. Rich in natural resources, the country has known both prosperity (if only for the elite) and poverty. For several decades after independence the nation's political life was a prototype of chronic instability. National governments came and went at gunpoint, threatening the new nation's territorial integrity. By mid-nineteenth century Mexico was heading toward a liberal government, which would have greatly reduced church power and the corresponding burdens of its colonial legacy. Political liberalism, however, gave way to the dictatorship of Porfirio Díaz (1876–80 and 1884–1911) and thence to the Mexican Revolution—the first of the world's great twentieth century revolutions. Out of the Revolution came a political system which had produced, since the 1930s, a political stability unmatched in Latin America.

Mexico's emergence from its colonial past has been conditioned by one factor no other Latin American nation shares: a 2000-mile border with the U.S. That proximity had produced benefits and liabilities (as a Mexican president once exclaimed, "Poor Mexico! So far from God, and so close to the United States!"). Having tasted bitter defeat on the battlefield, the people of Mexico have retained their dignity and pride—and now, having both discovered massive deposits of oil and been faced with a large-scale economic crisis, the country has encountered the risks involved in becoming a leading member of the international community. Mexico's future, like its past, arouses emotions of anxiety and hope.

Mexico After Independence

The Wars for Independence left Mexico in disorder and decay. Conditions were far worse in Mexico than in Argentina or Brazil, because the actual fighting had been so much more widespread and protracted in Mexico. The economy was in shambles. Spaniards had taken their capital out of the country. The gold and silver mines, once the pride of Spain's overseas empire, had fallen into disrepair. Insurgents and royalists had both made a point of killing technicians while thousands of miners had gone off to war; without sufficient supervision, the mines had flooded and machinery became utterly useless. Production plummeted to one-third its prewar level. Mining communities languished: Valenciana, for example, had 22,000 residents in 1810 and only 4000 in 1820. It would take another generation—and considerable sums of foreign investment—to restore the precious mines to full production.

The textile industry had also fallen on hard times, The scars of battle were visible throughout the country, especially the central valley. As one traveller recalled, there were "ruins everywhere—here a viceroy's palace serving as a tavern, where the mules stop to rest, and the drivers to drink pulque—there, a whole village crumbling to pieces; roofless houses, broken down walls and arches, an old church—the remains of a convent." Noting the toll on agriculture, too, another observer described how he and his companions "saw the houses roofless and in ruins blackened by fire, and had ridden over the plains still bearing faint traces of the plow; but the ranchers who tilled the ground had been murdered with their whole families during the war."

Roads had been neglected as well, so the country lacked a workable system of transportation and communication. Having ruled for 300 years, the Spaniards had managed to construct only three highways worthy of the name. Travel by stagecoach was difficult and hazardous, and transport—often by pack saddle—was costly and slow. This was a serious obstacle to economic integration.

Economic disorder meant there were very few jobs, and much unemployment. According to one estimate, about 300,000 men, most of whom had fought in the wars, had no job or income when the battles came to an end. This represented 15 to 30 percent of the entire adult male population! They were eager, often angry, and usually armed. They posed not only an economic problem, but a social threat as well.

Some of these veterans did find work. Others turned to crime (highway robbery being a particular favorite). Others stayed on in the army. Others drifted into unofficial, quasi-military units that provided support for local political bosses, generally known as *caudillos,* who were soon to play a dominant role in the Mexican political scene.

The wars also had a direct effect on Mexico's social structure. In the late 1820s the new government issued a decree expelling all Spaniards from Mexico. This ruling not only allowed the public to vent its hatred for the Spaniards; it also deprived the economy of an important source of capital. And it eliminated, at a single stroke, a leading segment of the nation's upper class or aristocracy. Now creole landowners, not Spanish-born, made up the upper echelons of Mexican society.

Economic transformations dating back to the Bourbon era, together with gradual recovery in the 1830s and 1840s, had made it possible for new groups to acquire wealth and status. Centered mainly in Mexico City, these aspirants, like most nouveaux rich, were ostentatious, putting on elaborate displays. As Fanny Calderón de la Barca, the English-speaking wife of a Spanish diplomat, later recalled, the new rich did not understand all the rules of social propriety: "But although there are cabinets inlaid with gold, fine paintings, and hundreds of rich and curious things," she observed in her memoirs, "our European eyes are struck with numerous inconsistencies in dress, servants, &c., in all of which there is a want of keeping very remarkable." In sum, early nineteenth century Mexico had a creole upper class with two parts: one consisted of old, traditional families who for the most part kept to their land; the other was new, drawn from commerce and the professions as well as land. And it was the new segment, the recently arrived, who became active in politics.

Poverty persisted among the vast majority of the population. Especially in the center and the south, Mexico had a classic peasantry—large masses of *campesinos,* or country people, who scratched out meager livings from the land. Largely of Indian origin, sometimes mixed-blood or *mestizo,* Mexico's peasants furnished labor for the agricultural sector. Many worked on haciendas, where they lived in virtual serfdom, and some went begging in the cities.

The existence of this underemployed peasantry also guaranteed Mexico a large surplus labor force. Partly for this reason, and partly because of anti-foreign sentiment, Mexican authorities did not encourage immigration from abroad. Unlike Argentina, Mexico never acquired a predominantly European-born working class. Nor did it undergo rapid population growth at any point in the nineteenth century. Starting with about 6 million residents in 1800, the country had about 7.6 million people in 1850; by 1900 the figure had climbed to 13.6 million, but even this represents a modest annual average growth rate of less than 1.2 percent over the 50-year period. Mexico's population explosion would not come until the twentieth century.

There were two institutional bases of power in Mexico after independence—the church and the military. The church had come through the independence wars with most of its immense wealth intact. According to at least one observer, the church may have controlled nearly one half the nation's land. The church earned regular income from rents on its vast real estate holdings, its investments were everywhere, and it was by far the largest banking operation in all Mexico. Its generous loans to large landowners not only guaranteed a steady income, but also created a firm alliance with the upper echelons of Mexican society. Small wonder that the church and its economic holdings would eventually become a target of opposition, particularly among those who failed to benefit from ecclesiastical largesse.

The second power base was the military, which dominated national politics. During the 40-year period from 1821 to 1860, Mexico had at least 50 separate presidencies, each lasting for an average of less than one year; 35 of these ill-starred regimes were led by army officers. The basic means of winning presidential office was through a military coup. And looming throughout this period was the tragicomic figure of Antonio López de Santa Anna, who held the presidency on nine separate occasions and who installed figureheads at other times.

Santa Anna was the most famous of Mexico's *caudillos.* These strongmen assembled their armed followers—miniature armies—who were primarily seeking wealth. Once they fought their way into national power, however, they often found that the treasury was running out (usually from previous military spending). Eventually the reigning *caudillo* band would break up and a new leader, with new followers, would seize power. The *caudillos* themselves did not bother with the arts of governance. That was left to a cadre of lawyers and professionals, many from Mexico City, who staffed the ministries (and in this, the same faces often reappeared: there were nearly 600 separate cabinet appointments between 1820 and 1860, but they went to only 207 individuals).

The North American Invasion

Crippled by the Wars of Independence, Mexico was a weak and vulnerable new nation. To the north lay another new nation, which had thrown off its English master fifty years earlier. Now the fledgling United States was rolling westward and southward, headed for the vast, virtually unpopulated northern domains of what was formerly the Viceroyalty of New Spain.

The Spanish had never found the resources to settle the north—the huge territories of California, the entire Colorado River valley and Texas. The best they could do was to create a network of religious missions, manned above all by the resourceful and loyal Jesuits. These sprawling lands became an obvious magnet for the restless North Americans. In 1821 Stephen Austin and a group of settlers moved into Texas, then a part of Mexico. Eventually chafing under central rule from Mexico City, the Texans revolted in 1835 and declared independence the following year. Attempting to crush the rebellion, Santa Anna led Mexican troops against the Alamo, killing the Texan defenders to the last man, but he later suffered defeat at San Jacinto and Texas remained independent. In 1845 the U.S. Congress voted to annex Texas, whose leaders promptly agreed.

The Mexicans saw the annexation of Texas as equivalent to an act of war by the U.S., and disputes over financial claims continued to complicate U.S.-Mexican relations. President James K. Polk sent American troops into a disputed border area, a step that Mexicans saw as invasion. When Mexicans counterattacked, Polk called it war. By consent of Congress—but with the opposition of such prominent legislators as John C. Calhoun and Abraham Lincoln—Polk had the war he and his supporters sought.

It was a total mismatch. Santa Anna was the hapless Mexican commander and at first his forces managed to resist American troops under Zachary Taylor, but in 1847 Winfield Scott led his columns directly from Veracruz up to Mexico City. Ordinary Mexicans joined in the effort to fight off the U.S. army, and young military cadets—since remembered as the "boy heroes of Chapultepec"—chose death rather than to surrender their national flag. But it was to no avail. Mexico lost. The price it paid was heavy.

The treaty of Guadalupe Hidalgo brought a formal end to the war in February 1848. By the treaty, the U.S. paid Mexico a modest settlement of $15 million and took the entire expanse of territory from Texas to California—about half of Mexico's national domain. This was a galling defeat, and its painful memory has never died in Mexico. Just as Americans are taught to "Remember the Alamo," Mexicans learn tales of valiant struggle against overpowering odds. The official name of the dispute offers a clue to sensibilities. In the U.S. it is called the "Mexican-American War," but in Mexico they call it "War of the North American Invasion."

The Mexican creole elite was deeply shaken by the loss. Their frustration erupted in a bitter attack by the Conservatives on the Liberals, the predominant faction in government since independence. The Conservatives, led by Lucas Alamán, maintained that Mexico had been humiliated because it had foolishly tried to adopt the values of the Anglo-Saxons to the north. What their nation needed, argued the Conservatives, was a return to its Hispanic tradition. Specifically, it needed to promote aristocratic ideals, protect the legal privileges of the military and the church, and create a constitutional monarch (perhaps by importing a European prince).

The Liberals, who continued to enjoy the advantage of power, fought back: in the mid-1850s, a flurry of new reforms, which caused the period to be labeled *La Reforma,* stripped power from the army and the church, and culminated in a new, notably liberal, constitution. Unfortunately the controversy was not restricted to speeches and laws. In 1858 the Conservatives counterattacked, opening almost twenty years of destructive civil war. Those years included the ill-fated empire (1863–67) ruled by Maximilian von Hapsburg of Austria. It literally enacted

229

the conservative formula. Not surprisingly, importing a foreign monarch aroused nationalist sentiments on which the Liberals quickly capitalized. Benito Juárez, the Liberal leader, led a successful overthrow of the empire and ordered the execution of the luckless Maximilian. The Liberals consolidated power under President Juárez until his death in 1872. A subsequent interval of instability was ended when one of the president's former associates seized power: General Porfirio Díaz.

The Díaz Era: Progress at a Price

For the 35 years from 1876 to 1911, Díaz proved himself to be a master of politics. He began with his military colleagues and followers and from there went on to create a broad coalition. He gave the regional *caudillos* room to maneuver, encouraging them to fight among themselves. As his presidency matured, he steadily built up the army. In order to maintain control of the countryside, where the vast majority of Mexicans lived, Díaz relied heavily on the feared *guardias rurales,* or rural police. In short, Díaz patiently built up the power of the federal government where it counted—in military and police power.

At first Díaz did not seem to represent anything new in politics. He was, after all, a product of the liberal movement. As time passed it became clear that Díaz was a liberal with a difference. He cultivated neutrality on the crucial question of the church, neither attacking it (like most liberals) or defending it. He conspicuously allowed his devoutly Catholic second wife to serve as a symbol of reconciliation toward the institution the liberals had pilloried.

In other respects Díaz stuck to liberal principles. In one of his most important and far-ranging measures, he ruled that the ban on corporate landholdings should apply to Indian villages. This opened vast new areas to speculators, ranchers, and political favorites. In 1894 Díaz helped the landowners even more by decreeing that unused lands, or *terrenos baldíos,* could be taken over for private exploitation. The crucial source of new capital was to come from abroad. Díaz and his leading ministers sought out prospective foreign investors, especially U.S. and British, and offered them generous concessions. All this was an obvious application of the principles of economic liberalism that had captured most Latin American elites in the closing decades of the nineteenth century. In Mexico the writers, technocrats, and intellectually inclined politicians who articulated these doctrines earned the label of the *científicos,* underlining their supposed link to Positivist philosophy.

Díaz proved his mastery of politics in that most fundamental of ways: he stayed in power far longer than any would have dared to predict. For three and a half decades he held the presidency, with only one interruption (Manuel González: 1880–84). He believed that he was giving Mexico the precious gift of political stability, which he saw as indispensable for economic growth. If that required some repression, it was for a good cause. A shrewd politician, Díaz avoided ever presenting himself as a dictator. He simply had the constitution amended, time and again, so that he could be re-elected to the presidency. Díaz knew how to appeal to the privileged sectors, how to make them loyal, how to orchestrate their support for the economic schemes that would raise their country to a "civilized" level.

Economic development was impressive. Railroads were a striking example. Díaz first tried to build them with public funds, but by late 1880 he was granting concessions to foreigners. In only four years the track in operation grew from 750 miles to 3600 miles. Mexico reached 12,000 miles of track by 1900. (On the other hand, paying interest and dividends on this foreign investment was a burden on the balance of payments.) Originally foreign-built, most railroads were taken over by the state in 1907.

As elsewhere in Latin America, foreign trade rocketed: ninefold between 1877 and 1910. The U.S. became Mexico's leading trade partner, as mineral exports expanded to copper and zinc, as well as silver and gold. Modest industrialization occurred, centered in textiles, cement, iron, and light consumer goods. Díaz set great store by the need to pursue economic policies that would maintain Mexico's creditworthiness in the U.S. and Europe. In 1895 the federal government produced a budget surplus, and for the rest of Díaz's regime all budgets were balanced. As celebrations for the independence centennial of 1910 approached, Díaz and his lieutenants could claim that they had realized in Mexico the Positivist ideal of "order and progress."

Economic activity varied in character from region to region, and this led to differing social structures. The north was primarily a mining and ranching area, where the workers were hired labor—miners, for instance, and cowboys. The central valley, by contrast, produced wheat and grain on both medium- and large-sized farms. Sugar was raised in the south-central region, particularly in the state of Morelos, where traditional peasant lands were being seized for use by the mills. Vast henequen plantations prospered in the Yucatán, where local natives were compelled to work as peons.

Under Díaz, Mexico never developed a strong entrepreneurial class. Concessions and favors came from the state, and capital came from abroad—England, France, and, of course, the United States. The middle sectors were extremely weak as well.

These social facts bore deep political significance. Elsewhere in Latin America middle-class professionals provided pressure and leadership for reformist movements, as in Argentina, and on occasion they drew support from fledgling industrialists, as in Chile. It appears that turn-of-the-century Mexico had the social ingredients for a revolution, but relatively little material for reform.

The economic progress of the Díaz years also had its cost. While the wealthy prospered and duly copied the ways of European aristocracy, the vast majority of Mexicans faced grinding poverty. Given its labor surplus, Mexico's wage rates remained very low. Indeed, one estimate (doubtless exaggerated) showed that average purchasing power in 1910 was only one-quarter the 1810 level. Mexico exported agricultural products, while production of most Mexicans' dietary staples—corn and beans (*frijoles*)—barely kept up with population growth. There could be no improvement in the notoriously low per capita consumption levels prevailing at the outset of the Díaz era. Vital statistics were alarming. In 1900, 29 percent of all male children died within their first year, and many of the survivors ended up working twelve hours a day in a sweatshop. Only a quarter of the population was literate.

This highly unequal economic "progress" drew repeated protest from workers, both urban and rural. There were strikes, sometimes fierce, especially where wage labor worked under industrial-type conditions. Between 1906 and 1908, for example, Mexican workers at the Cananea Copper Company repeatedly protested the higher wages given to U.S. laborers. Significant strikes occurred also among the railroad workers and at the Río Blanco textile mills. Labor protest was intensified by the international financial crisis of 1906–8. In the rural sector, peasants in the Morelos area bitterly resented losing their land to commercial cultivation of sugar and other market crops. In the north there was a similar reaction to the loss of land for railway construction.

Díaz and his advisers could pursue a consistent economic policy because they had created the most effectively centralized government Mexico had seen since independence. Decision making was centralized in Mexico City, at the expense of local or regional *caudillos*. Political office, especially at the federal level, was sought after by the higher level of society. Those who made it were envied, since economic gain so often required contact with the government. Díaz himself knew full well the kind of system he had promoted. Near the end of his regime he explained: "We were harsh. Sometimes we were harsh to the point of cruelty. But it was necessary then to the life and progress of the nation. If there was cruelty, results have justified it. . . . Education and industry have carried on the task begun by the army." Many of Díaz's opponents agreed on the need for national power, but denounced the way Díaz used it. Pressure was mounting, as frustration grew among the younger elite who were excluded from the Díaz coterie. Time was working against Díaz, but who could have predicted how his carefully constructed house would come tumbling down?

The Mexican Revolution

Few revolutions are precipitated by the oppressed. Far more often they begin with a split within the dominant elite. Disgruntled dissidents, frequently young, become angry enough to attack the system. So it was in Mexico in 1910.

One of the leading critics was Francisco I. Madero, of a family that had made a fortune in cattle and mining. It was also linked to Díaz's political machine. Evaristo Madero, Francisco's grandfather, had been governor of the state of Coahuila from 1880 to 1884, and the Madero family had cultivated a close friendship with José Y. Limantour, Díaz's long-time finance minister. Francisco got the best of a foreign education, studying in Paris and at the University of California. He returned to apply his skills in commercial agriculture, especially on the family's cotton plantation. He was a strong liberal in economics, which fit the Díaz era, but also in politics, which did not. His belief in political democracy soon alienated him from the rigidities of the late Díaz regime. He became an outspoken opponent, arguing that Mexico was ready for liberal democracy and that if Díaz chose to run for re-election in 1910 (as everyone expected), then the vice presidential candidate must come from outside the presidental clique.

Díaz was by now the captive of his own success. Why should he take seriously the lamentations of an ambitious and spoiled young oligarch? When the president failed to heed his message, Madero did the unthinkable: he entered the 1910 campaign as the candidate of the Anti-Reelectionist Party. Díaz now faced greater opposition than at any time in decades. His machine produced another victory, but it was far from effortless. The police had to jail 5000 of the opposition, including Madero. The young rebel, now emboldened, refused to recognize the legitimacy of Díaz's reelection. Instead, he issued (while in jail—which suggests Díaz hardly had an iron grip) his famous Plan of San Luis Potosí, and called for armed resistance. The rebel movement grew rapidly, as its troops took Ciudad Juárez (across the border from El Paso). Díaz now dropped the mask of the infinitely resourceful autocrat. In a surprising show of weakness, he capitulated and left the country in May 1911. A new presidential election was held and Madero triumphed. In 1912, he became the nation's president before delirious crowds in Mexico City. Democracy, it seemed, was on its way.

Francisco Madero and his fellow dissidents may have started the Mexican Revolution, but they did not long control it. Other rebels had larger goals: Emiliano Zapata, for example. Zapata had emerged as the rock-hard leader of landless peasants in the southwestern state of Morelos. They were the country dwellers who had seen their traditional

Emiliano Zapata gave determined
leadership to the revolutionary peasant movement that began in the state
of Morelos.

land rights taken away by the smooth-talking lawyers and speculators
using the new laws of "liberal" inspiration. These *zapatistas* (as they inevitably became known) saw the rebellion as a chance to restore justice.
That meant regaining their lands.

The *zapatistas* quickly became disillusioned with Madero, and with
reason. Why should this son of a great landholding family sympathize
with their cause anymore than the Díaz gang? In November 1911 Zapata and his followers in Morelos angrily attacked Madero in their *Plan
de Ayala.* "Having no intentions other than to satisfy his personal ambitions, his boundless instincts as a tyrant, and his profound disrespect"
for the Constitution of 1857, they said, Madero "did not carry to a
happy end the revolution which gloriously he initiated with the help of
God and the people." Instead, he let the Porfirian political machine
continue, thereby showing his indifference to the plight of the people.
The rural dwellers now had only one option: direct action. "We give
notice [that] . . . the *pueblos* or citizens who have the titles corresponding to those properties will immediately enter into possession of
that real estate of which they have been despoiled by the bad faith of
their oppressors, maintaining at any cost with arms in hand the men-
tioned possession." The *zapatistas* were as good as their word. These
rural smallholders had believed the Revolution would help them regain

their lands. When Madero failed to deliver, they contemptuously dismissed him and declared their own revolution.

Madero was hardly a true revolutionary. He was a would-be parliamentarian who thought Díaz's abdication would open the way to true democracy. Madero belonged in England or Scandinavia, not Mexico. He flinched at the thought—suggested to him by less squeamish rebels—that he should strike at his opposition before they struck at him. The mistake cost him his life in 1913. His killer was his own military chief of staff, Victoriano Huerta, a high-ranking general under Díaz. Huerta dragged the indiscreet U.S. Ambassador Henry Lane Wilson into his plot, thereby insuring that the U.S. would continue its notorious role in Mexican politics.

Huerta was a crude figure, who thought he could re-establish a version of the Porfirian regime. He tried to impose his authority across the aroused country, but soon met resistance. Many Mexicans who had been caught up in the revolt against Díaz now saw Huerta as the usurper. Opposition began to build, and as it gathered force it coalesced into the genuinely "revolutionary" phase of the Mexican Revolution.

One of the most powerful centers of resistance to Huerta was the northern state of Chihuahua, where Pancho Villa gained control. Villa was a rough-hewn ex-cattle rustler who had mobilized a small army. Unlike Zapata, with whom he was often compared, he led no peasant

In the north Pancho Villa created a powerful military juggernaut, but his personal flamboyance earned him a dubious reputation in Mexico and the U.S. (Courtesy of the Library of Congress.)

rebellion. Villa's supporters, at least initially, were small ranchers, unemployed workers, and cowboys: men who wanted jobs, not small plots of land. So it was not surprising that when Villa pronounced an agrarian reform, in December 1913, he called for confiscation of large haciendas, but not for their subdivision into plots. The state would administer the haciendas, and their commercial crops would help finance Villa's military machine.

Villa quickly put this idea into practice. It may have created administrative problems, but it achieved its goal. Money was produced and supplies were obtained (mainly from the United States, which remained the great arms supplier for all Mexican revolutionaries). Villa's army was well-fed and well-equipped. Indeed, Villa's followers now had a sure source of employment in his army, which emerged as a well-paid, professional, mercenary outfit.

There were other challenges to Huerta's bloody accession to power. One was in Madero's home state of Coahuila, where governor Venustiano Carranza mounted a strong resistance movement. Carranza, like Madero, was a dissident member of the elite, having risen to the level of senator during the regime of Díaz. A wealthy landowner, he had also been an interim governor. As the anti-Díaz forces slowly gathered strength in 1910, Carranza first cast his lot with Bernardo Reyes, another opposition candidate for president. During the campaign, however, he joined the "Anti-Reelectionist" group. Once in power, Madero rewarded Carranza by naming him governor of their home state, Coahuila.

Carranza contested Huerta's usurpation with little more than a counterclaim. Carranza's *Plan de Guadalupe* (March 1913) simply declared that Huerta held power illegitimately and that he, Carranza, should be recognized as "First Chief of the Constitutionalist Army." Once established, the new president would then convoke new elections. The *Plan* included no attempt to discuss larger socioeconomic or ideological questions. The *carrancista* movement looked like another *caudillo*-type rumbling. Support was scattered, mostly rural, obviously limited to the north.

All attention now centered on Huerta: Could he hold power? The opposition hammered away from the southwest (Zapata and the agrarian rebels) and the far north (Villa and his roaming army). Huerta's most dangerous enemy, however, was Carranza, the ultra-respectable elite politician. Mexico was now plunged into a bloody civil war that saw the federal army swell to more than ten times what it had been at the end of Díaz's rule. The *zapatistas* drew off Huerta's forces by their stubborn rebellion in Morelos, while the Constitutionalists in the north kept up their pressure. Eventually it was foreign intervention, not Mexican arms, that doomed Huerta. U.S. President Woodrow Wilson, determined not to recognize Huerta's government, had sent marines to occupy Veracruz after an incident involving the arrest of U.S. sailors. To counter the U.S. marines Huerta had to pull troops out of the civil war. Soon he saw his situation was hopeless. In early July 1914 he resigned, accusing the U.S. of having overthrown him.

By mid-1914 the Revolution was up for grabs. All of the forces that had overthrown Huerta gathered to discuss a possible coalition government. Carranza was immediately suspicious of the common agrarian origins of the Zapata and Villa forces. He withdrew from the negotiations, attacking the legitimacy of that putative "government," and set up his own regime in the Caribbean seaport of Veracruz.

The social fissures in the Revolution were now becoming painfully obvious. Villa, and especially Zapata, represented claims for radical social change. Carranza sensed that he would have to offer more than the liberal rhetoric that had sustained Madero. In a December statement Carranza began to edge leftward. He promised, without details, "legislation for the improvement of the condition of the rural peon, the worker, the miner, and in general the proletarian classes." The following month he pronounced an agrarian reform, calling for the restoration or creation of agricultural communities (*ejidos*), requesting procedures for restoring legal titles, and establishing a national agrarian commission. In February 1915 Carranza made his move toward labor: he got the anarcho-syndicalists—the best organized of the small urban labor movements—to agree that in return for favorable labor laws their Red Batallions would back the *carrancista* cause.

During 1915 the issue was joined. Villa, the most formidable of Carranza's military enemies, pressed forward for a quick victory. He met his match in Alvaro Obregón, Carranza's brilliant army commander from the northern state of Sonora. In mid-1915 Obregón decisively defeated Villa, who retreated to the hills of Chihuahua to continue a guerrilla war but no longer to offer a national threat. The *zapatistas* could not mount a sustained challenge to Mexico City, and withdrew into their native Morelos to hold out against federal incursions.

With his principal enemies safely at bay, Carranza could afford to call a constitutional convention in late 1916. In May 1917 he formally assumed the presidency. The stage was now set for the writing of the Mexican Constitution of 1917, a premier document of the Mexican Revolution.

Carranza himself had no radical ideas. He drafted a pale imitation of the Constitution of 1857, little more than a restatement of principles of classical liberalism. The convention delegates had other thoughts. They promptly took control and wrote a charter that was startlingly radical for this pre-Bolshevik era. Article 27 empowered the government to redistribute land. Article 123 announced rights for labor that had certainly never been heard of in North America. Article 3 subjected the church to new restrictions, which was a virtual straightjacket. Socialist overtones permeated the constitution. Suddenly it became obvious that what had started as a mere revolt of dissident elitists against Díaz was threatening to become a social revolution, to change significantly the power and property relationships in Mexico. After 1917 every aspiring political leader had to adopt at least a rhetorical posture in favor of Mexico's workers and the peasants.

The agrarian rebels—Villa and Zapata—continued to hold their strongholds and represent a possible threat to Carranza. Zapata was taken care of in 1919, murdered by *carrancista* troops in an ambush. The following year Carranza faced his own problem: he wanted to impose a little-known politician, Ignacio Bonillas, as his successor. In this Carranza was short-sighted. The "no reelection" slogan of the 1910 campaign had been its most powerful rallying call and it found explicit expression in the new constitution. Now Carranza was violating that rule in spirit by imposing a successor who would be his stooge. The Revolution reverted to its bloody practice: The valiant Obregón, the architect of victory over Villa, led an uprising. Carranza was forced to flee, and while on the run was assassinated by one of his own guards, probably acting on behalf of Obregón. The succession problem, which had led to Díaz's fall, was still far from solved.

Institutionalizing the Revolution

Obregón succeeded to the spoils of the presidency. The need was for reconstruction after years of civil war, but the world recession after World War I sharply reduced Mexico's export earnings and deepened a domestic economic slump. Nonetheless, the government launched an ambitious rural education campaign under the leadership of the noted intellectual José Vasconcelos. In the area of labor, the Obregón government bet heavily on the newly founded *Confederación Regional Obrera Mexicana* (CROM), which Obregón soon co-opted, while at the same time harassing the communist and anarchist-led unions. On land distribution Obregón was cautious, fearing a loss of production. The last of the original popular rebels, Pancho Villa, succumbed to a fusillade of bullets in 1923, and the era of effective demands for fundamental social reform was over for the moment. Obregón did make two important contributions to the stability of the revolution. He achieved an understanding with the U.S.—an agreement on how U.S. oil firms would be treated, in return for U.S. diplomatic recognition. Second, Obregón managed to transfer power peacefully to his successor, something no Mexican president had done since 1880.

The new president was another general from Sonora, Plutarco Elías Calles. This stolid officer-politician soon proved to be the man who would put the revolutionary political system on a solid footing. For Calles, however, the threat was from the right. Calling themselves the *cristeros* ("Christers"), Catholic militants presented the revolutionaries with the first broad-based, ideologically committed opponents of the secularizing Revolution. The *cristeros* were by no means limited to the wealthy defenders of the old economic order; they included many simple folk who saw the Revolution as the work of the devil, to be stopped only by the sword. This pious belief was reinforced by reactionary clergy, especially in the state of Jalisco, where they desperately needed foot soldiers in their crusade against the anti-clerical Revolution.

When the presidential term of Calles expired in 1928, Obregón, never politically reticent, presented himself for election anew. It was not a re-election, Obregón reassured Mexico, because he was not the incumbent. He won easily but did not live to enjoy his power play: before the inauguration he was assassinated by a religious fanatic.

Into the vacuum stepped the lame-duck Calles. He got the political leaders to agree on a new election and on the creation of a new party, the *Partido Nacional Revolucionário* (PNR). During the subsequent short-term presidencies of Emilio Portes Gil (1928–30), Pascual Ortiz Rubio (1930–32), and Abelardo L. Rodríguez (1932–34), Calles continued to be the power behind the scenes.

Most observers expected Calles to continue that role in the presidency of Lázaro Cárdenas, elected in 1934. Cárdenas was a relatively obscure army officer and politician from Michoacán who surprised everyone, promptly sending the stunned Calles into exile. It was the first of many moves that proved Cárdenas was going to be his own man.

Many peasants had grown cynical about the "revolutionary" goals of their rulers. Where was the land they had been so often promised? Cárdenas decided to make good on those promises. During his term (1934–40) he presided over the distribution of 44 million acres of land to landless Mexicans, almost twice as much as that distributed by all his predecessors combined. Cárdenas knew the dangers in simply distributing land without the necessary supporting services. All too often that led to subsistence agriculture, with the farmer able to feed his family but unable to produce a surplus for the market. That would create grave problems in the food supply to the cities, as well as for the export markets.

Cárdenas's solution was to rely heavily on the communal system of the *ejido*. It had the advantage of being genuinely Mexican, while being neither capitalist nor socialist. The land distribution was made to the

ejido, which was then the owner, even if plots were subsequently appor-
tioned for individual use. *Ejidos* could include hundreds, even thousands of families. The plans called for schools, hospitals, and financing,
which was to be provided by the newly founded *Banco de Crédito Ejidal.*
Not all the land distribution was made to *ejidos.* Individual peasants and
families got plots as well.

The huge distribution created an initial euphoria, as over 800,000
recipients saw a life-long dream realized. But the longer-term results
were not uniformly happy. Agricultural production for the market fell
in many areas, as had been feared. The social and financial services
promised by the government often never materialized in the volume
needed, despite some successes. The result was low productivity and
disorganization on many communal units and an insufficient integration into the market for many smaller units. Notwithstanding these
problems, Cárdenas earned enormous popularity among the peasants
for his boldness in distributing so much land. He had deeply reinforced the agrarian character of the Revolution.

Cárdenas also reorganized the party structure. Calles had led the way
by creating a stronger machine than he found upon entering office in
1924. In 1938 Cárdenas reorganized the official party and renamed it
the *Partido de la Revolución Mexicana* (PRM). It was now to be built
around four functional groups: the agricultural (peasant) sector, the
labor sector, the military sector, and the "popular" sector, which was a
residual category including primarily the middle class. In applying this
concept of functionalist representation, Cárdenas and his political ad-
visors were borrowing from corporatism, the political doctrine then in
vogue in Mediterranean Europe, especially Italy, Spain, and Portugal.

In this fashion Cárdenas devised a strategy for dealing with the lower
classes: mobilize and organize *both* the workers and the peasants, but
keep them apart from each other. Thus the creation of separate (and
competing) sectors for each group within the official party. This way
the government could maintain control of popular movements and
prevent the possible appearance of a worker-peasant coalition. (As of
the early 1980s, the regime appears to have achieved its goal.)

Cárdenas also took a more radical line in relations with the U.S. The
toughest issue was oil. In the early twentieth century, Mexico possessed
a significant percentage of the world's confirmed oil reserves. By the
1930s, foreign oil firms, mostly U.S. but some British, had huge investments in Mexico. The companies inevitably got into a wage dispute
with their Mexican employees, and it was finally carried to the Mexican
Supreme Court, which ruled in favor of the employees. The foreign
companies disregarded the court decision, assuming that now, as before, there must be a way around such legal problems in backward

Mexico. To everyone's surprise, the president intervened and announced the expropriation of the companies. The precipitating factor cited by Cárdenas was the companies' refusal to obey the Supreme Court decision. The legal basis given for expropriation was article 27 of the 1917 constitution, in turn based on the long-standing principle in Spanish law that all subsoil rights belong to the state (crown), not to the owner of the surface rights. The oil companies were infuriated. The U.S. firms demanded that President Franklin Roosevelt intervene on their behalf. Right-wing propagandists in the U.S. had a field day at the expense of the "atheistic" Mexican revolutionaries who had first attacked religion and were now attacking property.

In Mexico the news of expropriation provoked an ecstatic response. Mexican nationalist sentiment, never far below the surface, poured forth; Cárdenas was now an authentic hero for standing up to the gringos.

At first Roosevelt issued some angry demands to the Mexicans, but cooler heads prevailed in Washington. After all, Roosevelt's much ballyhooed "Good Neighbor" policy meant, at a minimum, no more U.S. invasions of Latin America. In fact, the Mexican government had always said it would compensate the companies. Dispute then centered on the value of the expropriated properties. The companies filed enormous claims, including the future value of all the oil in the ground they had owned. The long negotiations which followed favored the Mexican government, since the Roosevelt administration had early on ruled out government intervention on their behalf.

The companies were paid and the Mexicans created a state oil monopoly, *Petróleos Mexicanos* (PEMEX). It has since remained a high symbol of nationalism—above all, because its target had been the U.S. The oil companies and their friends in the U.S. government did not forget either. For another thirty years they enforced a world boycott against all Mexican oil and effectively obstructed the development of PEMEX's refining operations by getting it blacklisted with all leading foreign equipment suppliers. One reason the companies and the U.S. government thought they had to punish the Mexicans for their nationalist boldness was to prevent other Latin American governments from being tempted to similar expropriations. Mexico paid a price for standing up to Uncle Sam.

Cárdenas succeeded in giving the Revolution new life for many Mexicans. On the other hand, the wealthy sector—landowners and large merchants—hated him, much as their counterparts in the U.S. hated Franklin Roosevelt. In both countries the right saw these charismatic reformers as only preparing the way for radical leftism. Cárdenas gave his enemies ammunition with highly publicized gestures, such as granting asylum to Leon Trotsky in 1937 and welcoming Spanish Republican refugees fleeing Franco's vengeance at the end of the Civil War. But these were gestures on the world stage, not policies for Mexico.

Stability, Growth—and Rigidity?

Cárdenas would have been difficult for any politician to follow. The choice of his successor followed a pattern which has been repeated at the end of every six-year presidency since 1940: endless speculation, mostly ill-informed, over the likely nominee. The mechanics of choosing have varied, but it has remained essentially a negotiation among top-level political bosses, carried out in private, with frequent trial balloons to test public opinion. In short, perfect material for political rumor mills.

In 1940 the choice rested with Cárdenas, who had accumulated overwhelming influence in the official party. He chose neither of the two much-discussed front-runners (one radical and one conservative), but turned instead to his little-known minister of war, General Manuel Ávila Camacho. Clearly there was a consensus on steering the Revolution onto a moderate course.

In his campaign Ávila Camacho made it clear that he was not anticlerical; he even declared himself a believer. And he actually faced an opponent: Juan Andreu Almazán, candidate of the *Partido de Acción Nacional* (PAN), a fledging pro-clericalist party on the right. The official PRM candidate easily prevailed.

In several key policy areas Ávila Camacho soon proved more moderate than Cárdenas. One was land redistribution. Cárdenas had endeared himself to the Mexican peasantry by his much-publicized land grants, given almost invariably to the collective groups who were to form *ejidos*. Ávila Camacho targeted his distribution at individual families, rather than the *ejidos*, since he favored small-scale, single-family ownership. There was also a contrast in the total amount of land involved. Ávila Camacho distributed about 11 million acres, whereas Cárdenas had distributed 44 million acres.

In the labor field Ávila Camacho made another move away from the left. He replaced the official leader of the party's labor sector with Fidel Velázquez, who was openly hostile to the more militant union leaders and helped to make strikes more difficult. While autonomous union action was being discouraged, the government moved on another front: creating the *Instituto Mexicano de Seguro Social* (IMSS), a social security agency which provided workers with medical care through a network of clinics and hospitals. The coverage was limited to a few hundred thousand workers by the mid 1940s, but it was the precedent for a fringe benefit system which would be steadily extended to the best organized elements of labor.

In addition, Ávila Camacho faced the challenge of a spreading world war. Mexicans felt a strong sympathy for the Allied cause, but an almost equally strong suspicion of an automatic alliance with the United States. After Pearl Harbor the Mexican government broke off diplomatic relations with Japan, Germany, and Italy, but stopped short of declaring war. It was only the repeated sinking of Mexican ships by German U-boats that led the Ávila Camacho government to obtain a declaration of war from the national Congress in May 1942.

Mexico, along with Brazil, was one of the only two Latin American countries to supply combat forces to fight the Axis. The Mexican contribution was an air force squadron, trained in the U.S. and subsequently attached to the Fifth U.S. Air Corps in the Philippines. The squadron performed valiantly, and brought Mexico honor in the distant conflict with Japan. Mexico also supplied vital raw materials to the U.S. at government-controlled low prices. Another step would have grave importance for the future. After an explicit agreement between Presidents Franklin Roosevelt and Ávila Camacho, Mexico began sending agricultural workers north, to fill the gap left in the U.S. fields by the military draft. Spontaneous Mexican migration north had long been under way. As the war continued, the Mexican laborers (known as *braceros*) began to fill nonagricultural jobs as well—a development that aroused the opposition of U.S. organized labor. The war ended with an important precedent established: the officially endorsed northward movement of Mexican workers to perform jobs for which no Americans could be found. Yet there were enormous problems. The Mexicans, used to far lower levels of pay at home, were often willing to be cajoled (or forced) into conditions of employment inferior to what had been officially agreed upon. When the war ended, some 300,000 Mexicans had undergone the experience of working in the U.S. Although many had encountered prejudice and discrimination, most had earned much higher wages than was possible in Mexico. The promise of a higher income across the border, however tarnished, remained a constant attraction to impoverished Mexicans after the war.

With the end of World War II, Mexico saw industrialization as a way out of persistent poverty. The man the PRI chose to lead the way was Miguel Alemán, the first civilian president since the Revolution. One of Alemán's first acts was to reorganize the official party, now called the *Partido Revolucionario Institucional* (PRI). Adding the word "institutional" signalled a turn toward pragmatism. The party was made up of three sectors: peasant, worker, and popular, the form it has since retained. It has emerged as an utterly dominant official party, different from any other in Latin America.

The new president's hallmark was to be economic development. What Mexico most needed was infrastructure—roads, dams, communications, port facilities. Alemán therefore launched an ambitious program of public works, stressing irrigation and hydroelectric projects. There was also highway and hotel construction to facilitate the tourist trade from the U.S. This investment paid off, as tourism became an all-important foreign exchange earner for Mexico, although with cultural and social implications that Mexican nationalists found distasteful.

The Mexican economy did show significant growth. The foundations were laid by sharply increasing protection against imports. The short-run justification was to ease Mexico's severe balance-of-payments deficit, but the net effect was to provide a guaranteed market for domestic production—which made sense in a market as large as Mexico's. Domestic manufacturing responded with a spurt of growth, averaging 9.2 percent a year between 1948 and 1951. Agricultural production did even better in those years, averaging 10.4 percent. Inflation and a balance-of-payments deficit slowed the rate of growth in 1952. An additional cloud over Alemán's economic record was the constant charge of corruption.

The bosses of the PRI knew, when it came time to choose Alemán's successor in 1952, that they had a serious problem in improving the government's image. The man they chose was at least a partial answer. Adolfo Ruiz Cortines had been governor of Veracruz and later secretary of the interior in the Alemán presidency, yet he had managed to earn a reputation for honesty. Once elected president, Ruiz Cortines made good on a campaign pledge to root out grafters by firing a series of suspect officials.

The most important policies of Ruiz Cortines came in the economic sphere. Since the war, Mexico had been experiencing an inflation rate which was high for Latin America. The Mexican economic managers made a crucial decision. They opted for a "hard-money," low-inflation strategy, which meant setting an exchange rate (peso/dollar) and then managing their economy (by conservative fiscal and monetary policy) so as to maintain that exchange rate. The first step was to devalue the overvalued peso from 8.65 pesos to the dollar to 12.5 pesos to the dollar in 1954. This devaluation was larger than almost anyone expected. It gave an immediate stimulus to Mexican exports, now cheaper in U.S. dollars, and made Mexico cheaper for foreign tourists. Mexico quickly became known as a promising target for foreign investors.

When Ruiz Cortines left office at the age of 67, the king makers chose a successor two decades younger. He was Adolfo López Mateos, secretary of labor in the previous government. Since López Mateos had the reputation of being pro-labor, some thought the pendulum might be swinging back toward the center or even the moderate left. In fact,

Mexico was not highly unionized. The vast majority of lower-class citizens, especially the *campesinos,* had no organized means of protecting or promoting their own interests. The unions that did exist were closely tied to the regime itself. This contrasted sharply with Argentina, where Peronist trade unions had represented a base of political opposition since the mid-1950s, and with Chile, where worker movements identified with one or another political party. In Mexico, unions functioned as part and parcel of the political system.

Notwithstanding this pattern, López Mateos soon found himself facing an exception. He was quickly challenged by militant railworkers, who staged a major strike in 1959. Their leader, Demetrio Vallejo, was contesting the government-dominated structure of labor relations, not least since the railroads were government owned. He was demanding the right to genuinely independent union action. The workers followed the strike order and braced themselves for a long siege. López Mateos applied an old fashioned remedy: he arrested the leaders and ordered the workers back to work. The strike was broken and Vallejo remained in jail for years, an object lesson to other would-be militants.

The López Mateos government did not rely only on the stick in dealing with labor. It also instituted a profit-sharing plan under which many workers increased their take-home pay by five to ten percent a year. But this measure was typical of the PRI style of social policy: a beneficence granted on government initiative, not conceded under worker pressure. Given the fact that Mexico still had surplus labor, workers had little economic leverage. If they tried to organize independently, the apparatus was at hand to co-opt or repress them.

López Mateos nonetheless saw a need to change the course of the Revolution. He and his aides sought to distance his presidency from the pro-business administrations since 1940. The obvious starting point was land ownership. A chance to acquire land remained the greatest dream for Mexico's poorest rural dwellers. López Mateos ordered the distribution of approximately 30 million acres of land, giving him a land reform record second only to Cárdenas. Furnishing basic services (and credit) for these new landowners was much more difficult, and too seldom achieved. Nonetheless, revolutionary momentum had been resumed in a crucial realm.

In economic policy López Mateos continued the hard-money policies implicit in the 1954 devaluation. Investment remained high, and Mexico began raising capital abroad, above all in the New York bond market. The attraction was high interest rates, guaranteed convertibility (into dollars), and apparent political stability. The government succeeded in achieving extraordinarily low inflation, thereby making it possible to stick with its fixed exchange rate of 12.5 pesos to the dollar. Yet Mexico was by no means a 100 percent free market economy. Indeed, state intervention in the economy increased in the years of López Mateos. U.S.- and Canadian-owned electric companies were nationalized, for example, as was the motion picture industry, which had been largely U.S. controlled.

The López Mateos years (1958–64) brought some significant changes in other areas. In foreign affairs, the Mexican government succeeded in finding a definitive solution to the long-standing Chamizal border dispute with the U.S. A 1964 formal agreement between López Mateos and U.S. President Lyndon Johnson gave Mexico sovereignty over a long-disputed river bank territory in the area of El Paso. At the same time, López Mateos preserved independence on another issue: Fidel Castro's Cuba. After 1960 the U.S. was pushing incessantly for anti-Cuban votes in the Organization of American States. Mexico was the only Latin American country never to break relations with Cuba. It took pride in its refusal to bow to the U.S. call for a uniform response from its Latin American allies.

The official candidate to succeed López Mateos in 1964 was Gustavo Díaz Ordaz, whom many thought would swing the PRI back toward the right. He was from the state of Puebla, Mexico's Catholic stronghold. As the incumbent secretary of the interior he had earlier ordered the arrest of certain "radicals," including the world-famous artist David Alfaro Siqueiros.

Díaz Ordaz countered this expectation by pledging to continue the policies of his predecessor; he soon failed the first test. López Mateos had taken seriously the criticisms of the PRI's one-party system and pushed through a constitutional amendment that guaranteed opposition parties a minimum of congressional seats if they won a minimum national vote. Applying this principle in the 1964 elections, both the PAN (a right-oriented party) and the PPS (a left-wing party) had won seats in Congress, although still overwhelmingly outweighed by the PRI representation.

Díaz Ordaz began by honoring this reformist thrust. But the entrenched PRI soon made known their fury at the newly appointed leader of the party, Carlos Madrazo, who was attempting to open up the nomination procedures—always the critical link in a one-party electoral system. Responding to the party machine complaints, Díaz Ordaz fired Madrazo. The new hard line was further evident when the federal government annulled mayoral elections in two cities in the state of Baja California Norte which PAN candidates had won. The democratization of the one-party system had over-reached its limit.

Díaz Ordaz would have been lucky if mayoral elections had been his only political worry. But it was his fate to govern in the era of student protest that shook the western world in the late 1960s. The precipitating factor was Mexico's hosting of the summer Olympic games in 1968.

The government went all out to "sell" Mexico to the world. The Mexican left, always strong among students in Mexico City, was upset at the idea that the government might succeed in this public relations venture. There began a test of wills. A secondary school clash in Mexico City in July 1968 was met by brutal force from the riot police. Protest spread to the university in August. The government thought it saw a "subversive conspiracy," bent on disrupting the Olympic games. The national university in Mexico City went on strike. President Díaz Ordaz responded by sending army troops onto the campus, thereby violating its historic sanctuary status. The battle was joined. Could the student left stop the Olympic games?

The tragic rhythm of confrontation between students and troops continued. On October 2, 1968, a rally of students in the Mexico City section of Tlatelolco drew an unusually heavy contingent of security forces. An order to disburse was allegedly not observed and the police and paramilitary forces moved in. Later they claimed to have taken sniper fire from surrounding buildings. They began shooting and the crowd was caught in a murderous cross fire, as hundreds fell dead and many more wounded. The massacre at Tlatelolco sent a shudder through Mexico. There was no inquiry, no convincing explanation from

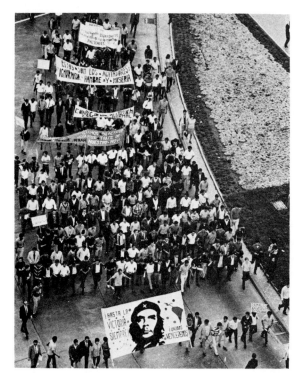

The student movement of 1968 began as a limited protest with an eclectic ideology, as suggested by the declaration of solidarity with Che Guevara during this peaceful march along the Paseo de la Reforma in Mexico City. It eventually became a tragic crisis for the nation's political system. (United Press International.)

the military or civilian authorities responsible for the slaughter. A chorus of critics said the massacre had proved the bankruptcy of the PRI monopoly on power. By the same token, the brutal show of force convinced virtually everyone that mass challenges to authority would only bring more wailing ambulances. The effect was chilling.

Despite the turmoil on the political front, the Mexican economy continued to boom. The Gross National Product grew at 6 percent a year, although the distribution of income remained troublingly unequal. Between 1950 and 1969 the income share going to the poorest tenth of the population dropped from 2.4 percent to 2.0 percent. Meanwhile, the richest tenth increased its share from 49 percent to 51 percent. The top two tenths widened their share at the expense of the bottom segments. By a standard measure of overall inequality (the Gini coefficient), Mexico's "miraculous" growth had only increased the maldistribution of income.

When the time came for the PRI bosses to nominate Díaz Ordaz's successor, they settled on Luis Echeverría, the secretary of the interior responsible for the security forces at Tlatelolco. It was hardly a choice likely to reunite embittered Mexicans. Echeverría tried to show a new face in his energetic campaign, and, after the usual landslide victory, plunged into his new duties. The sphere in which the new president sought to make his greatest mark was the one where he was soon most criticized: management of the economy.

Echeverría and his advisers wanted economic growth, but also better distribution of its benefits at the same time. An obvious place to begin, as always in Mexico, was the rural sector. Effort centered on infrastructure, such as rural electrification and the road system. In order to pacify consumers in the cities, the Echeverría government tightened the existing price controls on basic foodstuffs. In effect, the federal government was committing itself to an escalating subsidy on food for the urban masses. This could be financed only by draining the federal treasury or paying farmers below-cost prices for their goods. The latter would inevitably discourage production and the former would tend to be inflationary. As Echeverría's term continued, he resorted increasingly to short-term measures that would channel resources (wages, land, social services) to the poor.

At the same time the state was increasing its general control over the economy. In addition to direct spending through federal departments and ministries, the government allocated a large share of the budget—well over half in recent years—to dozens of special agencies and state-supported companies. The leading lending institutions, most conspicuously the *Nacional Financiera,* were operated by the government, and the manipulation of credit regulations endowed the state with considerable influence over the economy. As of 1970, for instance, the government controlled principal shares in 9 of the country's top 10 firms, in 13 out of the top 25, and in 16 out of the top 50. Most of the leading state-dominated firms were involved in credit banking, public services (telephone and electricity), or in high-cost infrastructural activities (such as steel or oil), so they did not always compete directly with the private sector.

While the Mexican state took active part in the country's capitalist economy, it retained considerable independence from the private sector. Much of this autonomy stems from the fact that Mexico's public leaders were, for the most part, professional politicians. They did not come from wealthy families and, after finishing school or university, they moved directly into political careers. In contrast to the United States, there was very little crossover of personnel between private corporations and public office. Consequently the Mexican state was not captive to any social group or interest. It tended to collaborate with the private sector, to be sure, but this was not always the case—a situation that gave the government considerable freedom of action.

While this process continued, the Mexican government faced a new problem: a guerrilla movement. Mexican politicians had long reassured themselves that their country was "different" from the rest of Latin America, where guerrillas were rife. After all, Mexico had already had its revolution. But Mexico was not immune. Guerrillas appeared, calling for violent action against the PRI and all its works. Beginning in 1971, they staged a series of bank robberies and kidnappings. The latter reached into the diplomatic corps: their victims included the U.S. consul general in Guadalajara and the daughter of the Belgian ambassador. In 1974 the father-in-law of the president was seized and held for ransom by militant guerrillas. In the state of Guerrero an ex-schoolteacher, Lucio Cabañas, led a guerrilla army that began to strike at will. They kidnapped the official (PRI) candidate for governor and defied the army by direct attacks on isolated outposts. It took a ten-thousand-man army more than a year to hunt down and kill the rebels and their leader. Despite predictions on the left, Cabañas had no successor in Guerrero or elsewhere, as the guerrilla threat faded. Why? Was it the genius of the co-optive system of the PRI? Or was it the repressive network developed over the decades as the government's counterpart to its participatory electoral machine?

But Echeverría's major problem was not with the guerrillas. It was with the economy. The weak point in Mexico's economic strategy was inflation. In crude terms, Mexico could not expect to guarantee the peso's convertibility at a fixed rate unless its inflation was no higher than the U.S. level. By 1973 Mexican inflation was running 20 percent and remained at that level in 1974. Mexico's costs, based on the 1954 exchange rate, were growing uncompetitive on the world market. Yet the government stuck with the fixed rate, which had been the bedrock of Mexican development and a powerful political symbol.

Above all, Mexico had to continue attracting foreign capital. It had become crucial in financing Mexican investment as well as helping the balance of payments. Since the Revolution began there had been significant change in the level and allocation of foreign investment in Mexico. Total direct foreign investment in 1911, on the eve of the Revolution, was about 1.5 billion dollars (in 1970 value). By 1940 the level was less than a third that amount. The decline could be traced to revolutionary turmoil, deliberate government policy, and the Depression. In the postwar era, however, the level soared to 2.8 billion dollars, with 80 percent from the U.S. And in sharp contrast to previous eras, when mining and communication-transportation were the dominant activities for foreigners, nearly three-quarters (73.8 percent) of this investment was in the manufacturing sector, mostly in critical industries: chemicals, petrochemicals, rubber, machinery, and industrial equipment. In this way Mexico has obtained a considerable share of the financial resources for economic growth from abroad—and foreigners, notably Americans, have assumed substantial if indirect influence on the direction of economic policy.

Commerce and tourism provided an additional type of dependence on the U.S. economy. About 60 percent of Mexico's international commercial transactions—imports as well as exports—were with the United States. About 85 percent of the income from tourism, needed so badly to offset balance-of-payments deficits, came from the United States. However much Mexicans wanted to achieve economic sovereignty, in fact they retained intimate ties to their northern neighbor. Nothing could have made this plainer than the economic crisis at the end of the Echeverría presidency.

Why was inflation plaguing Mexico? Many Latin Americans might have reversed the question: How had Mexico avoided it for so long? The answer was that the Mexican government, trying to please so many constituencies, was running large deficits, and financing them in an inflationary manner. There was also pressure from the balance of payments, which went into serious deficit by the middle of Echeverría's term of office. Mexico's continuing industrialization required heavy capital goods. But a relatively new import was even more worrisome: food. The economy's failure was in agriculture. Production had grown for selected foods (tomatoes, strawberries) for export, especially to the U.S., but output of basic foodstuffs, especially cereals, was falling short. Imports to meet this demand put an enormous burden on the balance of payments.

The reckoning came in Echeverría's last year as president. The drama centered on the greatly overvalued peso. With the government stubbornly maintaining its fixed rate of 12.5 to the dollar, every Mexican of means tried to convert his pesos into U.S. currency. The government's ever more frequent denials of devaluation rang hollow. In September of 1976, after capital flight had reached panic proportions, the government gave way. The peso was devalued by 60 percent. Government credibility was so low that a month later another devaluation of 40 percent was needed to settle the market. Could this incompetently managed devaluation convince investors (including Mexicans) to make new commitments in pesos? At the very least, Echeverría had cleared the decks for his successor. Mexico now had a new chance to put its foreign accounts in order. Success would depend, at a minimum, on maintaining a realistic exchange rate.

Echeverría ended his term in a flurry of histrionic gestures. Only eleven days before the end of his presidency, he expropriated rich farmlands in the north for redistribution to landless peasants. Panic spread among landowners. For the first time in years, Mexicans talked seriously about the possibility of a military coup.

Apparently Echeverría was motivated in part by a desire to win the secretary generalship of the UN, then up for election. Mexican politics suddenly seemed hostage to the ambition of one man. But the system—both in the UN and in Mexico—proved stronger than Echeverría. His term ended peacefully and on schedule. In retrospect, his presidency appears as merely another swing of the pendulum. (See Figure 7-1 for a schematic representation of the political positions of the presidents since 1934.)

The new president was José López Portillo, a leading moderate in Echeverría's cabinet. López Portillo made the moves to be expected of a new president shifting government policy back toward center. As the finance minister under Echeverría, he had presided over an economy that seemed to be wildly out of control. Mexico had growing deficits, both in its federal budget and in its balance of payments. Inflation had reached 30 percent. Although modest by Latin American standards, it was enough to erode confidence in the Mexican growth model, which had been based on guaranteed peso convertibility and free capital movement. López Portillo therefore gave first priority to that eternal task of restoring foreign confidence in his economy. Within weeks after his inauguration in December 1976, the new Mexican president traveled to Washington for a highly publicized visit with out-going President Gerald Ford and to address a joint session of the U.S. Congress. It was a powerful reminder that the Mexican elite still saw its fate closely linked to U.S. opinion.

López Portillo's presidency came to be dominated by economic issues. Just as he took office Mexico began discovering vast quantities of oil, and by 1980 López Portillo could announce that the country pos-

FIGURE 7-1 Presidencies and the Political Spectrum in Mexico since 1934

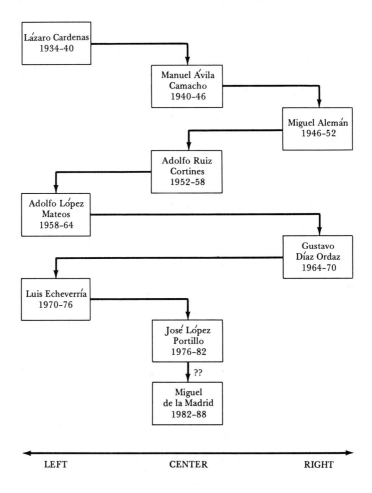

sessed proven reserves of 70 billion barrels and potential reserves of more than 200 billion. In a world beset by chronic shortages and soaring costs for energy, Mexico had suddenly acquired new international clout. Declared an ebullient López Portillo: "There are two kinds of countries in the world today—those that don't have oil and those that do. We have it."

Optimism and pride surged through the nation. Government officials declared their intentions to increase production only gradually, not rapidly, in order to avoid the sad experiences of Venezuela and Iran—where the influx of petrodollars spurred inflation and exacerbated social inequities. Exports grew and world prices mounted, however, and Mexico's petroleum earnings jumped from $500 million in 1976 to more than $13 billion in 1981. As shown in Figure 7-2, the dollar value of non-petroleum exports grew at a much less rapid rate. Somewhat in spite of itself, Mexico was becoming excessively dependent on oil revenues.

Economic problems persisted. Mexico was finding that the hard-money strategy which had worked so well between the mid 1950s and the late 1970s was no longer possible. The government could not get inflation below 20 percent, except for one year (1978), and by 1982 it shot up to almost 60 percent, an unprecedented rate for postwar Mexico. Another painful devaluation became inevitable in early 1982. Mexico had simply not adapted its financial system to inflation (as the Brazilians, for example, had managed to do).

Mexico had hoped to avoid all this by cashing in on its huge oil reserves, but the world slump in oil prices after 1981 reduced dramatically the projected foreign exchange earnings. The López Portillo government was therefore driven to heavy foreign borrowing, which raised the foreign public debt to $57 billion by the end of 1981. Most worrisome was the fact that the Mexican economy was still not producing jobs at a rate fast enough to absorb all the Mexicans entering the work force.

When faced by opposition, the Mexican regime's most frequent response was to bring its critics into the system—by offering a voice, a

FIGURE 7-2   Mexican Exports, 1970–81

Source: International Monetary Fund, *International Financial Statistics* (April 1977), 250–51; (April 1980), 268–69; (April 1983), 288–91.

job, or a policy concession. As one observer neatly summarized the government's approach: two carrots, maybe even three or four, then a stick if necessary. By embracing (and defusing) the opposition, the Mexican state managed to strengthen its support.

This tendency was especially clear in the political reforms sponsored by López Portillo. The changes covered a number of areas, including amnesty for political prisoners, but two innovations seemed particularly far-reaching: first, the rules for registration of political parties were made easier, so much so that the Communist Party gained official recognition; and second, opposition parties were guaranteed a total of at least 100 seats in an expanded, 400-member Chamber of Deputies. Such alterations seemed unlikely to lead to a fundamental change in the locus of power, but they at least provided an outlet—within the system—for the opposition. Preparations for the 1982 presidential campaign revealed the ambiguity so characteristic of Mexican politics: López Portillo was carefully reserving control over the selection of his successor, but a left-wing coalition was about to field a candidate. The official nominee turned out to be Miguel de la Madrid, a Harvard-trained technocrat and the minister of budget and planning under López Portillo, and he won a predictable victory in the elections of July 1982.

Before de la Madrid could take office on December 1, however, the Mexican economy was shaken by another devaluation crisis, similar to the one that shook the final months of the Echeverría presidency. Although inflation had soared to an annual rate of 100 percent, López Portillo's government had hoped its February 1982 devaluation of almost 100 percent would hold. But the world slump in oil prices had greatly reduced Mexico's ability to earn foreign exchange, which in turn raised doubts that it could maintain payments on the enormous foreign debt, which totalled $80 billion by the end of 1982. The result was all too familiar: massive capital flight (especially to the U.S.) and intense speculation over devaluation. The shift to multiple exchange rates came in time to consolidate Mexico's position with her foreign creditors, who in August had already had to swallow Mexico's unilateral suspension of payments on principal. The price of the "bridging loans" to stave off default was the acceptance of a tough IMF-approved plan to reduce sharply the public deficit—which had reached 15 percent of GDP—which in turn meant the end of government subsidies in such critical areas as food and public utilities.

By early 1983 de la Madrid had largely adopted the austerity program and had braced for the popular protest sure to result from the falling real income of most Mexicans. The debt burden loomed as overwhelming. Mexico was scheduled to pay in 1983 $43 billion in interest and amortization on its debt of $80 billion. Even with a rapid recovery of the world economy, extensive refinancing was inevitable, and that meant continuing pressure on Mexico to follow a deflationary economic policy. López Portillo had tried to make his parting devaluation more palatable by at the same time nationalizing the private Mexican banks. It is not clear what political magic de la Madrid can contrive for his presidency.

Like many other countries in Latin America, Mexico faces a formidable array of social and economic problems. Demographic growth since 1930 has produced a population explosion. The annual rate of increase in the 1960s was 3.3 percent and in the 1970s was 3.4 percent, one of the highest rates in the world. Though the rate of growth has declined recently it still seems likely that the current population, around 70 million, may double by the end of the century. About half the present population is under the age of 15—which means that for the immediate future there will be enormous demands for jobs and food.

Such pressures were mounting at a time when economic growth appeared to be slowing down. Like Argentina and Brazil, Mexico had come to a moment when economic growth could be harder to sustain. Investment was declining and social inequalities were on the rise. In contrast to the southern cone countries, however, Mexico has not yet resorted to pervasive, large-scale authoritarian repression.

Some key attributes of the Mexican political system—its restricted competition, its control of working-class movements, its autonomy from private interests and its tactical flexibility—help explain why Mexico has managed to avoid the violent trauma that has afflicted Chile and Argentina. Some analysts predict that the military may come to play a more visible role in national politics, but the general sense was that the system would survive the century.

In this a great deal depends, as usual, upon the United States. Mexico needs support and sympathy from the U.S. as well as helpful responses on specific issues. One particular pressing matter concerns the migration of Mexican workers to the U.S., most of whom cross the border illegally. This labor exodus is a crucial safety valve for Mexico. But it is a delicate social question for Americans and it is up to the U.S., of course, to decide whether to open its doors—and how much. As always, Mexicans find it difficult to escape the omnipresence of their neighbor to the north.

EIGHT

CUBA
Late Colony, First Socialist State

Cuba's historical development has been deeply affected by its location. Cuba is an island, lying astride a network of vital sealines that feed the rich Caribbean basin, extending from Florida to Guyana. Columbus discovered modern-day Cuba on his first voyage (1492) and it soon became a staging ground for the Spaniards' many expeditions to the Mexican and North American mainland. During the sixteenth and seventeenth centuries the island did not command much imperial attention, but its commercial and strategic importance grew in the eighteenth century with the expansion of the regular fleets between Spain and her American colonies.

The indigenous population, descended from immigrants from the Greater Antilles and the Bahamas, scarcely survived the first century of the Spanish colonization. Here, as elsewhere in Latin America, the European conquerors turned to black Africa for their labor supply. As a result, Cuba became a multi-racial society: by the twentieth century, according to one estimate, the population was 40 percent black, 30 percent white, and 30 percent mixed (including oriental and Indian).

Cuba's economy languished under the rigid mercantilist policies of the Spanish crown until the reforms of Charles III (1759–88) provided the stimuli that led to growth. The nineteenth century saw Cuba burst forth as an agricultural phenomenon. A brief coffee boom gave way to the cultivation of tobacco, which became a major crop by mid-century —a position it still holds, as Cuban cigars (*puros*) continue to be regarded as among the finest in the world.

But the most important source of wealth, the one that would shape the contours of Cuban society and history, was another product: cane sugar. Emphasis on sugar began in the eighteenth century and continued over time. By 1860 Cuba was producing nearly a third (500,000 tons) of the world's entire sugar supply. The human power to fuel this boom continued to come from the nightmarish slave trade which delivered more than 600,000 Africans in chains to Cuba between 1800 and 1865. Slavery itself lasted until 1886, longer than anywhere else in the Americas save Brazil.

Cuba's economic development has thus been typical of tropical America: a monocultural, slave-based, export-oriented agricultural society. In another respect, however, it was atypical. When Cuba was less than a decade away from the twentieth century it was still a colony. An earlier independence effort had failed in the bitter "Ten Years War" (1868–78), when the nationalist Cubans—those who rose against the Spanish—failed to rally the elite and were slowly ground down by Spanish troops.

Spain's continued political control of the island was becoming anachronistic, however, since by the 1880s Cuba's trade and investment was almost exclusively with the U.S. The U.S. economic interest in Cuba led to numerous offers to purchase the island country. The Spanish invariably refused, but some prominent Cubans strongly favored annexation by the U.S. Meanwhile, Cuba was drawn ever closer into the U.S. orbit.

A handful of Cuban nationalists who had never accepted their defeat in 1878 fled into exile and plotted a new rebellion. The most famous was José Martí, an eloquent revolutionary poet-lawyer whose long exile in New York produced Cuba's most memorable anti-American rhetoric. A new revolt for independence broke out in 1895. Cuba was soon engulfed in another savage war, with rebels and Spanish forces both resorting to scorched earth tactics. The war dragged on for three years. The Spanish resorted to brutal methods, such as the use of concentration camps, to liquidate the guerrilla-style patriots.

Given its huge economic stake in Cuba, the U.S. was unlikely to remain out of the struggle. The U.S. public was excited by sensationalist press accounts of Spanish brutality, and business and religious leaders demanded U.S. recognition of the rebels. The expansionist urge in the U.S. was fed both by those who stood to gain economically and by those who preached of a U.S. mission to rescue the Cubans from Spanish misrule.

Although President McKinley resisted pressure to intervene, events overtook him. In April 1898 the *USS Maine* mysteriously exploded in Havana harbor. The blast, which has never been satisfactorily explained, swept away the last vestiges of anti-war sentiment, and Congress promptly declared war on Spain. The "splendid little war" (as Teddy Roosevelt called it) lasted only seven months. The ill-equipped Spaniards went down to humiliating defeat. They had little choice but to grant Cuba independence in December 1898.

Dubious Independence

Cuba began her new status under U.S. military occupation, hardly favorable for developing a healthy sense of national identity. The U.S. authorities immediately disbanded the rebel army, thus removing the only potential source of armed opposition to U.S. rule. The occupation was a textbook example of what was regarded as "enlightened" intervention. The North Americans built badly needed schools, roads, sewers, and telegraph lines. But it was all in service of integrating the now "civilized" Cubans more closely into the U.S. orbit.

U.S. government leaders saw nothing contradictory in *their* presiding over Cuba's emergence as an independent nation. They saw economic, moral, and political responsibilities all going hand in hand. The Cubans were allowed, even encouraged, to choose a constitutional convention which produced a charter in 1901. But the U.S. government harbored doubts about the new country's ability to govern itself, so the U.S. forced the Cubans, under protest, to incorporate an amendment (the "Platt Amendment") which gave the U.S. the right to oversee the Cuban economy, veto international commitments, and intervene in domestic politics at Washington's discretion. This proviso remained in force until 1934, making Cuba an American protectorate.

Cuba's first president, Tomás Estrada Palma (1902–6), favored outright annexation by the U.S. He was typical of much of the Cuban elite which saw little advantage, and certainly no future, for an independent Cuba. Their willingness to embrace the Yankee encroachment aroused the bitterness and fury of those few Cuban nationalists who kept alive the flame of José Martí's dream of a Cuba free from Yankee dominance.

Estrada Palma won a second term by electoral fraud. The ensuing revolt, led by the defeated Liberals, brought a second U.S. military occupation (1906–9). The U.S. imposed an interim president, Charles Magoon, who oversaw a new election. Fraud recurred, however, triggering another U.S. military intervention in 1917. All these interventions presented opportunities for U.S. economic interests to deepen their hold over the Cuban economy. The Cuban governments gained a well-deserved reputation for venality and corruption; the Cuban political system was very far from having generated the democratic spirit which the U.S. idealists thought would result from U.S. occupation.

Overview: Economic Growth and Social Change

During Cuba's years as a protectorate, it underwent a great sugar boom. In the nineteenth century Cuba had rapidly emerged as one of the world's most efficient sugar producers, helped by the modern vacuum methods of refining. As output increased, sugar came to dominate Cuba's economy and, eventually, to have a lasting effect on class structure and social relationships.

By the early twentieth century, as shown in Figure 8-1, Cuba was producing several million tons of sugar per year—nearly one quarter of the world supply around World War I, about 10 percent of the total during the Depression years, close to 20 percent just after World War II. Throughout this entire period sugar exports earned approximately 80 percent of the island's foreign exchange. Such dependence on a single product obviously placed the Cuban economy in an extremely vulnerable position. If the harvest was poor (due to weather or other conditions) or demand was low (due to economic slowdown elsewhere) or prices were down (due to oversupply from other exporters) the Cuban economy would suffer. The variations in production from 1920 to 1959, and even later, illustrate some of the dangers of this situation.

Another feature of the sugar boom was concentration of ownership, especially in the hands of American investors. After the 1870s, the new technology, especially railways, stimulated a rapid reduction in the number of sugar mills (from 1190 in 1877 to only 207 in 1899), despite an increase in the cane hectarage. At the same time, the huge sugar estates began to spread. The independent growers, whose small and medium-sized farms had produced most of the cane before the 1870s, now sold out in growing numbers to the big sugar companies. By 1912 the latter controlled more than ten percent of all land in Cuba. By 1925 the number of sugar mills had dropped to only 184, and they controlled 17.7 percent of Cuban land.

This concentration of mill and land ownership was a natural result of the manner in which the sugar boom had proceeded. Under the shield of the protectorate, U.S. investors poured capital into the building of modern mills (*centrales*) and the consolidation of cane-growing lands. American-owned mills produced only 15 percent of Cuba's sugar in 1906, but by 1928 their share reached about 75 percent, thanks to loan defaults by Cuban owners; the figure then slacked off, and by 1950 it stood at 47 percent.

The technology of sugar production affected labor as well as ownership and management. Cultivation came to require a large-scale work force, especially at harvest time. Cane needs to be replanted only periodically, at intervals of 5 to 25 years. Therefore the principal need for labor is for the harvest, or *zafra,* a feverish three-month period of intense activity, mostly spent on the arduous cutting of cane with machetes. The rest of the year was known in Cuba as the *tiempo muerto,* the "dead season" of widespread unemployment and underemployment.

But workers had nowhere to go. Because of the enormous planta-

FIGURE 8-1 Sugar Production in Cuba, 1880–1978

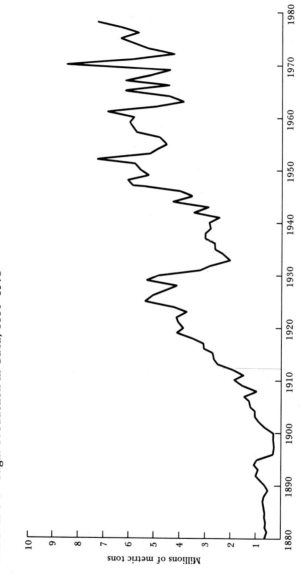

Sources: Manuel Moreno Fraginals, *El ingenio: complejo ecomico social cubano del azúcar* (La Habana: Editorial de Ciencias Sociales, 1978), III, Cuadro 1, pp. 37–40; and Arthur MacEwan, *Revolution and Economic Development in Cuba* (New York: St. Martin's Press, 1981), p 188.

A steam-driven engine hauls wagons of sugar cane to the mill around the turn of the century. (Courtesy of the Library of Congress.)

tions they could not lease or purchase small-scale plots of land for their own use. Managers wanted to keep them near the mills, available for work, and for this they devised several tactics. One was to raise cane on land owned by the *centrales* themselves, usually about 10 percent of the total, thus maintaining the presence of independent growers nearby who would share the problems of labor with them. Another was to let workers go into debt, so they would remain under obligation to the ownership. A third was to encourage the formation of modest urban settlements, called *bateyes*, that would create working-class communities.

As a result Cuba witnessed the appearance of a rural proletariat, a social group that differed greatly from a classic peasantry. To be sure, there were some isolated and self-sufficient peasant communities in Cuba, particularly in the rugged mountain regions, but they were not a predominant class. Workers in the sugar mills and in the *zafras* were laborers, not farmers. They were concerned more about wages and working conditions than the acquisition of land.

Moreover the rural laborers had intimate contact with the working class in the cities, most notably Havana. Despite the disincentives and inhibitions, they often migrated to urban areas, living in the kind of slum that has come to characterize many of Latin America's largest metropolises: known as *colonias populares* in Mexico and *favelas* in Brazil, they acquired in Cuba the suitable name of *llega y pon* ("come and settle"). And their residents were blighted by poverty and deprivation. By the 1950s close to 40 percent of the national population lived in cities. Only 40 percent of urban lower-class dwellings had inside toilets, only 40 percent had refrigeration of any kind, and as many as a dozen people lived in a single room.

Contact and communication between urban and rural elements of the Cuban working class would eventually have a decisive effect on the course of the country's history, because it permitted the sort of unified, class-wide social movement that has been found so rarely in Latin America. It is worth noting, too, that the church played only a minor role in Cuban society, and trade unions had a sporadic and precarious existence. In other words, the outlook and behavior of the Cuban laboring classes were not conditioned or controlled by existing institutions. Workers would, in time, be available for mobilization.

Meanwhile, the U.S. built up more and more control over the Cuban economy. Not only did U.S. capital take over major ownership of plantations and mills, the U.S. became by far the largest customer for Cuba's sugar exports—usually purchasing 75 or 80 percent of the total. This created a complex political dimension to Cuba's economic dependency on the U.S. On the one hand, U.S. investors in Cuba favored U.S. trade policies that helped Cuban sugar's competitive position in the U.S. market. On the other hand, U.S. beet sugar producers, as well as U.S. investors in non-Cuban sources of overseas sugar production, opposed favoritism for sugar imports from Cuba. To complicate matters further, U.S. sugar refiners might have wanted to favor Cuban raw sugar imports, while U.S. owners of sugar refineries in Cuba wanted favoritism only for refined imports. Through it all, Cuba was dependent upon U.S. decisions for the fate of its major industry. To make matters more dramatic, U.S. sugar import policy was invariably a topic of prolonged debate in Washington.

Newly independent Cuba had originally signed a reciprocal trade treaty in 1903 which gave Cuban sugar a 20 percent reduction from the existing U.S. tariffs. In return, Cuba gave U.S. exports reductions of 20 to 40 percent in Cuban tariffs. For the next thirty years U.S.-Cuban trade relations grew ever closer, as the Cuban economy was for all intents and purposes integrated into the U.S. economy. The Cuban currency was made interchangeable with the U.S. dollar. Cuban monetary policy was actually set by the Federal Reserve Bank of Atlanta, since the Cuban authorities had in effect surrendered any control over the movement of monetary assets between Cuba and the U.S.

The eager U.S. investor in Cuba might well have smiled over his good fortune, at least until the end of the First World War. The end of the war had brought a world food shortage and all food exporters, Cuba included, found themselves cashing in on near panic buying conditions for commodities. A crash then came in 1920. In a few months sugar prices fell to less than one-fifth of the record levels of May 1920 and in the following two years the value of the sugar crop declined to little more than one-quarter of the 1920 level. The decline continued through the rest of the 1920s, having a devastating effect on the rest of the economy, hitting especially those rural workers whose existence was precarious even in the best of times.

With the collapse of the world economy in 1929–30, Cuba soon suffered for its (somewhat involuntary) dependence on one trading partner. The U.S. Congress, under pressure from the domestic sugar beet producers, passed the Smoot-Hawley tariff in 1930, burdening Cuban sugar with new duties. This merely increased the pressure on the staggering Cuban sugar economy, which contracted severely. The only bright spot came with Franklin Roosevelt's assumption of power in Washington in 1933. Roosevelt and the Democratic Congress brought lower tariffs, as the Reciprocal Trade Agreement of 1934 cut duties on Cuban sugar imports, while Cuba gave increased favor to U.S. imports. Also in 1934 Congress mandated fixed quotas among domestic and foreign suppliers of the U.S. sugar market. Cuba's quota was 28 percent, a share that endured, with modifications, until 1960. It gave Cuba a privileged access to the U.S. market. It also made Cuba constantly subject to political or economic blackmail. Most important, it tied Cuba to the will of the U.S. Congress, which could change the legislation at any time. The quota was an economic bonus and a political liability. It symbolized all the vulnerability which "independence" had brought Cuba in the era of American dominance.

In sum, the reliance on sugar produced mixed blessings for Cuba's economy and society. It brought considerable prosperity to the island, especially in good *zafra* years, but only for a tiny fraction of the people as a whole—and it spawned enormous social and economic inequities. It attracted investment from abroad, but placed the country in a subordinate position to the international economy and especially the U.S. Also it created a volatile social structure, one in which rural and urban elements of a long-deprived working class maintained communication with each other. The top of the social pyramid was occupied not by resident landlords, as in classic haciendas, but by foreign entrepreneurs or native owners who often lived in Havana: the upper class was absentee. There was a sizable middle class, at least by Latin American standards, but it was an amorphous stratum that lacked cohesion and self-consciousness. As sociologist Maurice Zeitlin once observed, this combination of factors was bound to have its effect: "Large-scale enterprise in the countryside and the intermingling of industrial and agricultural workers in the sugar centrals permeated the country largely with capitalist, nationalistic, secular, anti-traditional values and norms of conduct. In this sense, the country was *prepared* for development—the only thing lacking being the revolution itself. . . ."

Politics: Corruption and Decay

The government the Cubans got in the 1920s and 1930s was among the most corrupt and brutal of the Republic's history. Gerardo Machado gained the presidency by election in 1925, and soon used his executive powers to make himself forever unbeatable at the ballot box. Machado's repressive measures and the growth of nationalist opposition, especially among students and urban labor, brought out the uglier realities of the U.S. protectorate. When the global Depression hit, Cuba's export-oriented economy suffered badly. The bottom dropped out of world sugar prices yet again, and the Cuban economy contracted even farther. Total income plummeted and unemployment mushroomed.

There was no shortage of political will to exploit the economic distress. Machado's opposition included a coalition of students, labor leaders, middle-class reformers, and disgruntled politicians, held together by a common hatred for Machado and a common aspiration for a more honest and more just Cuba. Armed plots abounded. Shoot-outs regularly punctuated Havana's nighttime. Machado's police and military bore down with more repressive measures. The U.S., so attentive to some other kinds of deviations from democracy in Cuba, stood by. Herbert Hoover's Republican administration, for all its supposed identification with business, was seeking to end the era of ruling the Caribbean via the U.S. marines.

Franklin Roosevelt's election victory brought an activist to the White House. While the U.S. assumed a more critical stance toward Machado, the Cubans took matters into their own hands. A successful general strike in August 1933 helped prod the army toward undercutting the dictator, who fled Havana. Now opinion began to polarize sharply. The young radicals dominant in the provisional government joined with army enlisted men, led by Sergeant Fulgencio Batista. This alliance took over the government, alarming Roosevelt's high-level envoy, Sumner Welles. The new civilian leader was Ramón Grau San Martín, a doctor-professor (the one faculty member to vote against giving Machado an honorary degree) and long-time hero to the student left, with whom he had invariably sided. "Soviets" were formed, followed by occupations of factories and farms. The new government proclaimed a socialist revolution.

Washington became deeply worried over the sharp leftward turn by her protectorate. U.S. navy ships took up stations off the Cuban coast; old style intervention seemed near. But a new strongman, eager to follow the Cuban formula for finding power and wealth, was already on stage. On signal from the U.S., Batista easily ousted Grau and the radicals. A front-man president acceptable to Washington was soon arranged, and the radicals, the nationalists, and the reformers watched with bitterness as Cuban politics returned to business as usual. U.S. hegemony was so certain that Washington had no trouble agreeing to abrogate the Platt Amendment in 1934. The U.S. naval base at Guantánamo, for example, was not affected.

For the next 25 years Cuban politics was dominated by Fulgencio Batista. Between 1934 and 1940 Batista ran his country through puppet presidents. He ruled directly from 1940 to 1944, then went back to a behind-the-scenes role as the one-time radical Grau San Martín returned to the presidency (1944–48). There was little left of Grau the idealist, and the spectacle of his descent into the nether world of Cuban political corruption merely deepened the disgust and moral fury burning in the radicals and nationalists. Grau's successor, another Batista front man, was Carlos Prío Socorrás (1948–52). Batista himself retook the presidential reins in a coup, and thenceforth ruled with dictatorial powers.

In reality, Cuban politics saw little change between 1934 and 1959. The futility of the electoral system was repeatedly demonstrated, as the perennial strongman (yesterday Machado, today Batista) worked his will. The honest opposition, far weaker than its true constituency, scrapped harmlessly. What had happened to the revolutionary fervor of 1933? Where was the coalition that had so frightened Washington? It had gone the way of all Cuban nationalist movements—rendered impotent by the unbeatable alliance of the Cuban elites, their political and military handmaidens, and Uncle Sam. If one had asked most Cubans in 1959 whether their little island had any chance of true independence, how many would have dared say yes? How many really thought Cuba could ever successfully assert its identity against the Northern Colossus? Very few. Most educated Cubans undoubtedly thought that the best their country could hope for was to win a few advantages at the margin—maximize Cuba's gain from her inevitable dependency on the U.S. What else could one hope? A startling answer soon came forth.

Fidel Castro and the Making of the Revolution

Born in 1927, Fidel Castro was the son of a successful Spanish immigrant, and he represented an old Cuban tradition—the heir of a *peninsular* who had "made America," as the Spaniards put it in the sixteenth century. But this immigrant's son was not interested in enjoying the comfortable life his background and training might have promised. He wanted to make a different America.

Fidel had followed the classic path—primary and secondary education with the Jesuits, then a law degree. He plunged into the turbulent world of student politics, where every brand of nationalism, leftism, and revolutionary thought could be found. He proved to be strong-minded, articulate, and ambitious. But he was not in the most radical ranks. Passionately nationalist, he steered clear of the communists, who were the best organized of the student groups.

Soon after graduation Fidel began traveling in Latin America, meeting other radical nationalists and learning about other political realities. His most dramatic experience came in Bogotá in 1948, when the colossal urban riot of the *bogotazo* turned the city upside down for two days. The triggering event had been the assassination of the charismatic leftist Colombian politician, Jorge Eliécer Gaitán. The populace rose as one and took over a city whose authorities had abdicated in terror. Fidel was swept up into the wave of popular outrage, and eagerly tried (unsuccessfully) to become a combatant. Those remarkable days must have given him a taste for the possibilities of popular mobilization.

Fidel Castro's first assault on Batista's state came straight out of the tradition of romantic Latin American revolutionaries. It was an attack on the 26th of July 1953, against the provincial army barracks at Moncada in the southeastern city of Santiago. Fidel led a band of 165 youths who stormed the garrison in what afterward could only seem a suicidal attack. They had hoped for surprise, but failed. Half the attackers were killed, wounded, or arrested. Fidel and his brother Raúl were among the few who got away. The government reaction was swift and ruthless. The police began slaughtering suspects. Fidel and Raúl decided to surrender, in hopes that would stop the killing. It did for the moment. The two were tried and sentenced to 15 years in prison. During the trial Fidel gave a long, impassioned, rambling speech ("History Will Absolve Me"), little noticed at the time but later to become a sacred text of the revolution.

The Castro brothers were lucky. They rotted in prison only eleven months before Batista granted amnesty in an attempt to please public opinion and improve the dictator's image. Fidel thus benefitted from a tactical concession by a government he was all the more determined to destroy. Given his freedom he immediately fled to Mexico to begin organizing a new revolutionary force. At this point there was little to distinguish him from the innumerable other Caribbean revolutionaries who plotted ineffectually against the Trujillos, Somozas, and Duvaliers—tyrants cut from the same cloth as Batista.

In 1956 Fidel set out with a new band of revolutionaries in the *Granma,* an ancient yacht whose name would later be immortalized as the title of revolutionary Cuba's official newspaper. With him once again was his brother Raúl, more politically radical than Fidel. Also aboard was Ernesto ("Ché") Guevara, a twenty-seven year old Argentine physician who had personally witnessed the CIA-conducted overthrow of radically anti-American Guatemalan President Jacobo Arbenz in 1954.

Fidel coordinated his voyage to coincide with the mobilization of anti-Batista forces on the island. They were to rise in communities close to the planned landing site. But the navigation went awry, so did the uprising, and the *Granma* beached in a swampy area. The eighty-two men struggled to get ashore. The next few days were a nightmare of thirst, hunger, and death at the hands of army units to whom they had been betrayed by local peasants. Seventy of the men were lost, but Fidel, Raúl, and Ché were not among them. They fled into the Sierra Maestra mountains in eastern Cuba, following their contingency plan. From the mountains, Fidel rebuilt his rebel band and once more launched his war against Batista.

For the next two months, until February 1957, Fidel's column was virtually lost to the world. Most of the Cuban press, encouraged by Batista's propaganda, thought Fidel was dead. What suddenly brought the rebels to notice was not their action against the government, but their discovery by a famous U.S. journalist.

Fidel and his co-conspirators knew that a key to toppling Batista would be the erosion of the dictator's foreign support, especially from the U.S. Fidel's contacts found the perfect vehicle: Herbert Matthews, a veteran foreign correspondent of the *New York Times* who had covered the Spanish Civil War and remained an unreconciled partisan of the Republican cause. Matthews was smuggled up to Fidel's mountain hideout and from there wrote a series of stories which exploded on the front page of the most prestigious newspaper in the U.S. Matthews' dramatic dispatches, which extolled the discipline, bravery, and commitment of the rebels, gave Fidel international status overnight. Readers around the world wondered: How could a fifty-seven year old foreign journalist elude the army's cordon and spend days with the supposedly nonexistent guerrillas? Suddenly Batista was on the defensive in world public opinion. He was in that most dangerous of realms— seen to be both brutal and impotent.

The following month, March 1957, Fidel received reinforcements. Fifty-eight new recruits joined the rebels, having been led in by the underground. Most of the guerrillas now in the Sierra Maestra were newcomers to the wild country, indeed to the countryside itself. Most, like Fidel, were from the middle class. They had joined up not because of a grand vision about transforming all Cuban society, but because they hated the brutality, corruption, and anti-nationalism of the politicians, who always seemed to serve the dictators. When they deserted the cities, however, they soon found another Cuba. However much they thought they knew about the "other" Cuba, they were unprepared for the realities in the mountains.

They found the peasants forced to scratch for a miserable living. The rebels took a strong interest in these people's fate because they needed peasant support to survive in the mountains. It was the first principle of the guerrilla: retain the sympathy of the local residents, not only for supplies, but also so they will not betray you to the authorities.

The rebel band was still, however, primarily middle class. A few peasants joined the rebels, but they never came in large numbers and they never held positions of leadership. This is hardly surprising. Most revolutions in history have been led by members of a counter-elite. This is not to say that participation and support from peasants was not important. But the *fidelista* phenomenon was middle class in origins and leadership. Its later directions were another matter.

Guerrilla warfare is a lonely and dangerous business. Month after month through 1957 the rebels managed the essential—to survive. But they failed to score seriously against the enemy. By December Fidel had become discouraged. His strategy was based on waiting for the urban uprisings. But over that front he had precious little control. How long could they wait in the mountains?

There were some encouraging signs in early 1958. In February the Cuban bishops issued a pastoral letter calling for a government of national unity. In March the U.S. government, under pressure for supplying arms to the repressive Batista regime, placed an embargo on arms shipments to both sides. This was a political slap to Batista, since it amounted to a partial withdrawal of legitimacy for the established government.

After a general strike failed to materialize in April 1958, Fidel decided to change his strategy. The guerrillas had to become more agressive. The strike failure also convinced Batista that he should now move, and the army launched a "liquidation campaign" the following month. It was a disaster. Whole army units were captured, along with secret codes and extensive supplies for arms. By August the army had withdrawn from the mountains, defeated by their own poor leadership and faulty training, and by superior intelligence and dedication on the rebel side.

Through the rest of 1958 a savage guerrilla war raged on. There were never any set battles, never any waves of peasants confronting Batista's soldiers. It was a war of hit-and-run, with bombings, sabotage, and harassment. Batista's response was counter-terror. Since he could seldom catch the guerrillas he sent his goons against the students and the middle class suspected of having links to the 26th of July Movement. In so doing, Batista was rapidly enlarging the support for Fidel. Here was the classic guerrilla tactic: goad the unpopular government into repressive measures, which then will serve to recruit new rebels against the government.

Support for Batista began to evaporate. As dictator his greatest card to play had always been his ability to keep order. Now even that was disappearing. Adding to the frustration and fury of the army and police was the fact that they could never pin down the enemy. They were unprepared for the kind of underground that could elude their network of regular informants. Torture and execution only produced new rebel adherents.

In November Batista carried out a presidential election, running a new front-man candidate in the hope that removing himself from the limelight might improve the situation. The result was a dramatic signal that the government had lost public support: most of the voters abstained. Here was the kind of political development that the rebels had been working for. Batista maneuvered desperately to hold on to his ebbing support from the Eisenhower administration. But the U.S., as in the case of the dictator Machado in 1933, now saw its enormous interests in Cuba endangered by the excesses of a rapacious and brutal dictator. Batista had outlived his time.

Batista had no desire to fight a losing cause to the end. He could see that his power was shrinking daily. His army and police had become both hated and derided. He had lost the all-important support from Washington. And the country had become so convinced of his fall that the economy was increasingly disrupted as businessmen and bankers waited for the inevitable. Suddenly, on New Year's Eve, he called his aides together, designated a successor president, and took off with a planeload of relatives for the Dominican Republic. The way was now cleared for Fidel's triumphal entry into Havana.

The guerrilla war had been so savage, the repression so fierce, the build-up so long, that Batista's sudden exit took the rebels by surprise. Crowds went wild in the cities, especially Havana. The red and black flags of the 26th of July Movement were everywhere.

Defining the Revolution

Euphoria is the only word to describe Havana's mood in the early days of 1959. Fidel had achieved genuine heroic status. The question now occupying the minds of the Cuban middle class, workers, peasants, foreign investors, the U.S. embassy, and other observers was: What kind of revolution would this be?

Fidel entered a political vacuum. The civil war had not only discredited Batista, it had besmirched the entire political class, all, to greater or lesser degree, compromised by the dictator. However important the urban conspirators, with their heroic tactics against the army and police in the last half of 1958, the momentum now lay with the men from the Sierra Maestra in the green fatigue uniforms. The visible power was the rebel army. It was to remain the key political institution thereafter.

Fidel's greatest asset, aside from his own formidable leadership gifts, was the desperate desire for change among his fellow Cubans. The most underprivileged, the rural poor, had never counted for anything in the electoral system. Working classes in the cities and towns had precious little more weight. The most restless and most important social sector was the middle class, which had produced the movement's leadership, such as Fidel and Raúl.

This class was ready to receive a new political message. They were first of all digusted by the old political cadre, and repulsed by the dictators (Machado, Batista) Cuba regularly produced. Second, they were moved by appeals for greater social justice. Third, they longed for a more independent Cuba. That meant a Cuba freer of the U.S. Could there be a Cuban nationalism that was not anti-American? In theory, perhaps; in practice, any assertion of Cuban national dignity was bound to collide with the Yankee presence.

1959 was a year of drama for the Revolution. For all his heroism, Fidel arrived as a political unknown. The government began as a triumvirate. Manuel Urrutia was president, José Miró Cardona was prime minister, and Fidel was commander-in-chief of the armed forces. The illusion of collegiality collapsed in February when Miró Cardona resigned, protesting his lack of real power. Fidel assumed Miró Cardona's post, portending the pattern of things to come.

The first major political crisis arose over what to do with the captured Batista officials who had been responsible for the worst of the repression. The revolutionaries resorted to arbitrary procedures in trying their victims, appealing to sentiments of "ordinary justice" to legitimize their executions. In the first six months of 1959 about 550 were put to death, following trial by various revolutionary courts. These executions, punctuated by cries of *paredón!* (to the wall!), worried the liberals in Cuba and their sympathizers abroad, especially in the U.S.

In April 1959 Fidel set out for New York, where he was to visit the UN headquarters. The trip was of extreme political importance, since U.S. opinion would be crucial for events in Cuba. From Fidel's standpoint, the visit was probably a success. He managed to project the image of a nationalist reformer, strongly opposed to foreign intervention, but also not a communist. He was careful to maintain only distant contact with the U.S. government (President Eisenhower refused any meeting and Vice President Richard Nixon had to receive the bearded revolutionary), while skillfully cultivating elite centers of opinion with, for example, a triumphant appearance in Harvard Stadium. Fidel hammered on the need for radical reform in Cuba, especially land reform. How could anyone who knew Cuban agriculture disagree?

Fidel returned to Cuba to carry out his most radical measure to date: the Agrarian Reform Law of May 17, 1959. The law eliminated the giant estates, expropriating farmlands over one thousand acres, with compensation to be paid in Cuban currency bonds in proportion to the declared value for taxes in 1958 (deliberately undervalued, as was the custom). No foreigners would henceforth be allowed to own agricultural land. The expropriated lands would be turned over to small private holders and cooperatives. A National Institute of Agrarian Reform (INRA) was created to implement these far-reaching measures. Critics in Cuba and abroad, especially in the U.S., began to raise the alarm. Was this not the first step to communism? Hadn't Fidel appointed a communist, Núñez Jiménez, as the operating head of INRA?

Political polarization heightened in June 1959. Fidel announced the discovery of a plot against the Revolution. Noncommunists among the supporters of Batista's overthrow now became increasingly alarmed. A former president of the Senate attacked the agrarian reform and called for the elections which Fidel had promised. Later that same month the commander of the air force, Major Pedro Díaz Lanz, resigned in protest over the alleged communist influence in the military. Díaz Lanz then fled to the U.S. and pushed hard his story that Fidel was a communist. Such defections strengthened the hand of the growing anti-Castro elements in the U.S.

In July Fidel staged what was to be a regular drama in revolutionary Cuba. He resigned the premiership in the midst of what he described as a political crisis brought on by the resignation of President Urrutia, whom Fidel had accused of joining Díaz Lanz in a conspiracy against the Revolution. Later in July there were huge rallies in Havana, where the carefully primed multitudes called for Fidel to return to the premiership. He bowed to their will.

Fidel was now in a strong enough position to speak his mind on the delicate subject of elections. He promised there would be no more elections for at least four or five years. In September Fidel returned to the United Nations in New York, this time to take a more radical line. Now he extolled neutralism as the only viable Third World stance in the Cold War. This time, in contrast to April, there were no contacts with the U.S. government.

Back in Cuba a case was brewing that would for many become a hallmark of the Revolution's radicalization. Major Huberto Matos, one of Fidel's oldest political allies and a long-time revolutionary, chose to break with the *fidelista* line. He resigned from the armed forces and issued a letter attacking the growth of communist influence. Fidel's response was swift. He jailed Matos and mobilized a huge propaganda campaign against him as a traitor to the Revolution. For the next decade and a half, Matos, locked away in prison, remained for the *fidelista* regime the supreme symbol of revolutionary deviationism. For many foreign observers, Matos remained the quintessential victim of Stalinist-style repression.

In the waning months of 1959 Cuba's line became more stridently anti-American. There were daily charges of Yankee-backed invasion plots to restore Batista. Such charges were by no means fanciful. Exiles were already flying missions from Florida, firing the cane fields and dropping anti-revolutionary leaflets. Although the White House and the State Department had not yet made up their minds about Fidel's intentions, the CIA and the Pentagon had long since ceased to have doubts. Meanwhile, Fidel had his eye on Washington—always the cockpit of decision in Cuban politics.

1960 proved to be an even more decisive year for the course of the Cuban Revolution. By the end of Fidel's second year in power, four basic trends had taken hold: (1) the nationalization of the economy; (2) a sharp swing to the Soviet bloc; (3) the establishment of an authoritarian regime; and (4) the launching of an egalitarian socioeconomic policy.

All Cuban nationalists had been angered over the years by the degree of U.S. control of the Cuban economy. It was inevitable that any Cuban government attempting to reassert Cuban control over its economy would collide with the U.S., both the investors and the government in Washington which had so often backed them up. The major clash came over oil, always an emotional economic issue in the Third World. When Fidel had discovered that he could buy crude oil cheaper from the Russians than from Venezuela, he ordered the U.S.-owned oil refineries located in Cuba to process the Russian crude. Although an old law obligated them to comply, they refused. Fidel promptly confiscated the U.S. oil companies. Partially in retaliation, President Eisenhower suspended the Cuban sugar quota in the U.S.

The Cuban government now followed by seizing virtually all the rest of U.S. property. That included electricity and telephone companies (another prime irritant to the nationalists), sugar mills, and nickel mines. The U.S. retaliated by embargoing all trade to Cuba, except medicines and foodstuffs. Other foreign firms in Cuba were also nationalized.

The nationalization campaign was not restricted to foreign owners. In the course of 1960 all major firms in Cuba were nationalized, including textiles, tobacco, cement, banks, and department stores. Agriculture took longer. The first move, in 1959, was against the sugar plantations and mills owned by Batista or his closest collaborators. But the shape of agricultural policy, always a tough problem for command economies, had not emerged by the end of 1960.

The swing to the Soviet bloc was neither a cause nor an effect of the clash with the U.S.; it was part and parcel of the same process. Initially it was a question of how far the Soviets might be willing to commit themselves in Cuba, so far from Moscow and so close to the U.S. backyard. The Russians proved bolder than almost anyone expected. In

February 1960, well before the full economic break with the U.S., the Soviets signed a trade agreement with Cuba, granting $100 million credit to buy equipment and promising to purchase 4 million tons of sugar in each of the coming four years. Fidel was now developing an alternative source of technology and equipment, and the Soviets were getting ready to integrate Cuba as a "socialist" ally in the Third World.

As 1960 continued, the Soviets added military weapons to the equipment headed for Cuba. Technical and artistic missions also arrived, to fill out the lesson in how to build a socialist society. By the end of 1960 Cuba's swing toward the East was decisive. Still, Fidel had not yet announced Cuba's total conversion to the Soviet brand of socialism, and foreign observers held conflicting views. Some, like Vice President Nixon, were convinced that Castro was a full-fledged communist. Others, sharing deep concern for social justice, hoped Fidel could find an independent path between the superpowers; if he failed, they argued, it would be because an intolerant U.S. pushed him into Russian arms.

Revolutionary Cuba's state was emerging in a piecemeal, ad hoc fashion. Fidel began by proclaiming his commitment to the old constitution, which Batista had repudiated by his coup of 1952. But by what institutions would or could the new Cuba be ruled? The problem was a classic, one that Salvador Allende would later encounter in Chile: How to carry out fundamental economic and social change when existing governmental institutions were set up to maintain the status quo.

Though the old legal system remained in place, for example, there was never any attempt to elect a new legislature. The 26th of July Movement could hardly provide an institutional base. It had never developed into a tightly knit organization, and it was far from a political party. From the start, Fidel relied on the most responsive and popular institution at hand: the revolutionary army.

In the fall of 1960 the government created an important new institution: Committees for the Defense of the Revolution (CDRs). Locally based citizens' groups, they were organized primarily for civil defense. The constant threat of invasion—by exiles and/or by the U.S.—necessitated such a measure. Since the Revolution also had enemies at home, the CDRs also had the task of monitoring the population for counter-revolutionary opinions or behavior.

That same year Fidel moved to eliminate or neutralize the key institutions of the former "bourgeois" order. By December the press had been brought into line, often through seizure by communist-controlled labor unions. Even the satirical *Bohemia,* long a mordant anti-Batista organ, fell victim. By December Fidel had gained power to appoint new judges at will, as the independent judiciary was phased out. The universities and the unions, once centers of opposition to the government, were also brought under absolute government control. A new law gave the minister of labor the power to "intervene," i.e., assume legal control over, any union. All private clubs and associations were subordinated to government direction. The church, although never strong in twentieth century Cuba, was watched closely, as the revolutionaries launched frequent attacks on "reactionary foreign priests." In 1961 the government nationalized all private schools, thereby removing one of the church's most important prerevolutionary roles.

The Revolution set out to create new institutions in place of the old. Fidel seemed to be everywhere. Mobilization was the inexorable theme: mobilization against invaders, mobilization against social and economic problems at home. All Cubans would become guerrillas. To achieve this goal a huge militia was created: by the end of 1960 it totalled 500,000 out of a total population of 6.7 million. It was, after all, an obvious way to organize the new Cuba. And none could doubt the identity of the commander in chief.

The only political party to survive the revolutionary transition was the Communist Party. Never a member, Fidel had throughout 1959 avoided any personal identification with the party. But he also made it clear that anti-communism would be considered counter-revolutionary. As 1959 continued, he increasingly turned to party members to handle such areas as agrarian reform. Their increasing participation did not, however, threaten Fidel's effective control of the party.

What most Cubans cared about was not political structure but how the Revolution would change their lives. On this score Fidel and his guerrilla companions kept their eyes fixed on the poor, especially in the countryside. The revolutionaries were determined to attack the legacy of the corrupt, capitalist Cuba: illiteracy, disease, malnutrition, and dilapidated housing. A year-long crusade in 1960 cut illiteracy rates in half (Cuba's illiteracy rate of 25 percent in 1959 was already low by Latin American standards), and it has virtually disappeared since then. Sensing the direction of the Revolution, the rich (and many from the middle class) began to flee, and the government acquired a windfall: the refugees abandoned assets—homes, offices, farms—that the state could now distribute.

In a typically populist move, Fidel began his government by freezing prices and ordering major wage increases (a step also taken by Perón in 1946 and Allende in 1970). This led to a buying spree, but the inventories soon disappeared. Batista had left $500 million in foreign exchange reserves. But that was quickly spent, especially on oil. So the era of seemingly painless redistribution was over by the end of 1959. In 1960 Cubans discovered the cost of the nationalist, egalitarian policies of the Revolution. For once in Cuban history, however, the huge inequalities of sacrifice had been eradicated.

But the number of defectors also grew. Most attacked the guerrillas for betraying the hope of rapid elections. Instead, they charged, Fidel and his clique were leading Cuba toward communist totalitarianism. Most probably were sincere. Some also thought it the best tactic to arouse the U.S.

Some people in the U.S. government needed little encouragement. By late 1959 a hard-line faction in the CIA and military intelligence saw Fidel as a Soviet foil who should be dealt with directly. The CIA began formulating an endless series of often bizarre conspiracies such as slipping Fidel an exploding cigar. All were aimed at disrupting or sabotaging the new government. All involved Cuban exiles, who were flooding into Miami. Therein lay one of the CIA's greatest vulnerabilities: working with exiles made security questionable. Fidel's intelligence apparatus, soon aided by the more experienced Soviets, cultivated its Miami contacts and neutralized much of the CIA's laborious plotting.

The most obvious strategy for the U.S. was to support an exile invasion of Cuba. That was how José Martí had arrived back in 1895, and it was the standard strategy in Caribbean-exile politics. Since late 1959 the CIA had been organizing anti-Castro exiles. In July 1960 the CIA empresario of the exile invasion, Richard Bissell, convinced President Eisenhower to approve the training of an invasion force. From that moment on, Bissell, a formidable intellect and bureaucratic in-fighter, became a super-advocate for the invasion.

The "toughness" of U.S. policy toward revolutionary Cuba became an issue in the 1960 presidential campaign, which featured Eisenhower's vice president, Richard Nixon, and the relatively unknown senator from Massachusetts, John Fitzgerald Kennedy. In their first televised debate, Kennedy took a more aggressive stance toward Cuba than Nixon, who knew of the invasion plan, which he did not wish to compromise.

It was Kennedy, the ostensibly tougher candidate, who won the presidency and inherited the "Cuban problem." Eisenhower broke diplomatic relations in January 1961, in response to Fidel's demand that the U.S. drastically reduce its embassy in Havana. In April, still inexperienced in foreign affairs, Kennedy found himself pressured to approve an exile invasion of Cuba. Wanting to do his anti-communist duty, but fearful of the possible effect on world opinion, the new president agonized. He finally gave the go-ahead, but demanded that there be no identifiable U.S. involvement: above all, no combat involvement of U.S. forces. It was an ironic concern, given the CIA's critical role, and it would have its effect on events.

As rumors mounted, an invasion force headed for Cuba in April 1961. The operation proved a misadventure from the beginning. After endless debate, President Kennedy reduced the exile-piloted air cover and vetoed the use of any U.S. planes. The invaders foundered in an ill-chosen bit of southern coast, on the Bay of Pigs, which Fidel happened to know well. The exiles were hopelessly disorganized. The hoped-for uprisings, which would supposedly paralyze the Cuban defenders, never materialized. The Cuban defenses proved more than adequate. The invasion brigades were quickly captured. They never had a chance to adopt their fall-back procedure—head for the mountains and mount a guerrilla operation.

The Bay of Pigs could not have been a greater triumph for Fidel and the revolutionaries. The U.S. had finally shown its intentions for what Fidel had always said they were: a desire to turn the clock back in Cuba. Although the CIA had tried to screen out the more unsavory ex-Batista types, the invaders included more than a few who had served the dictator. Fidel and his supporters seized on those names to prove that the U.S. wanted to restore the discredited dictator.

The failed invasion marked a watershed in U.S.-Cuban relations. Washington's most obvious strategy had failed. Cuba would not be the Guatemala of the Caribbean. What options were left for the aroused U.S.? Precious few. Now the issue shifted to the level of the superpowers. In July 1960, Khrushchev had rattled Soviet missiles in defense of Cuban socialism. In April 1961 Cuba didn't need Soviet help to repulse the CIA protégés. But would the Americans stop there?

The Soviets decided they must back up their threat by putting missiles in Cuba itself. The decision took almost everyone by surprise. Why would the Russians want to put intermediate-range missiles in the U.S. backyard, when their long-range missiles could easily reach the U.S. from Soviet launching pads? Yet the Soviets went ahead, and by October 1962 they were installing intermediate-range rocket bases in Cuba. This was an unprecedented challenge to the balance of military power. The U.S. demanded that the Soviets withdraw their missiles from Cuba, under sanction of a naval quarantine on all Soviet military shipments to Cuba. The world seemed to balance on the edge of nuclear war. After a fateful interval, Khrushchev complied. The missiles were withdrawn.

The superpower confrontation in the Caribbean had fateful implications for Cuba. First, Fidel himself was not consulted at any stage. The result was to make Cuba, in Latin American eyes, into a Soviet satellite in essential security matters. Second, the Soviets withdrew their missiles only because the U.S. (secretly) promised it would not invade Cuba. This was the least noticed and least understood result of the missile crisis: the Soviets had forced the U.S. to allow the socialist experiment in Cuba to proceed.

When Fidel then declared himself a Marxist-Leninist, in December 1961, the statement was an anti-climax. Whatever his ideological confessions, Fidel continued to be the overwhelmingly dominant personality in the Revolution.

Decade of Experiment

After defeating the Bay of Pigs invasion in 1961, the revolutionaries could concentrate on the economic tasks facing the new Cuba. The central fact was that the Cuban economy revolved around exporting sugar, especially to the U.S. The revolutionaries were determined to change that humiliating dependence. The chief architect was Ernesto Guevara, the Argentine physician-guerrilla who was the most creative theoretician among the revolutionaries.

Guevara drew up a Four Year Plan which called for agricultural diversification (de-emphasis on sugar) and industrialization (the manufacture of light consumer goods). Cuba launched this ambitious plan amid great fanfare. The Revolution would break the stranglehold of a monocultural export economy.

By 1962 the results had already proved disappointing. In part, Guevara and his youthful planners were reaping the whirlwind of the short-sighted policies of 1959–60. Stocks of consumer goods were exhausted, foreign exchange reserves were gone, and shortages were everywhere. Even worse, sugar production had taken a plunge. In 1961 the Cubans had produced 6.8 million tons of sugar, the second highest harvest in Cuban history. This output merely disguised the deliberate neglect the government was showing to sugar. They seemed to take it for granted. Cane fields were plowed under, new planting was delayed, fertilizer was forgotten. In 1962 the harvest dropped to 4.8 million tons and in 1963 it was only 3.8 million tons, the smallest since 1945. The fall was disastrous for export earnings.

The industrialization drive was also going badly. Cuba lacked the raw materials and expertise to rush into industrialization, even in light goods. Since 1960 the U.S. had enforced a strict economic embargo against Cuba, pressuring all U.S. firms (and their Latin American and European subsidiaries) to cease trade with Cuba. This embargo, enforced by U.S. legal measures, forced Cuba to depend largely on the Soviets and the eastern bloc for equipment. Direction was to come from highly centralized planning bureaucracies, modeled after Soviet and Czech patterns. The effort was ineffective and expensive. Even the Russians seemed uneasy about underwriting a socialist utopia in the Caribbean.

In mid-1963 the Soviets put their foot down. The Cubans must slow down the industrialization drive and improve their planning. They must recognize Cuba's comparative advantage: sugar. Cuban policymakers moved in this direction, not only because of Soviet pressure but also because they saw the need for change. Ché Guevara resigned, confessing his errors. Fidel, ever on the initiative, now embraced sugar, which he had so recently spurned. In 1963 he announced that in 1970 (later labeled the "Year of the Decisive Endeavor") Cuba would break all records for sugar production: it would harvest 10 million tons. Thus the famous target of 10 million tons.

Debate continued over strategies for economic development and political consolidation. Still active in the regime, Ché Guevara argued for an "idealistic" strategy, a Maoist approach that would totally eliminate the market and material incentives. The economy would be fully collectivized and directed by a centralized planning authority. A radical break with the capitalist past would require a "new man," a Cuban who would work for moral rewards (decorations, public praise) and thus reflect a new, higher level of political consciousness. Through dedication and sacrifice the "new" Cubans could contribute to the rapid construction of socialism. Here the Cuban leaders were going through the familiar dilemma of communist regimes: how to reconcile Marxist idealism with a pragmatic economic policy.

Guevara's idealists further argued that the construction of socialism at home required the aggressive promotion of revolution abroad. They wanted to prove that a guerrilla strategy could work throughout Latin America and perhaps the entire Third World. According to this voluntaristic vision, pragmatism and conventional institutions (political parties, labor unions) played only a minor role; the need was to create revolution *now*.

Guevara's main opponent in this debate was Carlos Rafael Rodríguez, an economist and long-time Communist Party member. Rodríguez took a practical approach. He favored a more measured use of central planning, partial reliance on market mechanisms, and autonomy left to the individual enterprises. He thought state firms should have to account for their expenses and earnings. In short, Rodríguez and his allies proposed a more conventional path, relying on material incentives instead of only moral ones. They favored also a strong party and a "flexible" policy toward Latin America. This meant a willingness to deal with regimes that Guevara saw only as targets for revolutionary opposition.

While the arguments went on, Cuba was returning to sugar. Even with the de-emphasis on industrialization, however, economic production was disappointing. 1964 yielded a 9 percent growth rate for most of the economy, and that was primarily catch-up from declines of 1961–63. In 1965 the figure slipped to 1.5 percent, less than the rate of population growth, and in 1966 became negative again (−3.7 percent). Indecision in basic policymaking was not building a dynamic socialism.

In 1966 Fidel brought the debate to an end. He endorsed Ché Gue-

Fidel Castro addresses a rally in the early 1960s; the doves, frequently used as a political symbol, represent the ideal of a society at peace. (Center for Cuban Studies, New York.)

vara's idealism. Cuba would make a gigantic collective effort accompanied by moral incentives. This immediately increased Fidel's own power, as he himself took charge of the now strengthened central planning apparatus. He and his trusted lieutenants plunged into the minutiae of economic management. Fidel selected and dropped favorite projects, often reacting impulsively on his never-ending visits to worksites around the island. The atmosphere recalled the early romantic days of the Revolution—endless rhetoric, euphoric dreams, celebration of the selfless "new man."

Along with this idealistic mobilization at home went a stepped-up commitment to revolution abroad. Cuba sought out guerrilla movements across Latin America, offering arms, training, expertise. Ché Guevara spearheaded the drive. Always a heroic figure, Ché became the nemesis of the CIA and the Latin American military. Unfortunately for Ché, however, he chose the *altiplano* (highlands) of Bolivia to start the spread of his "many Vietnams" in South America, and there met death in 1967 at the hands of U.S.-trained Bolivian Ranger troops. One important problem was his poor communication with the Bolivian Communist Party, which considered him a foreign adventurer who knew nothing of Bolivia. This rift mirrored the gap that had arisen between the Soviets and Cuba. Havana had strayed far from the prevailing Moscow line on exporting revolution.

By 1968 Fidel was pulling back from the Guevarist line. There had already been signs that Ché did not get full support from Havana during his ill-fated campaign in Bolivia. By supporting the Soviet invasion of Czechoslovakia in 1968, Fidel signalled a return to Soviet orthodoxy. He then began to downplay the export of revolution. However heroic Ché's death, the new policies suggested it might have been in vain.

On the domestic front, however, Guevarist policies continued intact. The spring of 1968 saw a "revolutionary offensive." The remainder of the private sector was nationalized, consumption was subordinated to investment, and Cubans were exhorted to give their all to reach the omnipresent target of 10 million tons of sugar in 1970.

The magic year came and all of Cuba was mobilized to cut cane. Even visiting Soviet sailors, much to their shock, were whisked off the docks to wield machetes. Everything was sacrificed to release labor for the cane fields. Sensing that the target was distant, the authorities left some of the 1969 harvest in the fields, hoping to improve the 1970 figure. At harvest time they tried to cut every available scrap. It was no use—the *zafra* reached only 8.5 million tons. It was a prodigious total, the largest in Cuban history, but it might as well have been half that amount. So much propaganda, so many promises. The entire fate of the Revolution had seemed to ride on the scales at the sugar mills. It was a mortal blow for the "voluntaristic" philosophy of Ché. The psychological toll was enormous. But Fidel, ever resourceful, was about to change policies again.

Cuba Since 1970

The failure of the 10-million-ton effort made Fidel's aboutface easier. Everyone could see that the "idealistic" model had failed. On July 26, 1970, Fidel confessed all. In a marathon speech (the "Let the Shame Be Welcome" speech), Castro took on his own shoulders the responsibility for the quixotic crusade for the super-harvest. He offered to resign, but the crowds cried no. The economic failure was obliterated by revolutionary theater.

Cuban policy now turned more pragmatic. First, there were to be new management and planning systems involving greater decentralization and more use of "profits" as a basis for decision making. Second, the private sector was to be given a greater role in both agriculture and services. Third, pay would now be linked to output, with premiums for needed skills. Finally, there was to be greater economic interaction with the West.

This more conventional economic policy was accompanied by a similar shift in institutional policy. The Communist Party was now strengthened, the unions and other mass organizations were reorganized and given a greater role. This move toward greater "orthodoxy," (i.e., closer resemblance to Soviet practice) affected culture as well. Central controls over education and mass media were strengthened.

Fidel began to sound like Khrushchev at his most obscurantist. In early 1971 Fidel launched furious attacks on "former friends" of the Revolution who had charged that Fidel's personalistic regime was leading Cuba toward economic defeat. One was the French agronomist René Dumont, who attributed Cuba's agricultural failures to Fidel's egomania and the helter-skelter militarization of the Cuban economy. The other critic, the Hungarian-born K.S. Karol, was more devastating because he had a deeper knowledge of Marxist thought and communist experience from which to gauge Fidel's limitations.

Also in early 1971 Fidel cracked down on the Cuban artistic scene by arresting the internationally known writer Heberto Padilla. Apparently under coercion, Padilla was forced to confess crimes against the Revolution. He later repeated his mea culpa before a writers' conference, which set the tone for a tougher standard of political loyalty now expected of all artists in revolutionary Cuba.

Part and parcel of this policy shift was an increasing approximation with the Soviet Union, which meant closer conformity to Soviet models of economic and political decision making. It had been under way since 1968, but the shift in domestic policy now made Cuba's overall stance more consistent. Radical experimentation was over. The inevitable logic of Cuba's enormous economic and military dependence on the Soviets was being played out. Fidel had now become a reliable ally of the U.S.S.R. in the Third World. Gone were the harsh attacks on the orthodox communist parties. As the decade of the 1970s began, the Cuban Revolution was approaching the Soviet model more closely than ever before.

As the Cuban Revolution entered the 1980s there could be no doubt that the one-time guerrillas had created a new society. There had been more than two decades to educate and train new generations in the commitment to an egalitarian, communitarian ideal. They had been able to train their own technicians, with Soviet and East European help, to replace the cadres that had fled the radicalizing regime. There had been time to make Cuba a formidable fighting force. No future would-be freedom fighter would be able to duplicate the epic of the *Granma*.

Cuba had also settled into an extreme economic dependence on the U.S.S.R., one that bore much resemblance to her one-time dependence on the U.S. A 1981 U.S. Department of Commerce study estimated that Soviet economic assistance to Cuba in 1979 totaled $3 billion and equaled about one-quarter of Cuban GNP. The integration of trade, both exports and imports, with the Eastern bloc was close to what it had once been with the U.S. Had Cuba merely traded one brand of dependency for another? In the most obvious sense the answer has to be yes. Yet the ties to the Soviet Union did not bring the direct ownership which had created such a nationalist backlash against U.S. economic penetration before 1959. Cuba, nonetheless, cannot do without trade with the capitalist West. Castro desperately needs capital goods and technology which only they can supply. To buy he needs hard currency, 85 percent of which Cuba earns from sugar sales on the open market. Cuba had run up a hard currency debt of $3 billion. Because of a fall in sugar prices, Cuba requested debt rescheduling in September 1982. There were some features of the world economy Cuba could not escape.

Beyond the statistics, however, there were more pressing questions. What were the consequences of this new dependency? We know that Fidel had echoed the Soviet-line denunciation of Solidarity in Poland ("the antisocialists and counter-revolutionaries") and praised the Soviet intervention against "the savage acts of provocation, subversion and interference against the revolution" in Afghanistan. But what were the deeper implications for Cuban society? The profound social revolution in Cuba had been possible only because of Soviet military protection and economic aid. It remains unclear whether Cubans now have more bargaining power with Moscow than they once had with Washington, since Soviet-Cuban relations occur in far greater secrecy than had relations with the U.S. Even basic data are hard to obtain. For reasons we may never know, the Soviets have found it worthwhile to subsidize Cuba. It is the ultimate irony of this nationalist revolution that after more than two decades it remains an economic ward of a distant superpower.

The Revolution has brought many changes to Cuba. For those who had lived with little hope in capitalist Cuba, the Revolution has brought a much improved standard of living. Socialist Cuba's greatest triumphs have been in serving basic human needs. Illiteracy has been wiped out, and a comprehensive school system created. Its teaching content is, not surprisingly, highly ideological, designed to inculcate the new socialist values. Basic health care, especially preventive care, has been extended to the lower sectors. Medical training has been geared to public health. Food distribution, always one of the most shocking reflections of social inequality, has been guaranteed by rationing. Minimum nutritional standards have been established and largely met for the entire population. The result is that life expectancy rose from 63 years in 1960 to

73 in 1980, and the infant mortality rate fell by more than two-thirds in the same period.

The role of women was another area of significant change. The tradition of *machismo* was especially strong in prerevolutionary Cuba and has proved a major obstacle to the feminist movement. To take a striking example, by mid-1980 only 19 percent of the Communist Party members and candidates for membership were women. Nonetheless, the Federation of Cuban Women (*Federación de Mujeres Cubanas,* or FMC) has gone a long way in changing opinion and behavior. The number of women in higher education and professional schools (especially medicine, where female students now outnumber males) has increased sharply. The FMC was instrumental in getting adopted in 1975 an egalitarian family code which obligated husbands to do half of all family chores. Any viewer of the Cuban film *Portrait of Teresa* knows this and other feminist goals will not be easily reached in Cuba. But where is that not true? Despite the perceptible change in Cuban attitudes, married women, especially those with children, have found it difficult to enter the full-time labor force. One reason is the cost and inconvenience of child care. Another is the fact that an additional income may bring few additional benefits, since consumer goods remain scarce.

Housing was the other basic need that had been so unequally distributed before 1959. Here the revolutionaries had trouble making rapid progress. It was easy enough to expropriate the residences of the wealthy and give them to special groups (like students). But new construction was slower and more expensive. In the short run, investment in new housing was not seen as a top priority. There the Cubans were following, perhaps inadvertently, the example of the Soviets, for whom the shortage of housing is a major social problem.

Ironically enough, Cuba's greatest economic failures have come in agriculture. In the early years of the Revolution that was understandable. The guerrillas were anxious to repudiate Cuba's long-time bondage to a single export crop. Guevara's great hope had been to diversify agriculture, as well as to industrialize. Even after the turn toward economic realism in 1963, food production lagged. According to a United Nations study, Cuba's agricultural performance for 1961–76 was tied with that of Chile for the worst in Latin America. In the mid-1960s this could be attributed to the effects of past neglect. By the end of the decade that explanation sounded weak.

As the 1970s closed, both the U.S. and the Cuban governments sought to improve their relations with one another. Fidel decided to let U.S. relatives of Cubans visit the island—the first time since early in the Revolution. And 100,000 relatives arrived in Cuba in 1979, loaded down with electronics and other consumer goods. Since these goods did not exist or were available only at high prices on the black market, many

Cubans realized how limited their consumer goods were after two decades of the Revolution.

This frustration undoubtedly contributed to what became a dramatic exodus from Cuba in 1980. The trigger was the Cuban government's decision to withdraw its guard at the Peruvian embassy, in response to a violent incident involving Cubans who charged the embassy barrier to gain asylum and, hopefully, safe conduct out of Cuba. Word suddenly spread that the embassy was unguarded and within twenty-four hours 10,800 Cubans rushed onto the embassy grounds, jammed in like cattle. The government, taken aback by the embarrassing surge of dissidents, announced they would all be allowed to emigrate, along with anyone else who cared to inform the authorities. The total eventually reached 125,000. Most went from the port of Mariel via small craft—many hardly seaworthy—provided by the Cuban community in Florida.

These 125,000 followed the previous waves of exiles, including the 260,000 who had left in the officially coordinated U.S.-Cuban program between 1965 and 1973. Why the exodus? Across the newspaper front pages and television screens in the U.S., West Europe, and the rest of Latin America were the images of almost 11,000 desperate Cubans crammed into the Peruvian embassy grounds, without food or water.

What at first seemed a public relations disaster was soon turned by Fidel into his own coup. He knew how to exploit the ambiguities and contradictions in the attitudes of the U.S. public, the U.S. Cuban community, and the U.S. government. He used the occasion to open another safety valve, getting rid of the discontents. They were overwhelmingly young, male, colored, and unskilled. Many had tangled with authority, some even imprisoned, mostly for defying Cuba's stern rules on work discipline, use of free time, and attitudes toward authority. Fidel also added a mixture of common criminals and mentally ill and retarded. Although not a large fraction of the overall exodus, they caused much anguish among the volunteer organizations trying to deal with the Cuban refugees in the U.S.

To refute the image of the desperate would-be exiles, hundreds of thousands of Cubans staged huge marches through Havana. By December Fidel could exclaim: "This time, the imperialists were stopped by our people's courage and could not skim off our specialists and trained personnel. This time they got our scum." But diplomats in Havana estimated that if Mariel had remained open perhaps 1,000,000 would have chosen to go to Florida. Whatever the exact potential, it was far larger than any foreign diplomat would have guessed before the April incident. The discontent could be partly explained as the frustration of Cubans who were weary of waiting for the higher standard of living promised for so long. Seeing the U.S. consumer goods brought in by the 1979 influx of relatives reinforced the lure of the

U.S.—often present in the minds of millions of Latin Americans in Mexico, Central America, and the Caribbean. The Cuban government was well aware of this discontent and in the wake of Mariel it supplemented the food rationing system with "free markets," and increased the supply of clothes available outside the ration markets. In fact, Mariel was a reminder for those both inside and outside Cuba that the Revolution was a dynamic process, which could and would be challenged anew.

A key to the Revolution's survival would be the ability to institutionalize the revolutionary process. In the 1960s Fidel drifted into reliance upon groups that had been born in the insurrection or were created to protect the new regime: the army, the militia, and the Committees for the Defense of the Revolution. The Communist Party was given a greater or lesser role at the initiative of Fidel and the top revolutionary leadership. With the turn toward orthodoxy in the early 1970s, the party assumed new importance.

The basic challenge for the revolutionaries was to transform leadership from a tiny elite of guerrilla veterans and party faithful to a growing base of loyal supporters. The most obvious means—and the one used in the Soviet model—was to broaden the base of the Communist Party. In 1975 this process began. Under the banner of "popular participation," grass-roots elections for regional assemblies were held. It was announced as an experiment with no long-term commitments. The idea was to build a representational structure at the local level.

What can such an effort produce? Obviously not a democratic system along European or American lines. Can it begin to guarantee the long-term survival of the Revolution without the charismatic leadership of the guerrillas, especially Fidel himself? Virtually no one, however hostile to the Revolution, thinks the socialist path in Cuba could be easily reversed. There are deep loyalties and heightened political consciousness, much stronger now than when the CIA grossly underestimated them two decades ago when planning the Bay of Pigs invasion. The succession to top power will be an important test. Is Fidel irreplaceable? The CIA and Kennedy brothers evidently thought so, or they would not have tried so hard to assassinate him. More important for the Cuban Revolution's survival than Fidel, however, is Soviet protection. The continued existence in its present form of the Caribbean's socialist showcase depends on the continued favor of one distant superpower against the hostility of the other.

NINE

CENTRAL AMERICA
Colonialism, Dictatorship, and Revolution

Central America has received scant attention from scholars in the United States. This neglect is partly due to the relative paucity of archives, libraries, and research centers in the nations of the isthmus. It is partly due to the smallness of the individual countries, which makes them appear less significant than Argentina, Brazil, or Mexico. And it is also due to the common assumption that the countries of Central America are backward: the least developed areas in a developing world. Dominated by dictators, the "banana republics" of the isthmus were viewed as sleepy relics of the past, the last places where popular revolt would strike.

The recent upheavals in Nicaragua and El Salvador have sharply challenged this image. If we discard modernization theory and instead follow an approach which places Central America within the context of the capitalist world economy, the history of the region begins to acquire new meaning. As we shall see, Central America came to develop classic plantation economies, and this fact had a decisive effect on social-class relations and political outcomes. The isthmus thus provides yet another variation on the interplay between socioeconomic change and political transition.

Central American history furthermore offers an opportunity to examine and comprehend the policies of the United States. Through trade, investment, invasion, and diplomacy, the U.S. obtained extraordinary influence over trends and events in the region. The use (and abuse) of this power not only yields insight into the behavior of the United States. It also enriches our understanding of the ways that Latin Americans have interpreted the motives and actions of the "colossus of the north."

Colonial Background

Nature endowed Central America with singular beauty. And from Guatemala to Panama, the isthmus exhibits many contrasts: a spectacular mountain range, studded by volcanoes of 10,000 feet or more; some arid zones; and verdant jungles along the coasts. Much of the soil is fertile and the year-round climate is temperate, warm in the mornings and cool in the afternoons. There are lakes in the mountainous areas but no major navigable rivers (with the possible exception of the Río San Juan in Nicaragua). Nor does either coast have adequate natural deep-sea harbors. Nature can bring calamity, too, through torrential rains, hurricanes, and violent earthquakes.

During precolonial times Central America was a meeting ground for Meso-American, South American, and Caribbean cultures. In contrast to Mexico and Peru, it was not the site of a centralized Indian empire. Indigenous peoples lived in stable, autonomous communities and engaged in trade with one another. After 500 B.C. a relatively advanced civilization appeared in the highlands of Guatemala and El Salvador, and it was greatly influenced by Olmec culture from the Veracruz-Tabasco coast of Mexico. Nahuatl settlements later followed, and classical Mayan culture appeared in the lowlands of northern Guatemala. The period from A.D. 600 to 900 marked the apex of the Old Maya Empire, as it was formerly called, though it did not constitute a highly organized political unit.

Spaniards first came to the area in 1501. Vasco Núñez de Balboa sighted the Pacific Ocean in 1513 and established his power in what is now Panama. In the 1520s, already under pressure from Spanish crown authorities, Hernán Cortés went as far south as Honduras. Pedro de Alvarado launched an expedition from Mexico City around this same time and, like other conquerors, he was able to take advantage of hostilities between two Indian groups, the Quichés and the Cakchiquels (who became his allies). As also happened elsewhere, the conquerors soon fought among themselves. Alvarado's column reached a stalemate in its encounter with the forces of Pedro Arias de Avila, better known as Pedrarias Dávila, who founded Panama City in 1524.

In the mid-sixteenth century the Spanish crown established the Kingdom of Guatemala as part of the viceroyalty of New Spain. The Kingdom included what later became Costa Rica, Nicaragua, El Salvador, Honduras, Guatemala, Belize (British Honduras), and the Mexican state of Chiapas. Its capital was the highland city of Antigua, Guatemala, then referred to as Santiago de Guatemala. Panama fell under the jurisdiction of Peru.

The diversity of Indian cultures meant that Spaniards penetrated Central America in stages, not all at once, and each conquest required

MAP 3 CENTRAL AMERICA

the establishment of a new government. The result was decentralization. Municipalities assumed day-to-day authority, and town councils
(*ayuntamientos*) became the most important governing bodies. Nomi-
nally under the control of distant viceroys, Spanish residents of the
isthmus functioned under separate royal orders for all intents and purposes.

The church followed closely on the heels of conquest. Secular and
regular clergy, especially Franciscans and Dominicans, took active part
in missionary efforts. By the late seventeenth century there were 759
churches throughout the area, which would acquire an archbishop in
1745. Early on, the church became a powerful source of authority.

Economic activity was modest. Mining was from the beginning a small-
scale operation. The first major export was cacao, though Venezuela
soon pre-empted this market. Indigo then took over as the leading export, and there was a bustling contraband trade in tobacco. In the 1660s
the English established a foothold at the mouth of the Belize River
(later British Honduras), which they used as a base for commerce in
dyewood and mahogany and for buccaneering raids. But for the most
part Central America was not a source of great wealth, and it received
correspondingly little attention from the Spanish crown.

The social structure was controlled, at the top, by a two-part elite.
One element consisted of Spanish-born bureaucrats (*peninsulares*) whose
political base was the imperial court (*audiencia*) in Guatemala; the other
consisted of locally born landholders (*criollos*) whose strength resided in town councils. At the bottom was the labor force, comprised
of Indians and African slaves. There also emerged a stratum of mixed-
bloods, known as *ladinos* in Central America, who worked as wage laborers or small farmers in the countryside and as artisans, merchants,
and peddlers in the towns. Near the end of the colonial era approximately 4 percent of the region's population was white (either Spanish
or creole), about 65 percent was Indian, and 31 percent was *ladino* (including those of black descent).

Independence: The Struggle for Unification

During the eighteenth century the Bourbon monarchy attempted to
reassert royal control of Spanish America, a move that everywhere reduced the political autonomy of the landed creole class. In Central
America a continuing decline in cacao production and a precipitous
drop in the indigo trade between the 1790s and the 1810s led to further discontent within the creole ranks. These factors heightened long-
standing differences between the imperial bureaucracy and the local
aristocracy, between the capital and the provinces.

As independence movements flourished elsewhere, Captain-General

José de Bustamante managed to maintain Spanish control of Central America, mainly by forging an alliance with *ladinos* and Indians against the upstart creoles. He was forced out in 1818, however, and Spain's adoption of a liberal constitution in 1820 sent repercussions throughout the area. In mid-1821 Agustín de Iturbide's declaration of the *Plan de Iguala* in Mexico forced the independence issue. Partly fearing "liberation" by Mexican troops, the socially conservative landowners decided to break with now-radical Spain, and in January 1822 proclaimed annexation of the isthmus to royalist Mexico. The following year Iturbide's abdication led to complete independence. Chiapas remained with Mexico. The other states, from Costa Rica to Guatemala (excluding Panama), became the United Provinces of Central America.

Despite discord and disagreement, Central America managed to separate itself from Spain—and from Mexico—in a relatively peaceful fashion. The peoples of the isthmus did not suffer nearly the same level of physical destruction that occurred elsewhere in the 1810s. And as a result, the colonial social order survived almost intact.

The isthmus thus achieved full independence as a politically unified republic. The ideal of unification had long inspired local patriots, and would continue to be a highly valued goal in years to come. But it also proved hard to sustain.

As happened elsewhere in Latin America, the Central American political elite divided into two factions: Liberals and Conservatives. The Liberals advocated continuation of reforms started by the Bourbon monarchy. They called for increased restrictions on clerical power, for the abolition of slavery, for the elimination of burdensome taxes, and for the promotion of economic development. They drew their support from emerging professional classes, white and *ladino,* and from upper-middle sectors excluded from the circles of the landed creole aristocracy. They espoused the idea of unification, too, and had considerable strength in the outlying provinces.

Conservatives stood for order, moderation, and stability. They upheld Hispanic institutions, especially the church, and they expressed suspicion of progressive reform. Led by creole landowners, they first advocated free trade, then reverted to a protectionist stance when they felt the impact of British commercial competition.

Violence erupted in the 1820s and Liberals appeared to have the upper hand. The constitution of 1824 bore resemblances to both the U.S. constitution and the Spanish constitution of 1812. In 1829 Liberal forces under Francisco Morazán of Honduras defeated a Conservative army, and in the wake of victory Liberals began a campaign to eliminate Conservatives from positions of power. Before long the tide would turn.

Rafael Carrera and Conservative Supremacy

The year 1837 brought shocks to Central America. In the mountain regions of Guatemala there began a massive rebellion, a peasant revolt that challenged the Liberal state. Village priests exhorted their poverty-stricken parishioners to join the uprising, proclaiming that a cholera epidemic—which started late the year before—was a sign of heavenly wrath. Indians flocked to the cause. Race war spread from Guatemala to the other provinces.

Leader of this movement was José Rafael Carrera, a *ladino* swineherd with no formal education. In mid-1837 he defined the goals of the revolt as: (1) reinstatement of traditional judicial procedures, (2) restoration of religious orders and ecclesiastical privilege, (3) amnesty for all those exiled in 1829, and (4) obedience to Carrera himself. His forces soon controlled Guatemala, and in 1840 he defeated Morazán.

The triumphant Carrera emerged as the dominant figure in Central American political life, a position he held until his death in 1865. Starting in 1839, the Guatemalan legislature proceeded to dismantle the Liberal program. Merchant guilds were reestablished, the archbishop was asked to return, education was turned over to the church. Roman Catholicism became the official state religion, and priests regained protection of the ecclesiastical *fuero*. Carrera maintained his grip on the military, and in 1851 he assumed the Guatemalan presidency as well. It was an era of Conservative ascendancy.

The Carrera revolt ushered in some lasting changes. A few Indians, but more especially *ladinos,* began to play active roles in political life. The white elite regained its social supremacy but lost its monopoly over the state. And under Carrera, the government abandoned the goal of trying to assimilate Indian masses. It adopted instead a policy aimed at protecting the Indians, much as the Spanish crown had done, and this policy helped contribute to the segregation that has persisted to this day.

The Carrera era also brought an end to the Central American confederation. In 1838 the congress declared each of the states to be "sovereign, free, and independent political bodies." The ideal of unification had come to be identified with the Liberal period of 1823–37 and was seen as a failure, so Carrera discarded the dream. At the same time, he sought to impose like-minded Conservatives in the (increasingly sovereign) states. In Nicaragua this impulse eventually culminated in one of the more bizarre episodes in the history of inter-American relations— the William Walker affair.

Geographical and economic considerations had long stimulated interest in the idea of an inter-oceanic route through Central

America. Having failed to discover a system of lakes and rivers connecting the Pacific Ocean and the Caribbean Sea, planners and visionaries pondered the possibility of an isthmian canal. The British and French gave early expressions of curiosity. The U.S. followed suit after taking Oregon and California, especially after the gold rush of 1849.

Because of its extensive lakes and the San Juan river, Nicaragua seemed a natural site for the canal project, and in late 1849 Cornelius Vanderbilt and his associates secured a concession from a Liberal government. Intrigue rapidly thickened. Costa Rica claimed jurisdiction over the proposed terminus at the eastern end of the route for the canal. Hoping to block their U.S. rivals, the British supported Costa Rica. By 1853 Conservatives had gained power in Nicaragua and, without conceding territorial rights, they chose to take sides with the British.

Frustrated Liberals turned to the U.S. for help. What they got was William Walker, the glib and intellectually gifted son of an austere, frontier-fundamentalist family from Tennessee. As a young man Walker studied medicine in the U.S. and Europe, then took up law in New Orleans. Under a contract with the Liberals, Walker hired a small army and invaded Nicaragua in 1855. He seized one of Vanderbilt's passenger vessels, won a quick victory, named himself head of the armed forces, and settled in as the country's authoritative ruler.

The U.S. government took a permissive view of these developments, openly tolerating intervention by a North American citizen in the affairs of another state. Walker staffed his forces with veterans from the 1846–48 war with Mexico, accepted support from Vanderbilt's business competitors, and invited migrants from the U.S. South—who brought slavery along. Opposition mounted from the British and from Conservatives in other states, however, and Walker was driven from power in 1857. He tried to return and met his death in 1860.

Thus ended the "National War," an event with long-lasting implications. It discredited both Liberals and the U.S., and helps explain why Conservatives stayed in power much longer in Nicaragua than in other parts of nineteenth century Central America.

Liberal Theory and "Republican Dictatorships"

After Rafael Carrera died in 1865 the Liberals began a resurgence. It had begun in the late 1850s, when Gerardo Barrios became president of El Salvador, and it soon picked up in other countries. In 1870 Tomás Guardia, an army officer, assumed the presidency of Costa Rica. In 1873 Justino Rufino Barrios took power in Guatemala, as did Marco Aurelio Soto in Honduras in 1876. The legacy of the Walker expedition delayed the Liberal comeback in Nicaragua until 1893, when José Santos Zelaya became chief executive.

Like other elites in late nineteenth century Latin America, the Central American Liberals believed in the notions of progress and economic development. They sought to integrate their countries with the rest of the world, to acquire the trappings of civilization, and to promote material improvement. In outlook they shared the views of Argentina's Generation of 1880 and, more particularly, of the Mexican *científicos*. In politics they would closely follow the example of Porfirio Díaz.

Notwithstanding their Liberal commitments, these leaders set up what came to be known as "republican dictatorships." They centralized authority, rigged elections, controlled institutions, and kept themselves in power for extended periods of time. They drew domestic support from the landed aristocracy and from some middle-sector elements. They forged close alliances with foreign interests—British, German, and North American. They modernized their military establishments and police forces, which they freely used to intimidate and suppress the opposition.

This pattern produced some social alterations. Where Conservative-Liberal distinctions were clearest (Guatemala and Costa Rica), they led to the near-total eclipse of power of old Conservative families. Where partisan lines were blurred (Honduras, El Salvador) some dynasties managed to hang on. Nicaragua proved to be an exception, as Conservative families had managed to consolidate their position by the time Zelaya came to power. Liberal ascendancy in general opened opportunities to middle-sector professionals and *ladinos* and, as we shall see, it fostered policies that led to the formation of new elites.

Moreover, it stripped the church of power and prestige. Its economic role was diminished and its legal privileges were abolished. As one historian wrote in the 1970s, "The major role the clergy had played in rural Central America became minor. This was one of the most important changes ever to take place in Central America." The demise of the church left an institutional vacuum in Central American society. It would eventually be filled, at least in part, by a new kind of Roman Catholic Church.

Overview: Economic Growth and Social Change

The economic program of the resurgent Liberals stressed the promotion of exports, especially of raw materials, in exchange for imports of manufactured goods. This entailed a reliance on agricultural production—and, in particular, on the cultivation of coffee and bananas.

Colonial Central America grew modest amounts of coffee. Costa Rica began serious production in the 1830s, shipping exports first to Chile and later to Europe. Guatemala promptly followed suit, and by 1870 coffee was the country's leading export, a position it has held ever since. El Salvador, Nicaragua, and Honduras joined the coffee trade in the 1870s and 1880s. Central American coffee exports have not risen to enormous volumes—never accounting for more than 15 percent of the world supply—but they have always been of high quality.

Coffee had important social consequences. Since it was grown in the cool highlands, along the mountain slopes, it did not everywhere require large-scale usurpation of land from the peasants. There were substantial takeovers in Guatemala and El Salvador, though perhaps less dramatic than occurred in Porfirian Mexico. In Honduras, Nicaragua, and Costa Rica most peasants lived in the lowlands, however, so dislocations were less common. Also many coffee plantations were modest in size, and they were usually owned by Central Americans. Foreign investors came to play an important part in coffee production in late nineteenth-century Nicaragua, and Germans acquired substantial amounts of coffee-growing land in Guatemala. But in general, coffee production remained in Central American hands.

Though liberal leaders sought to encourage immigration (more than Mexico's *científicos*), Central America never received the kind of massive, working-class influx that went to Argentina, Brazil, and the United States. Labor for coffee cultivation instead came from the mostly Indian and *mestizo* peasants. In time they fell into two groups: *colonos,* who lived on the plantation and leased small plots of land for subsistence cultivation; and *jornaleros,* day laborers who worked for wages while living at home and retaining control of some land. In either case they retained close contact with the earth and retained outlooks of traditional peasants, rather than forging class consciousness as a rural proletariat.

The banana trade would eventually become emblematic of Central American culture, but it had a small-scale start. In 1870 a New England sea captain named Lorenzo Baker began shipments from Jamaica to the east coast of the U.S., and in 1885 he joined with Andrew Preston to form the Boston Fruit Company. In the meantime Costa Rica had engaged Henry Meiggs, the dynamic railway entrepreneur, to lay track along the Caribbean coast in exchange for grants of land. Meiggs turned the contract over to two of his nephews, Minor Cooper Keith and Henry Meiggs Keith. In 1878 Minor Keith began shipping bananas to New Orleans, and soon established the Tropical Trading and Transport Company.

In 1899 the two companies merged, with Preston as president and Minor Keith as vice-president, to form a singular enterprise: the United

Fruit Company (UFCO). Here began a remarkable chapter in the history of U.S. investment, penetration, and control in Central America.

UFCO, or *la frutera* (the fruitery), as Central Americans called it, established a virtual monopoly on the production and distribution of bananas. Through government concessions and other means, the company acquired vast tracts of land in the hot, humid, sparsely settled Caribbean lowlands. Through the Meiggs connection it dominated transportation networks and owned a major corporation, International Railways of Central America. It built docks and port facilities. In 1913 UFCO created the Tropical Radio and Telegraph Company. *La frutera* possessed a large number of ships, widely known as the "great white fleet," and it had enormous influence on marketing in the United States. UFCO tolerated and even encouraged small-scale competition, but it was never seriously challenged in the decades after World War I.

The banana trade created enclave economies par excellence. UFCO supervisors and managers came from the U.S., most notably from the South, and black workers were imported from Jamaica and the West Indies. One result was to alter the racial composition of the eastern lowland population. Another was to create harshly enforced racial divisions within *la frutera* itself.

The industry became a giant foreign corporation. Some banana lands remained in local hands, but UFCO possessed control of technology, loans, and access to the U.S. market. Because of natural threats from hurricanes and plant disease, UFCO also sought to keep substantial amounts of land in reserve. These could usually be obtained only by government concession, a fact which required the company to enter local politics. The picture is clear: UFCO provided relatively scant stimulus for Central America's economic development, but became directly involved in local matters of state.

Coffee and bananas dominated economics after the turn of the century. As shown in Figure 9-1, the two products accounted for more than 70 percent of Central America's exports in 1913 and 1938 and nearly as much in 1960. The proportion declined by the early 1970s, as cotton and such other goods as meat, sugar, shrimp, refined petroleum (from refineries in Panama) and light manufacturers gained in importance, but the traditional products still carried great weight.

One implication of this fact is obvious: the Central America economy became thoroughly dependent on the export of two commercial crops, coffee and bananas. The economic fortunes of the isthmus now depended almost entirely on the vagaries of the international market. When coffee or banana prices were down, earnings were down, and there was little room for flexible response—since coffee and banana plantations could not be easily or quickly converted to producing basic foodstuffs (assuming that the owners wanted to do so, which was hardly

FIGURE 9-1   Principal Central American Exports, 1913–1972

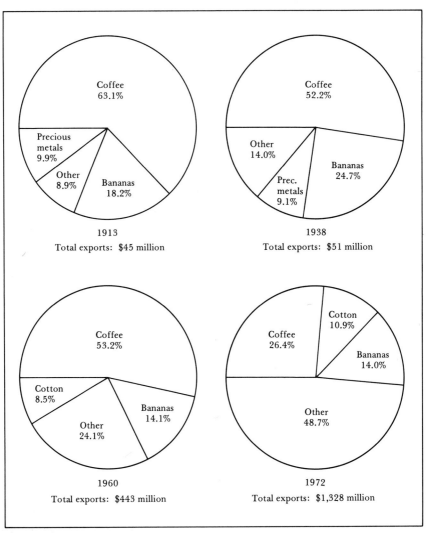

1913
Total exports: $45 million

1938
Total exports: $51 million

1960
Total exports: $443 million

1972
Total exports: $1,328 million

Source: Ralph Lee Woodward, Jr., *Central America: A Nation Divided* (New York: Oxford University Press, 1976), p. 257. Copyright © 1976 by Oxford University Press, Inc. Reprinted by permission.

the case). It is worth noting, too, that coffee consistently formed a larger share of exports than bananas, and UFCO could not control the coffee market. In strict economic terms only Costa Rica, Honduras, and Panama were "banana republics." Guatemala, El Salvador, and Nicaragua were mainly coffee countries.

The coffee-banana strategy moreover led to heavy reliance on trade with a single partner: the United States. In the late nineteenth and early twentieth centuries Central America had a flourishing trade with Europe—Germany, in fact, was the biggest coffee customer. But after World War I the U.S. asserted its supremacy. From the 1920s through the 1950s, as Table 9-1 demonstrates, the U.S. purchased 60–90 percent of the region's exports and provided a similar share of imports. The North American predominance in international transactions faded to 30–40 percent in the mid-1970s for most countries, which were doing more trade than before with each other and with western Europe. Nonetheless, the U.S. still had considerable commercial leverage over the nations of the isthmus.

The stress on agricultural exports and the persistence of peasant economies combined to discourage industrialization in Central America. The small scale of national markets presented another major obstacle to industrial growth.

In recognition of these difficulties, leaders of the isthmus decided to create the Central American Common Market (CACM) in 1960. The idea was to stimulate industrial development through a two-fold strategy; promoting free trade among member countries and creating common tariffs to protect infant enterprises. Costa Rica, El Salvador, Guatemala, Honduras, and Nicaragua formed the CACM membership; Panama did not belong because of its special status with the canal, but expressed from the start a continuing interest in association with the group.

The Common Market met with instant success. Commerce among the member countries multiplied, growing from 7.5 percent of all exports in 1960 to 26.9 percent by 1970. Manufacturing flourished—in

TABLE 9-1   Central American Trade with the United States, 1920–75 (as % of total)

	1920		1950		1975	
	Exports	*Imports*	*Exports*	*Imports*	*Exports*	*Imports*
Costa Rica	71	52	70	67	40	36
El Salvador	56	79	86	67	32	36
Guatemala	67	61	88	79	23	35
Honduras	87	85	77	74	47	46
Nicaragua	78	73	54	72	26	33
Panama	93	73	80	69	59	24

Sources: James W. Wilkie, *Statistics and National Policy,* Supplement 3, *Statistical Abstract of Latin America* (Los Angeles: UCLA Latin American Center, 1974), Table XV-3; James W. Wilkie and Peter Reich, eds., *Statistical Abstract of Latin America,* 19 (Los Angeles: UCLA Latin American Center, 1978), Table 2705.

such areas as electrical equipment, prepared foods, pulp and paper products, and fertilizers—as the isthmus embarked on the path of import-substitution industrialization. But CACM made little headway in the agricultural sector, where protectionist policies remained the rule, and it failed to meet the challenge of unemployment (which stood at 9.4 percent in 1970).

CACM also suffered from political disputes. Honduras had begun to complain about the distribution of benefits in the mid-1960s and withdrew from the market after an armed clash with El Salvador in 1969 (described below). Honduras has since negotiated bilateral agreements with the other countries—except El Salvador—but CACM lost a good deal of precious momentum.

Notwithstanding these efforts the regional economy has remained primarily agricultural, and its society has continued to be mostly rural. Around 1900 less than 10 percent of the population lived in cities. By 1970 the figure ranged between 20 and 40 percent (compared to 66 percent for Argentina, for example, and 61 percent for Chile). Even the biggest cities of Central America have been small by international standards. In 1970 Guatemala City, by far the largest, had well under a million inhabitants (731,000), and the other capitals had populations ranging from 200,000 to just over 400,000. Urbanization came late to Central America.

This delay has, in turn, produced a major social fact: Central America has never had a substantial urban working class. There are some workers in the cities, of course, and there have been sporadic efforts at unionization since the 1920s. But the de-emphasis on manufacturing and the smallness of the cities have not given rise to the scale of working-class movements that appeared in Argentina, Chile, Brazil, or Mexico. (In Nicaragua, for example, the unionized share of the economically active population in 1973 came to a paltry 2 percent.) A principal collective actor has been largely absent from the scene: just as Argentina has not had a classic peasantry, so Central America has lacked an urban working class.

Furthermore, the historical de-emphasis on manufacturing meant that the agricultural sector would never be challenged by an industrial sector. To be sure, CACM helped give shape and strength to a fledgling business group, but it did not lead to an outright assault upon the social order. Consequently there would be little incentive to form the sort of multi-class populist alliance that often emerges from sectoral conflict (as in Argentina, where Perón joined together industrial workers and entrepreneurs in a common attack upon the rural aristocracy). In the absence of an industrial threat, landlords and peasants, mostly Indian in Guatemala, faced each other in the Central American countryside. When conflict occurred, it would accordingly tend to follow class lines. Control of land would be the overriding issue.

The most active groups in Central America's cities have generally consisted of middle-sector merchants and professionals—lawyers, journalists, intellectuals, and students. They have not displayed much middle-class consciousness, but they have spawned some reformist political movements and produced a considerable number of civilian political leaders. As time passed their role in state and society steadily increased.

Despite this growth and development, the masses of Central America have remained poor. Per capita incomes are low (between 528 and 1,512 U.S. dollars in 1980) and wealth is tightly concentrated. As indicators of social welfare, national literacy rates reveal that in 1970 only 45–60 percent of adults could read and write in El Salvador, Guatemala, Honduras, and Nicaragua (Costa Rica, always the exception, was near to 90 percent). The proportion of young children (ages 7–13) who went to school was 70 percent or more for all countries but Guatemala—the largest country, where it was 50 percent. But this was more than offset by the low proportions of teenagers attending secondary schools: less than 20 percent in El Salvador, Guatemala, Honduras, and Nicaragua, only 33 percent in Costa Rica. If Central America's children were getting any education at all, their exposure to school was generally brief.

In time, this pattern of development and deprivation would exert tremendous pressure on the region's political systems. Understanding of this process requires a brief examination of each country's recent history.

Panama: A Nation and a Zone

Panama did not become an independent republic until after the turn of the century. During the 1800s it was a province of Colombia. Because of poor communications and distance from Bogotá it had become semi-autonomous. The energetic president of Colombia, Rafael Núñez, tried to assert central control during his tenure in office (1885–94), and partially succeeded. After his death the country fell into disarray, and Liberals and Conservatives began a frightful struggle that culminated in Colombia's "War of the Thousand Days" (1899–1903). The conflict ended with the Liberals in defeat, the economy in paralysis, the government near bankruptcy.

In view of these conditions Panama might have sought independence on its own, as it had long been chafing under rule from Bogotá. Ultimately, however, Panamanian sovereignty would not arise from an indigenous popular movement. It would grow out of big-power diplomacy and international intrigue.

At issue was an inter-oceanic canal, a time-honored vision for Central America. Plans went back as far as the seventeenth century. In 1878 the government of Colombia authorized a French group under Ferdinand de Lesseps, builder of the Suez Canal, to dig a route through Panama. U.S. engineers tended to favor Nicaragua, and a North American firm received a contract to begin digging in that country. The race was on. Then came the financial Panic of 1893, when both groups ran out of money and quit.

Popular opinion in the U.S. favored bold action in Latin America. The works of Rudyard Kipling spread deep convictions about the "white man's burden." Popularized versions of Social Darwinism helped convince North Americans they were among history's "fittest." The acquisition of Cuba and a Pacific empire through the Spanish-American War prompted interest in far-flung possessions. And in such magisterial books as *The Influence of Sea Power upon History* (1890), the historian-publicist Alfred Thayer Mahan forcefully argued that naval power was the key to international influence, a doctrine requiring a two-ocean navy for the U.S. After Theodore Roosevelt was elected president in 1900, it was clear that Washington would make a move. What kind?

Colombian politics led to resolution of the issue. As the War of the Thousand Days was nearing its end in 1903, Washington dispatched troops to quell disorder in Panama. This resulted in a diplomatic crisis which eventually produced the Hay-Herrán Treaty, an agreement that authorized the U.S. to build a canal in Panama. The U.S. Congress eagerly approved the document—but the Colombian legislature, unwilling to compromise national sovereignty, refused to go along.

The next step was insurrection. The de Lessups chief engineer, Philippe Bunau-Varilla, was continuing to push for a canal, and now he seized his chance. With Roosevelt's full knowledge, Bunau-Varilla started laying plans for a separatist rebellion in Panama. As the uprising began, U.S. ships prevented Colombian troops from crossing the isthmus to Panama City. The revolt was a success.

Within days Washington extended recognition to the newly sovereign government of Panama, and received Bunau-Varilla (still a French citizen) as its official representative. U.S. Secretary of State John Hay and Bunau-Varilla hastily signed a treaty giving the United States control of a ten-mile-wide canal zone "in perpetuity . . . as if it were sovereign." A pliant Panamanian legislature soon approved the document. Bunau-Varilla and administration lobbyists then turned their attention to the U.S. Senate, where pro-Nicaragua sentiment was still fairly strong. On the morning of the decisive vote Bunau-Varilla placed on each senator's desk a Nicaraguan postage stamp depicting a volcanic eruption, and the silent message took hold. The Senate approved the measure by a 66-14 margin, and the die was cast.

Panama thus acquired nationhood through big-stick diplomacy. Opened in 1914, the canal immediately became a major international waterway, and the government began receiving steady annuities. The

Canal Zone became a de facto U.S. colony, an area of legal privilege and country-club prosperity that stood in sharp and conspicuous contrast to local society. Outside the Zone, Panama developed the characteristics that typified Central America as a whole: dependence on agricultural exports (especially bananas), reliance on the U.S. market, and domestic control by a tightly knit landed oligarchy. Notwithstanding the Hay–Bunau-Varilla Treaty, the situation could not last forever.

In 1952 Col. José Antonio Remón became president and began renegotiation of the treaty of 1903. Three years later his efforts resulted in an agreement that increased the annuity payable to Panama, curtailed economic privileges for U.S. citizens, and sought to equalize wage rates for North Americans and Panamanians. But the question of sovereignty was left untouched. It came up in 1956, after Egypt's seizure of the Suez Canal. When President Ricardo Arias bitterly protested Panama's exclusion from a conference on the Suez crisis, Secretary of State John Foster Dulles frostily replied that the U.S. had "rights of sovereignty over the Panama Canal . . . to the entire exclusion of the Republic of Panama of any such sovereign rights, power, or authority."

Tensions and consultations continued. In January 1964 American students at Balboa High School raised a U.S. flag alone, without the accompaniment of a Panamanian banner, and large-scale rioting ensued. Ellsworth Bunker, U.S. Ambassador to the Organization of American States, charged that assaults on the Canal Zone came from mobs "infiltrated and led by extremists, including persons trained in Communist countries." Panamanian President Roberto F. Chiari broke off relations with Washington.

Tempers cooled and discussions resumed. In 1968 Dr. Arnulfo Arias won a disputed election, a campaign that he himself called "one of the most shameful in the history of the country." After holding office for merely 11 days he was overthrown by the National Guard, which set up a junta under Brigadier General Omar Torrijos Herrera. This marked a clear assertion by the Guard of hegemony in politics. It led to the emergence of Torrijos as the nation's strong man. And it yielded continuity in leadership, as Torrijos patiently pursued negotiations with the Nixon, Ford, and Carter administrations in the U.S.

The United States finally accepted a treaty that provided for complete Panamanian sovereignty over the canal by 1999. Ronald Reagan (before assuming the presidency in 1981) and other U.S. conservatives vigorously denounced the agreement as a "sellout," but Democratic President Jimmy Carter eventually obtained Senate approval. Intellectuals and statesmen throughout the hemisphere applauded the move. However briefly, U.S.–Latin American relations took a positive turn.

But Panama continued to have troubles of its own. Torrijos died in an air accident in 1981. On July 30, 1982, the civilian president Aristides Royo abruptly resigned, turning office over to the vice-president. Royo cited poor health but most observers believed that he had been dismissed by the National Guard, possibly because of Royo's inability to deal with labor unrest—or because of the presidential ambitions of the leader of the Guard, General Rubén Darío Paredes. Either way, one thing was clear: Men in uniform were in control.

Costa Rica: Fragile Democracy

Costa Rica has long been unique. Despite its name ("rich coast"), it was of minimal economic importance to Spain, and as the southernmost area in the kingdom of Guatemala it was relatively remote from the rest of Central America. Sparsely populated from the outset, it never developed a large-scale black or Indian subservient class. Nor did it have a wealthy landed oligarchy.

Coffee cultivation began on modest, family-sized farms in the 1830s. The flourishing commerce gave rise to a substantial and prosperous agrarian middle sector—and to a merchant class in the cities—without creating a landless peasantry. United Fruit established banana plantations on the east coast in the late nineteenth and early twentieth centuries, and bananas soon became the country's leading export.

For economic and demographic reasons Costa Rica emerged as a racially and socially homogenous society. By 1925 about 80 percent of the population was white, 4 percent was black (mostly workers on banana plantations), 14 percent was *mestizo,* and less than 1 percent was Indian. Middle-class culture prevailed, and racial conflict was largely absent.

Social consensus led to broad acceptance of constitutional politics. Early twentieth century governments fostered welfare programs (so Costa Rica, like Uruguay, inevitably came to be compared to Switzerland). Conservatives exchanged power with Liberals. There was not much to fight about, and democratic traditions began to take root.

Then worldwide depression in the 1930s bred social discontent. The National Republican Party came forward as an alternative to communism. The Liberal-Conservative distinction faded and, with leftist support, National Republicans won the presidential elections of 1936, 1940, and 1944. A progressive social security system and labor code were put in place.

Two leading factions then emerged. One was the vehemently anti-communist National Union Party, led by Otilio Ulate Blanco. The other was the left-of-center (but anti-communist) Social Democratic Party, organized by former Conservative José ("Pepe") Figueres Ferrer. In the 1948 elections both movements joined in a coalition against the National Republicans. Violence flared, disputes erupted, and Figueres assumed authority. Acting with vigor and decisiveness, he dissolved the army, levied new taxes, called a constituent assembly, and—as was occurring at this time elsewhere in Latin America—outlawed the communist Popular Vanguard. The dust settled and Ulate Blanco took office in 1949.

Figueres won the presidency in 1952 and normalcy returned. He stimulated agricultural exports and negotiated a new contract with United Fruit, under which the Costa Rican share of profits increased from 10 to 30 percent. With support from Washington he withstood an uprising in 1955. The election of 1958 went smoothly. Said Figueres after the loss by his party's candidate: "I consider our defeat as a contribution, in a way, to democracy in Latin America. It is not customary for a party in power to lose an election."

Subsequent events would bear out his claim. Voter participation in Costa Rica has generally been over 80 percent, one of the highest rates in the world (compared to 55–60 percent in the U.S.). And moderation has prevailed: less than 10 percent of the vote has gone to extremist candidates of left or right. In contrast to so much of Central America, Costa Rica has a strong and viable political center.

Economic straits, as always, put the system to a stringent test. Under the dubious administration of Rodrigo Carazo (1978–82) Costa Rica ran up a foreign debt of $4 billion U.S. dollars, enormous for a country its size. The growth rate declined from 8.9 percent in 1977 to −2.4 percent in 1981, during which year the local currency (the *colón*) was devalued by more than 400 percent. Unemployment climbed to 10 percent and appeared to be still rising.

The election in 1982 of Luis Alberto Monge, a cautious politician and fiscal conservative, offered hope that Costa Rica could weather its financial crisis. It would require firm direction. Whether Costa Rica's fragile democracy could meet the challenge was an open question.

Nicaragua: From Dynasty to Revolution

For much of its history Nicaragua has been a pawn of outside powers, especially the United States. During the nineteenth century it received unceasing attention from avaricious adventurers, many of whom sought to build a canal, and it endured the brief but ignominious presence of William Walker. The pattern would continue into the twentieth century.

The British conceded the Caribbean basin to the U.S. sphere of influence in the 1890s, and Washington eagerly seized the opportunity. The U.S. occupied Cuba, "took" Panama, and established a protectorate in the Dominican Republic. To justify these and future actions, Theodore Roosevelt proclaimed in 1904:

Any country whose people conduct themselves well can count upon our hearty friendship. If a nation shows that it knows how to act with reasonable efficiency and decency in social and political matters, if it keeps order and pays its obligations, it need fear no interference from the United States. Chronic wrong-doing, or an impotence which results in a general loosening of the ties of society, may in America, as elsewhere, ultimately require intervention by some civilized nation, and in the western hemisphere the adherence of the United States to the Monroe Doctrine may force the United States, however reluctantly, in flagrant cases of such wrong-doing or impotence, to the exercise of an international police power.

Known as the "Roosevelt Corollary" to the Monroe Doctrine, the rationale took on clear meaning: The U.S. could intervene in Latin America at will, in order to prevent intervention by Europe.

Nicaragua would soon find out what the dictum meant in practice. Washington had developed a strong dislike for José Santos Zelaya, the Liberal dictator who had staunchly resisted foreign control in negotiations over a canal route. In 1909 Zelaya ordered the execution of two North American adventurers. Secretary of State Philander C. Knox denounced Zelaya as "a blot on the history of his country" and expelled Nicaragua's ambassador from the U.S. In Nicaragua public pressure increased to where Zelaya stepped down from office.

Financial chaos ensued. European creditors began demanding payment on their debts. In desperation the new president, Conservative Adolfo Díaz, asked the U.S. to send military aid to protect North American economic interests from the threat of civil war within Nicaragua and to "extend its protection to all the inhabitants of the republic." Citing the Roosevelt statement, President William Howard Taft dispatched the marines. A plan for fiscal recovery obtained a guarantee from a New York banking conglomerate, which received control of the national bank and the railway system as security on its investment. Politically and economically, Nicaragua became a full-fledged protectorate of the United States.

This condition lasted till 1933. In the mid-1920s a dispute arose over presidential succession. The U.S. imposed the trusty Adolfo Díaz and agreed to supervise upcoming elections. As a result of this compromise, a Liberal named Juan Bautista Sacasa won the presidency in 1932 and called for the withdrawal of U.S. troops. The New York bankers had some time ago recovered their investment and Franklin Delano Roosevelt was about to proclaim the Good Neighbor policy. In 1933 the marines left Nicaragua.

But one Liberal activist, Augusto César Sandino, refused to abide by the bargain of the late 1920s. A fervent patriot, a nationalist and social moderate, Sandino had waged a guerrilla campaign againt U.S. intervention and Nicaraguan collaborationists. He gained a widespread pop-

Most Americans accepted the claim that the U.S. protectorate in Nicaragua was justified by the "Roosevelt corollary" to the Monroe Doctrine; the original caption for this cartoon was "cutting a switch for a bad boy." (McKee Barclay, *Baltimore Sun,* 1910. Courtesy of The Baltimore Sun.)

ular following but the U.S. worried about the presence of leftists among his supporters. U.S. marines joined in the campaign against him but he consistently eluded his pursuers. Even after U.S. forces left, Sandino continued the fight. With Sacasa firmly installed in the presidency, Sandino agreed to a meeting to try and reach a peace agreement. After leaving the presidential palace, Sandino and two supporting generals were seized by Nicaraguan National Guard officers and promptly executed. A genuine national hero, Sandino now became a martyr as well.

Political power resided not in the electoral system but in the National Guard, a domestic police force created during the U.S. occupation. At its head was General Anastasio ("Tacho") Somoza García, an ambitious and ruthless tyrant who had given the order to execute Sandino. He eventually unseated Sacasa and took over the presidency in 1937. Thus began the Somoza regime.

A wily politician, Somoza drew support from several sources: the National Guard, which he constantly nurtured and protected; the landed elite, with whose members he entered into numerous partnerships; and the United States, whose political power structure he knew so well how to manipulate.

Amassing an enormous fortune for himself and his family, Somoza promoted Nicaragua's economic growth and cultivated U.S. aid. He was struck by an assassin in 1956 and rushed to a hospital in the American-controlled Canal Zone. Ever grateful for Somoza's rabid anti-communism, President Eisenhower sent his personal surgeon to try to save the dictator's life. Somoza nonetheless succumbed.

The family enterprise endured. The elder son, Luis Somoza Debayle, took over and was elected to the presidency by an 89 percent majority in 1957. A trusted family associate, René Schick, assumed office in 1963. Four years later Luis Somoza died of a heart attack. Power then passed to Anastasio Somoza Debayle, a West Point graduate and, like his father, head of the National Guard. Self-seeking, ruthless, corrupt, Somoza clamped an iron rule on the country, but offended thoughtful Nicaraguans by his excesses. It was rumored, for example, that he exacted large-scale economic profits from the reconstruction of Managua after a devastating earthquake in 1972.

The complete absence of representative institutions meant that opposition to Somoza could take only one form: armed resistance. In the 1960s a strong guerrilla movement emerged, and it consisted of three major groups. One, known as Prolonged Popular War (GPP), formed in the early 1960s among rural peasants of the mountainous north. Second were the *Proletarios,* who splintered from the GPP in 1973 to carry the movement to workers and especially intellectuals in the cities. Third were the *Terceristas,* a politically moderate and anti-communist group led by Edén Pastora, renowned from his military exploits as the legendary "Commander Zero." Taking their name from Augusto César Sandino, the movements all combined to forge the *Sandinista* National Liberation Front.

After years of struggle the Somoza regime suddenly collapsed in 1979, just as Batista had given way in Cuba two decades before. Safely exiled in Miami, Somoza would lay the blame on forces beyond his control. "The Nicaraguan people have not thrown me out. I was thrown out by an international conspiracy that today has a majority of communists and that today desires Nicaragua to be a communist country." Anastasio, Jr., later met his death at the hands of assassins in Paraguay.

Once in power, the *sandinistas* proclaimed two broad policy goals. One called for implementation of an "independent and nonaligned" foreign policy, which meant no further submission to the U.S. The other envisioned the creation of a "mixed economy" in order to achieve socioeconomic justice.

The revolution got off to a promising start. President Carter invited

Nicaragua's leaders to the White House, sent $8 million in emergency relief to Managua, and secured an additional authorization from Congress for a $75 million aid package. Their domestic task was eased by the magnitude of the Somoza family fortune, which included about 20 percent of the country's cultivable land. It was therefore possible for the revolutionary government to nationalize these holdings and to initiate an agrarian reform without having to face the diehard opposition of an entrenched landed aristocracy.

The Nicaraguan revolutionaries quickly attacked the same social problems the Cubans had become famous for liquidating, such as illiteracy, inadequate preventive medicine and insufficient vocational and higher education. Nicaragua welcomed approximately 2500 Cubans (the count was carefully monitored by the CIA and State Department)—doctors, nurses, school teachers, sanitary engineers—to help the revolutionary government raise basic living standards. Cuban military, police, and intelligence personnel also arrived to help consolidate the regime against what the *sandinistas* (and Cubans) were convinced would be counter-revolutionary attacks from within and without.

The Nicaraguans also solicited help from the U.S., which responded in late 1979 with a very modest USAID program of $75 million. Far more important financial help came from West Europe—especially West Germany, France, and Spain. The Soviets, on the other hand, offered no hard-currency credits. The Nicaraguans therefore appeared as of early 1983 to have a better chance to avoid complete trade and financial dependence on one ideological bloc than did Cuba in 1959–61.

The Nicaraguan euphoria did not last long, however. In the U.S. the Republican Party electoral platform of 1980 formally deplored "the Marxist *sandinista* takeover of Nicaragua," and the Reagan administration thereafter began a persistent campaign to undermine the *sandinista* government. One key issue centered on intervention, as President Reagan and Secretary of State Alexander Haig accused Nicaragua of lending support to guerrillas in El Salvador; the Nicaraguans responded by accusing the U.S. of training anti-*sandinista* rebels in neighboring Honduras. Another disagreement focused on Nicaragua's military buildup from 20,000 to 50,000 troops (including reservists and militia): Washington contended this could only be intended for subversive purposes, while Managua insisted it was for legitimate self-defense. Nicaraguans grew apprehensive over this marked deterioration in relations with the United States. As junta member Daniel Ortega Saavedra remarked in August 1982, U.S. officials "leave open the possibility of invading or sending mercenaries against Nicaragua. . . . Our country has been invaded by the United States various times before, and we have every right to believe that, under the present circumstances, this could happen again."

There were internal difficulties too. After some hesitation the *san-*

dinista regime decided to postpone its first elections to 1985, six years after seizing power. The prominent newspaper *La Prensa* was shut down from time to time, and the government was sharply criticized by church authorities. Claiming that the state was too monolithic and too Marxist, some leading members of the original *sandinista* movement—including Edén Pastora—sought refuge in exile and joined the opposition. All in all, the political record was mixed: the *sandinista* regime was no doubt repressive in some ways, but it was also more open and less authoritarian than any Nicaraguan government within living memory. The course of the future was anyone's guess.

Honduras: Rule by Military

Honduras has undergone the least transition of all the Central American republics (or any of the other countries discussed here). Liberal-Conservative party rivalies have persisted to the mid-twentieth century, popular agitation has been minimal, and power has rested in the hands of a triangular alliance: landowners, foreign investors (mainly United Fruit), and the military. Because of its economic and political weakness Honduras has been especially vulnerable to outside influence. It remains, in many respects, a stereotypical "banana republic."

With vivid clarity, Honduran history reveals a fundamental fact of Central American political life: the emergence of the military as an autonomous caste, and as a supreme arbiter in national affairs. In Honduras, as elsewhere in the isthmus, a career in the armed forces (or national guard) offered chances for upward mobility to middle-sector *ladinos*. Land was already controlled by the aristocracy, the universities were restrictive, there was hardly any industrial development: an ambitious young person of middling origin had almost no other alternative. As a result recruits and cadets took immense pride in the honor and dignity of the military as an institution, and officers tended to look down on politicians and civilians. To this extent the armed forces stood apart from civil society—but their consent (if not support) was essential to the survival of any political coalition.

The leading figure in early twentieth century Honduras was Tiburcio Carías Andino, whose conservative-oriented National Party was prevented from taking the presidency in 1923. After some dispute Carías' candidate was permitted to govern till 1929, when the Liberals recaptured office. In 1932 Carías himself won the presidency, and he held that position till 1948.

In 1957 a group of young military officers supervised the election of Dr. Ramón Villeda Morales, a progressive Liberal who became an outspoken supporter of John Fitzgerald Kennedy and the Alliance for Progress. But senior commanders resented his reformist tendencies, and in 1963 they dismissed him in favor of armed forces leader Oswald

López Arellano, who ruled till 1975 (when he was toppled, of course, by a military coup).

Officers retained control until 1981. Partly as a result of international pressure, especially from the U.S., fairly open elections took place in that year. The candidate of the Liberal Party, Roberto Suazo Córdova, won 54.1 percent of the vote; the National Party once headed by Carías got 41.5 percent. The military decided to accept the result. Until further notice, at least, Suazo had a chance to govern.

Strife with neighboring countries has played an important part in Honduran history. During the 1960s, for instance, tensions with El Salvador mounted steadily. There had been longstanding, although minor, boundary disputes. The principal source of the trouble was economic: El Salvador was densely populated, with 390 persons per square mile, while Honduras had only 55 per square mile. *Salvadoreños* consequently went to look for jobs and land in Honduras, and the Hondurans understandably resented their presence. A 1963 law prohibited companies from employing more than 10 percent foreigners (that is, Salvadorans), and a 1968 decree prevented Salvadorans from gaining title to Honduran land.

Violence erupted in both capitals in 1969, when national soccer teams from the two countries played an elimination round in the World Cup competition. Antagonism reached such a point that the third and deciding game had to be played in Mexico. El Salvador won the contest, and frustrated Hondurans attacked Salvadoran residents in Tegucigalpa and other cities. El Salvador severed diplomatic relations and demanded reparations. So did Honduras. The case was going to the OAS when El Salvador claimed that Honduran planes had conducted bombing raids.

As the world looked on in astonishment, the so-called "soccer war" began in earnest and lasted two weeks. In one sense, it cast light on the political function of organized sport in Latin American society. In another, it revealed the latent hostility and rivalry among the republics of Central America.

More recently, Honduras has become embroiled in international disagreements over the character and course of the *sandinista* revolution in Nicaragua. Between 1980 and 1982 the U.S. nearly tripled its military assistance to Honduras, which had become a launching pad for counterrevolutionary guerrillas, some led by former *somocistas*. In mid-1983 a member of the *sandinista* junta openly charged that "the Honduran army and the military forces of the United States are involved in a military operation that threatens the territorial integrity of Nicaragua." The allegation was confirmed in the U.S. media, particularly by dispatches in the *Washington Post* and by a startling cover story in *Newsweek*.

Only time would bring the final outcome. Two points, however, stood beyond doubt: The armed forces retained ultimate power in Honduras, and the temptation to meddle in the affairs of other countries continued to exist.

El Salvador: From Stability to Insurgence

Oligarchic control eventually took hold in nineteenth century El Salvador. In 1863 Rafael Carrera launched an invasion from Guatemala and imposed a Conservative of his own liking, but Liberals countered with a successful revolt in 1871. Legal decrees in the 1880s prohibited the collective ownership of land by Indian communities and thus paved the way for the usurpation and consolidation of land by a tiny aristocracy— *las catorce,* the notorious "fourteen" families (which have meanwhile expanded in number and size). Coffee became the leading export crop, commerce flourished, and from 1907 to 1931 political power rested in the hands of a single family, the patriarchical Meléndez clan.

Peasants did not accept this passively. Angered by the loss of land, they staged four separate revolts between 1870 and 1900. The movements were crushed but they carried a message: like the *zapatistas* of Mexico, the peasants of El Salvador were willing to fight for their rights.

The ruling coalition of coffee-growing oligarchs, foreign investors, military officers—and church prelates—prevailed throughout the 1920s. The crash of 1929 had severe repercussions in El Salvador, since independent small farmers and plantation laborers suffered greatly from the drop in coffee prices. In 1931 a U.S. military attaché, Major A. R. Harris, filed this report:

> There appears to be nothing between . . . high-priced cars and the oxcart with its barefooted attendant. There is practically no middle class between the very rich and the very poor. . . . Roughly 90 percent of the wealth in the country is held by about one-half of one percent of the population. Thirty or forty families own nearly everything in the country. They live in regal splendor [while] the rest of the country has practically nothing. . . . A socialistic or communistic revolution in El Salvador may be delayed for several years, ten or even twenty, but when it comes it will be a bloody one.

It would not take that long.

On May Day 1930 a popular throng of 80,000 held a demonstration in downtown San Salvador against deteriorating wages and living conditions. The next year an idealistic landowner and admirer of the British Labour Party, Arturo Araujo, won the presidential election with the support of students, peasants, and workers. Somewhat naively, he announced that the Salvadoran Communist Party would be permitted to take part in municipal elections in December 1931. Exasperated by this prospect, the armed forces dismissed him from office on December 2 and imposed a right-wing general, Maximiliano Hernández Martínez.

The peasants broke out in rebellion. In late January 1932, as a chain of volcanoes erupted in Guatemala and northwest El Salvador, bands of Indians armed with machetes made their way out of the ravines and tangled hillsides down into the towns of the area. Led by Agustín Faribundo Martí, a dedicated communist who had fought alongside Sandino in Nicaragua, the peasants murdered some landlords and plunged the country into a state of revolt.

Hernández Martínez responded with ferocity. As military units moved in on the rebels the conflict took on the appearance of a racial war, as Indians—or anyone resembling Indians—suffered from the government attack. In the tiny country of 1.4 million inhabitants between 10,000 and 20,000 Salvadorans lost their lives.

The events of 1932 sent several messages. Peasants learned to distrust city-bred revolutionaries who might lead them to destruction. Indians began to seek safety in casting off indigenous habits and clothes. On the political level, leftists concluded that they could still cultivate followings in rural areas, especially in the absence of a reformist alternative. The right drew a stark lesson of its own: the way to deal with popular agitation was by repression.

A proto-fascist sympathizer, among the first to recognize the 1936 Franco regime in Spain, Hernández Martínez stayed on till 1944. Military officers seized power with the consent and blessing of *las catorce*. Major Oscar Osorio headed a moderate dictatorship in 1950–56. In 1960 his handpicked successor, Colonel José María Lemus, was overthrown by a civilian-military group with slightly leftist leanings under Colonel César Yanes Urías. Just one year later Yanes Urías was ousted by rightists under Lt. Col. Julio A. Rivera, whose Party of National Conciliation (PCN) took control of the state. This alliance of civilian conservatives and military officers would reign supreme till the late 1970s.

A reformist challenge finally came from José Napoleón Duarte, who founded the Christian Democratic Party (PDC). As mayor of San Salvador (1964–70), the dynamic and articulate Duarte built up a strong following among intellectuals, professionals, and other urban middle-sector groups. The PDC bore a commitment to peaceful reform through electoral means. Though Duarte may have won the presidential election of 1972, the recalcitrant military turned power over to one of its own, Colonel Arturo Armando Molina. Duarte himself was imprisoned, tortured, and exiled—but he did not take to the hills.

Conditions in the meantime worsened for the peasants. Coffee exports were thriving but the poor were suffering. About 80 percent of the people lived in the countryside, and by 1975 about 40 percent of the peasants had no land at all—compared to only 12 percent in 1960. Increasingly unable to gain access to the soil, the *campesinos* of El Salvador were getting ready to rebel.

The reform-oriented option gradually disappeared during the 1970s. The first attempt took the electoral road in 1972, and that was defeated by the military. The next step involved the formation of "popular organizations," apolitical groups that sought nonviolent routes to change. Sometimes organized by exiles like Duarte, they found support and stimulus from a revitalized institution: the Roman Catholic Church.

Indeed, the reawakening of the church has been one of the most decisive processes in contemporary El Salvador. The trend goes back to two events: the Second Ecumenical Council of the early 1960s (Vatican II), and the conference of Latin American bishops at Medellín, Colombia in 1968. The Medellín conference, particularly, denounced capitalism and communism as equal affronts to human dignity and placed the blame for hunger and misery on the rich and powerful. To redress these inequalities the bishops called for more education, increased social awareness, and the creation of *comunidades de base,* Christian communities of 12–15 people each.

These developments had a profound impact on the ecclesiastical hierarchy in El Salvador, then under Archbishop Oscar Arnulfo Romero. As one priest firmly explained:

> it is not communism to make the right to organize and defend oneself known to the peasants. They have a right to defend their interests and to promote the political order of their choice, to defend their rights effectively, to denounce abuse by authorities or agents of the powerful. It is simply carrying out the Gospel mandate, a duty the church must not refuse or avoid.

As repression mounted the church eventually acknowledged, in Romero's own words, "the case for insurrection . . . when all recourses to peaceful means have been exhausted." No one was immune to violence: in 1980 the archbishop himself was shot dead while administering high mass in the cathedral of San Salvador.

Nonetheless, the realignment of the Salvadoran church has far-reaching implications. Other partners still belong to the elite coalition: *las catorce* families, the military, and the foreign sector. But the church—at least, an influential segment of the church—has defected from the alliance and thrown its support to the masses. This has altered the structure of power.

But secular and religious grass-roots organizations met with continued repression in the mid-70s. The armed forces carefully controlled the elections of 1977, which turned the presidency over to General Carlos Humberto Romero. One of his most significant acts was to promote a "law to defend and guarantee public order."

The next phase in the deterioration of the political system began in October 1979, when a group of junior officers ousted Romero and set up a new government. At first the outlook was promising. The junta sought support from the "popular organizations." Given its commitment to human rights, the Carter administration greeted the regime with pleasure and relief.

Then things took a turn for the worse. Government repression persisted and killings continued at the rate of 1000 per month. The periodic estimates came from church and human rights groups who tried to monitor the slaughter. The cabinet resigned in protest, but the minister of defense—General José Guillermo García—hung on to his government post. The liberal wing of the Christian Democratic Party defected from the coalition. Now appearing undeniably conservative, the beleaguered Duarte took over as head of the government and announced a plan for land reform.

By this time the opposition moved underground. One group, the Democratic Revolutionary Front, was led by Enrique Alvarez, Minister of Agriculture in the first post–October 1979 junta. Another key element was the Farabundo Martí National Liberation Front—named for the leader of the 1932 uprising. In November 1980 Alvarez and five top associates were killed by government forces, an act that eliminated an entire cadre of reformist politicians. Guillermo Ungo stepped in to replace Alvarez, but the cause of moderate reform had suffered a devastating blow. Increasingly, guerrilla opposition to the regime took on a radical tinge.

The next month four North American women, three nuns and a lay worker, met a brutal death. The Carter administration protested vigorously and Duarte promised an investigation. In early 1981 the Reagan administration, more concerned with anti-communism than with social change or human rights, softened the U.S. demands. By mid-1982 a few low-ranking members of the National Guard were implicated in the crime, but a trial date had not been set. Thus the regime survived international furor.

Yet Washington pressed for elections in early 1982. The goal was to elect a constituent assembly that would in turn select an interim president, and the campaign had ominous signs. The right was led by a fiery ex-major, Roberto d'Aubuisson, whom former U.S. Ambassador Robert White had once called a "pathological killer." Known as "Major Bob" by his admirers, d'Aubuisson summarized his platform with a campaign slogan: "Another '32," meaning that it was time for El Salvador to repeat the slaughter of 1932. The center, or center-right, was represented by Duarte and his semi-conservative Christian Democrats. For its part, the Democratic Revolutionary Front—and the left as a whole—decided to boycott the elections. Ungo and his spokesmen argued that in the atmosphere of violence, leftist candidates were likely to be killed; voters would be intimidated; and the army would rig the results anyway. Consequently the election became a contest between the political right and the tattered remnants of the center.

Voter participation was remarkably high, if official statistics can be believed, and the results gave power to the right. Duarte's Christian Democrats won 35.3 percent of the votes, or 24 out of 60 seats in the constituent assembly. D'Aubuisson's party, the National Republican Alliance (ARENA), won 25.7 percent, or 19 seats, but managed to form a working coalition with other right-wing groups and take control of the assembly. "Major Bob" became the head of El Salvador's constitutional convention. The interim presidency went to Alvaro Magaña, an apolitical and soft-spoken economist who had for many years served as director of the National Mortgage Bank.

But the battle continued in the countryside. Guerrillas made periodic raids. Aided by U.S. military "trainers" (not called "advisers," in order to avoid association with Vietnam), government forces conducted sweeping search-and-destroy missions. Villagers and peasants grew fearful of both sides. By early 1983 the conflict appeared to favor the guerrillas. On its outcome hinged the future of El Salvador.

No less important was the battle for U.S. public opinion toward El Salvador. As of early 1983 the U.S. was supplying $205 million in economic aid and $26 million in military assistance, with higher requests pending in Congress. Few observers doubted that without this aid the regime in El Salvador would collapse. Growing opposition to the U.S. aid came from Congressional liberals and religious groups, especially the Catholic Church, still incensed over the 1980 killing of four American Catholic women in El Salvador, apparently with El Salvadorean army collusion, if not direct involvement. The intensity of U.S. opposition feeling could be seen in the bumper stickers that read "El Salvador is Vietnam in Spanish."

Guatemala: Reaction and Repression

Guatemala has a long history of strong-man rule. After Rafael Carrera died in 1865, Justino Rufino Barrios established a 12-year dictatorship (1873–85) and Manuel Estrada Cabrera followed with a 22-year, iron-fisted regime (1898–1920), the longest uninterrupted one-man rule in Central America. In 1931 General Jorge Ubico came to power, and immediately launched a campaign to crush the fledgling Communist Party. Instead of relying on coffee planters alone, Ubico built a tentative base among agrarian workers by abolishing debt slavery. The national police maintained law and order. As Ubico once said of his tactics: "I have no friends, only domesticated enemies."

A wave of strikes and protests led Ubico to resign in July 1944. He was replaced by a military triumvirate, and this in turn was ousted by

U.S. policy in Central America prompted a great deal of public controversy and debate in 1983. *Above,* cartoonist Tony Auth satirizes President Reagan's position and the hesitancy of the U.S. Congress in voicing opposition; *below,* Steve Benson dramatizes the left-wing threat to U.S. interests. (Reprinted with permission of the Washington Post Writers Group.)

a group of junior officers. Thus came the October Revolution of 1944, an event that signalled the beginning of a decade-long transformation.

In an open election the following year Guatemalans elected as president Juan José Arévalo Bermejo, an idealistic university professor who proclaimed a belief in "spiritual socialism." Arévalo oversaw the promulgation of a progressive new constitution in 1945, modelled in part on the Mexican charter of 1917, and he encouraged workers and peasants to organize. Industrial wages went up 80 percent between 1945 and 1950. Arévalo pushed education and other reforms as well. But the going was not easy: during his five-year term in office Arévalo weathered no less than 22 military revolts.

In 1950 Arévalo turned the presidency over to Colonel Jacobo Arbenz Guzmán, the minister of defense who led a center-left coalition in the elections of that year. A central figure in the October Revolution of 1944, Arbenz developed profound social concerns—partly at the insistence of his wife, María Vilanova, a wealthy Salvadoran who resembled Argentina's Evita Perón in her ambition for her husband to win political power through greatly increased social welfare benefits. Arbenz accepted Communist support, both during and after the election, but he was a reformer at heart. At his inauguration he spelled out his hopes for the country's future:

> Our government proposes to begin the march toward the economic development of Guatemala, and proposes three fundamental objectives: to convert our country from a dependent nation with a semi-colonial economy to an economically independent country; to convert Guatemala from a backward country with a predominantly feudal economy into a modern capitalist state; and to make this transformation in a way that will raise the standard of living of the great mass of our people to the highest level.

To achieve these goals, Arbenz said, Guatemala would need to strengthen its own private sector, "in whose hands rests the fundamental economic activity of the country." Foreign capital would be needed too, "as long as it adjusts to local conditions, remains always subordinate to Guatemalan laws, cooperates with the economic development of the country, and strictly abstains from intervening in the nation's social and political life." Finally, the new president declared, Guatemala would embark on a program of agrarian reform.

Arbenz set quickly to work. He authorized construction of a public port on the Atlantic coast and the building of an east–west highway. He convinced the legislature to approve an income tax—a watered-down version of a mild proposal, to be sure, but the first in Guatemalan history. He pushed for expanded public works and the exploitation of energy resources, including petroleum.

The centerpiece of the Arbenz administration was agrarian reform. Enacted in June 1952, the bill empowered the government to expropriate only uncultivated portions of large plantations. All lands taken were to be paid for in 25-year bonds bearing a 3-percent interest rate, and the valuation of land was to be determined according to its taxable worth as of May 1952. During its 18 months of operation the agrarian reform distributed 1.5 million acres to some 100,000 families. The ex-proporiations included 1700 acres owned by Arbenz himself, who had become a landowner through the dowry of his wife.

Almost immediately, Arbenz and the agrarian reform ran into a serious obstacle: implacable opposition from the United Fruit Company and from the U.S. government. *La frutera* had obvious reasons for resisting the reform. The company held enormous tracts of land in Guatemala, 85 percent of which was unused—or, as the company maintained, it was being held in reserve against natural catastrophes. And in arranging tax payments, UFCO consistently undervalued its holdings. (On the basis of tax declarations, the Guatemalan government in 1953 offered UFCO $627,572 in bonds in compensation for a seized portion of property; on behalf of the company the U.S. State Department countered with a demand for $15,854,849!)

Washington was deeply involved. Some of the ties were personal. Secretary of State John Foster Dulles and his brother, CIA director Allen Dulles, for example, both came from a New York law firm with close links to United Fruit. The company's Washington lobbyist was Thomas Corcoran, a prominent lawyer who was on close terms with President Eisenhower's trusted aide and undersecretary of state, General Walter Bedell Smith, himself once interested in a management position with UFCO. More important than personal ties, however, was the anti-communist doctrine developed in Washington.

The early 1950s had seen a well-articulated rationale on the needs of U.S. national security in a Cold War era. The U.S. had no choice, so the reasoning went, but to fight back against the Soviet Union and its client powers, which were dedicated to the overthrow not only of capitalism, but of all the Western democracies. The Third World (a term not yet used then) would be a favorite Soviet target, argued Cold War theorists, and would be subverted by communist parties or their fellow travelers. The most drastic challenges thus far had been in Europe (the Berlin Blockade, the Greek Civil War, the French and Italian elections) and in Asia (the Korean War, the fall of Nationalist China, and the Indo-Chinese civil war). Was Latin America to be immune?

U.S. policymakers had pushed a hard anti-communist line in relations with Latin America. The Rio Pact of 1947 had laid the groundwork for collective action, or so the U.S. hoped, against communist advances in Latin America, whether from within or without. In early 1953 John Foster Dulles was clearly worried about Latin America, where he said conditions "are somewhat comparable to conditions as they were in China in the mid-thirties when the communist movement was getting started. . . . Well, if we don't look out, we will wake up some morning and read in the newspapers that there happened in South America the same kind of thing that happened in China in 1949." The test came in Guatemala.

UFCO publicists and the Dulles brothers accused the Arbenz regime of being "soft" on communism, and branded it a threat to the U.S. security and to the free world at large. They cultivated fears that defeat in Guatemala might lead to a Soviet takeover of the Panama Canal. They warned that if Guatemala fell, then the rest of Central America might go as well (the "domino theory"). But the principal issue was agrarian reform. Such writers as Daniel James of *The New Leader* warned that communists would use the program as a stepping-stone to gain control of Guatemala. Whatever his intentions, the U.S. insisted, Arbenz was just a "stooge" for the Russians.

In August 1953 the U.S. decided to act. John Foster Dulles led a campaign in the OAS to brand Guatemala as the agent of an extra-hemispheric power (the Soviet Union) and therefore subject to OAS collective action under the Rio Treaty of 1947. When the Eisenhower administration pressed for this interpretation at a Caracas meeting of the OAS in early 1954 all it got was a declaration stating that communist domination of a member government would cause concern and should in theory lead to collective action—but with no specific mention of Guatemala.

The Arbenz government now saw that U.S. intervention was likely. The regime cracked down on domestic opposition and turned to Eastern Europe for small arms, which were en route by May. Meanwhile the U.S. government was demanding, in increasingly blunt language, compensation for U.S. property in Guatemala, meaning, of course, United Fruit.

Having failed to get OAS sponsorship for intervention in Guatemala, the Eisenhower government opted for covert action. The State Department had mounted the diplomatic offensive; now it was the turn of Allen Dulles and the Central Intelligence Agency. The CIA organized an exile invasion under an obscure renegade Guatemalan colonel, Carlos Castillo Armas. A rebel column of a few hundred men was assembled across the border in neighboring Honduras. They were equipped and directed by the CIA, which set up and operated a rebel radio station and provided a few World War II fighter planes to strafe Guatemala City. Under attack by these planes, and convinced that a large army was approaching the capital, Arbenz lost his nerve and gave up. The Castillo Armas rebels rolled into the capital virtually unopposed.

The new government purged communists and radical nationalists, reversed the expropriation of United Fruit lands, and dutifully signed a Mutual Defense Assistance Pact with the U.S. in 1955. The errant Central American republic had been brought back into line by a relatively cheap and efficient CIA operation. These were the postwar years of maximum U.S. influence, nowhere more conspicuous than in Central America.

The U.S. was strongly denounced by Latin American nationalists for its intervention in Guatemala, and to this day it is a symbol for Latin Americans of cynical U.S. action. As described twenty years later by a CIA officer who had been intimately involved in the overthrow of Arbenz: "Castillo Armas was a bad president, tolerating corruption throughout his government and kowtowing to the United Fruit Company more than to his own people. The United States could have prevented this with the vigorous exercise of diplomatic pressure on Castillo Armas to assure that he pursued social reform for the many rather than venal satisfaction for a few. Instead, Washington breathed a collective sigh of relief and turned to other problems." Even so, the fate of the Arbenz regime would serve as a warning to nationalist leaders who contemplated challenging U.S. corporations.

The 1954 coup marked a turning point in Guatemalan history. It virtually eliminated the forces of the political center (as represented by Arévalo and Arbenz). So the country had only a left and a right, and the right was in control. Coffee planters, other landowners, and foreign investors and their subsidiaries regained their power under the protection of neo-conservative military regimes. Since then individual rulers have come and gone but this alignment has persisted. Castillo Armas was assassinated in 1957. General Miguel Ydígoras Fuentes, who had lost to Arbenz in 1950, ruled from 1958 to 1963. Then came Colonel Enrique Peralta Azurdia. From 1966 to 1970 the presidency was held by Julio César Méndez Montenegro, a talented civilian who traced his political lineage back to Arévalo, but the armed forces kept him tightly in check. He was followed by Colonel Carlos Arana Osorio (1970–74), by General Kjell Langerud García (1974–78), and by General Romeo Lucas García (1978–82). In March 1982 power was seized by Efraín Ríos Montt, a flamboyant young officer and born-again evangelical Christian; in mid-1983 he was ousted by General Oscar Humberto Mejía Victores. The more the leaders changed, the more the system stayed the same.

One feature of this entire period, especially after the mid-1960s, was the frightful abuse of human rights. Paramilitary death squads, most notoriously *Mano Blanca* ("White Hand") and *Ojo por Ojo* ("Eye for an Eye"), carried on a murderous campaign against political dissenters. No less than 30,000 people were killed between 1966 and 1982. The government bore at least indirect responsibility for these killings, but worldwide protests did not bring much respite. As observers sadly noted: "Guatemala, impervious to outside pressures, has gone on practicing its form of politics in which there are no victors, only victims."

By the early 1980s Central America seemed far from realizing its dreams. The people of the isthmus were suffering poverty, they were enduring large-scale violence, and they were facing continuous outside pressure. Part of the solution might lie in unification, but even that goal appeared to be beyond reach. In one historian's phrase, Central America was still "a nation divided." But there were bright spots too: the tiny country of Belize (1980 population: 145,000), formerly British Honduras, achieved independence in late 1981; and there remained a hope that economic integration might create the conditions for long-term collaboration and unification. Despite continuing warfare across Central America, activists were striving to heal historical divisions and to achieve the potential that they believed to be rightfully theirs.

TEN

LATIN AMERICA, THE UNITED STATES, AND THE WORLD

The history of Latin America has by no means evolved in a vacuum. Ever since the time of Columbus the region has been constantly subjected to external forces. In the sixteenth century Spain and Portugal conquered and settled the continent with varying degrees of violence. During the seventeenth and eighteenth centuries Latin America became a pawn and a prize in European politics, as ambitious peoples from enterprising nations—England, France, and Holland—sought and seized strongholds in Iberia's New World. The early decades after independence marked a temporary decline in outside influence, as the new nations of Latin America turned inward and the expansionist powers of Europe focused their attention on more lucrative possessions in Africa, India, and Asia. From the 1880s onward, for the last century or more, the Latin American economies have been deeply integrated into the capitalist world-system, a system dominated by countries at the industrialized center—West Europe, the United States, and later Japan. To this extent Latin America has never escaped its dependency on the outside world. Despite persisting and valiant struggles to achieve autonomy, it has for the most part managed only to modify, not eliminate, the form, nature, and extent of its centuries-old dependency.

Even the name Latin America reflects an imperialistic legacy. The term was coined by the French in the 1860s, when they were supporting Maximilian in Mexico and laying the cultural groundwork for a political and economic offensive throughout Spanish and Portuguese America. They argued for a Latin essence—best embodied in French culture—which lay at the heart of Ibero-American civilization. This was not pure fancy, since French culture enjoyed enormous prestige among the New World elites.

Whatever the realities of the French claim to a homogeneous influence, Latin America began to exhibit a continental sentiment as early as the late eighteenth century. Indeed, the Spanish and Portuguese co-

321

lonial systems could hardly have failed to create a sense of common interest in the countries they spawned.

To understand modern Latin America's world position we must understand the nature of the Spanish and Portuguese colonial empires. Most important, the economic structures were mercantilist: designed to integrate the colonies totally into the mother country's economy. In Spanish America, that even meant no intra-colonial trade—all commerce from each region had to be with Spain alone. The practical effect was to distort the economic development of the colonies. Had they been able to trade more openly, they might have had considerably different economic options from those they inherited at the time of independence. (Portuguese America, too, was allowed to trade only with the mother country.)

The results of the Iberian mercantilist policies were cultural and psychological as well as economic. Spanish and Portuguese America had been nurtured on the model of closed societies. They were constantly on guard against political and economic inroads from European rivals, as well as against religious heresies emanating from Protestant Britain and the Low Countries.

Significant non-Iberian influences have left their mark on colonial Latin America. The 5.2 million slaves shipped from West Africa to South America, the Caribbean, Mexico and Central America brought a tradition different from either the Amerindian or the European. Despite the efforts of their European or *mestizo* masters, the Afro-Americans of Latin America made lasting marks on society and culture. The process went deepest in Brazil and the Caribbean, but was also important in Colombia, Venezuela, Mexico, and Central America. Languages, food, sports, and music all show profound and continuing African influence. The slaves engaged in rebellion as well, fleeing and founding runaway communities in Brazil and the circum-Caribbean, especially in Guyana and Curaçao. In the seventeenth and eighteenth centuries Brazil had flourishing runaway settlements, which by the nineteenth century had been either wiped out or absorbed by the growth of surrounding societies.

The Spanish and Portuguese American possessions might have continued well into the nineteenth century as colonies if it had not been for war in Europe. It was Napoleon's invasion of the Iberian mainland that provoked the crisis of loyalty in the New World. The crisis deepened, the monarchies were impotent, and creoles took charge of their own affairs.

Once the French were defeated, England emerged as the preeminent military, economic, and political power. The English moved at least part way into the vacuum created in the Americas. Their principal objective was economic—to promote Britain's commercial interests, which had relied on contraband trade throughout the eighteenth century. The basis for this activity would be England's strong network of economic institutions: the best available in shipping, banking, insurance, and investment capital. In effect, the British were seeking to replace the former Iberian colonial institutional infrastructure linking Latin America to the world economy. But they differed from Spain and Portugal in a key respect: they laid almost no territorial claims in Latin America. The English sought economic gain without the burden of direct political rule. It was an "informal imperialism," whereby Europe's chief investor and trader avoided the expensive link of territorial control—with its potential military entanglements.

What of the U.S.? It was by no means a hemispheric power in the early nineteenth century. On the contrary, the U.S. was unable even to prevent Washington (and the White House) from being devastated by the English in the War of 1812. Washington had significant contact in Mexico and the Caribbean, but even there it could not begin to rival English seapower.

Yet the U.S. had become at least a symbol of postcolonial success for Latin America creole elites. Most significantly, it had thrown off European control. Born in a revolution with a philosophical rationale from the Enlightenment, the U.S. demonstrated how a republic could emerge from European colonialism. The North American rebels had fought for the right of representation—something which Spanish and Portuguese Americans notably lacked. The federal structure of the U.S. was another feature that impressed the patriots among the creole elites of what were to become large countries such as Mexico, Brazil, and Argentina, where the reconciliation of regional autonomy with national power would become a longstanding issue of importance.

From Independence to Pan Americanism

The independent republics (plus the Empire of Brazil) of nineteenth century Latin America were an anomaly on the world scene. Along with Haiti and the United States, these Spanish- and Portuguese-speaking nations offered the first cases of successful rebellion against European rule in the Third World. Once independent, however, the new nations played but a minor role on the world scene in the 1800s. On the whole, they became absorbed in their own development.

That was not what Simón Bolívar, the great revolutionary of the independence wars, had hoped. He had a vision of a united Spanish America emerging from the anti-colonial wars. He dreamed that Spanish Americans could subordinate regional loyalties to unite into a single South American nation. But Bolívar's dream was denied. The rebellious colonies fractured along the lines of the old Spanish administrative units. Bolívar bitterly denounced his creole contemporaries for their provincialism. It was no use. Each new nation would have to find its own way in the world.

An early concern in postindependence Latin America was the nature of the relationship with the former mother countries. For Caribbean islands such as Cuba, Puerto Rico, and Jamaica, colonial rule continued. In Brazil, the former colony had become a "co-kingdom," with a monarch in Rio de Janeiro. The rest of Latin America had to adjust to the new reality of dealing with Spain as merely another distant European power. In fact, that could never be the case—the ties of blood and of such institutions as the church, higher education, publishing, still gave Spain a special place in Spanish America. Spain was now so divided between liberals and conservatives that it could no longer even attempt to project a single influence over its former American colonies.

The U.S. attempted to assert its power with the "Monroe Doctrine," promulgated by President Monroe in 1823. Originally aimed at czarist Russia's possible claims to the American Northwest, the doctrine became better known for its challenge to an apparent design of the European Holy Alliance to help Spain reconquer her former colonies. President Monroe firmly declared that "the American continents, by the free and independent condition which they have assumed and maintained, are henceforth not to be considered as subjects for colonization by any European powers." Further strictures warned the Europeans against using indirect means to extend their political power in the New World. As later put in a popular slogan, the basic message was clear: "America for the Americans."

In fact the message evoked indifference or scorn in Europe, some worry in Britain, and considerable sympathy in Latin America. Within the U.S. the Monroe Doctrine became highly popular and was a cornerstone of U.S.-Latin American policy for the next century. Within Latin America, however, the U.S. in the early nineteenth century lacked the economic and military power, as well as the political will, to make a significant impact.

France attempted to extend its influence in the brief 1838 military expedition to Mexico to enforce payment of damage claims against the Mexican government by French citizens. A negotiated settlement allowed the French to withdraw. Along with the British, the French also repeatedly blockaded the ports of the River Plate between 1838 and 1850. But it was Britain that exercised the predominant extrahemispheric influence during most of the nineteenth century. Britain had by far the most powerful navy, capable of asserting itself throughout Latin America, despite the fact the territory was 8000 to 12,000 miles from British ports. Second, Britain had the capital, the merchants, the bankers, and the insurance and shipping brokers to facili-

As World War I approached, the U.S. sought to assert its sphere of influence throughout the western hemisphere under the Monroe Doctrine. (Charles L. "Bart" Bartholomew [?], *Minneapolis Journal,* 1912. Reprinted with permission of the Minneapolis Star and Tribune Company.)

tate trade between Latin America and Europe, her great market. And Britain had an ideology—liberalism—which underlay her expansionism and which Latin America creole elites quickly assimilated. It offered a rationale for integrating Latin America into the world economy, which, not coincidentally, the British controlled.

Between the 1820s and the 1850s, the British pressed their advantage in Latin America. They quickly took over the financial and commercial services for the major countries. They rapidly arranged loans for governments and stock companies in Mexico, Brazil, Argentina, and Peru. But capitalist development of these South American republics proved more difficult than the British creditors had hoped. Most borrowers defaulted on their loans, and the London financial markets soon came to mark Latin America as a high credit risk.

Mexico was the one place where an extra-Latin American power other than Britain made an impact before 1850. There the U.S. pursued its "manifest destiny" by seizing huge chunks of Mexican territory. The

U.S. also made threats in the Caribbean and Central America, not re-
alized until later in the century. By mid-century the Caribbean and
Mexico, so close to the U.S., had come to be seen as special cases in
Latin America's relations with the world.

From 1850 to 1880 Latin America changed its posture toward the
outside world. Liberalism, both political and economic, gained increasing sway. In Argentina, for example, the nationalist Rosas was toppled
by his Argentine enemies, thanks in part to British and French intervention. As the Argentine liberals came to power, they installed in their
country such admired institutions of the English-speaking democracies
as the U.S. constitution and the U.S. public school system. The liberals
also believed in developing their country's economy by accepting foreign trade. That meant applying the principles of economic liberalism—minimal state interference with the market. In practice, that was
likely to reinforce Britain's predominant economic position.

A similar application of liberalism was being attempted in imperial
Brazil. Emperor Pedro II modelled his rule on the British monarchy,
although he exercised much more discretionary political power than
did Queen Victoria. The two parties in the Brazilian imperial parliament were modelled on Britain's two-party system; even congressional
speeches were filled with references to British constitutional precedents.

The years between 1850 and 1880 also saw French influence grow in
Latin America, especially in culture. French was the foreign language
most widely spoken by the elite, reflecting traditional practice in Europe itself. French cultural prestige in Latin America lasted well into
the twentieth century, remaining predominant in some countries until
the end of World War II, well after France's decline as a world power.
Why this resilience? Partly because France was spared the Latin American nationalist reaction directed at the British, partly because French
cultural values coincided with the Latin American elite's self-image.
However French and Latin elites might admire the economic prowess
of the Anglo-Saxons, they scorned the "materialistic" values that had
suffused Britain and the U.S. The French intelligentsia had produced
its own rationale in defense of their country against Britain—arguing
that France had a more humane vision of society than Britain's dehu-
manizing Industrial Revolution, and the Latin American elites identified with France's self-proclaimed cultural superiority.

The Rise of U.S. Influence

Between 1880 and the outbreak of World War I Britain lost her supremacy in Latin America. Other European powers, especially France
and Germany, increased their economic ties, competing with British

investors and merchants. But the most important challenge came from the U.S.

During these thirty-five years, U.S. influence spread southward. The deepest penetration was closest to home, in the Caribbean and Mexico. U.S. investors found the Mexico ruled by Porfírio Diaz to be attractive for investment and trade, and they poured capital into Cuba as well. Even before the Spanish-American War erupted in 1895, the U.S. had come to overshadow Spain in Cuba's economy.

U.S. entry into Cuba's revolt against Spain signalled a new phase in North America's relations with Latin America. After the Mexican-American War (1846–48) the U.S. continued to occupy and settle portions of the present-day Southwest. When the U.S. entered the war in 1898 and decisively defeated the Spanish, it was more than a military victory. It was a symbolic struggle that impressed all of Latin America. The time was long past when Latin American nations were absorbed only in their own problems.

The 1898 war was an independence battle by Cuban patriots against Spain. Other Latin Americans immediately sympathized with the Cubans. Yet the Yankees suddenly seized control of the rebellion. This naturally demoralized many Cubans, who had desperately hoped to defeat the Spaniards on their own. Furthermore, it underlined a common Latin American worry: Were the Spaniards and their American descendants inherently (i.e., biologically) weaker than the North Americans? Was the U.S. racially "destined" to take over Latin America?

A similarly agonizing self-appraisal had gripped Mexican elites after their humiliating defeat by the U.S. in 1846–48. They explained their weakness on the battlefield by linking it to supposed defects in their character, or, more ominously, their racial background. Now, in the 1890s, racism was at its height in the U.S. and Europe. The Jim Crow laws of the U.S. had institutionalized segregation, and the universities and churches overflowed with professors and preachers who calmly explained the scientific basis for believing in "inferior" and "superior" races.

These racist doctrines also penetrated Latin America. In country after country, leading intellectuals faithfully repeated the racist dogmas of the Europeans. Underlying such introspection was a lurking fear that some new conquistadors might take away their lands, manifested in the occasional nativist reaction against the British through the nineteenth century. The precipitating incidents were often petty, such as brawls by British sailors when ashore, but they called forth a deep hostility. The Latin American elites knew that both the British and the North Americans often viewed them with contempt.

It is therefore not surprising that the crushing defeat of the Spanish by the U.S. in 1898 deeply troubled the Latin Americans. Having seized

Puerto Rico and Cuba (the latter as a protectorate), it was widely asked, how much farther would the Yankees go? The pessimists in Mexico had long believed that the U.S. had designs on more of their land.

United States expansionism into the Caribbean showed that the Latin American fears were not entirely groundless. The U.S. search for a satisfactory transcontinental canal site revealed what the Yankees would do to achieve their economic and geopolitical interests. President Theodore Roosevelt, that arrogant embodiment of North American imperialism, rode roughshod over objections to his site for the canal in a northernmost section of Colombian territory extending northward into Central America. Thus was born the new nation of Panama, and the canal was built between 1904 and 1914. The U.S. got its canal, but it took the bogus creation of a new republic.

Between 1880 and 1914 the U.S. also attempted to create a new hemisphere-wide alliance of nations. It began with the ambitious plans of the U.S. Secretary of State James Blaine. On his initiative the First Pan American Conference was held in Washington in 1889. Between 1826 and 1864 there had been five congresses, all attracting only a limited number of countries. The 1889 meeting was the first to involve all the Latin American nations and the U.S. Ironically, this was when the U.S. began its imperialist offensive in Latin America.

Out of the 1889 conference came an authorization for a "Commercial Bureau of the American Republics," from which emerged the Pan American Union and later the Organization of American States (OAS). Accomplishments were limited primarily to commercial issues.

The U.S. diplomatic, economic, and military offensive into Latin America after the 1880s prompted a strong reaction among Latin American intellectuals and students. The Spanish-American War aroused José Enrique Rodó, Uruguayan-born and one of the most celebrated of these militant critics of the U.S. In 1900 he published *Ariel,* a slim essay in which he contrasted North America's excessive materialism to Latin America's superior cultural sensitivity. Of the U.S. he charged: "Her prosperity is as great as her inability to satisfy even a middling concept of human destiny. . . ."

Rodó's ideas had great influence in Spanish America, whose elites were well prepared to hear of their spiritual superiority. They were also spurred to think in terms of a Latin American identity arising from the cultural unity toward which Rodó was groping. The theme was picked up and spread widely by such writers as the Argentine Manuel Ugarte, who wrote newly elected President Woodrow Wilson in 1913 to demand that "the stars and stripes cease to be a symbol of oppression in the New World." Other famous intellectuals caught up in this pan Latin American reaction were José Martí of Cuba (whose critique began in the 1870s), Rubén Darío of Nicaragua, and Rufino Blanco-

TABLE 10-1   U.S. Investment in Latin America, 1897–1914 (millions of dollars at end of year)

	Caribbean Countries	Mexico and Central America	South America	Total
1897	4.5	221.4	37.9	304.3
1908	220.2	713.0	129.7	1,062.9
1914	329.0	946.7	365.7	1,641.4

Source: United Nations, Economic Commission for Latin America, *External Financing in Latin America* (New York: United Nations, 1965), p. 14.

Fombona of Venezuela. Their writings were published throughout the continent in what was one of Latin America's most culturally integrated eras. Many themes from this anti-*yanqui* movement have survived in inter-American relations down to our day.

European influence continued to be highly important in Latin America between 1880 and 1914, despite the growing U.S. role. One need only look at the size of investment and trade. Table 10-1 demonstrates the magnitude of North American investment, which came to embrace the Caribbean and South America as well as Mexico and Central America. Even so, as Table 10-2 indicates, Britain was far and away the most important single source of capital on the eve of World War I; France and Germany were also prominent.

Another important sphere of European influence was military training and technology. From the time of their independence wars Latin American elites had known that they lacked military skills and advanced weaponry. To defeat the Spanish garrisons, usually undermanned and cut off from resupply, the patriots often had to hire or appeal to foreign soldiers and sailors.

TABLE 10-2   Long-Term Foreign Capital Investment in Latin America, 1914 (millions of dollars)

Origin	Foreign Private Investment (and External Public Debt)	Percentage
Britain	5066	51.9
France	1013	10.4
Germany	367	3.8
U.S.	1487	15.2
Others	1821	18.6
Total	9754	100.0

Source: United Nations, Economic Commission for Latin America, *External Financing in Latin America* (New York: United Nations, 1965), pp. 16–17.

As the nineteenth century continued, other European military establishments offered examples to ambitious Latin American rulers. In both Chile (1885) and Argentina (1899), for example, German military missions were contracted for extended periods to introduce new weapons and teach their use. Equally important, they taught new methods of staff organization and command. In Brazil the rapidly growing state of São Paulo contracted in 1905 for a French mission to train the state militia, which included cavalry. These European missions were expected, above all, to transmit the new professionalism that had transformed the military in Europe. War was no longer a matter for aristocrats; now it was a serious business which required thorough scientific and technical training.

What did this transfer of military "professionalization" imply for Latin America? First, it had enormous consequences in politics, as the "professionalized" armies became more active, ironically, in the constitutional realms of Chile, Argentina, and Brazil. The political implications would become obvious only after World War I.

The Consolidation of U.S. Influence

The First World War, although of no direct concern to Latin America at the outset, fundamentally changed the region's relationship with the world. For one thing, it accelerated Britain's decline as the most important economic force in the hemisphere. Drained by the long and costly hostilities on the continent, England had to draw on her overseas investments to pay for the war. Furthermore, Britain had begun to experience a long-term decline in world economic competitiveness.

Second, the war highlighted the dynamic U.S. economy, based on a continent full of resources and now mature enough to become a net exporter of capital. The decisive U.S. intervention in the war proved it now held the balance of economic and military power: European powers could never again disregard the U.S.

Latin America was essentially a bystander in the conflict. The U.S. pressed hard to use the war as an occasion to strengthen its political influence in Latin America, but with varying results. Only eight Latin American republics declared war on Germany: Brazil (the only major country), Cuba, Costa Rica, Guatemala, Haiti, Honduras, Nicaragua, and Panama. Another five broke diplomatic relations: Bolivia, the Dominican Republic, Ecuador, Peru, and Uruguay. Seven nations remained neutral: Argentina, Chile, Colombia, Mexico, Paraguay, El Salvador, and Venezuela.

By the conclusion of World War I, U.S. power and influence in Latin America were clearly on the rise. The U.S. now exercised virtual hegemony in the Caribbean basin, as could be seen in the military occupations of Nicaragua (1912–25), Haiti (1914–34), the Dominican Republic (1916–24), and Cuba (1917–23). Even when the U.S. did not occupy these countries, it deeply influenced their development, wielding veto power over their domestic politics. Most of the elites in these countries took U.S. hegemony for granted; indeed, they would have been surprised to think the world could have been otherwise.

The two exceptions to this pattern were Mexico and Cuba. In Mexico, the Revolution of 1910 threatened to change the country's relationship with the U.S. Washington was disturbed over the direction taken by the Revolution, and made repeated interventions, including the military landing at Veracruz in 1914 and the sending of General John J. Pershing's column in 1916 to pursue Pancho Villa's irregulars. Yet the Revolution succeeded in giving the Mexicans an élan, a pride, a degree of mobilization that would eventually help check the traditional brand of U.S. intervention. It nonetheless remained true that the Mexican people could do little without taking due account of the continuous pressure of that powerful neighbor to the north.

Cuba was a different case. There the U.S. had established a protectorate after ending its military occupation in 1902. This U.S. presence generated a nationalist reaction, erupting most often among students at the University of Havana. Although easily suppressed, they represented an important dissenting opinion within the elite, and in the 1930s they seized center stage in Cuban politics.

The world Depression hit Latin America hard. New capital ceased flowing into the region, and foreign investors found it hard to repatriate profits. Country after country defaulted (or declared a unilateral moratorium) on their debts.[1] The reason was obvious. The collapse of the world economy had reduced demand for the primary products on which Latin America depended for its foreign exchange earnings. Suddenly these countries had no way to earn the dollars, pounds, marks, or francs to repay their foreign creditors. So Latin Americans could not now expect to receive any net inflow of capital. Even more important, they would be short of foreign exchange to pay for the imports essential to domestic economic development, especially industrialization.

The 1930s were thus a time when Latin American countries had to look inward. Not coincidentally, it was a period of high nationalist feeling. With the options for foreign economic help so reduced, it was logical to concentrate on domestic resources. Argentina, Brazil, and Mexico, for example, all took steps to increase national control over the oil industry. Mexico went the farthest, when in 1938 President Cárdenas nationalized all foreign oil firms. Argentina had already created an au-

---

1. With the exception of Argentina, Haiti, and the Dominican Republic.

tonomous government oil enterprise in the 1920s, while in Brazil the state oil enterprise was given its definitive shape in 1953.

The 1930s also brought one new import to Latin America: fascist ideology. The clearest version came from Italy, where Mussolini's movement grew in response to the emerging revolutionary left—especially the syndicalists and the communists. With the rise of Nazism in Germany, European fascism gained an even more powerful exemplar. Especially important for Latin America was the fact that Spain and Portugal had both fallen prey to authoritarian regimes (Franco after 1936 in Spain and Salazar after 1928 in Portugal) which had corporatist, many would say fascist, overtones.

Europe's swing to the right gave ammunition and prestige to those anti-democratic and anti-liberal groups in Latin America that had their own reasons for wanting to create authoritarian governments. None of the Latin American "fascist" movements were exact copies of European cases. In Brazil, the Integralists were a primarily middle-class movement, preaching the need for order, with an essentially corporatist message. Argentina had several rightist paramilitary groups that resembled European fascism, but the deepest influence was in the military. The secret "lodges" within the officer corps produced initial stimulus for the Peronist movement, which owed part of its inspiration to the Italian model. But Peronism never gained a doctrinal and organizational form like that of Italian fascism. In Mexico there was a small rightist movement, *sinarquismo,* which showed European influence; it also drew primarily on right-wing Christian sentiment. In Chile, finally, there was a National Socialist party, clearly an imitation of the Nazi party, which provoked a furious response from the Chilean left.

None of these parties or movements came close to winning power in the 1930s. In Chile and Mexico they faded, as the civilian political system proved capable of containing and absorbing them. In Argentina fascist sentiments were overshadowed by the Peronist movement, once World War II entered its final phase. In Brazil the Integralists almost appeared to be on the threshhold of power in 1936, but they were swept away by Vargas's *Estado Nôvo* in 1937.

As the 1930s continued, Latin America became a staging ground for geopolitical competition. The Germans and the Italians both looked to Latin America to increase their economic and political influence. The Italians were especially active in Brazil and Argentina, where large Italian communities offered a possible base of operations. The Mussolini government sought to keep the Latin American republics pro-Italian. That meant stimulating and reinforcing anti-British (and, by extension, anti-U.S.) opinion. The Italian government also contributed directly to Brazilian fascists, by using its embassy to pass large sums of money to the Integralists.

As the most powerful partner in the European Axis, Hitler's Germany was even better situated to exert pressure in Latin America. The Nazi regime used its fully owned subsidiary airline, Condor, and its diplomatic service to create a network of agents and contacts throughout South America. Hitler and his more aggressive advisers convinced themselves that Latin Americans of German descent were eager to join the Fatherland and create separatist territories, alert to Berlin's every direction.

But the Germanic population in Brazil proved to be extremely loyal to its New World nation. The effect of Nazi measures in Brazil was just the opposite of what the Germans had intended: the Vargas government adopted stringent new laws requiring that all school classes be taught in Portuguese, thereby eliminating the exclusively German language schools in the south of the country. The result was to accelerate the assimilation of the German descendents in Brazil.

The Axis powers were of course not the only outside nations engaging in this geopolitical competition. For many years the U.S. military had regarded Latin America as a vulnerable flank. This provided the military rationale for expansion in the Caribbean: the need to protect vital sea lanes. The vast, virtually unpatrolled boundary with Mexico was another area difficult to defend. The Panama Canal gave the U.S. an additional danger zone. What was needed, some officers thought, was an arc of military security stretching into northern South America.

As Nazi Germany built its war machine, U.S. officers cast a more worried look at the Latin American flank. With Japanese power growing in the Pacific, the U.S. was faced with the likelihood of a two-ocean war. Latin America could now be menaced from both east and west. The U.S. therefore examined its hemispheric ties in a new light: How could Washington gain maximum support from the Latin Americans in case of war?

Part of the answer would depend on cultural relations. Latin America between the wars saw a sharp rise in cultural programs sponsored by foreign governments. Because of their enormous cultural prestige, the French had the favored position. French was still the most widely spoken foreign language, and Paris was the point of reference for artists and writers of Latin America. Latin American universities, primarily copied from Iberian models, came under increasing French influence. In Brazil, for example, when the *paulistas* wanted to found a new university—the University of São Paulo, in 1933—they sent a delegation to France. In response, Paris sent a mission of leading professors in the social sciences, including such luminaries as Claude Lévi-Strauss, Jacques Lambert, and Pierre Monbeig. The French government established a fellowship program for study in France; similar programs also emerged elsewhere in Latin America.

While European influence remained dominant among elites, North American influence was making great inroads through mass media—the unchallenged vehicles of popular culture in our century. By the 1930s Hollywood films were the craze throughout Latin America. U.S. film stars such as Jean Harlow and Clark Gable were household names in even provincial towns, as Argentine novelist Manuel Puig's *Betrayed by Rita Hayworth* poignantly shows. U.S. music, especially jazz, had a similar effect. The dynamic, fluid, dazzling and futuristic North American society proved fascinating, although engendering a split between elite and popular reactions to the U.S. which was to deepen and prove increasingly important over time.

As the war broke out in Europe, the U.S. government stepped up its recruiting of military and political allies in Latin America. Franklin Roosevelt's government sought: (1) military bases, especially in the Caribbean and on the Atlantic coast of South America; (2) guaranteed accessibility to vital raw materials, such as natural rubber and quartz; (3) willingness to join the U.S. in an alliance against the Axis, should the U.S. join the fight; or (4) at the very least, a neutrality that would prohibit hostile extra-continental powers from creating footholds in their countries.

The U.S. largely achieved these aims. The inter-American system, emerging with painful slowness since the 1880s, was now harnessed to the security interests of the U.S. The U.S. military got the use of valuable bases, especially in Brazil, and U.S. war industry got access to the vital raw materials it needed.

World War II greatly increased U.S. influence in Latin America. Germany and Italy, once important powers in the region, were discredited: Italy, by its blustering lurch for new territory in North Africa; Germany, by the horrendous suffering its war machine unleashed on Europe. Fascism was a bankrupt legacy by 1945. Only the anomalous survival of Franco in Spain and Salazar in Portugal kept alive the right-wing ideology, and neither country, ironically, had great political influence in Latin America.

The British and French, although victors in the war, were gravely weakened. Both had to liquidate overseas investments to pay for the war. Neither had the resources or the will in 1945 to compete for influence in distant Latin America. The net result was that 1945 saw U.S. influence at an all-time high in Latin America.

The Zenith of U.S. Influence

The U.S. emerged from the Second World War with greatly increased prestige and authority. The war brought the U.S. economy out of the Depression and into a massive industrial effort. Unlike Europe or Japan, however, the U.S. suffered no war damage at home. Her economy was intact and prosperous. In 1945 the U.S. accounted for half the world's manufacturing output and about two-thirds of global exports. The U.S. had built up the most imposing arsenal the world had seen, capped by the atomic bomb—the "ultimate weapon," which only the U.S. possessed. The war also provided the U.S. with a network of alliances that offered a strong power base in postwar international politics.

With the war over, many Latin American politicians hoped the newfound U.S. interest in Latin America would pay off. They expected increased attention to their problems, especially the obstacles to economic growth. After all, the U.S. could now afford to look south, where it would be logical to consolidate its greatly increased influence.

But it was not to be. U.S. government policy virtually lost track of Latin America after 1945. Attention focused, instead, on rebuilding Europe and Japan. The Truman administration (1945–53) and the Congress, along with farsighted business leaders, realized that an economically sound Europe was essential for a prosperous U.S. The Marshall Plan of 1947 appealed to the U.S. public on both humanitarian and economic grounds and helped to direct attention primarily toward Europe.

What about Latin America? It simply did not seem significant to U.S. policymakers. The Latin American specialists in the State Department and the military services found themselves downgraded or transferred. The Truman administration apparently assumed it would continue to receive loyal backing from Latin America, almost as a matter of course.

This relative U.S. indifference was broken again by an outside threat. As U.S. relations with the Soviets began to cool in 1946, the Truman administration decided to mount a Cold War offensive in Latin America. It assumed two aspects. First was pressure to get Latin American governments to sever diplomatic relations with the Soviet Union. This was remarkably successful, as every country with the exception of Mexico, Argentina, and Uruguay followed suit. The second aspect was to press Latin American governments to outlaw the local communist parties. Although not highly publicized in the U.S., the success of this campaign demonstrated how responsive the Latin American political elites still were to U.S. direction.

The Truman administration also decided to make more permanent the military alliance created during the war. A special 1945 meeting of hemispheric foreign ministers in Mexico City agreed on the need to redesign the Pan American system. The first step was taken in 1947, when delegations approved a treaty (the "Rio Pact") defining an attack on any American state, from inside or outside the hemisphere, as an attack on all, requiring collective measures to counter the aggression.

The second step was taken in Bogotá, Colombia, in March of 1948, when a new body was created: the Organization of American States (OAS). The structure included a legal charter creating a council to deal with day-to-day business, inter-American conferences every five years, and foreign ministers' consultative meetings to handle threats to the hemisphere. A bureaucratic infrastructure took shape as the General Secretariat and the Pan American Union. OAS member states committed themselves to continental solidarity (which the U.S. wanted) and total nonintervention (which the Latin Americans wanted), along with the principles of democracy, economic cooperation, social justice, and human rights. In short, the U.S. and Latin America created the world's most highly articulated regional association. Not surprisingly, the member states expected very different things from it.

The OAS got an important test when war broke out in Korea in 1950. The U.S. had troops stationed in South Korea and was thus immediately drawn into the conflict. As North Korean troops streaked south, the U.S. convinced the UN Security Council to brand North Korea as the aggressor. The Truman government then turned to the OAS, asking it to define the North Korean attack as aggression against the U.S.—thereby obligating the OAS members, by the Rio Pact, to join the battle. What the U.S. wanted was additional legitimacy and military contributions from Latin America.

The other OAS members balked at this appeal, except for Colombia, which sent a battalion of infantry. In their speeches the Latin Americans showed much more concern for their own economic problems than for the military clash in distant Korea. The OAS produced a compromise: in return for a commitment to improve their military defenses and increase military cooperation, the Latin Americans got a U.S. promise that it would submit proposals for solving the hemisphere's economic problems.

To U.S. policymakers the Korean War demonstrated that their battle with communism was world-wide, not just in Europe. The "fall" of China in 1950 further dramatized the point. In 1951 the Truman administration and Congress accordingly decided to extend to Latin America the U.S. Military Security Program of 1949, originally aimed at Europe. From 1952 to 1954 the U.S. signed bilateral mutual defense assistance pacts with ten Latin American countries: Ecuador, Cuba, Colombia, Peru, Chile, Brazil, the Dominican Republic, Uruguay, Nicaragua, and Honduras. (Argentina and Mexico were conspicuous by their absence.) Under these agreements the U.S. was to exchange military equipment and services in return for Latin American promises to expand defense capacities, to send strategic materials to the U.S., and to restrict trade with the Soviet bloc.

The implications of these new defense arrangements were far-reaching. The U.S. was tying Latin America's armed forces into the U.S.

web—once possessing American equipment they would depend on the U.S. for parts, replacements, and ammunition. Furthermore, by frequent contact with U.S. military, in training programs and joint exercises, the Latin American officers could be expected to identify closely with the U.S. No less important, the U.S. was offering far more equipment than the recipient countries could have bought through the normal appropriations of their governments. The armed services thereby gained power in their societies without having to fight budget battles at home. These U.S. military links were a revival of the structure the Roosevelt administration had created on the eve of U.S. entry into World War II. Now, in the early 1950s, the U.S. was building on its wartime prestige to expand and consolidate its influence.

One other country earned great prestige during the war: the Soviet Union. The Soviets had lost far more of its population (20 million) and endured much more suffering than the U.S. Many Latin Americans admired the endurance and fortitude of the Russian people, and some of that admiration was transferred to the Latin American communist parties, which enjoyed a flurry of popularity in 1945. The Brazilian Communist Party, for example, won 10 percent of the vote in the presidential election of 1946. Later that year three members of the Chilean cabinet were communist, and there were communist members of the national congress in Cuba, Colombia, Peru, Ecuador, Brazil, Chile, Bolivia, Uruguay, and Costa Rica.

The Truman administration began pursuing an aggressively anti-Soviet line in Latin America as early as 1946. The chain of bilateral military pacts was only one of the instruments to mobilize the Latin Americans against the Soviets. Since military officers were normally a bulwark of anti-communist and anti-Soviet opinion, the U.S. hoped to tie this pro-U.S. element even tighter and strengthen its anti-communist resolve. Military pacts and training programs now gave the U.S. a monopoly on foreign links among Latin American military.

At first glance this penetration might look similar to the relationship the Soviets established with its East European satellites after 1945. The Soviets, however, achieved a far greater integration of its client nations' military structure into the Soviet one—with direct link-up of command structure, communication systems, and Soviet intervention in day-to-day operations. The Soviets were especially careful in screening candidates for higher command positions. They took further advantage from the fact that large numbers of their own troops were still stationed in many of the satellites. Although the Soviet control of its satellites' military was more pervasive and complete, it resembled the U.S. in Latin America in that both superpowers had little opposition.

The Truman administration also expressed an interest in technical and economic help for Latin America, as a partial replication of the

Marshall Plan—the oft-cited prototype of American overseas aid. But the situations proved to be very different. The Marshall Plan was directed at nations which were physically devastated but still possessed the most important economic ingredient of all: skilled and experienced manpower. An investment in these European countries—Britain, France, Italy, West Germany—could and did have a quick pay-off. These industrial economies revived and were poised to participate in the rapid growth of world trade that was to occur after 1950.

The economic problem in Latin America was more fundamental. There was relatively little industry even in the largest countries. There was an enormous shortage of skilled labor and technological know-how. Infrastructure (roads, railroads) was often lacking. Economists did not know how to stimulate rapid economic development in such areas as Latin America.

Whatever the labels, economists and planners soon found that simply supplying more capital, in the form of dollars or investment goods, was not the answer. Economic development was (and is) a complex process that requires adjustment at every societal level. The Truman administration favored a sympathetic look at the problem. In his 1949 inaugural speech President Truman proposed (in his address it was "Point Four," a label which then stuck) a U.S. government-coordinated technical assistance program to aid developing countries. This was in response partly to Latin American complaints that the U.S. was ignoring their fundamental economic problems, while concentrating its attention on Europe.

Before Truman's Point Four program had a chance to go far, the Democratic Party was turned out of the White House by the 1952 electoral victory of General Dwight D. Eisenhower. The Republicans brought a new philosophy, especially in international economics. They took a strongly laissez-faire stance, and thought government's first obligation was to let the free market operate. President Eisenhower's secretary of the treasury, Cleveland businessman George Humphrey, soon made clear that this free-enterprise philosophy would rule out any large-scale economic aid overseas, even through low-interest government loans. An equally cold shoulder was turned to current proposals for commodity agreements, designed to stabilize world-market prices for such products as coffee and cocoa—primary products of great importance to Latin America. Above all, said the Republicans, Latin Americans must not discourage private foreign investment, which in these years meant primarily U.S. investment. (See Figure 10-1 for data on the growth and location of postwar American overseas investment: Latin America attracted the largest regional share of U.S. investment in 1950, though it would be far surpassed by Canada and West Europe by the 1970s.)

FIGURE 10-1   U.S. Overseas Investment, 1950 and 1977

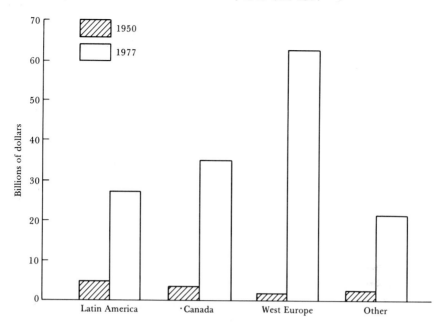

Sources: *New York Times,* 23 January 1967; and U.S. Department of Commerce, *U.S. Direct Investment Abroad* (Washington: U.S. Government Printing Office, 1981), Table B, pp. 6–7.

This Republican orientation toward Latin America provoked a strong reaction among reformist and development-minded younger politicians and technocrats in Latin America. Not coincidentally, Latin America was now beginning to produce its own analysis of its economic problems. This diagnosis was to help Latin American elites define their relationship to the outside world. Ideological competition was turning intense once again. In the 1930s the confrontation had pitted fascism and corporatism, linked to growing Axis power in Europe, against economic and political liberalism, linked to the U.S. and Britain. Now, in the 1950s, it was radical nationalism and Marxism versus neo-liberalism, with a position in between that we have called reformist developmentalism.

The Nationalist Impulse

Nationalism had deep roots in Latin America. In early form it contributed to the rebellion against Spain and Portugal in the early nineteenth century. During the course of the nineteenth century, however, few nationalists were prepared to resist foreign economic intrusions.

The dictator José Gaspar Rodríguez de Francia of Paraguay (1814–40) was one, as were his successors from the López family (1844–70). But Paraguay was a relatively insignificant country, and its defiance of British economic power made little difference to the rest of the continent. The occasional outbreaks of economic nationalism in Chile and Argentina before mid-century left little permanent effect. The nineteenth century saw the triumph of economic liberalism in Latin America. Its export-oriented strategies were based on the law of comparative advantage. A few nationalist voices cried out against this strategy, but without much practical impact.

It was not until the 1930s that the economic nationalists could hope to capture policymaking. One of their targets was oil exploration and production. Some nationalists, such as Alejandro Bunge in Argentina and Roberto Simonsen in Brazil, also argued vigorously for industrialization. They reasoned that their countries could never gain control of their economic future until they industrialized. In other words, they should break with a simple-minded application of the law of comparative advantage, which restricted them to exporting primary goods to pay for imported finished goods. They must create the productive capacity to survive slumps in the world economy, such as the 1929 crash.

The pro-industrialization arguments began to influence government policy in the 1930s in Brazil and Chile and, to a lesser extent, in Argentina. In all three countries the state took the initiative by creating public enterprises (state oil and steel companies in Argentina and Brazil, CORFO in Chile, PEMEX in Mexico). This greatly increased the state role in the economy, which was anathema to believers in liberal economic doctrine.

After World War II economic liberalism staged a comeback in Latin America. In part it was tied to the resurgence of political liberalism. It flourished also because the world demand for primary products was strong in 1946–47, boosting foreign exchange earnings of the Latin American economies. By the early 1950s, however, they had all run into trouble. The world demand for primary products became erratic, and their prices fluctuated dizzily. The pro-industrializationists reappeared, arguing that economic liberalism was no solution for Latin America's future.

In the 1950s the debate was joined by an articulate new Latin American voice: the Economic Commission for Latin American (ECLA), a United Nations regional agency created in 1948. It was to be a secretariat of technicians, primarily economists, who were to analyze systematically the economic problems of the Latin American region and its individual countries. Its executive secretary was Raúl Prebisch, a talented Argentine economist who had played a key role in the creation of the Argentine central bank in the 1930s. ECLA was located in Santiago, Chile, in a deliberate effort to obtain distance from the U.S.-dominated atmosphere of the OAS headquarters in Washington, D.C.

ECLA became an aggressive participant in the analysis of Latin America's relationship to the world economy. One of its major accomplishments was to train a generation of Latin American economists who learned, during their time with ECLA, to see their countries' problems in a continental perspective. They also got to know their counterparts in other nations and were able to compare notes on the problems and possibilities of economic policymaking. Essentially, ECLA helped to produce a Latin American mentality in economic analysis.

It would be misleading to imply that ECLA had a single message. It was careful to confine its publications to technical analyses of past economic trends, along with discussion of current policy options and projections of the effects of likely policy choices. Yet the choice of topics and the direction of the analysis showed the strong influence of Prebisch and his disciples.

The Prebisch-ECLA thesis, as it became known, was that the world economy since the 1880s had been working systematically to the disadvantage of the countries that relied on the export of primary products. It was argued that the prices of finished goods went up faster than prices for primary goods, so the developing countries found themselves in a steadily deteriorating position vis-à-vis the industrial countries. The way out of this dilemma? First, adopt international commodity agreements to protect primary-product exporters from huge market-price fluctuations. Second, the larger developing countries should industrialize.

These conclusions were never stated as such in ECLA documents, which had to remain technical studies produced by a branch of the UN bureaucracy. But they were the unmistakable implications, and they were widely recognized as such.

These arguments provoked fierce responses, both in Latin American and the U.S. They irritated the Eisenhower administration (1953–61), which saw ECLA as a beehive of deluded statist thought, 'promoting policies likely to harm private enterprise. In fact, the Prebisch-ECLA analysis furnished ammunition for centrist politicians such as Vargas, Kubitschek, Frondizi, and Frei. Above all, ECLA gave reform-minded Latin Americans the confidence to shape their own development strategies, knowing they could call on an intellectual resource which was authentically Latin American.

In other words, ECLA offered a milestone in Latin America's search for self-knowledge. This was an important step, since Latin American analysts and politicians had long felt at a disadvantage when facing the economists, bankers, and businessmen of the industrial world.

The other important intellectual force gaining new strength in the

1950s was Marxism. To understand the force of Marxism in Latin America one has to look closely at the history of the communist parties, since they were the primary channels of Marxist thought, at least into the 1960s. It is true that there were a few influential non-communist party Marxist thinkers and politicians, of whom Peru's José Carlos Mariátegui was the most famous and influential. But they were the exceptions. It was the orthodox communist parties, affiliated with the Comintern in the 1920s and 1930s, which did most to spread the Marxist message. By the early 1950s they had lost the prestige that rubbed off from the Red Army in 1945. They were a negligible force in elections, except in Chile. They had some strength among student organizations and labor unions, but in general they suffered from identification with Stalinism.

Their Marxist analysis was a relatively crude form of economic determinism. Its application to individual countries was spelled out by the local parties, acting on Moscow's instructions. Few Latin Americans completely accepted the party line. When the communists moved to tap sentiments of economic nationalism, however, they could mobilize a wider following. Nationalist sentiment was usually directed against the U.S., on which the communist parties concentrated their fire. The communists and many Marxists sought to develop a clearly anti-imperialist (meaning, above all, anti-American) political stance. Nonetheless, Marxist thought was relatively isolated in Latin America in the 1940s and early 1950s, closely identified with a network of communist parties under Soviet discipline.

A crisis in the 1950s furnished strong evidence for the anti-imperialist argument. As described in Chapter 8, the U.S. strongly opposed the reformist program of Colonel Jacobo Arbenz in Guatemala. The CIA-organized exile invasion of Guatemala in 1954 imposed Carlos Castillo Armas as president, who promptly reversed the expropriation of United Fruit lands, and dutifully signed a mutual defense assistance pact with the U.S. in 1955. The Soviets, for their part, merely stood by and watched. A similarly managed coup succeeded in Iran in 1953, ousting Mossedegh and reinstating the Shah. With its power and wealth, the U.S. was flexing muscle on a global scale.

Especially in Latin America, the State Department could count on a solid phalanx of Latin American votes in the UN. The dogma of free enterprise continued to dominate U.S. hemispheric policy, despite a chorus of Latin American voices calling for international commodity agreements, a multi-lateral development bank for the Americas, and expanded accessibility to technology. Democratic reformers in Latin America, such as José Figueres in Costa Rica, Rómulo Betancourt in Venezuela, and Eduardo Frei in Chile, urged the U.S. to encourage democracy and social reform. The U.S. had too often favored the dictators, argued Figueres, thereby nurturing the kind of extreme leftism that emerged in Guatemala. Time was growing short—"one minute to midnight," as Figueres liked to announce dramatically.

Such pleas fell on deaf ears in Eisenhower's Washington until Vice-President Nixon traveled to Latin America in 1958. The trip was largely ceremonial, to attend the inauguration of President Arturo Frondizi of Argentina, with stops in seven other South American countries. Nixon's well-publicized past as a virulent anti-communist made him a natural target for student leftists in Latin America. Despite repeated warnings from his security staff, Nixon insisted on making his public appearances. There were demonstrations everywhere, but they were especially ugly in Lima and Caracas. On one occasion Secret Service agents had their guns drawn against a mob attacking Nixon's car when the driver just succeeded in whisking the shaken vice-president away. The events got world-wide publicity, and Washington worried over the possible causes of such anti-American feeling. The first important revisions in U.S.–Latin American policy began to appear in 1959, when the U.S. government dropped its opposition to the creation of an Inter-American Development Bank. There were also plans to expand U.S. bilateral aid. But events in the Caribbean soon overtook this modest change in official U.S. thinking.

Increasing the International Options?

During his guerrilla war against the dictator Batista, Fidel Castro had presented himself as a democratic reformer, fighting tyranny to restore representative democracy. Once in Havana, however, Fidel moved steadily to the left. He knew that any threat to U.S. investment—or to the U.S. political hegemony—in Cuba would bring U.S. intervention. Early in 1959, Fidel made overtures to the Soviets; by the end of the year Cuba was receiving economic aid from Moscow. By the end of another year Cuba had completed an almost total switch in trade relations—from overwhelming trade dependence on the U.S. to overwhelming trade dependence on the Soviet Union. Soviet military aid has also begun pouring into Cuba. The Soviets were obviously now willing to take a far bigger gamble than they ever contemplated in Guatemala in 1954.

The U.S. reaction foreseen by Fidel now began. The attempted landing at the Bay of Pigs in early 1961 might have succeeded if President Kennedy had ordered use of U.S. navy air cover, but Washington said no. The dilemma was all the more acute because the Kennedy administration was working frantically to produce a new and more enlightened Latin American policy.

The U.S. was humilated: first by the failure of the anti-Castro invaders, second by the clumsy cover used to conceal U.S. involvement. The defeat left Fidel stronger than ever. He had dramatic proof that the U.S. presented a constant threat to Cuba's security. He could now crack down against all domestic opposition.

The failed invasion also confirmed the entry of the other superpower into the hemisphere. The long-discussed U.S. fear—Soviet penetration of the Americas—was now fact. If the Soviets were willing to supply the Cubans, how many other guerrilla movements in Latin America might hope for the same support? That worry goaded the Kennedy policymakers to speed up the formulation of their new Latin American program.

The new policy, as announced in 1961, had two distinct aspects. The first was a major multi-laterally sponsored economic and social development program, christened the "Alliance for Progress." It was to involve both economic growth and social reform, to be carried out by democratic governments. Each Latin American nation would have to submit a detailed development plan to a council of nine "wise men," economists and technocrats. The U.S. government promised to provide public funding, up to $20 billion over ten years. It also promised to push the multi-lateral authorities and private investors in the U.S. and Europe to increase their capital flows to Latin America. The U.S. launched this new policy in a blaze of publicity, including a gala White House dinner for the Latin American diplomatic corps.

Considerable groundwork for this new program had been laid by the Eisenhower administration. Yet the dramatic embrace of the cause of social reform, and the willingness to press for public funds, would have been difficult for a Republican administration. In effect, the U.S. government was now adopting the logic put forward by ECLA and by the democratic reformers, such as Figueres and Betancourt. To the surprise of many of its detractors, the U.S. government was now claiming the leadership of a peaceful social revolution in Latin America.

The second aspect of the Kennedy administration's new Latin American policy was less publicized. It was a stepped-up counter-insurgency program by which the U.S. government would help Latin American governments fight guerrilla movements. The Kennedy policymakers were not betting on economic development and social change alone. Even the most committed reformer, they reasoned, might run afoul of a well-organized guerrilla opponent. Conventional military and police could not do the job alone. New methods were needed, such as the British had perfected in their successful anti-guerrilla campaign in Malaya. The Kennedy mystique was therefore now applied to the creation of a new, elite corps of counter-insurgency experts. They were given a distinctive green beret, and told that training counterpart forces in the Third World would be one of their main tasks.

As part of this effort to protect favored governments, the U.S. increased its military supply and training programs. There was a premium on modernizing the military, making them capable of the rapid and coordinated action needed to fight well-trained guerrillas. A new element was also added: the training and equipping of police forces to control urban riots and sabotage, and improvement of their techniques of interrogation and record retrieval. This activity was housed in the U.S. Agency for International Development (USAID) and bore the euphemistic label of "public safety."

The theory behind this two-pronged U.S. policy was that the U.S. had an interest in identifying and supporting strongly reformist leaders, giving economic aid to achieve growth, and at the same time offering the means to defeat armed domestic opponents who might have Soviet or, more likely, Cuban help. The U.S. was now betting on the anti-communist reformers to ride the historical tide in Latin America, and to produce more prosperous, more egalitarian, and therefore stronger nations with interests compatible with those of the U.S. Soviet penetration would be stopped, the U.S. sphere of influence would be preserved, and everyone in the hemisphere could be better off.

The Alliance for Progress was born to widespread applause. The glamor and eloquence of the new U.S. president, contrasting sharply with the pro-big business image of Eisenhower, excited Latin American imaginations. Liberals in the U.S. and Europe were thrilled, as were those long-time critics of U.S. policy who had excoriated Uncle Sam for always siding with the dictators.

Then Cuba hit the headlines again. The CIA, apparently with clearance from the White House (or at least Robert Kennedy), tried several plots to assassinate Castro. All failed. Meanwhile Fidel tightened his grip on Cuba, and looked to spread the revolution elsewhere in Latin America.

The Soviets became emboldened by U.S. weakness at the Bay of Pigs and decided to act. During 1962 they flooded Cuba with military equipment, including missiles—hardly a defensive weapon, since the missiles were too close to be detected by the U.S. warning system. The U.S. got the OAS to approve a blockade against all ships carrying offensive weapons to Cuba. There followed a frightening face-off, and the Soviets finally agreed to remove the missiles, but only when the U.S. promised to lift the blockade and pledged not to invade Cuba in the future.

The "missile crisis" of October 1962 had great implications for Latin America's relations with the U.S. and the world. First, the Soviets had been forced, by threat of direct U.S. attack on their Cuban installations, to give up the strategic advantage they tried to win by stealth. In effect, the Soviets were ratifying anew the U.S. strategic military hegemony in Latin America outside of Cuba.

Second, the U.S. had promised to keep hands off of—at least by direct invasion—the "first socialist experiment in the Americas." Fidel now knew he could concentrate on building socialism at home and exporting revolution abroad. Nonetheless, he needed a large security force to ward off CIA and exile-sponsored raids, as well as to prevent Cubans from fleeing the island.

Castro was in a good position to extend support—including money, materials, and training—to revolutionaries elsewhere in Latin America. Cuba became a "platform" for the export of revolution. A prime target was Venezuela, where President Rómulo Betancourt was a prototype of the democratic reformer the Kennedy administration sought in Latin America. In November 1963 the Venezuelan government announced its discovery of arms sent to Venezuela from Cuba, and asked the OAS to act. The Venezuelans charged that the arms were intended for local guerrillas, precisely the kind of anti-democratic forces Washington had said would justify U.S. counter-insurgency aid. The OAS dutifully endorsed the Venezuelan charge and, in July 1964, asked member nations to sever all diplomatic ties with Cuba and to suspend all commercial and transportation links. Cuba was to be an outcast nation in the hemisphere. All OAS members complied, except Mexico, which had reason to want the U.S-Cuban stalemate to continue, since it had partially replaced Cuba both as tourist attraction and as a supplier of sugar.

The pattern for Cuba's role in the hemisphere was now set. Backed up by an extraordinary Soviet subsidy—far greater per capita than the U.S. subsidy to any of its client regimes in Latin America—the Castro regime pressed ahead on two fronts. One was the difficult task of constructing socialism in Cuba, far more difficult than most revolutionaries had foreseen in 1960. The second was the promotion of revolution abroad. It was best exemplified by Ché Guevara, who soon found that, like the achievement of socialism at home, the promotion of revolution abroad was easier said than done.

The *fidelistas* were by no means the only source of the call to revolution in Latin American during the 1960s. Just as Soviet penetration via the Cuban revolution shattered the U.S. hegemony in the hemisphere, so the Sino-Soviet split in world communism fragmented the revolutionary left. Back in the 1940s and 1950s, the Latin American left had been dominated by national communist parties, almost all under Moscow's direction. In the late 1950s, however, the split between Peking and Moscow created new opportunities for Latin America revolutionaries. The Chinese communist dissidents gave inspiration to Latin Americans long dissatisfied with the bureaucratized orthodox communist parties. They yearned for revolution now, not in some distant era when "objective conditions" would be favorable. Revolutionaries of this bent arose in every major country in the 1960s. Almost invariably they met a bloody end.

Democratic Reformers and the Alliance for Progress

The framers of the Alliance for Progress banked on an improbable combination of favorable factors: elected governments promoting economic growth while achieving social reform. If Latin America had all the problems its analysts so often described, how could politicians suddenly produce the consensus necessary to carry out such ambitious programs? Why would the wealthy and privileged stand by? Could economic growth be achieved if governments mounted social reform threats to established producers?

Elsewhere we have seen the fate of democratic reformers in Chile, Brazil, Argentina, and Peru. In Chile, Frei (1964–70) fell far short of his goals in key areas such as land reform and redistribution. Power then passed to a more radical reformist, Salvador Allende (1970–73), under whom politics polarized dangerously and the economy spun out of control, due in part to U.S. economic warfare against Chile. Reformism—of which Allende was still a representative—had failed dramatically. Chile's repressive military regime after 1973 was exactly what the Alliance for Progress was designed to avoid.

In Brazil, Jânio Quadros (1961) at first appeared to be the dynamic vote-getting reformist Brazil needed. But he resigned after only seven months in office, opening a three-year political crisis that culminated in a coup against his ineffectual successor, João Goulart (1961–64). The military-dominated governments after 1964 emphasized economic growth, with little effort toward social reform. The result was an increase in social inequality, combined with a steady move in the 1960s away from direct elections—a path the architects of the Alliance for Progress would have thought was an invitation for trouble.

In Argentina, the best hope for democratic reformism was Arturo Frondizi's government (1958–62), but it was soon jeopardized by a highly unpopular anti-inflation program and became a casualty of the longstanding Peronist-military confrontation. None of the succeeding governments in Argentina came close to the model envisioned in the Alliance for Progress.

Venezuela, one of the few countries to maintain a continuous civilian government, was a bright spot for the U.S.-promoted reformist policy. Yet it produced little significant social reform and its relevance was always compromised by its windfall of oil revenues.

In Peru, President Fernando Belaúnde Terry (1963–68) looked like a democratic reformer, and he bet on economic development, especially by opening up the Peruvian Amazon. But he ran afoul of nationalists in the military and also met severe economic difficulties. He was then deposed in a military coup led by General Juan Velasco Alvarado, whose military regime carried out a land reform more radical than any contemplated by Belaúnde. Velasco was in turn replaced by a more pro-private-sector military regime, which allowed elections again in 1980, and Belaúnde, long in exile in the U.S., was re-elected to the presidency. But the economic odds were stacked against his reformist government.

Colombia was another country where U.S. planners placed great hope. The president from 1958 to 1962, Alberto Lleras Camargo, was an articulate and attractive Liberal Party politician from a prominent Colombian family. His cadre of economists and technocrats prepared the kind of detailed economic and social plans called for in the Alliance for Progress. They won large loans from the U.S. government and the multilateral agencies, and Colombia was soon labelled a "showcase" for democratic reformism by enthusiastic U.S. observers. Unfortunately, the hopes proved premature, as the Colombian government achieved little reform in crucial areas such as land redistribution. Although economic growth was forthcoming, precious little of it benefitted the rural sector or the mushrooming shanty towns around the cities. By the mid-1960s Colombia had become a prime example for U.S. congressional critics, such as Senator J. William Fulbright, who found far too few of the Alliance aims accomplished in this "showcase" country.

Events in the Dominican Republic brutally exposed the contradictions in U.S. policy. The assassination in 1961 of Rafael Trujillo, one of the Caribbean's most notorious dictators, opened the way for a free presidential election—won by Juan Bosch, a popular reformer whose ideas certainly fit the mold of the Alliance for Progress. Despite U.S. support, Bosch was deposed by a military coup in 1963. Another armed revolt in 1965 triggered fears in the Lyndon Johnson administration that a Castro-like regime might emerge, which would be a disaster both for Johnson's foreign policy and for his standing with U.S. domestic opinion. Johnson listened to all his advisers and then sent in 20,000 U.S. troops. They were joined by troops from Brazil, now ruled by a military government anxious to show its Cold War zeal.

A new civilian, Joaquín Balaguer, was elected president in 1966 and the U.S. and Brazilian troops left. But the U.S. had aroused resentment in much of Latin America for the heavy-handed manner in which the Johnson administration demanded (and just barely got) OAS blessing for the U.S. intervention. It wasn't quite the 1920s again, but it certainly wasn't the bright new era John Kennedy had envisioned in 1961.

Clearly, the Alliance for Progress had failed as of 1970. The expectations had been too high, given the political realities of the decade.

Furthermore, the goal of promoting democracy soon conflicted with the goal of preventing any more Cubas. In Brazil, for example, the U.S. became convinced that President João Goulart was leading his country dangerously leftward and Washington therefore quickly endorsed a military-civilian conspiracy when it overthrew him. By the end of the decade the Brazilian military regime had joined the ranks of the highly repressive, with little pretense of social reform; nevertheless it continued to be the largest beneficiary of U.S. aid.

In Argentina between 1963 and 1966, the U.S. found itself dealing with the ineffectual civilian government of Illia, which was succeeded by the repressive regime of General Onganía. But here too a general had his attractions for Washington, as did his military successors, because they were cracking down on the growing guerrilla movement.

The ideology of the Alliance for Progress was set by John F. Kennedy and the "New Frontiersmen," although President Lyndon B. Johnson pledged to continue the basic policies when he took office in November 1963. The election of Richard Nixon in 1968 brought a change in U.S. policy. Although Nixon maintained a rhetorical commitment to democracy and social reform, at heart he and his advisers favored a return to the more traditional Republican stance of leaving economic development primarily to the private sector. The Nixon administration also increased military aid, acting on the advice of Governor Nelson Rockefeller, whose 1969 presidential mission to Latin America pointedly noted that "a new type of military man is coming to the fore and often becoming a major force for constructive social action in the American republics." The implications were obvious.

Nixon was the first U.S. president to have to deal with an elected Marxist head of state in Latin America. Salvador Allende's victory in 1970 was a test for the U.S., publicly committed to social reform but strongly opposed to leftist movements. Although Allende's regime never reached a revolutionary stage, the Nixon administration was determined from the day of Allende's election to use every means ("make the economy scream" was one of Nixon's suggestions to CIA Director Richard Helms) to prevent his inauguration or, failing that, to speed his overthrow.

The U.S. discouraged new private investment in Chile and obstructed, wherever possible, Chile's access to financing from multi-lateral agencies such as the International Monetary Fund, the World Bank, and the Inter-American Development Bank. At the same time, President Nixon ordered the CIA to develop and carry out a secret plan for harassing the Chilean government. At least $10 million was spent in subsidies to the Chilean opposition press (especially the militantly anti-Allende *El Mercurio*) and to opposition groups, including many strikers who helped paralyze the Chilean economy in 1972–73. Seen in the context of all Allende's problems, the U.S. effort was probably of marginal importance. It was the Chilean military and the Chilean middle and upper classes who rose up against the Popular Unity government. They needed no lessons from the U.S. in why and how to do it. But the U.S. increased the sense of seige felt by the Allende government and encouraged the opposition to believe generous U.S. aid awaited them after a coup.

Not the least important result of the Allende era was the wide publicity about the U.S. covert activities. The official documentation of a U.S. Senate Select Committee in 1975 and subsequent journalistic revelations confirmed that the U.S. was still ready to intervene in the way Latin Americans had so long claimed.

In retrospect, these events reveal long-run continuities and transitions in the United States posture toward Latin America. Over the past 150 years, it appears that the form and extent of U.S. involvement in the region has passed through four separate stages (these stages refer only to U.S.-Latin American relations, whereas the overall subdivisions in this chapter refer to Latin America's relationship to the entire world).

Stage 1 (1819–80): Territorial Aggrandizement. Early in the nineteenth century the United States, itself a fledgling republic, engaged in outright territorial expansion at the expense of Latin America. The U.S. purchased Florida from Spain in 1819, just as the Wars of Independence were entering their final phase, and thereafter began its campaign to obtain land from Mexico—from the annexation of Texas in 1844 to the war of 1846–48 to the Gadsden Purchase of 1855. In the 1850s other expansionist efforts flourished and faltered, such as the Ostend Manifesto of 1854 (which set down terms for the purchase of Cuba) and William Walker's filibustering expedition in Nicaragua, and then the land-grabbing impulse started to fade. Throughout this era the U.S. jealousy attempted to exclude Europeans from Latin America, principally through the Monroe Doctrine of 1823.

Stage 2 (1880–1932): Investments and Protectorates. Economic growth and industrial development in the U.S. kindled the new type of interest in Latin America, as North American entrepreneurs looked to the region for raw materials and markets for their goods. The political prerequisite for economic investment was stability (and/or Washington's influence), and for this reason the U.S. created and sustained a string of "protectorate" states throughout the Caribbean—in Cuba, Haiti, the Dominican Republic, Panama, Nicaragua, and Central America in general. The U.S. also attempted to control the outcome of the Mexican Revolution, as Woodrow Wilson justified the dispatch of U.S. marines by vowing "to show those Latins how to elect good men," but eventually had to settle for indirect forms of leverage. In South America the U.S. came to rely more on diplomacy than naked force, but negotiations could still be heavy-handed and one-sided. As Teddy Roosevelt had once declared, in dealing with Latin America the United States should "speak softly and carry a big stick."

Stage 3 (1932–72): Good Neighborhood and Economic Aid. U.S. entanglements in World War II and the Cold War prompted still another redefinition of national interest in Latin America, one that stressed the importance of "good will" among hemispheric neighbors while the U.S. was locked in bitter struggles with rival world powers. The economic development of Latin America came to be seen as a key element in this strategy, since it would reduce the temptation for dissatisfied Latins to align themselves with unfriendly camps (first Nazi Germany, then Communist Russia). Franklin Roosevelt's announcement of the Good Neighbor policy occurred as these tensions were still on the horizon, but the implementation of his principles picked up appreciably during and after World War II. The idea of good-neighborliness reached its peak with John Kennedy's pronouncement of the Alliance for Progress in the 1960s. For the most part the U.S. refrained from overt military intervention (with conspicuous exceptions in Cuba and the Dominican Republic), preferring instead to rely on covert operations (as in Guatemala). Increasing emphasis was placed on diplomatic negotiation, promoting private trade and investment, and, under Kennedy, on government-to-government aid for economic development.

Stage 4 (1972 to the present): Waning Influence. For the last decade or so, U.S. influence in Latin America has been on the decline, as nations of the region have achieved more independence and autonomy, in part by playing the international superpowers off against each other. Japan has entered the commercial scene, trade with Europe and the Soviet Union has continued to increase, investment now comes in from diverse areas. Latin American leaders have attempted to manage and reduce their dependency by a strategy of diversification, so their countries would become partially dependent on a variety of outside nations and external influences, rather than wholly dependent on a single power: the U.S. On occasion the U.S. stoutly resisted this trend, as shown by its attempt to destabilize the Allende government in Chile. (Such undercover action revealed that the threat and use of force had become much more subtle and selective than in the "big stick" era, but it nonetheless remained a constant feature of U.S. policy.) From the viewpoint of Latin America, however, diversification seemed to many like a workable and realistic approach. It also underlined one basic truth of hemispheric relations: What is good for Latin America may not be good for the U.S.

The Economic Dimension

By 1960 West Europe and Japan were entering Latin America as major investors and traders. Another increasingly important force were the multinational corporations (MNC's). Firms such as International Telephone and Telegraph (ITT), Philips, and Royal Dutch Shell had such far-flung assets that they were no longer identified with any one country. Their multi-country base of operations meant they could exploit fully the widely varying national laws and regulations, often playing off one country against another while channeling business among branch firms. Multinationals predominated, especially in high technology areas. In some key sectors, such as pharmaceuticals or computers, countries had little alternative but to allow the multinationals to enter. Any transfer of the relevant technology was difficult to negotiate, since the MNC's had no incentive to give away the source of their high profits.

As time passed, Latin America was unable to devise an effective strategy for this problem of technology transfer. The United Nations sponsored studies of it, but came up against the hard fact that advanced technology in industrialized countries is produced by private firms which use it to make profits. They are unwilling to sell the technology, and insist on marketing it themselves. Distribution and sales require direct investment, leading to eventual profit remissions that can, in principle, far exceed the original investment. Furthermore, the MNC may be able to wield monopolistic power in the local market, charging prices higher than a competitive market would have allowed.

Attempts by individual countries (or even country consortia) to develop advanced technology have faced long odds. The research facilities and experience of an IBM or Bayer are hardly within the reach of hard-pressed scientists and researchers in Latin America. In consequence, the terms of transfer of technology have become one of the central issues in the relationship of the Latin American economies to the industrialized world.

By the 1980s another major vulnerability had become evident in the Latin American economies: their huge indebtedness, especially to private U.S. and West European banks, but also to the World Bank and the Inter-American Development Bank. The causes were several. First, most countries, especially the net oil importers, have run persistent trade deficits which have had to be financed by foreign loans. This is not surprising, since Latin America is at a stage of economic development that requires outside capital. If properly invested, this assistance can vitally aid the individual countries' economic development. Such was the case with the U.S., which before 1900 was a net importer of capital.

A second reason for borrowing was to import primary goods. With the sharp increase in oil prices after 1974, all Latin American countries except the net oil exporters (Bolivia, Ecuador, Venezuela, post-1975 Mexico, and post-1978 Peru) found their oil bill escalating alarmingly. Food, especially cereal grains, was also imported from elsewhere. This reflected the failure of many Latin American countries to keep agricultural output at least equal to population growth.

Third, borrowing was needed to pay the interest and principal on the existing debt. Obviously this practice could lead to a vicious circle, especially when new interest rates were higher than those on the expiring debt. Finally, in some cases the borrowers found themselves the target of hard-selling bankers, whose hefty Eurodollar balances had been swollen with deposits from the oil exporters. Thus Latin America soon proved a principal outlet for the huge Eurodollar surplus that emerged in the 1970s.

This heavy borrowing is not worrisome as long as the borrowers increase their export capacity and thus their ability to earn the foreign currency to service the debt. But any significant lag in strengthening the export capacity presents ground for concern. Even if export capacity grows satisfactorily, the debtor governments find they spend much time simply managing the debt. For such countries, the foreign creditors, led by private bankers from New York, Chicago, London, and Paris, have become key decision makers because they determine whether and on what terms they will continue to lend.

In the late 1970s foreign indebtedness grew dramatically in Latin America. Brazil and Mexico, the two most dynamic economies, led the way. Their heavy borrowing made it possible to pursue higher growth strategies than otherwise would have been possible. But by the early 1980s both had run up against very high interest rates and were forced to reduce growth in order to curb trade deficits and thus keep down the net increase in foreign borrowing. Both had wagered heavily on their ability to earn their way out of massive foreign debt, with Mexico betting on oil and Brazil betting on its diversified export capacity.

The 1981–82 world slump in oil prices, along with its own reckless economic policies, brought Mexico perilously close to formal default in August 1982. Brazil, supposedly a stronger borrower, ran into a similar crisis in December 1982. In both cases emergency loans were quickly arranged from the U.S., the IMF, and U.S. and European private banks. Both Mexico and Brazil suspended amortization payments on foreign debt, as Argentina had done earlier in 1982.

Suddenly Latin America's financial crisis looked big enough to pull down the entire world economy. By December 1982 four of the world's largest debtors were Latin American—Brazil ($87 billion), Mexico ($80 billion), Argentina ($43 billion) and Venezuela ($28 billion)—and there was a strong suspicion that the official totals were underestimates.

Latin America's debt crisis involved the U.S. and Europe in a vital way because the private creditors included over 1400 banks for Mexico and 1110 for Brazil. That tied the heart of the U.S. and European economies into Latin America in an unprecedented manner. The only solution to the crisis was a recovery of the world economy, thereby enabling the debtors to earn the hard currency needed to get their debt servicing (payment of interest and amortization of principal) down to a manageable level.

Latin America in the World of the 1980s

In the 1980s Latin America projected itself onto the world stage more than ever before in this century. There were the more than 50,000 Cubans in Africa, as military and social service personnel in Angola, Mozambique, Ethiopia, and a half dozen other African republics. The Cubans were there to prove the superiority of socialist ways, backed by Soviet military support. Here was a new dimension to Latin American relations with the world: a Latin American country taking the initiative outside the continent, representing the cause of the Third World (as interpreted by Havana) in another ex-colonial setting. However compromised by the Soviet sponsorship, these Cuban initiatives represented a unique effort by a more advanced part of the Third World to reach out to a less advanced region.

By the 1980s Latin America was receiving recognition on the world stage in other ways. Until July 1982, Argentina was the defending champion of world soccer, having won the world cup in Buenos Aires in 1978. In tennis, Argentines Guillermo Vilas and José Luis Clerc had shown their prowess against the best of the U.S. and West Europe. The secretary generalship of the UN went to a Peruvian diplomat, Javier Pérez de Cuéllar. The Latin American novel had become an artistic and commercial success in the U.S. and Europe, with Carlos Fuentes (Mexico), Gabriel García Marquez (Colombia), Jorge Amado (Brazil), and Julio Cortázar (Argentina) impressing North American and European readers and critics. World-renown poets included Gabriela Mistral (Chile) and Jorge Luis Borges (Argentina). Leading composers of music were Carlos Chávez (Mexico), Alberto Ginastera (Argentina), and Heitor Villalobos (Brazil).

There were also dramatic changes in the sphere of economic thought. Many of the 1980s policymakers in Latin America turned to the free-market economic doctrines best publicized by Milton Friedman of the University of Chicago, who had long argued for fixed monetary policies and strong control over all sources of public spending. Friedman became a guru for reigning technocrats in Chile and Argentina, where application of his policies led to major recessions. But Friedman argued that the long-run consequences could justify the short-run sacrifices.

It looked like a return to the economic liberalism of nineteenth century Latin America, as the rapid reduction of tariffs staggered Argentine and Chilean industry. Meanwhile, the burden of anti-inflation programs in both countries was borne disproportionately by the workers.

Mexico and Brazil followed more pragmatic policies, but still faced a huge shortfall in jobs available relative to new entrants into the labor market. Nowhere had the combination of economic growth, social reform, and political democracy taken hold. The 1960s vision of the developmental reformists still seemed very far in the distance.

Hispanic Culture Within the United States

The U.S. in the 1980s found itself facing a new dimension in its relationship with Latin America. Suddenly the U.S. discovered it had one of the largest Spanish-speaking populations in the hemisphere. The 1980 census placed the "Hispanic" population at 14.6 million, but most knowledgeable observers thought it was at least 20 million, if all the illegal immigrants (labelled "undocumented" in more circumspect official language) were included. That meant that only Mexico, Argentina, and Colombia had larger Spanish-speaking populations in the western hemisphere.

According to the 1980 census, New York City, for example, had 1,406,000 Hispanics, primarily from Puerto Rico and the Caribbean. This was an increase from the 1970 total of 1,200,000, achieved despite the fact that the total New York City population declined during that decade. Los Angeles recorded 816,000 in 1980 and Chicago, seldom considered a heavily Hispanic area, had 422,000 Hispanics. In the Los Angeles and Chicago public school systems Hispanic students came to outnumber whites. Hispanics compose 19 percent of the population in California, the nation's most populous state, and 21 percent in Texas, the third most populous state. In much of south Florida, especially in the greater Miami area, Hispanic influence (essentially Cuban) clearly predominates. Most significant of all, between 1970 and 1980 the U.S. Hispanic population increased by more than 50 percent. In many cities in the Southwest the Hispanic population is growing faster than either the blacks or the "Anglos" (as non-Hispanic whites have been labelled). The increase occurs not only by birth but also by the influx of new immigrants.

There is reason to believe that these Hispanics will retain their language and culture longer than did previous generations of non-English speaking immigrants into the U.S. The painful question of how—if at all—to preserve non-U.S. culture has been faced by millions of non-English speaking immigrants to America. Waves of Europeans were filtered through the public schools of New York, Philadelphia, Chicago,

Cleveland, where everyone assumed that the only language at school was English. Indeed, immigrant parents often forbade their children to speak the Old World language because they were so anxious to make their children into Americans. The result, of course, was that usually the second and certainly the third generation immigrant lacked any knowledge of his ancestral language—German, Polish, Italian, or Greek. All wanted to be Americanized, and language was the first instrument at hand.

The Hispanics in the U.S., on the other hand, have reached center stage at a different moment in U.S. history. They followed the 1960s activism of the black movement, which belatedly generated a new legitimacy for the cultural traditions of ethnic minorities. Operating in this climate of opinion (which mixes Anglo guilt and sympathy), Hispanics have successfully campaigned to institute bilingualism in schools and public facilities. The logic is that the Spanish-speaking Americans, by their number and by their past discrimination, deserve the opportunity to continue using their language. Most important, it is argued that Hispanic children are often disoriented and demoralized when faced with an all-English language school. Maintaining some instruction in Spanish will help build their confidence and forge links between their culture and the wider U.S. society.

Bilingualism in public schools is officially intended to enable Spanish-speaking children to have their subjects in Spanish, at the same time as learning English. The argument is that children can learn biology or mathematics just as well in Spanish as in English. The final objective is for the child to finish high school fully competent in both English and Spanish. Critics of the system charge that all too often, especially in schools with a high percentage of Spanish speakers, students never learn correct English and may not learn Spanish grammar either. If true, they enter the job market with a grave disadvantage.

Whatever the case, there are millions of Spanish-speaking Americans who cannot command enough English to conduct essential business. In response the U.S. federal government now publishes in Spanish as well as English a wide range of official announcements and forms. City, county, and state authorities in key areas—including northern cities such as Chicago and Kansas City—have had to hire Spanish-speaking staff. In effect, the U.S. now has large regions and urban pockets where Spanish has official sanction as a second language.

This is bound to have implications for U.S. society. New York City, Newark, Miami, and Los Angeles all have regular television programming in Spanish, and the entire U.S. Southwest from Texas to Los Angeles has a cable TV network connected directly to Mexican national television. Television, like bilingualism, will help maintain a live Hispanic culture.

Politics is another area where Hispanic power is beginning to be felt. Like blacks, Hispanics have tended to be apathetic about politics. Long suspicious of the Anglo world, they often did not see any point in voting. Recently, however, Hispanic voters have begun to bring their numbers to bear. In San Antonio, Texas, for example, Henry Cisneros was elected mayor in 1981, the first ever of Mexican-American descent. New Mexico elected a Mexican-American governor, Jerry Apodaca, and Arizona did the same in electing Raúl Castro to the governorship. In New York City the Hispanics are steadily increasing their influence in the Democratic party. In Miami, the Cuban-American community has achieved prominence in sectors of commerce, banking, and real estate, and represents a political force as well.

This growing Hispanic presence in the U.S. will influence how the North American public thinks about key issues in our relationships with Latin America. One of the most pressing is the issue of undocumented workers. The largest number comes from Mexico, although the Dominican Republic, Haiti, and Central America have also produced significant numbers. Their status in the U.S. has become a highly complex question, especially during a recession, involving multiple considerations of their contributions to the U.S. economy, as well as their use of public services and the competition they pose in the labor market. If the influx continues, then it will replenish and enlarge the U.S. Hispanic community. If the U.S. government moves to reduce or eliminate the influx, then it will probably meet strong opposition from the Hispanic community and from the Mexican government, which may use its sale of oil and natural gas to the U.S. as a bargaining weapon. Whatever the final outcome, the U.S. will find it has already imported some of Latin America's problems. The U.S. citizen therefore can no longer afford to ignore Latin America.

There is another key issue which ostensibly is not Latin American: the status of Puerto Rico. Puerto Rico now exists as a U.S. commonwealth only by virtue of having been conquered in the Spanish American War and then ceded by a Spain too weak to resist U.S. military might and money. Puerto Rico's current status is a potentially explosive issue, both in domestic U.S. politics and in U.S. Caribbean policy. Its commonwealth status is inherently unstable. The contrary poles toward which Puerto Rican activists seek to push it are full statehood or complete independence. Approving either would require a significant struggle among U.S. decision makers. The approximately 2 million Puerto Ricans in the U.S. could undoubtedly become involved and the issue could prove very divisive in U.S. politics.

Since the 1960s Latin America has been drawn increasingly into the wider world. U.S. hegemony in Latin America, at its height from 1940 to 1960, is clearly on the wane. Extra-hemispheric forces, such as West Europe, Japan, and the Soviet Union, have come to play a greater role in Latin America than at any time in this century. The military deterrent of a distant superpower, the USSR, has prevented the U.S. from liquidating a troublesome regime in Cuba, thus cancelling out what had long been a standard instrument of U.S. domination in the Caribbean and Central America.

On the other hand, the *fidelistas* failed in their crusade to spread revolution in the hemisphere. Even in Central America, the Nicaraguan revolutionary regime (and probably the El Salvadorean, if the guerrillas win) depends primarily not on Cuba or Soviet aid, important though they may be, but on help from West Europe. So pluralism may yet be an option for Latin America. Governments may be able to negotiate their way into gaining help from a broad spectrum of foreign sources. Past experience suggests that the only way to escape from dependency is to increase the options. Gabriel García Márquez, one of Latin America's most famous contemporary writers, stated the issue eloquently in his 1982 Nobel Prize acceptance speech:

> Why is the originality so readily granted us in literature so mistrustfully denied us in our different attempts at social change? Why think that the social justice sought by progressive Europeans for their own countries cannot also be a goal for Latin America, with different methods for dissimilar conditions? No: The immeasurable violence and pain of our history are the result of age-old inequities and untold bitterness, and not a conspiracy plotted 3000 leagues from our homes. But many European leaders and thinkers have thought so, with the childishness of old-timers who have forgotten the fruitful excesses of their youth as if it were impossible to find another destiny than to live at the mercy of the two great masters of the world. This, my friends, is the very scale of our solitude.

WHAT FUTURE FOR LATIN AMERICA?

Predicting the future is always risky, more so for Latin America. The continent has repeatedly been described as on the verge of miraculous development, only to disappoint the optimists. In 1912 Lord Bryce, after a tour of South America, predicted its temperate area "will be the home of rich and populous nations, and possibly of great nations." In 1910 another English traveller located Brazil "upon the road that leads, surely though slowly, to a future of great prosperity." Over seventy years later the certainty has faded.

It has been frequently maintained that education would solve all of Latin America's problems. Ignorance and illiteracy held back the Latin Americans. If they could only follow the U.S. and West European example with state-supported mass education! But which have been the most educated nations in Latin America? Argentina, Chile, and Uruguay. And those countries produced Latin America's most brutally repressive military dictatorships of the 1970s. Their elegant constitutions were torn up, their congresses closed, their courts rendered a sham. How could this be so?

But if prediction is treacherous, it is also necessary. As we follow the historical development of Latin America, we cannot help but wonder about the rest of the story. And since the U.S. will continue to have vital interests in Latin America, we cannot ignore the possible implications of future Latin American developments for the U.S. and its citizens.

Prediction has other virtues too. As we strain to think ahead, we have to think again about the past. To estimate a future balance of forces, one has to assess their past and present weight. If urban labor has been subject to manipulation in Brazil, will it continue to be that way? Why did the Chilean coup of 1973 take thousands of lives, whereas the Brazilian coup in 1964 took almost none? One must ponder these historical questions before considering possible scenarios for the 1980s and 1990s.

And with some care, we can hope to identify sources of change and determine a probable range of results.

Preparing To Predict: Comparative Analysis

Let us begin by a retrospective survey of the country studies presented in this book. In Chapter Two we offered a schematic outline of historical transformations in Latin America since the 1880s, and in subsequent chapters we traced the history of individual countries and regions. One of our concerns throughout has been to focus on (a) each country's location in the world economy, (b) the social structure associated with each pattern of economic activity, (c) the kind of coalition among classes or groups that might result, and (d) the political consequences deriving from all these factors.

We attempt to approach this problem through a systematic comparative analysis, and this requires a comprehensive conceptual framework. At the conclusion of Chapter Two we presented a series of questions for consideration in each of the country case-studies. Central to these interrogations was a focus on the structure and alignment of social classes. To make these issues more explicit, we now offer an abstract analytical scheme.

The central idea entails a classification of social strata along two separate dimensions: urban-rural position and class status. There are, in this view, six such groups:

- the *urban upper class,* consisting primarily of industrialists, bankers, financiers, and large-scale merchants—or, in Marxist terms, the upper bourgeoisie;
- the *rural upper class,* mainly landowners;
- the *urban middle class,* a heterogeneous stratum including professionals, teachers, shopkeepers, and so on—otherwise known as the petty bourgoisie;
- the *rural middle class,* not often noticed in Latin America, one that includes small farmers as well as merchants in rural areas;
- the *urban lower class,* principally an industrial working class or proletariat, but a stratum that also includes growing segments of unemployed migrants from the countryside; and
- the *rural lower class,* either an agrarian proletariat or a traditional peasantry—some of whose members may take part in the national economy, some of whom (especially in indigenous communities) may subsist outside the reaches of the marketplace.

The groupings in the "lower class," often known as the "popular classes" in Latin America, represent by far the largest segments in society. These are poor people, undereducated and sometimes malnourished, and they have been systematically deprived of the benefits of development.

One additional social actor—not a class or stratum, but a critical group nonetheless—consists of the *foreign sector.* This includes private inves-

FIGURE 11-1   Hypothetical Array of Social Actors

Social Classes		Foreign Sector	National Institutions
Urban	Rural		

Upper: Industrialists, bankers | Large landowners | Foreign investors, merchants | State

Middle: Merchants, professionals, intellectuals | Small farmers | Foreign governments | Church

Lower: Workers, unemployed migrants | Peasants

tors and corporations as well as foreign governments and military establishments. Though sometimes divided against itself, the foreign sector has often wielded enormous power in Latin America.

To enhance their relative position, these social actors typically compete for control of major institutions. The most crucial institution, at least in recent times, has been the *state,* which commands large-scale resources and usually claims an effective monopoly on the legitimate use of force (only a government, for example, can put a citizen in jail). One key group within the state is the military; another consists of party politicians (if they exist); another is composed of technocrats and bureaucrats. Also important as an institution has been the Roman Catholic Church.

Figure 11-1 provides a general picture of these groups and institutions. It does not depict the outlines of any specific Latin American society. It is an abstract scheme, a hypothetical means of illustrating the subject of concern.

To apply the framework to any historical situation we need to ask the questions first posed in Chapter Two. In abbreviated summary they are:

• What are the principal social classes? Which ones are present and which ones are absent?
• Which social classes have the most power?
• Which groups are allied with which? On what basis?
• How autonomous is the state? Is it captive to any of the social classes, or is it independent?
• What are the predominant factors on the international scene? What, in particular, is the position of the United States?

To demonstrate these possibilities we next present schematic analyses of political and social transitions in each of the areas covered in Chapters Three through Nine. We concentrate here on relatively recent developments, though the method could just as well apply to earlier periods in time. This is an interpretive exercise, we emphasize, not a definitive statement; it requires estimates and judgments that should provide discussion and debate. Nonetheless we think the approach provides strong confirmation of our basic arguments: that political outcomes in Latin America derive largely from the social class structure, that the class structure derives largely from each country's position in the world economy, and that a comparative perspective on these phenomena can help elucidate the variations and the regularities in Latin American society and politics.

Our first application deals with Argentina, where the economic dominance of beef and wheat produced two major social results: the absence of a peasantry, especially in the pampa region, and the importation of working-class labor from Europe. In the years before Perón the state and the foreign sector were mostly in league with landed interests, as shown in Figure 11-2. (Solid arrows represent relatively firm alliances; broken arrows represent fragile or partial coalitions.) Even the Radicals who governed with urban middle-class support in 1916–30 tended to favor the cattle-raising oligarchs.

For economic and demographic reasons Argentina's urban working class suddenly began exerting pressure on the political system in the 1930s, but there was no possibility of a class-based alliance with a peasantry; the most likely allies, instead, were newly emergent industrialists ready to challenge the landowning aristocracy and its foreign connections. The preconditions thus existed for an urban, multi-class coalition of workers, industrialists, and some segments of the middle class. It took the political instinct, the populist rhetoric, and the personal charisma of Colonel Juan Perón to make this alliance a reality, and he used a corporatist state structure to institutionalize it. One reason for its initial success was that the landowners had no peasantry with which to form a common conservative front. A reason for its ultimate failure was that limited industrial growth led to class-based worker-owner conflict within the coalition itself.

Starting in 1966 and again in 1976, the military seized the state and attempted to impose a "bureaucratic-authoritarian" regime. The dominant alliance has consisted of military officers, foreign investors, local industrialists, and landowners. Workers have been repressed and forcibly excluded from power. The middle sectors have played a waiting game.

Chile is quite a different case. It has contained every type of social actor, including a peasantry (and migratory rural proletariat) and a

FIGURE 11-2 Political and Social Coalitions: Argentina

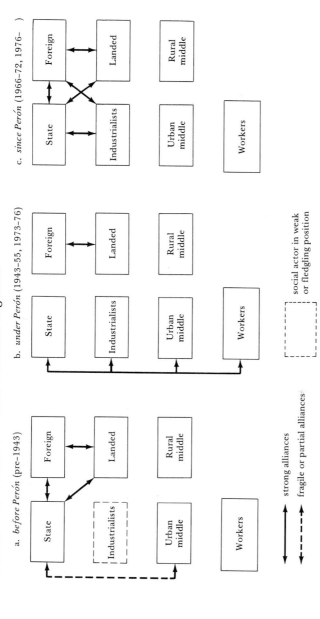

a. *before Perón* (pre-1943)

b. *under Perón* (1943–55, 1973–76)

c. *since Perón* (1966–72, 1976–   )

strong alliances

fragile or partial alliances

social actor in weak
or fledgling position

Before Perón (a) a coalition of landed and foreign interests controlled the state and obtained support from leaders of the urban middle class; under Perón (b) a populist coalition of urban workers and new industrialists—with some middle-class participation—dominated the state, to the virtual exclusion of foreigners and landed oligarchs; after Perón (c) an alliance of foreign interests, landowners, and industrialists led technocrats and the military to impose a "bureaucratic-authoritarian" regime.

Note: Here and in subsequent figures, the foreign sector is depicted as a single unit, since the economic and political interests of individual foreign powers have usually tended to coincide.

working class that by 1900 was well-organized, at least by Latin American standards. Foreign interests, especially the copper companies, collaborated with an upper class that, in contrast to Argentina, was deeply involved in finance and industry as well as land. Though political parties represented specific social groups the state generally retained substantial independence.

So there existed elements of a powerful socialist movement. Party politics could (and did) lead to ideological polarization. The alliance of the foreign sector with the upper class added a nationalistic dimension to anti-aristocratic resentment. A broad-based coalition of workers and peasants seemed possible: hence the triumph and euphoria of the early Salvador Allende government. Chile's socialist movement was not able, however, to expand its support much beyond its industrial working class

FIGURE 11-3   Political and Social Coalitions: Chile

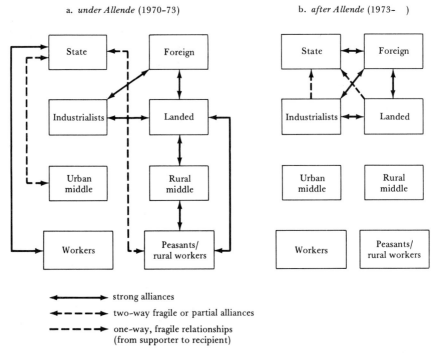

a. *under Allende* (1970–73)   b. *after Allende* (1973–   )

⟶ strong alliances

◂ ─ ─ ─ ▸ two-way fragile or partial alliances

─ ─ ─ ▸ one-way, fragile relationships
(from supporter to recipient)

Under Allende (a) a political movement based largely on urban workers gained control of the state—against the opposition of foreign interests, industrialists, and a multi-class array of rural groups; after Allende (b) a coalition of industrialists and landowners joined with foreign interests, most conspicuously the U.S., to create a military-dominated bureaucratic-authoritarian state that has shown remarkable autonomy in the domestic arena (hence the broken one-way arrows).

FIGURE 11-4   Political and Social Coalitions: Brazil

a. *under Goulart* (1961-64)   b. *after Goulart* (1964-   )

←——————→ strong alliances

←— — — → fragile and partial alliance

——→ ←—— potential alliance (but not achieved)

Under Goulart (a) the state mobilized support from both workers and peasants, raising the specter of a potential worker-peasant alliance; after Goulart (b) a bureaucratic-authoritarian state relied on numerous constituent groups and retained considerable allegiance from the urban middle class.

base. Allende supporters failed especially to convert many of the lower middle class. Urban and rural elements of the upper class, on the other hand, maintained their solidarity, partly through family connections, and landowners managed to get support from other strata in the countryside. U.S. undercover intervention further hastened the downfall of Allende's regime. (See Figure 11-3.)

Since 1973 the Chilean military, like its counterpart in Argentina, has established a bureaucratic-authoritarian system. The ruling coalition includes industrialists, landowners, foreign investors, and a state that possesses extraordinary power. Staffed by generals and technocrats, especially the "Chicago boys," the Chilean government has set about its course determined to prevail over any and all opposition.

Brazil presents a similar picture. Under Vargas the *Estado Nôvo* organized urban workers under the auspices of state control. In the early 1960s his protegé, João Goulart, stepped up the mobilization of the workers—and also fomented (or at least permitted) the organization of peasants in the countryside. The prospect of a worker-peasant alliance antagonized both the upper class and foreign interests, depicted in Figure 11-4, and prompted the military to intervene in 1964 and to establish a prototypical bureaucratic-authoritarian regime. Despite waves of repression that hit every social sector (although to highly differing degrees), the Brazilian government has succeeded in retaining more residual middle-class support than its counterparts in Argentina or Chile, and this explains in part why the process of liberalization (*abertura*) has gone farther there.

In Peru the period from 1948 to the mid-1960s witnessed a close association between the state (especially under Odría), foreign capital, landowners, and—to the extent that they existed as an identifiable power

FIGURE 11-5   Political and Social Coalitions: Peru

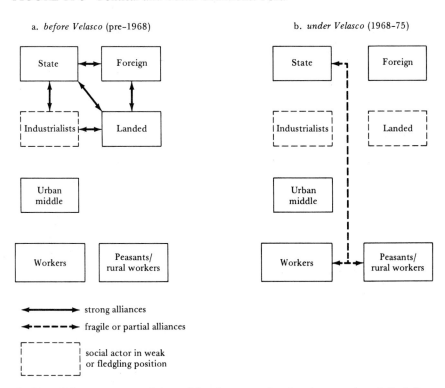

a. *before Velasco* (pre-1968)

b. *under Velasco* (1968-75)

Before Velasco (a) a coalition of landowners, foreign interests, and fledgling industrialists controlled the state; under Velasco (b) the state succeeded in weakening the landed oligarchy and attempted to mobilize support from workers and peasants through a corporate structure (without forging a horizontal lower-class alliance) but could not do so on a long-term basis.

FIGURE 11-6   Political and Social Coalitions: Mexico

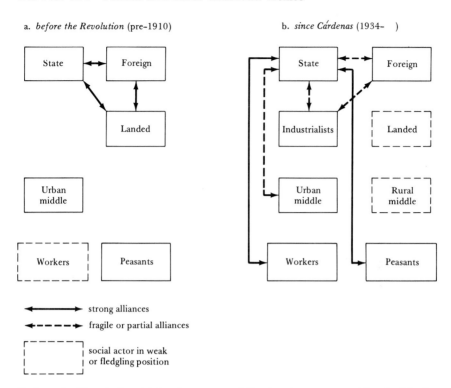

a. *before the Revolution* (pre-1910)   b. *since Cárdenas* (1934-   )

⟵⟶ strong alliances

⟵ - - - ⟶ fragile or partial alliances

social actor in weak
or fledgling position

Before the Revolution (a) landowners and foreign interests combined with the military and contemporary technocrats (the *científicos*) to gain control of the state; since the 1930s (b) the ruling coalition has consisted of a delicate balance among foreign interests, local industrialists and financiers, and the state—which has kept a firm hand over workers and peasants while cultivating some support from the urban middle class.

group—local industrialists. (See Figure 11-5.) The urban middle sectors took an ambivalent stance, sometimes supporting APRA or Belaúnde's Popular Action, but not challenging the overall structure of power. Left out of the ruling alliance were organized workers, migrants in the shantytowns and, of course, the peasants who finally took up arms in the sierra.

The revolutionary military regime under Velasco Alvarado (1968–75) dismantled this coalition and built an entirely new one, based on state-sponsored mobilization and control of workers and peasants against the formerly ascendant groups: especially foreign investors and aristo-cratic landowners, the latter being gravely weakened by agrarian re-form. The state was conspicuous for its autonomy, and no sector was immune from its intervention. Ultimately, the reformist military proved unable to institutionalize its corporate structure and thus consolidate its ties to workers and peasants. Subsequent governments—under Morales Bermúdez (1975–80) and Belaúnde (1980-present)—have gradually returned significant shares of power to factions of the pre-1968 elite. The success of this strategy has yet to be determined.

Mexico offers a different combination. Prior to the Revolution of 1910 the country had no indigenous industrial elite or rural middle-sector; there was a nascent but unorganized working class. As shown in Figure 11-6 the ruling coalition, under the *Porfiriato,* included three groups: landowners, the foreign sector, and the state.

The Revolution ruptured this coalition and, through agrarian reform, weakened the rural elite. The state increased its authority and, from the 1930s onward, encouraged the formation of an industrial bourgeoisie. The post-revolutionary governments drew popular sup-

FIGURE 11-7   Political and Social Coalitions: Cuba

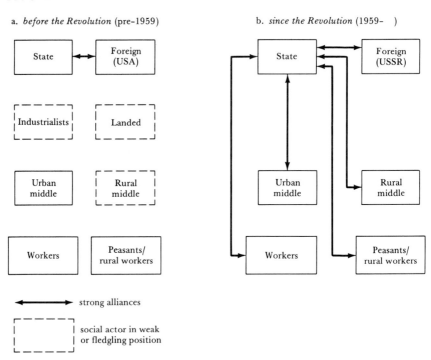

a. *before the Revolution* (pre-1959)   b. *since the Revolution* (1959-   )

Before the Revolution (a) a weak state relied on the U.S. for sustenance and support; the post-revolutionary state (b) has dislodged the upper class (much of which migrated to the U.S.) and mobilized support throughout the rest of Cuban society, but still receives assistance and protection from a foreign power.

port from both workers and peasants, and under Cárdenas developed its strategy for dealing with the masses: the state would organize workers and peasants in such a way as to keep them apart. The PRI developed separate "sectors" for workers and peasants, reflecting the regime's obsession with heading off any spontaneous, class-based politics.

Cuba's monocultural society reveals still another profile. Foreign (that is, United States) domination of the sugar industry meant that, for all practical purposes, there was hardly any local upper class. Workers in the mills and on plantations formed an active proletariat, as pictured in Figure 11-7, and migration strengthened ties between laborers in the cities and the countryside. Unions were weak, the army was corrupt, and the state, under Batista, was a pitiful plaything of U.S. interests.

Cuba possessed elements of a socialist movement, one that could capitalize on anti-imperialist sentiments. There was another secret to Fidel's eventual success: his movement would meet very little resistance, except for the foreign sector—whose proconsuls did not use all the resources at their disposal. Since 1959 Fidel and his lieutenants have revamped the island's social structure, eliminating vestiges of the old upper class, organizing middle- and lower-class groups in cities and the countryside, and implementing a "command" economy. To achieve this Fidel has had to rely heavily on foreign support. This time, however, it came from the Soviet Union. The bonds of dependency continue to exist.

In partial resemblance to Cuba, most of Central America prior to the 1970s typified a traditional "plantation" society: landlords (but here resident, not absentee) and peasants in the rural sector, a fledgling urban middle class, and a ruling alliance consisting of an aristocracy, foreign interests, and a dictatorial state fully supported by the church. In the last decade or so, two major developments have taken place, especially in Nicaragua and El Salvador (the latter is portrayed in Figure 11-8). First, political leaders from the middle classes have sought support from peasants. Second, perhaps even more important, the Roman Catholic Church has openly and courageously espoused the cause of the poor. Except for Nicaragua, the state in Central America remains in league with the landed elite and foreign interests, but the patterns of alliance have undergone significant change. Political struggles in the near future will reveal the implications of this realignment.

In addition to placing each of the country studies within a comparative framework, this overview can offer several basic clues for predicting trends and outcomes. One is that *a large share of influence on Latin America's future development will continue to come from outside the region.* Economic growth (or decline) at the industrial center of the capitalist world-system will have major effects on demand for Latin American goods, and could thus affect the power relationships between groups

FIGURE 11-8   Political and Social Coalitions: El Salvador

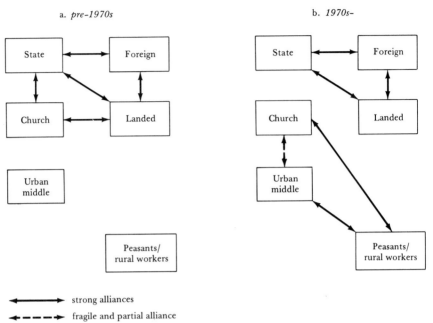

a. *pre-1970s*   b. *1970s–*

⟵————————⟶   strong alliances

⟵— — — —⟶   fragile and partial alliance

Prior to the 1970s (a) El Salvador was dominated by an alliance of landowners, foreign interests, and the military, with the approval of a conservative church hierarchy; by the mid-1970s (b) a middle-class reformist movement was seeking support from peasants and leading clerics pronounced their solidarity with the dispossessed.

in the producing countries. Whether Cuba or Central America embarks on industrialization, for instance, depends not only on local planning and resources; it also depends on the actions of the U.S. and the U.S.S.R. As the world becomes ever more interdependent, it is less and less likely that this situation will change.

Second, the action of any particular social group or class will depend not only on its own growth and strength. *It will depend on what is happening among other social groups.* It is reasonable to suppose, for instance, that the urban working class will increase in most countries of Latin America. But this alone will not determine political outcomes. Those will depend in large part on the other groups in each society: on what other groups are present, on the nature of alliances, and on the resulting power arrangements. A socialist movement succeeded in Cuba and failed in Chile not only because of their differing degrees of internal cohesion, but also because of different bases and degrees of opposition.

This stricture applies especially to middling groups, often called middle classes or sectors. They are bound to grow. But their political activity is likely to depend, in very large part, on the power relationships among other major groups in each society. *Latin America's middle classes have tended to react to political opportunities, rather than to initiate structural transformation, and there is no reason to expect this to change.* The middle-class movements of the 1890–1910 period represented attempts to gain access to power, not to implement structural change; even Francisco Madero, the "apostle" of the Mexican Revolution, had limited goals of his own. Ever since that era, middle-class parties—in Argentina, Chile, Brazil, and elsewhere—have taken a responsive stance. To be sure, some *individuals* from these strata (and the upper-class elites) have assumed leadership of popular and revolutionary movements, but *collective* behavior has been cautious, tentative, and often incoherent. By itself, the expansion of the middle sectors will not determine patterns of political change. In conjunction with other factors, though, it could become a decisive force.

on what happens in Latin America between now and the year 2000 and presumably beyond. To assess the implications of this fact, we must first anticipate the social and economic environment that is most likely to prevail.

Dimensions of Change: Demography and Economics

One of the most important factors is the size and growth of Latin America's population. This will determine the overall demand for resources (especially food) and for employment, services, and political participation. The specter of a "population explosion" has long haunted visions of the continental future, and not without reason. According to one estimate, for instance, the population of Latin America—about 364 million in 1980—could swell to more than 600 million by the year 2000, well over twice the projected size of the United States. An expansion of this magnitude would place enormous strain on Latin American society, and many observers have predicted such dire outcomes as famine, disorder, and disarray.

It is important to realize, however, that the prospects vary widely from country to country. Between 1970 and 1980 the population of Mexico increased at an average annual rate of 3.4 percent (which means a doubling of the population every 21 years!). The rate for Chile was 1.6 percent, and for Cuba it hovered around 1.3 percent (which would take nearly 60 years for doubling). On the basis of recent growth rates, Table 11-1 displays a set of low and high projections for major countries of the region. Brazil, it appears, may have almost 200 million in-

TABLE 11-1   Population Projections for Major Countries of Latin America, 1980–2000 (in millions)

	Population 1980	Projected Annual Growth Rates (Low and High Estimates)[a]	Population 1990	Population 2000
Argentina	27.1	1.5%	31.5	36.5
		2.0	33.0	40.3
Brazil	126.4	2.0	154.1	187.8
		2.5	161.8	207.1
Chile	11.5	1.5	13.3	15.5
		2.0	14.0	17.1
Cuba	10.6	1.0	11.7	12.9
		1.5	12.3	14.3
Mexico	70.0	3.0	94.1	126.4
		3.5	98.7	139.3
Peru	17.7	2.0	21.6	26.3
		2.5	22.7	29.0
Central America	22.4	3.0	30.1	40.5
		3.5	31.6	44.6

[a] Estimates represent low and high boundaries that have been placed above and below actual growth rates observed in 1970–81 (see Table 12-1 in Statistical Appendix). Compare these projections with forecasts in World Bank, *World Development Report 1982* (New York: Oxford University Press, 1982), Table 17, pp. 142–143.

Source for 1980 data: James W. Wilkie and Stephen Haber, eds., *Statistical Abstract of Latin America,* 21 (Los Angeles: UCLA Latin American Center, 1981), Table 104.

habitants by the end of this century, when it will be comparable in size to the U.S. population of about 260 million. Argentina, Cuba, and Chile need not worry about inordinate demands on resources, at least in so far as attributable to population growth. Mexico and Central America offer cause for concern.

Changes in population growth rates have multiple causes. Modern history has shown that urbanization and rising incomes are generally accompanied by reduced birth rates. Important also are social attitudes and availability of contraceptives. The most dramatic case of recent change in demographic growth rate in Latin America is Cuba, which between 1958 and 1980 saw its birth rate decline 46 percent. At 14 births per thousand population, Cuba's rate is comparable to or lower than that of most developed nations. This can be explained by the transformation in social structure and economic conditions, as well as by the scarcity of housing and the cost of child care. The Cuban government has made contraceptives freely available, as well as abortion on demand, although women are strongly advised against using abortion as a means of birth control.

Elsewhere in Latin America the picture on birth control is more complicated. There is much resistance to it—not so much because of Catholic teachings, but because poor people in traditional society tend to see large numbers of children as a positive benefit. High infant mortality rates induce parents to have lots of babies so that some, at least, will survive. And children not only count as mouths to feed; at an early age they can begin to work, in fields or elsewhere, and contribute to the family income. And parents have generally looked forward to being supported in their old age by their children. Within this traditional outlook a reluctance to use contraceptives—even if they are available— is entirely reasonable.

The problem, moreover, does not merely involve the number of births in coming years. A critical concern must deal with young people who are already here and who will be seeking jobs within the predictable future. In high-growth countries such as Mexico nearly half the population is under the age of 15. Within the next two decades, therefore, the pressure for employment will be immense. Demographic trends convert quickly into social realities.

Will the regional economy be able to support this kind of population? Economic development will no doubt continue. There is good reason to expect that Latin America's manufacturing output will steadily expand, perhaps amounting to one-third of Latin America's output by the end of the century, while the relative importance of agriculture and mining will decline. The question is whether economic production will increase more or less rapidly than the population. Here the prospects are unclear.

And capitalist economic growth seldom produces economic equality, especially in the early phases. On the contrary, it often tends to concentrate wealth in small sectors of the population—especially in "dependent" societies, where economic expansion so often takes place within restricted enclaves or "pockets." Though indirectly, the Hudson Institute projections dealt with this issue by classifying social sectors as urban-rural or active-inactive (that is, whether people take active part in the process of economic production). According to this estimate, displayed in Figure 11-9, the rural population is likely to decline from 61 percent in 1950 to only 27 percent by 2000; because of technological advances the rural-active group would be only 6 percent and the rural-inactive would account for 21 percent. By the end of the century Latin America will be overwhelmingly urban, 73 percent. But because of natural growth, migration from the countryside, and the shortage of jobs, the urban-inactive sector may well amount to *nearly half* the total population. This group may remain politically inactive for a while, but the long-run prospects are nonetheless unsettling. The cities may well become seedbeds of discontent.

Moreover, by early 1983 virtually all of Latin America was staggering

FIGURE 11-9 Projected Composition of Latin American Population, to Year 2000

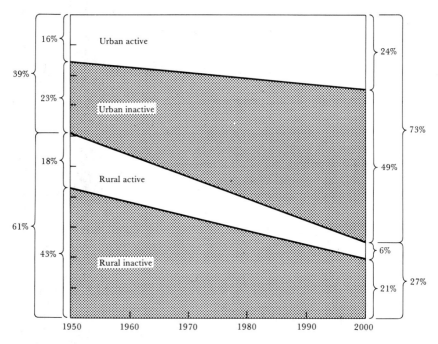

Note: Projection based on census trends as of late 1960s. The terms "active" and "inactive" refer to formal participation in the market economy; members of the "inactive" group are often under- or unemployed, but they take frequent part in informal economic activities.

Source: Hudson Institute, *Prospective International Issues*, vol. IV, *Long-Term Prospects for Latin America*, HI–840–BN/4/1 (N.Y., 1967), p. 15.

under a massive burden of foreign debt payments. Argentina, Mexico, and Brazil had all suspended repayments of principal and were feverishly negotiating more loans. The stakes were high. Avoiding default required deflationary policies bound to produce years of negative or low economic growth rates. That was likely to guarantee, sooner or later, a strongly nationalistic political response. It was ironical that Latin America, so long on the margin of the international scene, should have taken center stage as a chief actor in the melodrama of world capitalism's fight to maintain its own solvency.

Looking Ahead: Political Responses

Economic misery alone does not create revolution. Otherwise Haiti would long ago have become a political tinderbox. And in the 1970s, it was children of the middle and upper classes who joined guerrilla movements in Uruguay and Argentina, not the poorest segments of society.

What is the revolutionary potential of the popular masses in Latin America? In the southern countries—Argentina, Chile, Uruguay—the military has shown its capacity to monopolize power against the opposition of organized labor. Will this hold true for the short run only? Or will it last more than 5 or 10 years?

Argentina's labor movement has shown an extraordinary ability to survive, but, owing to its populist and Peronist orientation, it has never shown much interest in revolution. Its concerns are bread-and-butter issues—wages and working conditions—and it will continue to be a powerful actor on the Argentine political stage. Chile also had a thriving union movement before the 1973 coup and, despite continuous repression since the coup, it is highly likely to re-emerge as a substantial force.

In Brazil the experience has been different. Brazil has been a labor surplus country throughout this century. That has worked against unionization, even in the dynamic center-south region. The Brazilian government has followed a shrewd mixture of repression and co-optation to keep the major unions under control. The years 1979 and 1980 brought a new worker militancy in São Paulo that threatened this hegemony. But a recession in 1981–82 threw the unions off balance, and nothing suggests that the Brazilian labor movement has reached the degree of class consciousness or organizational experience evident in Argentina and Chile. Yet the Brazilian urban workers have emerged as a major unknown. They are not "revolutionary" as such, but it is unclear how they will tip the economic and political balance in Brazil over the next decade or two.

Mexico, like Brazil, is a labor surplus economy. Urban workers know that if they strike there are plenty of new arrivals from the countryside ready to take their jobs. As in Brazil, the government has been shrewd in using co-optive measures to corrupt the union leadership. Where it has come to confrontation, the Mexican government has not hesitated to repress the workers and imprison their leaders for long periods. Mexico appears to have tighter control over the working class control than does any other major Latin American country. It seems safe to assume that Mexican labor will prove unable to bend history to its will.

None of the major political shifts in Latin America has been directly brought about primarily by workers. They have been able, once mobilized, to throw their weight, as in Argentina. But the working class per se has not been able to seize control of events. It tried in Chile and failed. And in Cuba, the *fidelista* rebellion was carried out completely independently of organized labor, which was dominated by the Communists. The guerrillas were predominantly middle class, with no initial links to the organized working class. To say that organized labor is unlikely to take the initiative in Latin America is not to deny that it will fight for the bread-and-butter rights of its members. It will do so, at great cost to the leadership, as has occurred under the military governments in Argentina, Chile, and Brazil. But this is not the same as revolution.

And the peasantry? The revolutionary potential of rural workers is obviously difficult to measure. It fueled the Mexican Revolution at crucial stages, and it has left its mark on Chile (land invasions in the Frei and Allende presidencies), Bolivia (in the revolution of 1952) and Peru (the guerrilla movement that helped provoke the military revolution of 1968), to mention only a few cases. Could there be a new agrarian rebellion in rural Mexico? There were guerrilla movements in Mexico in the 1970s, but the government suppressed them with only a small army. Could rebellion spread from Central America northward? Could guerrillas in Guatemala export revolution into the bordering Mexican state of Chiapas? This possibility has caused the Mexican military to strengthen greatly its military garrison in Chiapas and other southern outposts.

What about the middle classes? In the 1950s the middle classes were repeatedly "discovered" by U.S. scholars, who solemnly declared that the growing middle class would serve as a ballast to insure a gradual reformist approach to the deep-seated problems of the region. A sizable middle stratum did emerge after World War II, especially in Argentina, Chile, Mexico, and Brazil. In the latter two the middle class was much smaller in proportion to the total population, but that still meant a large number in absolute figures.

The problem with the Latin American middle classes was that they resided in Latin America, not the U.S. or Europe. That meant that their relation to other classes was completely different from the U.S. or Europe. Above them was a rich and powerful upper class, whose life style they often envied. Below was an immense lower class—in Mexico, Brazil, and Chile perhaps 65 or 75 percent, in Argentina 50 percent. In crises the middle classes tended to identify with the upper class, as happened in Chile in 1973, in Brazil in 1964, and in Argentina in 1976. The middle classes apparently became frightened at the prospect of losing income, status, and property.

In calmer times these middle classes could be expected to vote for representative government and reformist leaders, as shown whenever relatively open elections have been held in Brazil since 1964. The tendency is to favor coups in a crisis but elections when the dust clears. This has posed a constant problem for the military officers who carry out the coups. The middle classes will remain important, not least because they produce so many of the technocrats who frame policy in the military-dominated regimes (and in Mexico, which has its own system for recruiting administrators).

What about industrialists? In country after country the business community has proved to be timid and uncertain. Though manufacturing output will increase, Latin American entrepreneurs are so preoccupied with surviving—against the formidable odds of inflation, government regulations, and foreign competition—that they have not proven to be a major political force. In times of crisis they have sided with the military and the middle classes. Businessmen have only rarely played the reformist role of the "progressive national bourgeoisie" envisioned in Marxist theory. Instead, they have faced increasing pressure both from the state sector and from foreign firms. In many cases they have chosen to associate with foreign companies to get capital and technology, thereby undermining a potential role as independent national spokesmen. They are vulnerable and on the defensive, unlikely to take the initiative.

What about the church? This institution bears close watching. In Brazil and Chile and Central America the church has created, among the lay population, an extraordinary new consciousness and mobilization. The momentum lay not with the clergy, but with the congregations. The "theology of liberation" was the church's more dramatic reaction to the "social question" in Latin America. But the subsequent experience of dictatorships, with repression directed especially at the liberal churchmen, exerted a profound effect on the politically active classes in Latin America. Here we are dealing with an unknown. It will depend on how the new religious awareness is transferred into political terms.

The military is another key group. Today it is difficult to remember the enthusiasm generated by the "progressive" Peruvian military after the Peruvian coup of 1968. Given the experience of the 1970s, the Latin American military now present themselves as the repressive praetorians protecting the privileged in all too many countries. Even if the Brazilian generals honor their commitment to "open" the Brazilian political system, the Latin American armed forces have in general served to arrest socioeconomic reform. It is difficult, if not impossible, to discern the progressive tendencies of the Latin American military in the early 1980s.

So the prospects for revolution are not encouraging. Guerrilla movements have been defeated in Argentina, Mexico, Chile, Brazil, Peru, Venezuela, and Uruguay, to name only the more obvious. In general, the chances for revolution will depend on two factors: the capacity for workers and/or peasants to create a class-based popular coalition, and the power of the opposition. Outside of Central America, where the ruling oligarchies have begun to reveal weaknesses, the conditions do not seem very ripe. But the best way to test this prognosis is to think through the possible combinations and coalitions of the social actors that have been discussed one by one in this section.

Latin America: Capitalist or Socialist?

Since the early 1950s the Latin Americans have found themselves the target of ideological competition between the U.S. and the Soviets. When Cuba went Marxist-Leninist in 1960–61, it gave the Soviets a potential "showcase" for socialism in the Americas. The U.S. responded with its own offensive in Latin America, promoting both reform-oriented economic growth and counter-insurgency. We have traced the effects of these policies and it is now time to speculate about the future course of this competition.

In nineteenth century Europe the Marxist-oriented political movements argued passionately over the proper tactics for achieving a socialist society. A radical wing urged revolutionary methods, including violence when necessary. The capitalists and their apologists would never be willing to give up a society from which they profited so handsomely, argued the radical Marxists. Moderates maintained that it was possible to move steadily toward socialism by working within the legal structure, especially where there was representative government.

This argument deeply split the European left, creating a division between the revolutionaries and the democratic socialists. Out of the latter came such important political parties as the German Social Democrats, the British Labor Party, and the French Socialist Party. The revolutionaries remained fragmented until the Russian Revolution in 1917 gave a new focus. The victorious Bolsheviks created an international command structure to coordinate (and, as it soon turned out, to dominate) newly formed communist parties around the world. Most of the revolutionaries entered the communist parties, although important dissident factions survived, such as the Trotskyists.

This argument over the revolutionary versus the "peaceful" path to socialism carried over to Latin America. Interestingly, the communist parties of Latin America up to 1959 promoted the "peaceful" path in domestic politics, with two exceptions: El Salvador in 1932 and Brazil in 1935. The communist legacy in Latin America is therefore not revolutionary. Indeed, in many countries young radicals in the post-1945 era began to move leftward after rebelling against the bureaucratized and conservative local communist party.

How did revolutionary socialism come to the Americas? Through a middle-class lawyer, Fidel Castro, who organized an armed revolt of a kind Latin America knew well. Once in power Fidel became a passionate advocate of the revolutionary path. Indeed, it was the fear of his example that propelled the U.S. to take its countermeasures in Latin America.

Is Cuba the future of Latin America? No doubt nationalists and socialist revolutionaries in Latin America will continue to find inspiration in Cuba's evident success at achieving high minimum standards for its population in health care, education, and job availability. They will also probably continue to admire Fidel's stand against the U.S., which has never stopped harassing the Cuban government.

But other aspects of the Cuban socialist experiment make it less attractive. Most obvious is the huge Soviet subsidy (running at $3 billion a year in 1979) which in per capita terms is one of the largest in the world. The Soviets continue such an outlay because of Cuba's symbolic importance—"only 90 miles away" from the U.S. This subsidy obviously has costs for Cuba, such as the need to follow Soviet direction on both domestic economic policies and foreign policy. So while Fidel's Cuba can be said to have survived the deadly hostility of the U.S., it has not attained the independence which Latin American revolutionaries passionately desire. This point gains weight when we remember that the Soviets have generally been very cautious about revolution elsewhere in Latin America. By the same token, Cuba's close identification with the Soviets tends to reduce its attraction for Latin American revolutionaries.

This is not to say that the Cubans will lack influence in Latin America. The *fidelista* government will undoubtedly help armed revolutionaries elsewhere in the Americas through money or arms or both. But such aid is likely to be discrete and subordinate to overall Cuban (and Soviet) foreign policy goals.

The only successful armed revolution since Cuba has been in Nicaragua in 1979. There the guerrillas had a vital asset: Anastasio Somoza's dictatorship had begun to lose support from even the wealthiest sector. The rich were disillusioned and embittered at the dictator's greed in taking even more than "his share" from the funds and supplies sent from abroad after the devastating earthquake of 1972. The armed rebels, among whom the *Sandinista* National Liberation Front was the most effective, were thus able to count on wide support.

Are other countries in Latin America likely to produce socialist governments soon? Central America seems the most probable area—with El Salvador's well-based guerrilla movements. Divisions within the oligarchy of wealthy families would accelerate a rebel victory. If such serious splits do not develop, then a drawn-out struggle would be one of the most important tests of revolutionary potential in Latin America.

Is socialism likely by the "peaceful" road? In 1970 Chile seemed to present that option. Yet the experiment was not allowed to run the six years of Allende's presidential term. After only 33 months the military snuffed out the left coalition's chaotic government in a brutal coup. Was that the end of parliamentary socialism in Latin America? Many said so. After all, Chile seemed to be a European-style nation where civilian power predominated and the rule of law was deeply rooted. Here, if anywhere, the "peaceful road" seemed possible. True, Allende's coalition had won only 36 percent of the popular vote in the presidential election, and the opposition controlled the Congress, but hopes were high in 1970. Virtually no one then predicted the coup that came in 1973. Its practical effect was to cast a dark cloud over the "peaceful road."

Two major countries where the left has recently been able to organize relatively freely are Mexico and Brazil. The Mexican prospect for socialism remains bleak because of the overwhelming effectiveness of the government political machine—not just the PRI, but the apparatus of the huge state sector. In Brazil the left also has to work against a political machine adept at co-optation and division. In Brazil, as in Mexico, the established political elite has skillfully argued against "divisive" ideological positions. This has proved especially effective among the middle classes, always susceptible to patriotic appeals of this kind.

The Prospects for Capitalism

Latin America has no capitalist counterpart to Cuba. The reason is to be found in the economic history of the region. In the late eighteenth century elements of free-market capitalism were emerging in Latin America. In the nineteenth century a fraction of the elites sought to eliminate the vestiges of colonial privilege and introduce a market-oriented economy, geared to foreign trade. The more radical of these reformers wanted to reduce all social relationships to a market definition. Since this was easiest in countries without Indians, it was far simpler in Argentina than in Mexico. The attempt to accelerate that process helped provoke the rural rebellions in the Mexican Revolution.

This transition to capitalism has dominated Latin America in our century. It was sharply modified after the 1930s, as state intervention in the economies increased. In every major country the central government used such instruments as state oil companies, government marketing institutes, and special loan programs. The state role was so great by the early 1970s that one could no longer speak of textbook capitalism in Latin America, but of a *hybrid* capitalism. It had three sources of capital: private national, state, and foreign (usually multinational). When foreign capital came in to supplement national capital, national elites saw a danger that foreigners would gain too much economic power. So the state gained an increasing share of responsibility. The result is a market economy with many more artificial constraints than the nineteenth century liberals would have ever envisioned.

This hybrid capitalism aroused the fury of twentieth century economic liberals. Throughout Latin America, but especially in the south, economists and businessmen of extreme laissez-faire views had long fought against the growing state role. Thanks to military coups in Argentina in 1976 and Chile in 1973, they won control of economic policymaking. They sought to reduce drastically the government sector by selling off state enterprises and opening the national market by slashing tariffs and regulations.

Does this return to a more pure capitalism have a future in Latin America? As in the case of socialism, the odds are against it. These policymakers have held power thanks only to repressive military regimes. The fate of the authoritarian military regimes, in turn, depends very much on the balance in the world ideological struggle. Since these regimes fly in the face of long traditions of economic nationalism and state intervention, their staying power may be doubted. No less important, the liberal economic policies must work by their own definition— yet they ran into deep trouble in Argentina and Chile in 1982, and their prospects look poor elsewhere.

The most likely path for capitalist regimes is closer to the Mexican or Brazilian model, both hybrid capitalist systems. They have two major vulnerabilities. One is inequality of income and wealth. Both Mexico and Brazil have maintained high economic growth for the last four decades, yet their income inequality has also increased. This can be politically destabilizing insofar as it is seen as being unjust by the middle sectors, which tend to produce most revolutionaries.

A second vulnerability is its uncertain ability to maintain development. The legitimacy of mixed capitalism flows from its capacity to generate growth. If that is appreciably interrupted, the elite may question the capitalist system itself. A likely cause for such a slowdown would be a world slump severe enough to rock the peripheral economies. One result of the 1929 crash was a much reduced legitimacy for political and economic liberalism. Theoretically, at least, that could occur again.

To minimize these risks, hybrid capitalism itself may pursue various paths. One key factor depends on the relative weight of private, national, state, and multinational participation. Another concerns the *nature* of the public sector role. At one extreme, the state could operate in much the same manner as a private entrepreneur (as has already occurred); at the other, it could nationalize specific sectors of the economy and run them on a non-profit basis. Still another option would be to foster joint worker-manager ventures and large-scale "profit-sharing" schemes. In summary, we anticipate the further spread of hybrid capitalism in Latin America, but we suspect that it may produce considerable latitude in the range of social policy. It may also coexist with a corresponding variety of political regimes.

What Will Happen to the Non-European Cultures in Latin America?

Few can study Latin America without becoming fascinated with its kaleidoscopic mixture of races and peoples. A question soon arises: Will the unusual, the different, the exotic, be homogenized into national amalgams that lack the originality of the Indian, African, or provincial cultures? What about the Mexican Indians of Chiapas, or the Indians of the Peruvian altiplano, or the blacks of Brazil's Bahia? Will they disappear?

It is not easy to argue that they will survive. Latin America is hardly immune from the process of social homogenization so familiar in the industrial world. Television and radio have eroded regional and provincial barriers and concentrated attention on "national" models, as in the highly popular television soap operas (*telenovelas*). There is also a relentless economic pressure on the ethnic holdouts to learn the national language and adopt national cultural ways. In Mexico, for example, the proportion of the population still speaking only an Indian language had dropped to 2 percent by the early 1970s. Incorporating these Indians into the Spanish-speaking population has been a prime goal for Mexican governments. In the process, however, ethnic traditions have been lost. Could it be otherwise? The Mexican government, more than any other in Latin America, has attempted to preserve indigenous traditions (partly to earn tourist dollars, since "native" customs are an attraction). There has also been a genuine desire to preserve a measure of Mexico's unique pre-Hispanic culture. The pursuit of social development, however, tends to work against these goals.

In Brazil the most important non-European tradition has been African. Indeed, African slaves so penetrated every region of Brazil that its modern culture is indelibly stamped with the African presence. Can it survive the relentless process of national cultural assimilation? It seems to persist as an underground influence, especially in religion. The context is Brazil's multi-level religious world. On top is the Roman Catholic Church, official in every respect. Underneath lie the worlds of *umbanda,* spiritism, and Afro-Brazilian sects such as *candomblé* and *macumba*. In these counter-establishment religions the African influence is alive and vital. In the case of Brazil, at least, the African element has so permeated the national culture that its survival, if in an assimilated mode, seems assured.

The only areas where Indian cultures seem likely to survive for long are in the Andes, southern Mexico and Guatemala, where Indian populations appear sufficiently concentrated to help preserve traditional social identities. In general, however, urbanization in Latin America is engulfing or liquidating the rural and the provincial. The most likely outcome is that these nations will all emerge with primarily European cultures, with scattered remnants of the indigenous and African influence. This seems no more surprising than the annihilation of American Indian culture in the U.S. or the relentless obliteration of regional culture in North America. In the last analysis, few elites inside or outside Latin America set store by the preservation of African or Indian culture. And where does it rank in the ratings of the World Health Organization or the International Monetary Fund? The picturesque may interest tourists, but it becomes an impediment to reducing illiteracy or infant mortality. In the modern world, capitalist or socialist, cultural heterogeneity seems to count for little.

The Potential for Regional Conflict

Latin America has not seen frequent wars in the twentieth century, although some long-standing conflicts have remained alive. Among the most important are the Falklands/Malvinas dispute between Argentina and Britain, the Argentina-Chile clash over the Beagle straits, the Peru-Chile tension in 1979–82 over the lands taken by Chile in the War of the Pacific, and the Venezuela-Guyana boundary conflict. The potential for armed conflict is probably increased by a rise in arms purchases by Latin America, which tripled between 1969 and 1978. A key question must be whether any of these Latin American countries is likely to have the atomic bomb in the near future.

Argentina has the most advanced nuclear physics capacity. Although such matters are shrouded in secrecy, by the middle to late 1980s the Argentines may well have produced their own atomic bomb. Argentina's humiliating defeat by Britain in the Falklands/Malvinas war certainly gave her a new motivation. The Brazilians are next closest, and the threat of an Argentine bomb would probably push them to produce one also. Will this make conflict in the Río de la Plata basin more likely, especially in view of the long-standing Argentine-Brazilian politics-military rivalry? The enormity of atomic weapons undoubtedly creates inhibitions about their use. On the other hand, desperate governments become far more dangerous when they possess weapons of mass destruction. Over the course of the near future, however, it seems unlikely that atomic weapons in South America will lead to any radical change in the international relationships.

What about possible conflict on the U.S.-Mexican border? Can the huge flow of undocumented migrants continue without a U.S. reaction? This volatile question must be seen in the context of U.S. policies toward the entire Caribbean basin. Here the question is the degree to which the U.S. is willing to continue serving as the escape valve for those who flee from poverty and/or policital repression. The key variable will be the attitude of the U.S. public. Will hard economic times, which brought increased protectionism in U.S. trade policy, lead to tougher curbs on undocumented migrants? There are some signs of this, and U.S. dependence on Mexican oil could make it into a volatile issue.

What about Central America? It had become a center for ideological conflict in the early 1980s. Polarization in Nicaragua and El Salvador seemed to be self-reinforcing. How far would the U.S. go in sponsoring an overthrow of the *sandinista* regime in Nicaragua? How far would Nicaragua or Cuba go in trying to prevent a defeat of the guerrillas by the U.S.-financed government of El Salvador? Not least important was the apparent brake on the Reagan administration from a wary Congress and a suspicious U.S. opinion.

Finally, what about potential conflict between the U.S. and Cuba? The U.S.-U.S.S.R. agreement ending the 1962 missile crisis included a U.S. pledge not to invade Cuba. Some in the Reagan administration have wanted to rescind that agreement. The Cuban regime has been very much aware of such thinking in the U.S. and sought to reassure Washington that it was not exporting revolution. The Cuban-U.S. face-off remains the most dangerous flashpoint in Latin America, because it immediately involves both superpowers. Both have shown caution in the 1970s. Will they do so in the 1980s and 1990s?

Latin America's Contribution to the World

Given its political and economic constraints, what is Latin America likely to contribute to the human experience? It has already made its mark in literature. Gabriel García Márquez, Carlos Fuentes, Jorge Luis Borges, Jorge Amado—the "boom" in Latin American literature has led to its translation into major European languages. Mass paperback editions have facilitated wide distribution. Music is another artistic realm of Latin American excellence. Afro-Brazilian and Afro-Cuban music have penetrated North American popular music, giving an unmistakable style and rhythm.

Latin Americans have been conspicuous for their impressive contributions in athletics. In soccer, the most universally played sport, Brazil is the only country to have won the world cup three times. Argentina won the cup in 1978. Even small Latin American countries such as Uruguay have taken home the world cup. European soccer clubs bid into the millions of dollars to lure Latin American stars.

Theology and church organization have seen impressive innovation in Latin America. The highly controversial "theology of liberation" is largely a Latin American phenomenon—an attempt by Latin American theologians to reconcile their religious tradition with the political and economic pressures around them. No less important are the rapidly burgeoning laymen's groups ("ecclesiastical base communities") which represent a reawakening in Latin American nations that had long seemed sunk into religious apathy. It is worth remembering that the Church, both through its clergy and its laymen, played a key role in Brazil's redemocratization in the 1970s. In Chile the church has also served as a rallying point for resistance to a repressive military regime. This oppositionist role has brought the Church back onto center stage, and reminded democrats everywhere that one of Latin American society's most traditional institutions can still be highly relevant in the modern world.

Latin America has also made a great contribution in the field of race relations. Notwithstanding persistent cruelty to non-Europeans, Latin America produced societies in which mixed bloods have enjoyed great mobility. The *mestizos* of Mexico, Central America, and the Andean region represent a new social category born out of the mixture of European and Indian. Although racism still exists in many guises, mobility has been remarkable. The same can be said for the mulatto in Brazil, Cuba, Colombia, and other Caribbean nations. To find a contrast one need only look to North America. Of course prejudice and discrimination still occur in Latin America, especially against the "pure blood" Indians and very dark-skinned people in general. Yet the relative social harmony is notable, especially in light of the miserable record left by the Europeans in so many parts of today's Third World.

In the future, as in past centuries, the fate of Latin America will depend largely on its relationship to the centers of international power. The region will continue to cope with the implications of subordination and dependency. Meanwhile outsiders will continue to be startled and fascinated by what García Márquez called "the unearthly tidings of Latin America, that boundless realm of haunted men and historic women, whose unending obstinacy blurs into legend."

STATISTICAL APPENDIX

TABLE 12-1   Selected Social Indicators

	Population Size (millions)		Annual Population Growth Rate (%)		Urbanization (%)[a]		Per Capita Income[b]
	1900	*1980*	*1900–10*	*1970–81*	*1900*	*1970*	*1980*
Argentina	4.6	27.0	4.3	1.5	24.9	66.3	$2,331
Brazil	18.0	126.4	2.2	2.5	8.7	39.5	1,523
Chile	3.0	11.5	1.2	1.6	19.9	60.6	1,950
Cuba	1.6	10.6	1.0	1.3[c]	25.0	43.4	840
Mexico	13.6	70.0	1.0	3.4	9.2	35.2	1,800
Peru	3.0	17.7	3.0	2.1	6.0	40.3	655
Central America:							
Costa Rica	0.3	2.3	1.5	2.8	8.5	27.0	1,512
El Salvador	0.8	4.8	2.1	3.0	6.0	20.5	639
Guatemala	0.9	7.1	2.1	2.9	~	16.1	749
Honduras	0.4	3.6	2.8	3.2	~	20.2	528
Nicaragua	0.4	2.7	2.6	2.4	~	31.0	825
Panama	0.3	1.9	2.4	2.4	6.8	39.4	1,116
United States	76.1	221.6	1.9	0.8	25.9	64.0	8,612

[a] Population is communities of 20,000 or more inhabitants, as percentage of national total.
[b] In U.S. dollars of 1980.
[c] Figure for 1970–80.

Sources: *Statistical Abstract of Latin America*, 19, Table 623, and 21, Tables 104, 623, 634; Inter-American Development Bank, *Economic and Social Progress in Latin America: The External Sector* (1982), p. 346; World Bank, *World Development Report 1982* (New York: Oxford University Press, 1982), Table 17, pp. 142–143; *Boston Globe*, 12 January 1983.

HEADS OF STATE

Argentina

1861	Bartolomé Mitre
1865	Marcos Paz
1868	Bartolomé Mitre, January 2–October 12, 1868
	Domingo F. Sarmiento, October 12, 1868–October 12, 1874
1874	Nicolas Avellaneda
1880	Julio Argentino Roca
1886	Miguel Juárez Celman
1890	Carlos Pellegrini
1892	Luis Sáenz Peña
1895	José E. Uriburu
1898	Julio Argentino Roca
1904	Manuel Quintana
1906	José Figueroa Alcorta
1910	Roque Sáenz Peña
1913	Victorino de la Plaza
1916	Hipólito Irigoyen
1922	Marcelo Torcuato de Alvear
1928	Hipólito Irigoyen
1930	José Félix Uriburu
1932	Augustín P. Justo
1938	Roberto M. Ortiz
1940	Ramón S. Castillo
1943	Arturo Rawson, June 5–7
	Pedro P. Ramírez, June 7–March 9, 1944
1944	Edelmiro J. Farrell
1946	Juan Domingo Perón
1955	Eduardo Lonardi, September 23–November 13
	Pedr Eugenio Aramburu, November 13–May 1, 1958
1958	Arturo Frondizi
1962	José María Guido
1963	Arturo Illía
1966	Juan Carlos Onganía
1970	Roberto Marcelo Levingston
1971	Alejandro A. Lanusse
1973	Hector Cámpora, May 27–July 13
	Juan Domingo Perón, October 12–July 1, 1974
1974	María Estela (Isabel) Martínez Perón
1976	Jorge Rafael Videla
1981	Roberto Viola, March 29–December 22
	Leopoldo Fortunato Galtieri, December 22–June 17, 1982
1982	Reynaldo Benito Antonio Bignone

Brazil

1831	Dom Pedro II
1889	Manoel Deodoro da Fonseca
1891	Floriano Peixoto
1894	Prudente de Morais Barros
1898	Manoel Ferraz de Campos Salles
1902	Francisco de Paula Rodrigues Alves
1906	Affonso Augusto Moreira Penna
1909	Nilo Peçanha
1910	Hermes da Fonseca
1914	Wenceslau Braz Pereira Gomes
1918	Délfim Moreira da Costa Ribeiro
1919	Epitácio da Silva Pessòa
1922	Artur da Silva Bernardes

1926	Washington Luís Pereira de Sousa
1930	Julio Prestes, October 24–November 4
	Getúlio Dornelles Vargas, November 4–October 31, 1945
1945	José Linhares
1946	Eurico Gaspar Dutra
1951	Getúlio Vargas
1954	João Café Filho
1955	Carlos Luz, November 8–11
	Nereu Ramos, November 11–January 31, 1956
1956	Juscelino Kubitschek
1961	Jânio Quadros, January 31–August 25

	Ranieri Mazzilli, August 25–September 8
	João Goulart, September 8–April 2, 1964
1964	Ranieri Mazzilli, April 2–15
	Humberto de Alencar Castello Branco, April 15–March 15, 1967
1967	Arthur da Costa e Silva
1969	Military junta (Augusto Hamann Rademaker Gruenewald) August 31–October 25
	Emílio Garrastazu Medici, October 30–March 15, 1974
1974	Ernesto Geisel
1979	João Baptista Figueiredo

Chile

1876	Aníbal Pinto
1881	Domingo Santa María
1886	José Manuel Balmaceda
1891	Jorge Montt
1896	Federico Errázuriz
1901	Germán Riesco Errázuriz
1905	Rafael Rayas
1906	Pedro Montt
1910	Elías Fernández Albano, August 16–September 6
	Emiliano Figueroa, September 6–September 18, 1911
1911	Ramón Barros Luco
1915	José Luis Sanfuentes
1920	Luis Barros Borgoño, June 25–December 23
	Arturo Alessandri, December 23, 1920–September 8, 1924
1924	Military junta headed by Gen. Luis Altamirano
1925	Military junta led by Carlos Ibáñez del Campo, January 23–March 21, 1925
	Arturo Alessandri, March 21–October 1, 1925
	Luis Barros Borgoño, October 1, December 1925
	Emiliano Figueroa Larraín, December 1925–May 4, 1927
1927	Carlos Ibáñez del Campo
1931	Pedro Opazo Letelier, July 26–27, 1931

	Juan Esteban Montero Rodríguez, July 27–August 18, 1931
	Manuel Trucco Franzani, August 18–November 15, 1931
	Juan Esteban Montero Rodríguez, November 15, 1931–June 4, 1932
1932	Arturo Puga, June 4–12, 1932
	Marmaduque Grove, June 12–16, 1932
	Carlos Dávila Espinoza, June 17–September 13, 1932
	Bartolomé Blanche Espejo, September 13–October 2, 1932
1932	Abraham Oyanedel, October 2–December 24, 1932
	Arturo Alessandri Palma, December 24, 1932–December 24, 1938
1938	Pedro Aguirre Cerda
1941	Geronimo Méndez Arancibia
1942	Juan Antonio Ríos Morales
1946	Alfredo Duhalde Vázquez, June 27–October 17, 1946
	Juan A. Irabarren, October 17–November 3, 1946
	Gabriel González Videla, November 3–1946-November 3, 1952
1952	Carlos Ibáñez del Campo
1958	Jorge Alessandri Rodríguez
1964	Eduardo Frei Montalva
1970	Salvador Allende Gossens
1973	Augusto Pinochet Ugarte

Costa Rica

1876	Tomás Guardia
1882	Próspero Fernández
1885	Bernardo Soto y Alfaro
1889	Durán

1890	José Joaquím Rodríguez
1894	Rafael Iglesias Castro
1902	Ascensión Esquivel Ibarra
1906	Cleto González Víquez

1910	Ricardo Jiménez Oreamuno
1912	Cleto González Víquez
1914	Alfredo González Flores
1917	Federico Tinoco Granados
1919	Julio Acosta García, May 7–August 13
	Juan Bautista Quirós, August 13–May 8, 1920
1920	Julio Acosta García
1924	Ricardo Jiménez Oreamuno
1928	Cleto González Víquez
1932	Ricardo Jiménez Oreamuno
1936	León Cortés Castro
1940	Rafael Angel Calderón Guardia
1944	Teodoro Picardo Michalski

1948	Santos León Herrera, April 19–May 8, 1948
	José Figueres, May 8, 1948–November 8, 1949
1949	Otilio Ulate Blanco
1952	Alberto Oreamuno Flores
1953	José Figueres
1958	Mario Echandi Jiménez
1962	Francisco José Orlich
1966	José Joaquín Trejos Fernández
1970	José Fugueres
1974	Daniel Oduber
1978	Rodrigo Carazao
1982	Luis Alberto Monge Alvarez

Cuba

1899	Gen. John R Brooke, January 1–December 23 } Gen. Leonard Wood, December 23–May 20, 1902 } U.S. Occupation
1902	Tomás Estrada Palma
1906	William Howard Taft, September 29–October 13 } Charles Edward Magoon, October 13–January 28, 1909 } U.S. Occupation
1909	José Miguel Gómez
1913	Mario García Menocal
1921	Alfredo Zayas
1925	Gerardo Machado Morales
1933	Carlos Manuel de Céspedes, August 12–September 5
	Council of Five, September 5–September 10
	Ramón Grau San Martín, September 10–January 15, 1934
1934	Carlos Hevía, January 15–18
	Manuel Márquez Sterling, January 18
	Carlos Mendieta Montefur, January 18–December 11, 1935
1935	José A. Barnet y Vinageras

1936	Miguel Mariano Gómez Arias, May 20–December 24
	Federico Laredo Bru, December 24–October 10, 1940
1940	Fulgencio Batista y Zaldívar
1944	Ramón Grau San Martín
1948	Carlos Prío Socarrás
1952	Fulgencio Batista y Zaldívar
1959	Manuel Urrutia Lleo, January 2–July 17 [Fidel Castro de facto head from here on]
	Osvaldo Dórticos Torrado, July 17–December 3, 1976
1976	Fidel Castro Ruz becomes President of Council of States

El Salvador

1876	Rafael Zaldívar y Lazo
1885	Francisco Menéndez
1890	Carlos Ezeta
1894	Rafael Gutiérrez
1898	Tomás Regalado
1903	Pedro José Escalón
1907	Fernando Figueroa
1911	Manuel Enrique Araújo
1913	Carlos Meléndez
1914	Alfonso Quiñones Molina
1915	Carlos Meléndez
1919	Jorge Meléndez
1923	Alfonso Quiñones Molina
1927	Pío Romero Bosque
1931	Arturo Araujo, March 1–December 4, 1931

	Maximiliano Hernández Martínez, December 4, 1931–August 29, 1934
1934	Andrés Ignacio Menéndez
1935	Maximiliano Hernández Martínez
1944	Andrés Ignacio Menéndez, May 9–October 21, 1944
	Osmín Aguirre y Salinas, October 21, 1944–March 1, 1945
1945	Salvador Castañeda Castro
1948	Manuel de J. Córdova
1949	Oscar Osorio, January 4–October 22, 1949
	Oscar Bolaños, October 22, 1949–September 14, 1950
1950	Oscar Osorio

1956 José María Lemus
1960 Military junta (Miguel Ángel Cas-
      tillo)
1961 New military junta (Aníbal Por-
      tillo)
1962 Eusebio Rodolfo Cordón, January
      25–July 1
      Julio Adalberto Rivera, July 1–
      July 1, 1967

1967 Fidel Sánchez Hernández
1972 Arturo Armando Molina
1977 Carlos Humberto Romero
1979 Jaime Abdul Guitíerrez, Adolfo
      Arnoldo Majano & junta
1980 José Napoleón Duarte
1982 Alvaro Alfredo Magana (provi-
      sional president)

Guatemala

1873 Justo Rufino Barrios
1885 Alejandro Sinibaldi, April 2–15
      Manuel Lisandro Barillas, April
      15–March 15, 1892
1892 José María Reina Barrios
1898 Manuel Estrada Cabrera
1920 Carlos Herrera
1922 José María Orellana
1926 Lázaro Chacón
1930 Baudillo Palma, December 13–16
      Manuel Orellana C., December
      16–31
      José María Reyna Andrade, De-
      cember 31–February 14, 1931
1931 Jorge Ubico
1944 Military junta (Federico Ponce
      Vaidez), July 1–October 21
      Jacobó Arbenz Guzmán, Decem-
      ber 12–March 1, 1945

1945 Juan José Arevalo
1951 Jacobó Arbenz Guzmán
1954 Carlos Díaz, June 27–29
      Elfego J. Monzón, June 29–July 8
      Carlos Castillo Armas, July 8–July
      26, 1957
1957 Luis Arturo González López, July
      27–October 25
      Guillermo Flores Avendaño, Oc-
      tober 28–March 2, 1958
1958 Miguel Ydígoras Fuentes
1963 Enrique Peralta Azurdia
1966 Julio César Méndez Montenegro
1970 Carlos Arana Osorio
1974 Kjeli E. Laugerud García
1978 Fernando Romeo Lucas García
1982 Efrain Ríos Montt
1983 Oscar Humberto Mejía Victores

Honduras

1876 Marcos Aurelio Soto
1883 Luis Bográn
1891 Pariano Leiva
1893 Domingo Vázquez
1894 Policarpo Bonilla
1899 Terencio Sierra
1903 Manuel Bonilla
1907 Miguel R. Dávila
1911 Francisco Beltran
1912 Manuel Bonilla
1913 Francisco Bertrand
1915 Alberto Membreño
1916 Francisco Bertrand
1920 Rafael López Gutiérrez
1924 Fausto Dávila, March 27–31
      Vincente Tosta, April 1–February
      2, 1925

1925 Miguel Paz Barahona
1929 Vicente Mejía Colindres
1933 Tiburcio Carías Andino
1949 Juan Manuel Gálvez
1956 Roque I. Rodríguez
1957 Ramón Villeda Morales
1963 Osvaldo López Arellano
1971 Ramón Ernesto Cruz
1972 Oswaldo López Arellano
1975 Juan Alberto Melgar Castro
1978 Policarpio Paz García & Junta
1982 Dr. Roberto Suazo Córdova

Mexico

1876 Porfirio Díaz
1880 Manuel González

1884 Porfirio Díaz
1911 Francisco León de la Barra, May

25–November 6, 1911
Francisco Madero, November 6, 1911–February 18, 1913
1913 Victoriano Huerta
1914 Venustiano Carranza
1920 Adolfo de la Huerta, May 21–December 1, 1920
Alvaro Obregón, December 1, 1920–December 1, 1924
1924 Plutarco Elías Calles
1928 Emilio Portes Gil

1930 Pascual Ortiz Rubio
1932 Abelardo Rodríguez
1934 Lázaro Cárdenas
1940 Manuel Avila Camacho
1946 Miguel Alemán
1952 Adolfo Ruiz Cortines
1958 Adolfo López Mateos
1964 Gustavo Díaz Ordaz
1970 Luis Echeverría Alvarez
1976 José López Portillo
1982 Miguel de la Madrid Hurtado

Nicaragua

1879 Joaquín Zavala
1883 Adán Cárdenas
1887 Evaristo Carazo
1889 Roberto Sacaza
1893 Innere Wirren
1894 José Santos Zelaya
1909 José Madriz
1910 José Dolores Estrada
1911 Juan José Estrada, January 1–May 9
Adolfo Díaz, May 9–December 31, 1916
1917 Emiliano Chamorro Vargas
1919 Diego Manuel Chamorro
1923 Bartolomeo Martínez
1925 Carlos Solórzano
1926 Emiliano Chamorro Vargas, January 15–November 11
Adolfo Díaz, November 11–January 1, 1929
1929 José María Moncada

1933 Juan Bautista Sacasa
1936 Carlos Brenes Jarquín
1937 Anastasio Somoza ("Tacho")
1947 Leonardo Argüello, May 1–26, 1947
Benjamín Lacaya Sacasa, May 26–August 15, 1947
Victor Román y Reyes, August 14, 1947–May 6, 1950
1950 Anastasio Somoza ("Tacho")
1956 Luis Somoza Debayle
1963 René Schick Gutiérrez
1966 Lorenzo Guerrero Gutiérrez
1967 Anastasio Somoza Debayle ("Tachito")
1972 Governing junta for Somoza family
1974 Anastasio Somoza Debayle ("Tachito")
1979 Francisco Urcuyo junta: Daniel Ortega and others

Panama

1904 Manuel Amador Guerrero
1908 José Domingo de Obaldia
1910 Carlos Antonio Mendoza, March 1–October 1
Federico Boyd, October 1–October 4
Pablo Arosemena, October 4–February 2, 1912
1912 Rodolfo Chiari, February 2–March 7
Pablo Arosemena, March 7–October 1
Belisario Porras, October 1–October 1, 1916
1916 Ramón Maximiliano Valdés
1918 Ciro Luis Urriola, June 3–October 1
Pedro Antonio Díaz, October 1–12

Belisario Porras, October 12–January 30, 1920
1920 Ernesto Tisdel Lefevere, January 30–October 1
Belisario Porras, October 1–October 1, 1924
1924 Rodolfo Chiari
1928 Florencio Harmodio Arosemena
1931 Harmodio Arias, January 2–16
Ricardo J. Alfaro, January 16, 1931–October 1, 1932
1932 Harmodio Arias
1936 Juan Demóstenes Arosemena
1939 Agusto S. Boyd
1940 Arnulfo Arias
1941 Ernesto Jaén Guardia, October 9, 1941
Ricardo Adolfo de la Guardia, October 9, 1941–June 15, 1945

1945 Enrique Adolfo Jiménez
1948 Domingo Díaz Arosemena
1949 Daniel Chanis, July 28–November 20
       Roberto Chiari, November 20–25
       Arnulfo Arias, November 24, 1949–May 10, 1951
1951 Alcibíades Arosemena
1952 José Antonio Remón Cantera
1955 José Ramón Guizado, January 3–15

Ricardo M. Arias Espinosa, January 15–October 1, 1956
1956 Ernesto de la Guardia, Jr.
1960 Roberto F. Chiari
1964 Marco Aurelio Robles
1968 Arnulfo Arias Madrid, October 1–October 11
       Omar Torrijos, October 11–September, 1980
1980 Ricardo de la Espriella

Peru

1886 Andrés Avelino Cáceres
1890 Remigio Morales Bermúdez
1894 J. Borgoño, May 1–August 10
       Andrés Avelino Cárceres August 10–March 19, 1895
1895 Manuel Candamo, March 21–September 8
       Nicolás Pierola, September 8–September 8, 1899
1899 Eduardo López de Romaña
1903 Manuel Candamo
1904 Serapio Calderón, May 7–September 24
       José Pardo y Barreda, September 24–September 24, 1908
1908 Augusto B. Leguía
1912 Guillermo E. Billinghurst
1914 Oscar Benavides
1915 José Pardo
1919 Augusto B. Leguía
1930 Manuel Ponce, August 25–27, 1930
       Luis M. Sánchez Cerro, August 27, 1930–March 1, 1931
1931 Ricardo Leoncio Elías, March 1–5, 1931
       Gustavo A. Jiménez, March 5–11, 1931

David Sámanez Ocampo, March 11–December 8, 1931
       Luis M. Sánchez Cerro, December 8, 1931–April 30, 1933
1933 Oscar Benavides
1939 Manuel Prado y Ugarteche
1945 José Luis Bustamante y Rivero
1948 Zenón Noriega, October 29–30, 1948
       Manuel A. Odría, October 31, 1948–June 1, 1950
1950 Zenón Noriega, June 1–July 28, 1950
       Manuel A. Odría, July 28, 1950–July 28, 1956
1956 Manuel Prado y Ugarteche
1962 Military junta led by Ricardo Pérez Godoy
1963 Nicolas Lindey López, March 3–July 28
       Fernando Belaúnde Terry, July 28–October 3, 1968
1968 Juan Velasco Alvarado
1975 Francisco Morales Bermúdez
1980 Fernando Belaúnde Terry

SUGGESTIONS FOR FURTHER READING

These reading suggestions are arranged by the chapter sequence in the text, which necessarily leads to overlap in coverage. Some suggestions listed for the country (and Central American) chapters are also relevant for the Prologue, Chapters I, II, X, and the Epilogue. Readers interested in a specific country within the context of these chapters should look also at the suggestions by country chapter.

The following titles were chosen to provide interesting and profitable reading for the novice student of modern Latin America. For that reason books only in English are included. We have avoided unwieldy "definitive" works. Our objective is to suggest books that will actually be read. The listing correlates closely with the themes developed in each chapter of the text. Readers who wish greater detail will find a wealth of leads in most of the suggested books.

Prologue   Why Latin America?

U.S. stereotypes about Latin America as seen in our newspaper and magazine cartoons since the late nineteenth century are laid out in John J. Johnson, *Latin America in Caricature* (Austin: University of Texas Press, 1980). The same author produced the best-known application of modernization theory to Latin America in his *Political Change in Latin America: The Emergence of the Middle Sectors* (Stanford: Stanford University Press, 1958). A cultural approach to Latin American politics is exemplified in Howard J. Wiarda, ed., *Politics and Social Change in Latin America: The Distinct Tradition* (Amherst: University of Massachusetts Press, 1974).

Dependency analysis has spawned much literature and considerable controversy. The classic formulation remains Fernando Henrique Cardoso and Enzo Faletto, *Dependency and Development in Latin America*, trans. Marjory Mattingly Urquidi (Berkeley and Los Angeles: University of California Press, 1979). Useful anthologies include James Cockcroft, André Gunder Frank, and Dale L. Johnson, eds., *Dependence and Underdevelopment: Latin America's Political Economy* (Garden City: Doubleday/Anchor, 1972), which is a collection of thematic essays, and Ronald H. Chilcote and Joel Edelstein, eds., *The Struggle with Depen-*

dency and Beyond (New York: John Wiley, 1974), which includes case studies of Guatemala, Mexico, Argentina, Brazil, Chile, and Cuba. Penetrating critical analyses of both dependency and modernization are included in Heraldo Muñoz, ed., *From Dependency to Development: Strategies to Overcome Underdevelopment and Inequality* (Boulder: Westview Press, 1981).

The essential starting point for understanding the Chicano experience in the U.S. is Rodolfo Acuña, *Occupied America: A History of Chicanos,* 2nd ed. (New York: Harper & Row, 1981). Feelings for the Puerto Rican cultural heritage can be found in such works as María Teresa Babín and Stan Steiner, eds., *Borinquen: An Anthology of Puerto Rican Literature* (New York: Random House, 1974). For more on the "Third World"—both its defining characteristics and its grim reality—see Paul Harrison, *Inside the Third World: The Anatomy of Poverty,* 2nd ed. (Harmondsworth: Penguin, 1981). Economic geographers have much to tell us about man's historic relationship to his Latin American environment, such as Arthur Morris, *Latin America: Economic Development and Regional Differentiation* (London: Hutchinson, 1981).

Chapter One   The Colonial Foundations, 1492–1880s

The literature in English on colonial Latin America has grown so rapidly that any short list is bound to be arbitrary. The best introduction to the pre-European cultures is Friedrich Katz, *The Ancient American Civilizations* (New York: Praeger, 1972). The all-important Iberian skills at navigation, ship design, and weaponry are nicely outlined in J. H. Parry, *The Age of Reconnaissance* (Cleveland: World, 1963). Bernal Díaz del Castillo, one of Cortes's foot soldiers in the conquest of Mexico, wrote a fascinating account "from the bottom up" in *A True History of the Conquest of New Spain,* trans. by A. P. Maudslay (New York: Farrar, Straus & Cudahy, 1956). Too often the "conquest" is seen only from the European viewpoint. An excellent corrective is Miguel Leon-Portilla, ed., *The Broken Spears: The Aztec Account of the Conquest of Mexico,* trans. by Lysander Kemp (Boston: Beacon Press, 1961). A pioneering study of how the native peoples adjusted to European rule while also preserving a sense of community and a capacity to resist exploitation is found in Steve J. Stern, *Peru's Indian Peoples and the Challenge of Spanish Conquest: Huamanga to 1640* (Madison: University of Wisconsin Press, 1982). A landmark study of the effect of the Portuguese penetration on the Brazilian native peoples is John Hemming, *Red Gold: The Conquest of the Brazilian Indians, 1500–1760* (Cambridge: Harvard University Press, 1978).

The rationale of the Iberian colonial New World empires is imaginatively analyzed in Stanley and Barbara Stein, *The Colonial Heritage of Latin America: Essays on Economic Dependence in Perspective* (New York: Oxford University Press, 1970). The functioning of the Spanish American bureaucratic system—with all its famous corruption and inefficiency—is lucidly portrayed in John Leddy Phelan, *The Kingdom of Quito in the Seventeenth Century: Bureaucratic Politics in the Spanish Empire* (Madison, University of Wisconsin Press, 1967). Phelan also wrote an important study of a late colonial revolt in *The People and the King: The Comunero Revolution in Colombia, 1781* (Madison: University of Wisconsin Press, 1978), which examines a possible connection between a local grievance and the later impulse for independence from Spain. The all-important role of the church is examined in the anthology edited by Richard E. Greenleaf, *The Roman Catholic Church in Colonial Latin America* (New York: Alfred A. Knopf, 1971). On women there is a useful collection edited by Asuncion Lavrin, *Latin American Women: Historical Perspectives* (Westport, Conn.: Greenwood, 1978), which includes some coverage of the colonial era.

For colonial Brazil there is no substitute for Gilberto Freyre's classic *The Masters and the Slaves* (New York: Alfred A. Knopf, 1946). For the history of the slave trade one should consult Philip D. Curtin, *The African Slave Trade: A Census* (Madison: University of Wisconsin Press, 1969), which is only slowly being superseded by new research.

The origins and travail of independence in Spanish America are described in John Lynch's broad-ranging *The Spanish-American Revolutions, 1808–1826* (New York: Norton, 1973). A comparable effort for Brazil is A. J. R. Russell-Wood, ed., *From Colony to Nation: Essays on the Independence of Brazil* (Baltimore: Johns Hopkins University Press, 1975).

Chapter Two   The Transformation of Modern Latin America, 1880s–1980s

The most widely read economic history of this period is Celso Furtado, *Economic Development of Latin America: Historical Background and Contemporary Problems,* 2nd ed., (Cambridge: Cambridge University Press, 1976), which reflects the author's structualist preconceptions. A contrasting picture, covering the world economy and Latin America's role, is offered in W. Arthur Lewis, *The Evolution of the International Economic Order* (Princeton: Princeton University Press, 1978), which stresses market forces. The specific context of third world development is sketched in Paul Bairoch, *The Economic Development of the Third World Since 1900* (London: Metheun, 1975).

The outlines of the emerging import-export economies are suggested in the case studies in Roberto Cortes Conde, *The First Stages of Modernization in Spanish America* (New York: Harper & Row, 1974). Carlos Diaz Alejandro, *Essays on the Economic History of the Argentine Republic* (New Haven: Yale University Press, 1970), is the finest study for any country economy in this era. An important monograph on a key topic in Brazil, of great importance also to Argentina, is Thomas H. Holloway, *Immigrants on the Land: Coffee and Society in São Paulo, 1886–1934* (Chapel Hill: University of North Carolina Press, 1980).

The starting point for labor history in this era is Hobart A. Spalding, Jr., *Organized Labor in Latin America: Historical Case Studies of Urban Workers in Dependent Societies* (New York: Harper & Row, 1977), which includes country-by-country coverage. The implications of pre-1930 labor history for the modern era are explored in Thomas E. Skidmore, "Workers and Soldiers: Urban Labor Movements and Elite Responses in Twentieth-Century Latin America," In Virginia Bernhard, ed., *Elites, Masses, and Modernization in Latin America, 1850–1930* (Austin: University of Texas Press, 1979).

Readers interested in intellectual history will find an excellent guide in Martin S. Stabb, *In Quest of Identity: Patterns in the Spanish American Essay of Ideas, 1890–1960* (Chapel Hill: University of North Carolina Press, 1967). There has been a rapid increase in research and publishing on women in Latin American history. A stimulating collection can be found in June Nash and Helen Icken Safa, eds., *Sex and Class in Latin America* (New York: Bergin, 1980). For a wide-ranging monograph by a leading researcher, see Elsa M. Chaney, *Supermadre: Women in Politics in Latin America* (Austin: University of Texas Press, 1979).

The long-standing debate over the inherent nature of Latin American political systems is elegantly continued in Claudio Veliz, *The Centralist Tradition of Latin America* (Princeton: Princeton University Press, 1980), who finds centralism to be the principal theme.

A vivid if sometimes hyperbolic look at all of Latin America on the eve of World War II can be found in John Gunther, *Inside Latin America* (New York: Harper, 1941).

On the post-1945 history of anti-inflation programs (often called "stabilization" policies) there is Rosemary Thorp and Laurence Whitehead, eds., *Inflation and Stabilisation in Latin America* (New York: Holmes & Meier, 1979), which includes case studies of all major countries.

The argument in our chapter on the transformation (1880s–1980s) has been much influenced by Guillermo O'Donnell, *Modernization and Bureaucratic-Authoritarianism: Studies in South American Politics* (Berkeley: Institute of International Studies, University of California, 1973) and David Collier, ed., *The New Authoritarianism in Latin America* (Princeton: Princeton University Press, 1979).

Chapter Three   Argentina: From Prosperity to Deadlock

One of the most stimulating histories of Argentina is Ysabel F. Rennie, *The Argentine Republic* (New York: MacMillan, 1945). The best synthesis since Rennie is James R. Scobie, *Argentina, a City and a Nation*, 2nd ed., (New York: Oxford University Press, 1971). The relevant chapters of Arthur P. Whitaker, *The United States and the Southern Cone: Argentina, Chile and Uruguay* (Cambridge: Harvard University Press, 1976) contain the careful judgments of a long-time dean of Argentine history specialists in the U.S.

To understand nineteenth-century Argentina and the origins of modern Argentine nationalism one must start with the famous strongman Rosas, who has received his best scholarly biography in John Lynch, *Argentine Dictator: Juan Manuel de Rosas, 1829–1852* (Oxford: Oxford University Press, 1981). The classic explanation of nineteenth-century Argentina's economic base is Miron Burgin, *The Economic Aspects of Argentine Federalism, 1820–1852* (Cambridge: Harvard University Press, 1946). The interaction of interest groups and government policymaking for one sector between 1900 and 1946 is explored in Peter H. Smith, *Politics and Beef in Argentina: Patterns of Conflict and Change* (New York: Columbia University Press, 1969).

Carlos F. Diaz Alejandro, *Essays on the Economic History of the Argentine Republic* (New Haven: Yale University Press, 1970) is the premier economic history on modern Argentina, with penetrating analyses of agricultural development, industrialization, tariffs, and inflation. Much of Argentine history is mirrored in the history of its capital city, whose social and economic development has been expertly traced by James Scobie in *Buenos Aires: Plaza to Suburb, 1870–1910* (New York: Oxford University Press, 1974).

One of the most puzzling political phenomena of modern Argentina is the rise and decline of the Radical Party, admirably analyzed for the early twentieth century in David Rock, *Politics in Argentina, 1890–1930: The Rise and Fall of Radicalism* (New York: Cambridge University Press, 1975). No institution has been more important in modern Argentina than the military, which is studied in depth in Robert A. Potash, *The Army and Politics in Argentina, 1928–1945* (Stanford: Stanford University Press, 1969), and his *The Army and Politics in Argentina, 1945–1962* (Stanford: Stanford University Press, 1980).

Juan and Eva Perón aroused such emotions that objective history writing about them has been slow to appear. That has begun to change, as can be seen in the excellent collaborative work edited by Frederick C. Turner and José Enrique Miguens, *Juan Perón and the Reshaping of Argentina* (Pittsburgh: University of Pittsburgh Press, 1983). The first scholarly biography of Perón is Joseph A. Page's ambitious *Perón: A Biography* (New York: Random House, 1983), which is both well written and well documented. There is a similar study of Eva Perón, if on a smaller scale, by Nicolas Fraser and Marysa Navarro, *Eva Perón* (New York: Norton, 1980). A persuasive analysis of Perón's labor policies is given in Samuel L. Baily, *Labor, Nationalism and Politics in Argentina* (New Brunswick: Rutgers University Press, 1967).

One of the most persistent questions about Argentina is why such an economically developed country should have been plagued by authoritarian regimes since 1945. The origins of that apparent breakdown are clearly laid out in Peter H. Smith, *Argentina and the Failure of Democracy: Conflict among Political Elites, 1904–1955* (Madison: University of Wisconsin Press, 1974). Guillermo O'Donnell's analysis of "bureaucratic authoritarianism" (see reference in Chapter II) compares Brazil and Argentina as cases of industrializing societies subject to a new kind of military coup. The relationship between regime type and economic policy in Argentina is carefully examined for 1945–76 in Gary W. Wynia, *Argentina in the Postwar Era: Politics and Economic Policy Making in a Divided Society* (Albuquerque: University of New Mexico Press, 1978).

Chapter Four   Chile: Democracy, Socialism, and Repression

Brian Loveman has produced a reliable general history of Chile in *Chile: The Legacy of Hispanic Capitalism* (New York: Oxford University Press, 1979). The history of the agrarian sector between 1850 and 1940 is traced in Arnold J. Bauer, *Chilean Rural Society: from the Spanish Conquest to 1930* (Cambridge: Cambridge University Press, 1975). One aspect of that story is brought up to the 1970s in Brian Loveman, *Struggle in the Countryside: Politics and Rural Labor in Chile, 1919–1973* (Bloomington: University of Indiana Press, 1976).

The best economic history, necessarily sketchy for pre-1930, is Markos J. Mamalakis, *The Growth and Structure of the Chilean Economy: From Independence to Allende* (New Haven: Yale University Press, 1976). The interpretation of nineteenth century Chile revolves around the interpretation of President Balmaceda and the civil war of 1981. The best documented and best argued—although not universally accepted—interpretation is to be found in Harold Blakemore, *British Nitrates and Chilean Politics, 1886–1896: Balmaceda and North* (London: Athlone Press, 1974). Labor's struggle for bargaining rights, as well as bread and butter gains, is well portrayed in Peter DeShazo, *Urban Workers and Labor Unions in Chile, 1902–1927* (Madison: University of Wisconsin Press, 1983), which emphasizes the Anarchist-led unions. An excellent overview of labor relations—with their penetration by differing political influences—up to 1970 is given in Alan Angell, *Politics and the Labor Movement in Chile* (London: Oxford University Press, 1972).

The historical role of the military is examined in Frederick M. Nunn, *Chilean Politics 1920–1931: The Honorable Mission of the Armed Forces* (Albuquerque: University of New Mexico, 1970). After the 1973 coup Nunn reexamined that subject in *The Military in Chilean History: Essays on Civil-Military Relations, 1810– 1973* (Albuquerque: University of New Mexico Press, 1976).

An economic issue of utmost political significance since the turn of the century has been foreign ownership of Chilean mines. For a political scientist's sophisticated analysis of how the U.S.-owned copper companies came to be completely nationalized in 1971, see Theodore H. Moran, *Multinational Corporations and the Politics of Dependence: Copper in Chile* (Princeton: Princeton University Press, 1974).

One of the most penetrating studies of any Latin American political party is given in Paul W. Drake, *Socialism and Populism in Chile, 1932–52* (Urbana: University of Illinois Press, 1978). The party is the Socialists, which attracted many former Anarchists and later moved to the left of the Chilean Communist Party.

The last twenty years of Chilean history have proved highly controversial, and not simply because they are the closest to us. Paul Sigmund, a scholar sympathetic to the Christian Democrats and critical of Allende, has traced the process of political radicalization in *The Overthrow of Allende and the Politics of Chile, 1964–1976* (Pittsburgh: University of Pittsburgh, 1977). For a systematic comparative analysis of the economic policies and political bases of three presidents—a Conservative (Allesandri), Christian Democratic (Frei), and Popular Front (Allende) president—see Barbara Stallings, *Class Conflict and Economic Development in Chile, 1958–1973* (Stanford: Stanford University Press, 1978), which is sympathetic to the Allende government. The most systematic critique of Allende from the left is Ian Roxborough, Phil O'Brien, and Jackie Roddick, *Chile: The State and Revolution* (London: Macmillan, 1977). For a participant's firsthand report by an American Marxist economist on how the Unidad Popular government functioned and the odds it faced, see Edward Boorstein, *Allende's Chile: An Inside View* (New York: International Publishers, 1977). One of the most balanced pictures of the process leading to the coup of 1973 is found in Arturo Valenzuela, *The Breakdown of Democratic Regimes: Chile* (Baltimore: Johns Hopkins University Press, 1978).

Few would deny that the Catholic Church has played a pivotal role in twentieth century Chile. The history of that role is lucidly analyzed in Brian H. Smith's *The Church and Politics in Chile: Challenges to Modern Catholicism* (Princeton: Princeton University Press, 1982).

One of the most valuable attempts to rethink the Allende years is Federico C. Gil, Ricardo Lagos E., and Henry A. Lansberger, eds., *Chile at the Turning Point: Lessons of the Socialist Years, 1970–1973* (Philadelphia: ISHI, 1979), which includes chapters by a wide range of scholars and former Allende government members. The autobiography of Chile's Nobel laureate in poetry is a fascinating journey through the artistic worlds of Latin America and Europe: Pablo Neruda, *Memoirs* (New York: Farrar, Straus and Giroux, 1977). It is also an eye-opener about political persecution, since Neruda was a long-time Communist Party militant.

Chapter Five   Brazil: Development for Whom?

E. Bradford Burns, *A History of Brazil,* 2nd ed. (New York: Columbia University Press, 1980) is a sure-handed survey, with extensive suggestions for further reading. The most important general interpretation of Brazil's economic history is Celso Furtado, *The Economic Growth of Brazil* (Berkeley: University of California Press, 1963), which stops in the early 1950s. The more recent years are covered in Werner Baer, *The Brazilian Economy: Growth and Development,* 2nd ed. (New York: Praeger, 1983), which includes a wealth of data.

For nineteenth century Brazil, Gilberto Freyre has provided a fascinating portrait in *The Mansions and the Shanties: The Making of Modern Brazil* (New York: Alfred A. Knopf, 1963), which is continued into the early twentieth century in Freyre's *Order and Progress: Brazil from Monarchy to Republic* (New York: Alfred A. Knopf, 1970). One of the finest microstudies for any area of Latin America is Stanley J. Stein, *Vassouras: A Brazilian Coffee County, 1850–1900* (Cambridge: Harvard University Press, 1957). A provocative if not always convincing account of industrial growth is given in Warren Dean, *The Industrialization of São Paulo, 1880–1945* (Austin: University of Texas Press, 1969).

The English influence on Brazil's transition to a major agro-exporter is well described in Richard Graham, *Britain and the Onset of Modernization in Brazil, 1850–1914* (Cambridge: Cambridge University Press, 1968). Thomas Holloway's study of immigration (reference for Chapter II) provides a well-documented analysis of how two million European immigrants were drawn to and integrated into the booming coffee economy of São Paulo. Joseph Love, *São Paulo in the Brazilian Federation, 1889–1937* (Stanford: Stanford University Press, 1980) offers an excellent overview of Brazil's economically most important state, emphasizing how political leaders were recruited and how they shaped both the state and national economies. There are companion volumes on Minas Gerais by John Wirth (1977) and Pernambuco by Robert Levine (1978).

For the Vargas era (1930–54) the most important studies are R. M. Levine, *The Vargas Regime: The Critical Years, 1934–1938* (New York: Columbia University Press, 1970); John D. Wirth, *The Politics of Brazilian Development, 1930–1954* (Stanford: Stanford University Press, 1970), which includes a chapter on the creation of Petrobras, the national oil enterprise; Stanley E. Hilton, *Brazil and the Great Powers, 1930–1939: The Politics of Trade Rivalry* (Austin: University of Texas Press, 1975); and John W. F. Dulles, *Vargas of Brazil* (Austin: University of Texas Press, 1967). *The Brazilian-American Alliance, 1937–1945* (Princeton: Princeton University Press, 1973) by Frank McCann ably describes the wartime alliance that, in the most immediate terms, enabled the U.S. to turn back the Nazi U-boat menace in the Atlantic. For an analysis of the political process from Vargas's overthrow in 1945 to the military coup of 1964 see Thomas E. Skidmore, *Politics in Brazil, 1930–1964: An Experiment in Democracy* (New York: Oxford University Press, 1967).

President Kubtischek's construction of Brasília in 1957–61 captured the world's imagination, but the reality proved a mixed blessing, as is made clear in Norma Evenson, *Two Brazilian Capitals: Architecture and Urbanism in Rio de Janeiro and Brasília* (New Haven: Yale University Press, 1973) and David G. Epstein, *Brasília, Plan and Reality: A Study of Planned and Spontaneous Urban Development* (Berkeley: University of California Press, 1973).

The all-important role of the army in the 1945–67 era is admirably analyzed in Alfred Stepan, *The Military in Politics: Changing Patterns in Brazil* (Princeton: Princeton University Press, 1971). The subsequent military role in the post-1964 authoritarian system is analyzed in Peter Flynn, *Brazil: A Political Analysis* (Boulder: Westview, 1978). For other critiques see the collection edited by Alfred Stepan, *Authoritarian Brazil: Origins, Policies, and Future* (New Haven: Yale University Press, 1973) and Thomas C. Bruneau and Philippe Faucher, eds., *Authoritarian Capitalism: Brazil's Contemporary Economic and Political Development* (Boulder: Westview, 1981). A well-written analysis of the painful human trade-offs in Brazil's capitalist strategy is Sylvia Ann Hewlett, *The Cruel Dilemmas of Development: Twentieth-Century Brazil* (New York: Basic Books, 1980). A highly subtle analysis of the role of foreign capital in the post-1964 regime is given in Peter Evans, *Dependent Development: The Alliance of Multinational, State, and Local Capital in Brazil* (Princeton: Princeton University Press, 1979).

An excellent analysis of the labor relations system in the pre-1964 era can be found in Kenneth Paul Erickson, *The Brazilian Corporative State and Working-Class Politics* (Berkeley: University of California Press, 1977). Updating that topic for the later 1970s is John Humphrey, *Capitalist Control and Workers' Struggle in the Brazilian Auto Industry* (Princeton: Princeton University Press, 1982), the first study based on research on the shop steward level.

The finest introduction to Brazilian race relations is Carl N. Degler, *Neither Black Nor White: Slavery and Race Relations in Brazil and the United States* (New York: Macmillan, 1971), although his hypothesis of the "mulatto escape hatch" is now under fire. A pioneering work on the links between Africa and Brazil is offered in José Honório Rodrigues, *Brazil and Africa* (Berkeley: University of California Press, 1965). Of the many works on abolition the most penetrating is Robert Conrad, *The Destruction of Brazilian Slavery, 1850–1888* (Berkeley: University of California Press, 1972).

The Brazilian elite's attempt to reconcile racist science and the reality of their multi-racial society is described in Thomas E. Skidmore, *Black into White: Race and Nationality in Brazilian Thought* (New York: Oxford University Press, 1974). For the reflection of the "whitening" ideal in Brazilian literature, see David T. Haberly, *Three Sad Races: Racial Identity and National Consciousness in Brazilian Literature* (Cambridge: Cambridge University Press, 1983).

Chapter Six Peru: Soldiers, Oligarchs, and Indians

An able survey of Peruvian history is given in Frederick B. Pike, *The Modern History of Peru* (London: Weidenfeld and Nicolson, 1967). Economic history is covered superbly in Rosemary Thorp and Geoffrey Bertram, *Peru 1890–1977: Growth and Policy in an Open Economy* (New York: Columbia University Press, 1978). Jonathan V. Levin, *The Export Economies: Their Pattern of Development in*

Historical Perspective (Cambridge: Harvard University Press, 1960) includes a study of "Peru in the guano age" as a prototype of an export enclave economy. The effects of rapid economic change on the highland population is sympathetically described in Florencia E. Mallon, *The Defense of Community in Peru's Central Highlands: Peasant Struggle and Capitalist Transition, 1860–1940* (Princeton: Princeton University Press, 1983). The political implications of these economic changes are spelled out in Peter F. Klarén, *Modernization, Dislocation, and Aprismo: Origins of the Peruvian Aprista Party, 1870–1932* (Austin: University of Texas Press, 1973). That story is carried forward in Steve Stein, *Populism in Peru: The Emergence of the Masses and the Politics of Social Control* (Madison: University of Wisconsin Press, 1980).

Recent history writing about Peru has been dominated by attention to the military regime which seized power in 1968. Part of the background is given in Richard Charles Webb, *Government Policy and the Distribution of Income in Peru, 1963–1973* (Cambridge: Harvard University Press, 1977). One of the most careful portraits of the post-1968 regime is the collection edited by Abraham F. Lowenthal, *The Peruvian Experiment: Continuity and Change under Military Rule* (Princeton: Princeton University Press, 1975). Lowenthal and Cynthia McClintock edited a follow-up volume: *The Peruvian Experiment Reconsidered* (Princeton: Princeton University Press, 1983). A well-known political scientist's categorization of Peru's political experiment is laid out in Alfred Stepan, *The State and Society: Peru in Comparative Perspective* (Princeton: Princeton University Press, 1978).

For a discussion of the rural sector, see Howard Handelman, *Struggle in the Andes: Peasant Political Mobilization in Peru* (Austin: University of Texas Press, 1975) and Cynthia McClintock, *Peasant Cooperatives and Political Change in Peru* (Princeton: Princeton University Press, 1981). For a study of the relationship between the military government and urban squatters, see David Collier, *Squatters and Oligarchs; Authoritarian Rule and Policy Change in Peru* (Baltimore: Johns Hopkins University Press, 1976). The most incisive analysis of the military government's economic policy is E. V. K. Fitzgerald, *The State of Economic Development: Peru Since 1968* (Cambridge: University Press, 1976).

For insight into the thinking of a guerrilla who was an important voice of the highland Indians, see Hugo Blanco, *Land or Death: The Peasant Struggle in Peru* (New York: Pathfinder Press, 1972). Modern Peru's most influential political thinker was the maverick Marxist José Carlos Mariategui, whose work on Indians and land is translated in *Seven Interpretive Essays on Peruvian Reality* (Austin: University of Texas Press, 1971).

One of Peru's most pressing questions has been the fate of its large Indian population. For an overview of that vexing problem see Thomas M. Davies, Jr., *Indian Integration in Peru: A Half-Century of Experience, 1900–1948* (Lincoln: University of Nebraska Press, 1974).

Chapter Seven Mexico: The Taming of a Revolution

Mexico is fortunate in having a detailed, well-balanced, and up-to-date one-volume history in Michael C. Meyer and William L. Sherman, *The Course of Mexican Hisotry*, 2nd ed. (New York: Oxford University Press, 1983). It includes chapter-by-chapter bibliographies in both English and Spanish. For coverage of the century between independence and the 1910 Revolution there is the convenient anthology in W. Dirk Raat, ed., *Mexico: From Independence to Revolution, 1810–1910* (Lincoln: University of Nebraska Press, 1982). Charles A. Hale, *Mexican Liberalism in the Age of Mora, 1821–1853* (New Haven: Yale University Press, 1968) is the best study of liberalism in Latin America.

An excellent lead into the Mexican elite's self-image may be found in John S. Brushwood, *Mexico in Its Novel: A Nation's Search for Identity* (Austin: University of Texas Press, 1966). There is a wealth of local color, as seen by a European, in Fanny Calderon de la Barca, *Life in Mexico,* ed. Howard T. Fisher and Marion Hall Fisher (Garden City: Doubleday, 1966).

The subject of foreign participation in the economic boom of the *Porfiriato* is treated in David M. Pletcher, *Rails, Mines, and Progress: Seven American Promoters in Mexico, 1867–1911* (Ithaca: Cornell University Press, 1958). The infamous rural police of Profírio Diaz's era are given a careful reexamination in Paul J. Vanderwood, *Disorder and Progress: Bandits, Police and Mexican Development* (Lincoln: University of Nebraska Press, 1981).

Explanations of the Revolution have come to dominate twentieth century Mexican historiography. A valuable study of early ideas is James D. Cockcroft, *Intellectual Precursors of the Mexican Revolution* (Austin: University of Texas Press, 1968). No scholar was more successful than Frank Tannenbaum in portraying what the revolution meant to those at the bottom. His evocative powers are evident in *Peace by Revolution: Mexico After 1910* (New York: Columbia University Press, 1933) and *Mexico: The Struggle for Peace and Bread* (New York: Alfred A. Knopf, 1950). Tannenbaum knew many revolutionary leaders and traveled widely in Mexico to see at firsthand who supported the revolution. The atmosphere of the era can be sensed from the magnificent illustrations in Anita Brenner, *The Wind That Swept Mexico: The History of the Mexican Revolution of 1910–1942* (Austin: University of Texas Press, 1971).

The finest study of the agrarian revolution is John Womack, Jr., *Zapata and the Mexican Revolution* (New York: Alfred A. Knopf, 1968). The first decade of the revolution is well covered in Charles Cumberland, *Mexican Revolution: Genesis under Madero* (Austin: University of Texas Press, 1952) and in his succeeding volume, *Mexican Revolution: The Constitutionalist Years* (Austin: University of Texas Press, 1972). How the revolution changed from a military movement into one-party system is explored in Edwin Lieuwen, *Mexican Militarism: The Political Rise and Fall of the Revolutionary Army* (Albuquerque: University of New Mexico Press, 1968). Lázaro Cardenas has long been seen as a major hero of the Revolution, but his presidency has been subjected to a revisionist critique in Nora Hamilton, *The Limits of State Autonomy: Post-Revolutionary Mexico* (Princeton: Princeton University Press, 1982).

One of the most influential attempts by an outside scholar to rethink the meaning of Mexico's one-party system is Roger D. Hansen, *The Politics of Mexican Development* (Baltimore: Johns Hopkins University Press, 1971). For a systematic rethink by a cross section of U.S. and Mexican scholars, see José Luis Reyna and Richard S. Weinert, eds., *Authoritarianism in Mexico* (Philadelphia: ISHI, 1977). A recent view of Mexico's economic prospects is given in Jorge I. Dominguez, ed., *Mexico's Political Economy: Challenges at Home and Abroad* (Beverly Hills: Sage, 1982). Any analysis of the PRI must begin with its methods of recruitment, which are given their first systematic analysis (for 1910–1976) in Peter H. Smith, *Labyrinths of Power: Political Recruitment in Twentieth-Century Mexico* (Princeton: Princeton University Press, 1979). The basic source on Mexican economic history is Clark W. Reynolds, *The Mexican Economy: Twentieth-Century Structure and Growth* (New Haven: Yale University Press, 1970).

Central to Mexican history has been conflict with the U.S., which is traced in Karl M. Schmitt, *Mexico and the United States, 1821–1973: Conflict and Coexistence* (New York: John Wiley, 1974). The long drawn-out battle over oil is carefully analyzed in Lorenzo Meyer, *Mexico and the United States in the Oil Controversy, 1917–1942,* trans. by Muriel Vasconcellos (Austin: University of Texas Press, 1972).

Mexican intellectuals have written moving accounts of their collisions with their national reality, as in José Vasconcelos, *A Mexican Ulysses: An Autobiography* trans. by William Rex Crawford (Bloomington: Indiana University Press, 1963). Vasconcellos, who had grown up on the U.S. border, later became a highly nationalist Minister of Education and a presidential candidate. The most famous interpretation of Mexican national character is Octavio Paz, *The Labyrinth of Solitude: Life and Thought in Mexico,* trans. by Lysander Kemp (New York: Grove Press, 1961). Paz produced a sequel in *The Other Mexico: Critique of the Pyramid,* trans. by Lysander Kemp (New York: Grove Press, 1972).

Chapter Eight   Cuba: Late Colony, First Socialist State

Anyone studying the history of Cuba becomes rapidly indebted to Hugh Thomas for his superbly researched and highly readable *Cuba: The Pursuit of Freedom* (New York: Harper & Row, 1971). For the nineteenth century background one of the most penetrating works is Ramiro Guerra y Sanchez, *Sugar and Society in the Caribbean* (New Haven: Yale University Press, 1964), an indictment of the spread of latifundia in the sugar cane sector. The economic context of nineteenth century slavery is spelled out in Franklin W. Knight, *Slave Society in Cuba During the Nineteenth Century* (Madison: University of Wisconsin Press, 1970). The dominant figure in Cuban history is still José Martí, the subject of a recent biography by John M. Kirk, *José Martí: Mentor of the Cuban Nation* (Gainesville: University of Florida Press, 1983).

The origins of the Revolution of 1959 are skillfully described in Ramon Eduardo Ruiz, *Cuba: The Making of a Revolution* (New York: Norton, 1970). Cuba's relationship to the U.S., which was crucial to the growth of Cuban nationalism, is lucidly outlined in Robert F. Smith, *The United States and Cuba: Business and Diplomacy, 1917–1960* (New Haven: College & University Press, 1960). The ill-fated government of Grau San Martín in 1933 was in many ways a dress rehearsal for 1959. That story is well told in Luis A. Aguilar, *Cuba 1933: Prologue to Revolution* (Ithaca: Cornell University Press, 1972).

Much mythology has been generated over Batista's fall. The most painstaking reconstruction of the "politico-military factors" leading to a rebel victory is Ramon L. Bonachea and Marta San Martín, *The Cuban Insurrection, 1952–1959* (New Brunswick: Transaction, 1972), which does not support the more extreme Fidelista claims for a totally rural guerrilla victory. The most sophisticated attempt to link Cuba's pre-1959 condition to the socialist transformation undertaken by the revolutionaries is James O'Connor, The *Origins of Socialism in Cuba* (Ithaca: Cornell University Press, 1970).

A systematic comparison of Cuba before and after 1959 is offered in Jorge I. Dominguez's fact-filled *Cuba: Order and Revolution* (Cambridge: Harvard University Press, 1978). An earlier collaborative volume edited by Carmelo Mesa-Lago, *Revolutionary Change in Cuba* (Pittsburgh: Pittsburgh University Press, 1971) well illumines the first decade of the Fidelista regime. One of the most interesting close-up portraits of Fidel is offered in the profusely illustrated *Castro's Cuba, Cuba's Fidel* (New York: Random House, 1969) by Lee Lockwood. The passionate debates over "material" versus "moral" incentives is documented in Bertram Silverman, ed., *Man and Socialism in Cuba: The Great Debate* (New York: Atheneum, 1973).

The indispensable starting point on the economic record of the Fidelista government is Carmelo Mesa-Lago, *The Economy of Socialist Cuba: A Two-Decade Appraisal* (Albuquerque: University of New Mexico Press, 1981) and his *Cuba in the 1970s: Pragmatism and Institutionalization,* rev. ed. (Albuquerque: University of New Mexico Press, 1978). For a study by an able economist sympathetic to the revolutionary government, see Arthur MacEwan, *Revolution and Economic Development in Cuba* (New York: St. Martin's Press, 1981).

Cuba's greater visibility on the world scene, beginning in the mid-1970s, has stimulated much analysis, as in Cole Blasier and Carmelo Mesa-Lago, eds., *Cuba in the World* (Pittsburgh: University of Pittsburgh Press, 1979), which is dated but nonetheless valuable. A similar collaborative work, focusing on the Caribbean, is Barry B. Levine, ed., *The New Cuban Presence in the Caribbean* (Boulder: Westview, 1983). The most systematic attempt to look at how when Cuba tried to "export" the revolution is found in Carla Anne Robbins, *The Cuban Threat* (New York: McGraw-Hill, 1983), which was written in the hope of making U.S. policy toward Cuba more flexible.

For a wide-ranging anthology of articles about post-1959 Cuba, see Irving Louis Horowitz, ed., *Cuban Communism,* 4th ed. (New Brunswick: Transaction, 1981), which is broader than the title implies. The Federation of Cuban Women has worked hard to change the traditional female role in their Latin society. A favorable view of their efforts is offered in Margaret Randall, *Women in Cuba: Twenty Years Later* (New York: Smyrna Press, 1981). A fascinating series of individual portraits, based on in-depth interviews, are painted in Oscar Lewis, Ruth M. Lewis, and Susan M. Rigdon, *Four Women: Living the Revolution: An Oral History of Contemporary Cuba* (Urbana, Ill.: University of Illinois Press, 1977). This project produced two other volumes, *Four Men* (1975) and *Neighbors* (1978).

Chapter Nine Central America: Colonialism, Dictatorship, and Revolution

Central America has been relatively neglected by North American historians until recently. With the explosion of guerrilla movements in the late 1970s, along with the deepening involvement of the U.S., we have been deluged with "instant" books often lacking in historical perspective and documentation. The best starting point for this region is Ralph Lee Woodward, Jr., *Central America: A Nation Divided* (New York: Oxford University Press, 1976), which includes a forty-three-page guide to the literature on Central America. The colonial background has been mapped in Murdo J. MacLeod, *Spanish Central America: A Socioeconomic History, 1520–1720* (Berkeley: University of California Press, 1973) and by Miles L. Wortman, *Government and Society in Central America, 1680–1840* (New York: Columbia University Press, 1982).

One constant theme in Central America has been the attempt to unify the isthmus. Much of the story is told in Thomas L. Karnes, *The Failure of Union: Central America, 1824–1960* (Chapel Hill: University of North Carolina Press, 1961). The hope for a new version of union in a Central American Common Market is traced in Gary W. Wynia, *Politics and Planners* (Madison: University of Wisconsin Press, 1972). Alas, the Common Market has proved no more successful than most previous attempts at lasting unification. Examples of the perennial intrusion of foreign entrepreneurs into Central America are laid out in William J. Griffith, *Empires in the Wilderness: Foreign Colonization and Development in Guatemala, 1834–1944* (Chapel Hill: University of North Carolina Press, 1965).

Guatemala, the largest and potentially richest country of Central America, has recently attracted attention from historians. The outstanding work before this "boom" was Richard N. Adams, *Crucifixion by Power: Essays on the Guatemalan National Social Structure, 1944–1966* (Austin: University of Texas Press, 1970). The U.S. role in the overthrow of President Arbenz in 1954 has been documented in Stephen Schlesinger and Stephen Kinzer, *Bitter Fruit: The Untold Story of the American Coup in Guatemala* (Garden City: Doubleday, 1981) and Richard H. Immerman, *The CIA in Guatemala: The Foreign Policy of Intervention* (Austin: University of Texas Press, 1982). Although both books tap unpublished sources, Immerman is the more judicious in his use of hearsay and undocumented evidence.

A highly useful overview of Nicaraguan history is given in Thomas W. Walker, *Nicaragua: The Land of Sandino* (Boulder: Westview, 1981), whose views are made clear in the subtitle. Essential for understanding the durability of the Somoza dynasty is Richard Millett, *Guardians of the Dynasty: A History of the U.S. Created Guardia Nacional de Nicaragua and the Somoza Family* (Maryknoll: Orbis Books, 1977). Among the many books describing Nicaragua since 1979 is Henri Weber, *Nicaragua: The Sandinist Revolution,* trans. by Patrick Camiller (London: Version, 1981), which stresses the need to retain a pluralist model of revolution.

The unhappy republic of El Salvador has descended into a bloody civil war, with much meddling by outside powers. El Salvador has a long-standing tradition of repression of popular opposition, as can be seen in Thomas P. Anderson, *Matanza: El Salvador's Communist Revolt of 1932* (Lincoln: University of Nebraska Press, 1971). For a recent synthesis of political history since 1948, see Enrique Baloyra, *El Salvador in Transition* (Chapel Hill: University of North Carolina Press, 1982). For an insight into a major reformist force, see Stephen Webre, *José Napoleon Duarte and the Christian Democrat Party in Salvadorian Politics: 1960–1974* (Baton Rouge: Louisiana State University Press, 1979). A rich anthology on the background to the civil war of the 1980s is offered in Marvin E. Gettleman, et al., *El Salvador: Central America in the New Cold War* (New York: Grove Press, 1981). Among the many collective efforts to give perspective on the civil war is *El Salvador: Background to the Crisis* (Cambridge: Central America Information Office, 1982).

The 1969 "soccer war" between Honduras and El Salvador came as a lightning bolt, illuminating the tensions in Central America. It has been analyzed in William H. Durham, *Scarcity and Survival in Central America: Ecological Origins of the Soccer War* (Stanford: Stanford University Press, 1979) and Thomas P. Anderson, *The War of the Dispossessed: Honduras and El Salvador, 1969* (Lincoln: University of Nebraska Press, 1981).

The U.S. presence hovers over Central America, making every domestic political decision a possible conflict with Uncle Sam. The past record is spelled out in Jenny Pearce, *Under the Eagle: U.S. Intervention in Central America and the Caribbean* (London: Latin American Bureau, 1982). For the attempt by a distinguished authority in U.S. foreign policy analysis to explain the context, see Walter LaFeber, *Inevitable Revolutions: The United States and Central America* (New York: Norton, 1983).

Chapter Ten Latin America, the United States, and the World

Few scholars have looked at Latin America's changing relationship with the outside world as a whole. A useful approximation is Harold Eugene Davis, et al., *Latin American Diplomatic History: An Introduction* (Baton Rouge: Louisiana State University Press, 1977), which covers the nineteenth and twentieth centuries. In *The Foreign Powers in Latin America* (Princeton: Princeton University Press, 1972), Herbert Goldhamer compares foreign influences in the 1960s. Coverage by country is given in Harold Eugene Davis, et al., *Latin America Foreign Policies: An Analysis* (Baltimore: Johns Hopkins University Press, 1975).

U.S.-Latin American relations have generated an enormous bibliography, mostly from a conventional diplomatic history point of view. The most succinctly informative is Federico G. Gil, *Latin American-United States Relations* (New York: Harcourt Brace Jovanovich, 1971). A highly useful, if narrowly defined, diplomatic history is Graham H. Stuart and James L Tigner, *Latin America and the United States*, 6th ed. (Englewood Cliffs: Prentice-Hall, 1975). Among the many specialized studies are Lester D. Langley, *Struggle for the American Mediterranean: United States-European Rivalry in the Gulf-Caribbean, 1776–1904* (Athens: University of Georgia Press, 1976) and his *The United States and the Caribbean in the Twentieth Century* (Athens: University of Georgia Press, 1982). The standard source on the 1930s is Bryce Wood, *The Making of the Good Neighbor Policy* (New York: Columbia University Press, 1961), although his picture has been revised by such authors as Lloyd C. Gardner, *Economic Aspects of New Deal Diplomacy* (Madison: University of Wisconsin Press, 1964); David Green, *The Containment of Latin America: A History of the Myths and Realities of the Good Neighbor Policy* (Chicago: Quadrangle Books, 1971); and Irwin F. Gellman, *Good Neighbor Diplomacy: United States Policies in Latin America, 1933–1945* (Baltimore: Johns Hopkins University Press, 1979).

Much of the post-1945 era has been covered in F. Parkinson, *Latin America, the Cold War, and the World Powers, 1945–1973: A Study in Diplomatic History* (Beverly Hills: Sage Publications, 1974) and in Samuel L. Baily, *The United States and the Development of South America, 1945–1975* (New York: Franklin Watts, 1976). Baily is far more critical of U.S. policy than Parkinson. For examples of two U.S. liberals who grew alarmed over "the threatening cloud—communism plus castroism," see William Benton, *The Voice of Latin America* (New York: Harper & Row, 1961) and Adolf A. Berle, *Latin America: Diplomacy and Reality* (New York: Harper & Row, 1962). That "cloud" (Benton's phrase) did much to stimulate creation of the Alliance for Progress, whose first decade is critically examined in Jerome Levinson and Juan de Onís, *The Alliance that Lost its Way* (Chicago: Quadrangle, 1970). Studies on relations between the U.S. and individual countries include Harold F. Peterson, *Argentina and the United States, 1810–1960* (New York: University Publishers, 1964) and Robert Wesson, *The United States and Brazil: Limits of Influence* (New York: Praeger, 1981), which concentrates on the 1960s and 1970s.

The nineteenth century was Britain's heyday in Latin America, as can be seen in J. Fred Rippy, *British Investments in Latin America, 1822–1949* (Minneapolis: University of Minnesota Press, 1959); H. S. Ferns, *Britain and Argentina in the Nineteenth Century* (Oxford: Clarendon Press, 1960); and Alan Manchester, *British Preeminence in Brazil* (Chapel Hill: University of N. Carolina Press, 1933), which covers the first half of the nineteenth century. World War II virtually finished off any major role for Britain in Latin America, as can be seen in R. A. Humphreys, *Latin America and the Second World War*, 2 vols. (London: Athlone, 1981–1982). The first volume covers 1939–1942 while the second covers 1942–1945. We often tend to forget how long a direct Spanish influence persisted in Latin America. A good reminder is Fredrick B. Pike, *Hispanism, 1898–1936: Spanish Conservatives and Liberals and Their Relations with Spanish America* (Notre Dame: University of Notre Dame Press, 1971).

The role of the Central Intelligence Agency in Latin America got wide publicity after the exposé by a former CIA agent with many years of service in Latin America, Philip Agee, *Inside the Company: CIA Diary* (New York: Stonehill, 1975). Another agent with long Latin American service—including key roles in the Guatemalan coup of 1954 and the Bay of Pigs in 1961—has written a sophisticated defense of the CIA, by implication blaming its disasters on the poor judgment of its political masters: David Atlee Phillips, *The Night Watch: 25 Years of Peculiar Service* (New York: Atheneum, 1977).

In the 1970s human rights became a highly controversial issue in the U.S.-Latin American relations. The most comprehensive study of this question is Lars Schoultz, *Human Rights and United States Policy Toward Latin America* (Princeton: University Press, 1981). Schoultz favors greater emphasis on human rights, a position roundly condemned by Jeane J. Kirkpatrick in *Dictatorships and Double Standards: Rationalism and Reason* (New York: Simon & Schuster, 1982). The thoughts of a younger generation of U.S. academics are collected in Richard Newfarmer, ed., *From Gunboats to Diplomacy: New U.S. Policies for Latin America* (Baltimore: Johns Hopkins University Press, 1983).

A convenient source on ECLA thinking is the anthology *Development Problems in Latin America: An Analysis by the United Nations Economic Commission for Latin America* (Austin: University of Texas Press, 1970), which includes excerpts from the more influential ECLA documents. There is a vast literature by Latin Americans attacking the U.S. (and Europe) for exploiting Latin American resources while keeping it economically dependent and politically impotent, as in Eduardo Galeano, *Open Veins of Latin America: Five Centuries of the Pillage of a Continent* (New York: Monthly Review Press, 1973) and Alonso Aguilar, *Pan-Americanism from Monroe to the Present: A View from the Other Side* (New York: Monthly Review Press, 1968). For the very different view of a Venezuelan conservative, see Carlos Rangel, *The Latin Americans: Their Love-Hate Relationship with the United States* (New York: Harcourt Brace Jovanovich, 1977).

Epilogue   What Future for Latin America?

A very useful overview of Latin America's demographic history can be found in Nicolas Sanchez-Alboronoz, *The Population of Latin America: A History* (Berkeley: University of California Press, 1974). A representative example of demographic research on Latin America is J. Mayone Stycos, *Ideology, Faith, and Family Planning in Latin America: Studies in Public and Private Opinion on Fertility Control* (New York: McGraw-Hill, 1971).

Data on the widespread income inequality can be easily located in Alejandro Foxley, ed., *Income Distribution in Latin America* (Cambridge: Cambridge University Press, 1976). A very useful survey of labor throughout Latin America is given in James Dunkerley and Chris Whitehouse, *Trade Unions in Latin America: A Case for Solidarity* (London: Latin American Bureau, 1980). The finest recent survey of agriculture is Alain de Janvry, *The Agrarian Question and Reformism in Latin America* (Baltimore: Johns Hopkins University Press, 1981).

On peasants and their politicization, the best single source is a collection of articles edited by Rodolfo Stavenhagen, *Agrarian Problems and Peasant Movements in Latin America* (Garden City: Doubleday, 1970). An excellent starting point on the church is the collective volume edited by Daniel H. Levine, *Churches and Politics in Latin America* (Beverly Hills: Sage Publications, 1980). On the military there is another collection edited by Brian Loveman and Thomas M. Davies, Jr., *The Politics of Antipolitics: The Military in Latin America* (Lincoln: University of Nebraska Press, 1978).

Brazil and Mexico lend themselves well to comparative analysis, as can be seen in Sylvia Ann Hewlett and Richard S. Weinert, eds., *Brazil and Mexico: Patterns in Late Development* (Philadelphia: ISHI, 1982). The sharp swing in the 1960s and 1970s toward monetarist policies is examined in Alejandro Foxley, *Latin American Experiments in Neoconservative Economics* (Berkeley: University of California Press, 1983).

For a wide-ranging examination of many aspects of the U.S.-Mexican border, see Stanley R. Ross, ed., *Views Across the Border: The United States and Mexico* (Albuquerque: University of New Mexico Press, 1978). There is no substitute for reading the great Latin American writers, but their works can become even more interesting after reading Luis Harss and Barbara Dohmann, *Into the Mainstream: Conversations with Latin American Writers* (New York: Harper & Row, 1967). For a good introduction to race relations see H. Hoetink, *Slavery and Race Relations in the Americas: Comparative Notes on Their Nature and Nexus* (New York: Harper & Row, 1973).

The wave of military coups and economic reversals in the 1960s and 1970s led many scholars to think together about Latin America's future and the strategies likely to bring the greatest benefit to the largest number. Good examples are Margaret E. Crahan, ed., *Human Rights and Basic Needs in the Americas* (Washington: Georgetown University Press, 1982) and Heraldo Muñoz, ed., *From Dependency to Development: Strategies to Overcome Underdevelopment and Inequality* (Boulder: Westview Press, 1981).

INDEX